JH

D1637047

WITHDRAWN

CHRISTIAN HISTORY AND
INTERPRETATION:
STUDIES PRESENTED TO
JOHN KNOX

CHRISTIAN HISTORY AND INTERPRETATION: STUDIES PRESENTED TO JOHN KNOX

EDITED BY

W.R.FARMER
Professor of New Testament Studies, Perkins School of Theology, Southern Methodist University

C.F.D.MOULE
Lady Margaret's Professor of Divinity, Cambridge University

R.R.NIEBUHR
Florence Corliss Lamont Professor of Divinity, Harvard University

CAMBRIDGE
AT THE UNIVERSITY PRESS
1967

Published by the Syndics of the Cambridge University Press
Bentley House, 200 Euston Road, London, N.W. 1
American Branch: 32 East 57th Street, New York, N.Y. 10022

Library of Congress Catalogue Card Number: 67–15306

Printed in Great Britain
at the University Printing House, Cambridge
(Brooke Crutchley, University Printer)

CONTENTS

v

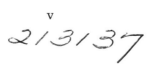

Contents

Contents

We should like to thank John H. Popper, New York, for permission
to reproduce the portrait of John Knox as a frontispiece.

vii

TABULA GRATULATORIA

S. Aalen
Elizabeth Achtemeier
Paul J. Achtemeier
James Luther Adams
James B. Adamson
S. Agourides
Kurt Aland
N. Alexander
B. W. Anderson
G. W. Anderson
James M. Ault
John W. Bachman
J. Arthur Baird
William Baird
E. Bammel
R. S. Barbour
William Barclay
A. Barr
James Barr
T. Barrosse, C.S.C.
Markus Barth
William A. Beardslee
G. R. Beasley-Murray
Dwight M. Beck
Johan C. Beker
V. Nelle Bellamy
P. Benoit, O.P.
Earl F. Berg
James W. Bergland
Hans Dieter Betz
E. F. F. Bishop
Matthew Black
E. C. Blackman
Edward P. Blair
Wm Barnett Blakemore
Gray M. Blandy
Josef Blinzler
M.-E. Boismard
G. H. Boobyer
Jack Stewart Boozer
Myles M. Bourke
M. Bouttier
W. C. Bower
Walter Russell Bowie

John Wick Bowman
W. J. Bradnock
Cora Brady, R.S.C.J.
S. G. F. Brandon
F.-M. Braun, O.P.
Herbert Braun
Brailsford R. Brazeal
Blanche M. Britton
R. E. Brown, S.S.
Robert McAfee Brown
W. R. F. Browning
F. F. Bruce
Harry M. Buck
Rudolf Bultmann
T. A. Burkill
Millar Burrows
B. C. Butler, O.S.B.
George A. Buttrick
Henry J. Cadbury
G. B. Caird
Robert Lowry Calhoun
J. Cambier, S.D.B.
J. Y. Campbell
Michael Cantuar.
(A. M. Ramsey)
M. Carrez
L. Cerfaux
Henry Chadwick
Frederick L. Chenery
Henry Clark
Kenneth Clark
J. J. Collins, S.J.
Carsten Colpe
Ernest C. Colwell
T. Corbishley, S.J.
Bruno Corsani
Rena S. Craig
C. E. B. Cranfield
O. Cullmann
Frederick W. Danker
D. Daube
G. Henton Davies
J. G. Davies
Donald G. Dawe

I. de la Potterie, S.J.
G. Delling
A.-M. Denis, O.P.
Robert C. Dentan
A.-L. Descamps
Simon J. DeVries
Clarence Dickinson
Erich Dinkler
Frank S. Doremus
Tom F. Driver
Randolph H. Dyer
John H. Elliott
E. Earle Ellis
W. Eltester
S. Ifor Enoch
Morton S. Enslin
C. F. Evans
O. E. Evans
A. Feuillet
Floyd V. Filson
Jack Finegan
Fred L. Fisher
J. A. Fitzmyer, S.J.
Daniel J. Fleming
W. F. Flemington
Georges Florovsky
W. Foerster
J. Massingberd Ford
Harry Emerson Fosdick
G. Friedrich
G. W. S. Friedrichsen
R. H. Fuller
Victor Paul Furnish
Winfred E. Garrison
Fred D. Gealy
Jacob Geerlings
A. George, S.M.
A. Geyser
Langdon Gilkey
S. MacLean Gilmour
F. Wilbur Gingrich
J. Gnilka
Eugene V. N. Goetchius
Edwin M. Good

E. Grässer
Holt H. Graham
David Granskou
Frederick C. Grant
Robert M. Grant
K. Grayston
E. M. B. Green
Jack C. Greenawalt
H. Greeven
D. R. Griffiths
W. Grundmann
Feliks Gryglewicz
Aileen Guilding
E. Haenchen
F. Hahn
Paul L. Hammer
R. J. Hammer
Robert T. Handy
A. T. Hanson
Walter Harrelson
Edward G. Harris
Everett F. Harrison
Van A. Harvey
Henrietta Harvin
G. Haufe
Arnold W. Hearn
Raeburne S. Heimbeck
Frank W. Herriott
A. J. B. Higgins
Earle Hilgert
D. Hill
Toshio Hirunuma
Edward C. Hobbs
T. Holtz
S. H. Hooke
Morna D. Hooker
Paul W. Hoon
Robert L. Horn
P. E. Hughes
A. M. Hunter
C.-H. Hunzinger
J. Philip Hyatt
Marguerite Hyer
Ralph Douglas Hyslop
Charles W. Iglehart
Herbert C. Jackson
S. Jellicoe
Joachim Jeremias
Robert Clyde Johnson

R. Francis Johnson
Sherman E. Johnson
Leander E. Keck
Howard C. Kee
J. Spencer Kennard, Jr
Edwin O. Kennedy
Noel Q. King
G. Klein
James A. Knight
Helmut Koester
Robert A. Kraft
Richard Kroner
W. G. Kümmel
J. Kürzinger
Richard Kugelman, C.P.
G. E. Ladd
George M. Landes
Friedrich Lang
A. R. C. Leaney
Robert E. Lee
Paul Lehmann
Ronald Leicester
(R. R. Williams)
Barnabas Lindars, S.S.F.
G. Lindeskog
Bernard M. Loomer
Earl A. Loomis, Jr
Mary Ely Lyman
S. Lyonnet, S.J.
Harvey K. McArthur
J. D. McCaughey
John Macquarrie
Georg Maldfeld
J. Mánek
J. Marsh
James Alfred Martin, Jr
James P. Martin
R. P. Martin
W. Marxsen
Edouard Massaux
B. A. Mastin
Herbert G. May
R. Mayer
Benjamin E. Mays
J. S. Mbiti
Sidney E. Mead
Bruce M. Metzger
Robert M. Meye
Paul W. Meyer

O. Michel
Robert I. Miller
C. L. Mitton
J. Molitor
H. W. Montefiore
Robert M. Montgomery
Jules L. Moreau
Leon Morris
H. K. Moulton
James Muilenberg
A. Victor Murray
F. Mussner
B. D. Napier
W. Neil
C. Ellis Nelson
William Stuart Nelson
C. F. Nesbitt
E. Nestle
Reinhold Niebuhr
B. Noack
Morgan Phelps Noyes
Dan O'Connor
Schubert M. Ogden
G. Ogg
J. C. O'Neill
E. F. Osborn
H. P. Owen
Pierson Parker
V. Parkin
G. J. Paul
J. R. C. Perkin
Norman Perrin
W. Pesch, C.S.S.R.
C. Stewart Petrie
Otto A. Piper
T. E. Pollard
Frederick A. Pope, Jr
Frank W. Price
Alexander C. Purdy
Howard L. Ramsey
M. W. Redus
Frank O. Reed
K. H. Rengstorf
C. R. Renowden
J. Reuss
Howard Rhys
Alan Richardson
Cyril Richardson
Donald W. Riddle

Tabula Gratulatoria

H. Riesenfeld
B. Rigaux, O.F.M.
Martin Rist
B. J. Roberts
T. A. Roberts
James M. Robinson
K. Romaniuk
W. Rordorf
Lawrence Rose
J. Coert Rylaarsdam
E. P. Sanders
J. A. Sanders
Ernest W. Saunders
H. Sawyerr
Martin H. Scharlemann
Richard L. Scheef, Jr
Paul Scherer
R. Schippers
H. Schlier
J. Schmitt
R. Schnackenburg
W. Schneemelcher
Johannes Schneider
Robert E. Seaver
Oscar J. F. Seitz
Massey H. Shepherd, Jr
Helen H. Sherrill
Roger L. Shinn
Edward F. Siegman,
  C.PP.S.

S. S. Smalley
C. W. F. Smith
D. Moody Smith,
  Jr
Morton Smith
R. Gregor Smith
T. C. Smith
Ralph W. Sockman
Matthew Spinka
G. Stählin
David M. Stanley, S.J.
Ludwik Stefaniak
Krister Stendahl
J. S. Stewart
Charles R. Stinnette,
  Jr
G. Strecker
G. M. Styler
Frank E. Sugent
Ray Summers
J. P. M. Sweet
Arthur L. Swift
Theophilus M. Taylor
Vincent Taylor
Samuel Terrien
George F. Thomas
Burton H. Throck-
  morton, Jr
E. J. Tinsley
Lawrence E. Toombs

E. Trocmé
Mary A. Tully
John W. Turnbull
Joseph B. Tyson
Ruel W. Tyson, Jr
Henry P. Van Dusen
B. Van Elderen
A. Vanhoye, S.J.
W. C. van Unnik
P. Vielhauer
J. J. Vincent
A. Vögtle
G. Wagner
R. C. Walls
A. M. Ward
R. A. Ward
George W. Webber
Eugene S. Wehrli
Edward N. West
D. E. H. Whiteley
Henry Nelson Wieman
Amos N. Wilder
R. Dwight Wilhelm
Walter Wink
John Woolwich
(J. A. T. Robinson)
Alec Wyton
J. E. Yates
M. Zerwick, S.J.
H. Zimmermann

xi

JOHN KNOX AT UNION

JOHN C. BENNETT

John Knox's twenty-three years at Union Seminary were the period of his greatest creativity. His teaching profoundly influenced his students both in his own field of New Testament studies and in systematic theology. His most original work was always closely related to problems which were central in theological debate. In this respect his carefulness and humility kept him from asserting himself outside the area of his own most intensive studies but these led him to distinctive positions on such issues as the relation between faith and history and especially the way in which we should understand the historicity of Jesus, the origin and meaning of the Church, and the relationship between justification and new life in Christ. He spoke through the interpretation of New Testament texts and especially through his understanding of Paul, but always it was John Knox reporting a discovery that came from living with the texts. As a former student has put it: He never 'allowed secondary literature to become an end in itself'. He had absorbed it in such a way as to enrich and correct his study of the New Testament itself but it seldom became the main subject of his teaching or his writing. He thought with freedom and often with boldness but his thought was inspired by what he believed to be the true interpretation of the New Testament.

Knox had his own method of demythologizing, long before Bultmann was much discussed, which came from his church-centred piety and his own way of assimilating the teachings and methods of the Chicago school. In contrast to Bultmann, who interpreted the kerygma in terms of the personal existence of the individual, Knox found the key to interpretation of the New Testament in the corporate experience of the Church. One of the remarkable aspects of Knox's teaching was that the New Testament Church was his Church and not merely the subject-matter of historical sociology. There is in him an unusual union of piety and scholarship. His students and his colleagues have always felt this about him as a person. However, one cannot say that in an external way his piety or his own theological stance determined the results of his research, for always he was rigorously honest and open. One of his students writes of him: 'Critical independence and integrity were not so much enjoined as revealed. Though solutions were tenaciously sought, questions were brought no further toward a conclusion than the data would permit; and one saw that frequently that was very little. Yet every case must be judged on its merits, and one realized how varied are the degrees of probability.'

Knox taught at Union when Paul Tillich was leading his students into the perpetual debate about Jesus as an historical figure. Tillich's students carried away contrasting emphases from his lectures and were engaged in furious arguments about what he meant. His thought always seemed to remain on a knife edge and even readers of his books continue to argue as to how far for Tillich the historical reality of Jesus was essential for faith. There was a parallel debate about Knox's thought. Yet in his case the situation was different because of his central emphasis on the historicity of the New Testament Church which remembered Jesus Christ and the origin of which was part of the 'event', Jesus Christ. There could be no doubt about the facticity of the historical core of the New Testament and its importance for faith but there always remained a good deal of uncertainty about the possibility of any knowledge of Jesus Christ as an historical figure that enabled the Christian to find in him a criterion by which to judge the Church. If Tillich was at one extreme in the Union Seminary debate of the period, President Henry Van Dusen was at the other in his insistence on the centrality of the historical Jesus. Tillich, who always tended to absorb the thought of others into his system, felt close rapport with Knox on this subject and Van Dusen always felt that Knox tended to lose Jesus in the Church. I am sure that the debate about the real meaning of the thought of both Tillich and Knox will continue.

Another continuous debate at Union Seminary was between the Reinhold Niebuhr of that period and, again, President Van Dusen over the relationship between justification and sanctification or, with different nuances, between grace and law. Here Knox intervened in the debate quite clearly and decisively. He understood fully the emphasis on justification and he had his own brilliant analysis of Paul's thought on this subject but he always insisted on the essential place of law, sanctification, character, moral achievement. I remember his chapel sermons on this subject which combined a powerful correction of the one-sided emphasis on justification with his own fresh way of stating the dialectic which Niebuhr also sought to maintain in a different way. I felt then and I feel now that, influential as Knox was on theological thinking, in this area he should have been listened to even more as a most perceptive systematic theologian. He always had the advantage of being able to appeal to Paul, who was also the chief authority for those who seemed to have a one-sided emphasis on justification! One of his students says of Knox that though he was 'congenial to the theological realism of the 1940s', he counterbalanced 'the extreme tendencies of the so-called neo-orthodoxy'.

During several years when I taught the basic course in Systematic Theology, I used as one of the required readings in Christology Knox's volume entitled *On the Meaning of Christ*. Whether one is fully satisfied with his understanding of the place of the historical Jesus in the 'Christ event', Knox does provide most systematically in that volume alternatives to the traditional Christological categories which I have found most meaningful.

His colleagues have always marvelled at John Knox's productivity. He published fourteen volumes while at Union. These were relatively short books for Knox never felt it necessary to argue in his writings with many of his predecessors or contemporaries. He usually took the secondary materials for granted. Before he came to Union he had done his book on Marcion and also his study of Philemon. He had already proved that he had a gift for the detective type of scholarship in dealing with the origin and authorship of biblical writings which he had learned from his teacher Edgar Goodspeed and others. Some of this type of scholarship appears in his books of the Union period but mostly he devoted himself to the analysis and interpretation of biblical theology. I always felt that more than most scholars he came to know Paul by living with him and reflecting continually on his thought, always doing his own thinking about Paul's problems as his own problems while he listened to Paul.

He lived a very disciplined life, choosing only those outside engagements which seemed to belong to his own vocation. In later years at Union he limited the variety of his activities because of health though there were few days on which he was unable to carry his full responsibilities. His natural reserve, that may have seemed to some to represent considerable detachment, was combined with a willingness to enter into many of the activities of the Seminary that seemed to him to be most important. One of his students has written: 'There was not only his heavy involvement as Director of Studies...but he was frequently on student-faculty panels—sometimes discussing curriculum, sometimes such theological issues as "New Testament Miracles"...He was also very regular in his attendance at Chapel when others preached—and his singing of the hymns is one of the distinctive and lasting memories I have of Chapel at Union.'

One aspect of this disciplined life was his early rising and his colleagues could know when they were having breakfast that John Knox had already written his five hundred words or more for the day, that already through him Union Seminary had made a significant contribution to the thought of the Church. Such continuous daily writing year after year, when the writer can devote what are for him the best hours of the day to it, does bear wonderful fruit. Often the immediate stimulus for his writing was an engagement to deliver a series of academic lectures to be given at another institution. This often controlled the form of the book, keeping it concise and its style direct and its subject-matter relevant. His books are not generally 'popular' in the pejorative sense with which that word is sometimes applied to books by scholars, but they are clear and without the technical apparatus which limits the book to specialists. His books contain many fresh contributions to *thought* about the results of scholarship by one who knows those results at first hand.

John Knox was most involved in the life of the Seminary during his thirteen years as Director of Studies. This position has since been given the title of Dean of Instruction and it should have had this title when Knox held the position. He was in fact the academic dean for the B.D. students. Union in its curriculum has always given priority to its B.D. students and so during his years as Director of Studies Knox was at the centre of the academic administration of the Seminary with a great deal of committee work, including for a time the chairmanship of the Committee on Admissions, a most exacting responsibility. He was involved in an extensive correspondence and

John C. Bennett

torical research, for its critical potency, for its open-endedness, d at the same time for its intrinsic limits.'

Knox was one of the most effective preachers in the Seminary hapel though such a characterization will shock his humility. or some reason he refused to preach in the chapel on Sunday. This may have been partly a result of his diffidence and partly the result of his questioning the Seminary's having chapel on Sunday in competition with the churches. I can remember a number of occasions when he preached during the week or at special services. His sermons were very carefully wrought and read with great force, often with passion. Naturally his sermons were expository and they always involved a fresh canvassing of a vital theological or ethical issue. His particular analysis of the text often contained surprises and I find myself remembering something substantial from his sermons many years after. I suppose that the sermons of which I speak were not for the average congregation but they were preached with great effect to the Seminary community. In some form the material in his sermons was often included later in his books. As always he limited himself to areas of thought and application that belonged to his own most characteristic reflexion. Unlike many of his colleagues he was reticent in moving out into discussions of current public issues. I often wished that he would speak out more on such issues but I respected his diffidence about speaking outside the sphere of his own special vocation. When he did speak on social issues it was often in the context of the Church's own integrity. Quite naturally he spoke in these terms about the problems of fellowship and justice as between the races. As a Southerner who had at one time been Chaplain at Fisk University the racial issues were always on his mind and conscience. Even in this area I noticed a non-political cast of mind, again in contrast to many of his colleagues.

It was during the later years of his period at Union Seminary that John Knox became an Episcopalian. He had always spoken with warmth and piety about the ministry and influence of his father in the Methodist Church, but for a man who made the Church so central in his scholarship and thinking he never seemed to be a strong churchman as a Methodist. As I have said, his dealing as a scholar with the Church as the key concept in the New Testament was combined with a strong sense that the New Testament Church

in many hours a week of interviews with
in writing the official, diplomatic but kinc
He had a strong sense of order and of the si
but he combined with this what one of his stu
empathy for students'. This administrative
experience all of the dilemmas concerning g
concerned him so much as a biblical theologian
greatest respect from the students, and his collea
much his quite natural wish to be relieved of th
responsibilities after he had had what was sur
them.

Always on administrative issues his mind was aler
ment much trusted as a member of the faculty. He w
faculty meetings and in these and on other occasions, wi
to assert himself, it was usually after a ritual of self-c
which at times aroused amusement because it was as muc
as it was inappropriate, but then he would speak and he
views about policy with great confidence and even stubt
What I have called his sense of order and of the significance
cedents always proved to be useful and influential when he p
pated in the debates of the faculty. There was sometimes an aus
about his devotion to academic principles which was too mucl
the majority of the faculty but if he was voted down it was o
after several forceful and even eloquent speeches by him. Administ
tors would often try out their ideas on Knox and would be ver
much encouraged when he was on their side!

I have been impressed by the extent to which students emphasize
that as a teacher Knox always encouraged them to think and speak
for themselves. As one of them says: 'He prefers helping students to
develop their own capacities for independent judgment.' He adds
that Knox, 'instead of becoming the centre of a personality cult,
focuses the attention of his students on the subject being studied'.
Another writes: 'Toward students Professor Knox was an attentive
listener and reader, requiring only commitment to the evidence and
hard thinking. One could argue with him freely.' This same student
who has devoted much of his own career to the problems surrounding the historicity of Jesus says: 'Beyond the many specific insights,
one gained from him an ineradicable feeling for the seriousness of

was his Church. His own confidence in the historical base of Christianity came from his participation in the Church, the founding of which belonged to the Christ-event. His friends who watched him very gradually move toward the Episcopal Church felt that he was seeking a Church which celebrated continuity and tradition in its faith and worship and which at the same time would give him the full theological freedom which he often exercised with unusual boldness. I am not an Episcopalian but I can understand such a feeling about that Church. The Episcopal students at Union, of whom there have long been many especially among graduate students, asked him to be their adviser while he was becoming an Episcopalian. He and his family joined a small but very vital Episcopal Church a few blocks down the hill from the Seminary in Harlem, a Church which is remarkable for its interracial character and its service to the whole community. In due course he received Episcopal ordination. It is significant that he was soon joined in this same pilgrimage by way of this same local congregation by his Scotch Presbyterian colleague, John Macquarrie, who has dedicated to Knox his *Principles of Christian Theology*. In his preface Macquarrie mentions especially his indebtedness to Knox's 'profound insights into the nature of the Church' This is one of many indications that John Knox has been a teacher of his colleagues as well as his students.

JOHN KNOX: *CURSUS VITAE*

1900   Born in Frankfort, Kentucky.

1919   A.B., Randolph-Macon College.

1919–24 Minister in the Methodist Episcopal Church, South, serving several parishes in West Virginia and in Baltimore, Maryland, with an interim of study at Emory University.

1924–7   Assistant professor of Bible, Emory University.

1925   B.D., Emory University.

1928–9   Methodist pastorate, Bethesda, Maryland.

1929–36 Minister, Fisk University.

1935   Ph.D., University of Chicago.

1936–8   Managing Editor, *Christendom*.

1938–9   Associate professor of N.T., Hartford Theological Foundation.

1939–42 Associate professor of Homiletics, University of Chicago.

1942–3   Professor of Homiletics and N.T., University of Chicago.

1943–66 Baldwin Professor of Sacred Literature, Union Theological Seminary (Director of Studies, 1945–57).

1944   Became member of the New York East Conference of the Methodist Episcopal Church; Ayer Lecturer, Colgate-Rochester Divinity School.

1946/7   William Belden Nobel Lecturer, Harvard University.

1948   Litt.D., Randolph-Macon College.

1949   Quillian Lecturer, Emory University.

1950   Jackson Lecturer, Southern Methodist University.

1952   McFadin Lecturer, Texas Christian University.

1952–3   Fulbright Lecturer, Cambridge University.

1954   Guest Lecturer, Butler University School of Religion.

1955   Hoover Lecturer, University of Chicago.

1956   S.T.D., Emory University; Shaffer Lecturer, Yale University; Gray Lecturer, Duke University.

1957   Carew Lecturer, Hartford Theological Foundation; Convocation Lecturer, Eden Theological Seminary

1960   Ingersoll Lecturer, Harvard University; Willson Lecturer on Christian Education, Nashville, Tennessee; Frank and Mary Miller Lecturer in Homiletics, United Theological Seminary.

1962   Ordained to the ministry of the Protestant Episcopal Church; Bohlen Lecturer, Philadelphia, Pennsylvania.

1963   James W. Richard Lecturer, University of Virginia; D.D. degree, Glasgow University; D.D. degree, Philadelphia Divinity School.

1965   Francis B. Denio Lecturer, Bangor Theological Seminary. S.T.D. degree, General Theological Seminary.

1966–   Professor of New Testament at the Episcopal Theological Seminary of the Southwest in Austin, Texas.

BIBLIOGRAPHY OF THE WORK OF
JOHN KNOX

COMPILED BY JOHN COOLIDGE HURD, JR

NOTE: On John Knox's work through 1962 see Dennis E. Nineham, 'Theologians of Our Time: 6, John Knox', *Exp Times* 74 (1962/3), 234–8. The abbreviations for the names of journals in this and in subsequent annotations follow the system used by *New Testament Abstracts*.

BOOKS AND ARTICLES

1929   '"He shall Be Like a Tree"', *The Christian Century*, 46, 21 (22 May 1929), 680–1.

1930   'Why the Revival Did Not Come', *The Christian Century*, 47, 47 (19 Nov. 1930), 1415–16.

1932   *'He Whom a Dream Hath Possessed': Some Aspects of Religious Living.* New York: Ray Long and Richard R. Smith, Inc., 1932. Pp. x + 121.

——   'God Is Still Building His World', *Christian Advocate* (Nashville, Tenn.), 93, 36 (2 Sept. 1932), 1128–30.

——   '"...When There is no Peace"', *Christian Advocate* (Nashville, Tenn.), 93, 50 (9 Dec. 1932), 1576–7.

1934   '"Ugly Ducklings"', *Christian Advocate* (Nashville, Tenn.), 95, 23 (15 June 1934), 744–5.

1935   *Philemon Among the Letters of Paul: A New View of Its Place and Importance.* (The University of Chicago: A Dissertation Submitted to the Faculty of the Division of the Humanities in Candidacy for the Degree of Doctor of Philosophy, Department of New Testament and Early Christian Literature, 1935.) Chicago: The University of Chicago Press, 1935. London: Cambridge University Press, 1935. Pp. x + 59. [Enlarged and republished, 1959.]

For comment and response see: Edgar J. Goodspeed, *Christianity Goes to Press* (New York: The Macmillan Company, 1940), pp. 8, 12, 57, and 83; P. N. Harrison, 'Onesimus and Philemon',

AnglTheolRev 32 (1950), 268–94; H. Greeven, 'Prüfung der Thesen von J. Knox zum Philemonbrief', *TheolLitZeit* 79 (1954), 373–8; C. Leslie Mitton, *The Formation of the Pauline Corpus of Letters* (London: The Epworth Press, 1955), *passim*; Edgar J. Goodspeed, *The Key to Ephesians* (Chicago: The University of Chicago Press, 1956), pp. xiv–xvi; C. F. D. Moule, *The Epistles of Paul the Apostle to the Colossians and to Philemon* ('Cambridge Greek Testament Commentary', ed. C. F. D. Moule; Cambridge: The University Press, 1957), pp. 14–18; and Walter Schmithals, 'Zur Abfassung und ältesten Sammlung der paulinischen Hauptbriefe', *ZeitNTWiss* 51 (1960), 225–45.

1936   'A Note on II Thessalonians 2: 2', *Anglican Theological Review*, 18 (1936), 72–3.

—— 'A Conjecture as to the Original Status of II Corinthians and II Thessalonians in the Pauline Corpus', *Journal of Biblical Literature*, 55 (1936), 145–53.

—— '"Fourteen Years Later": A Note on the Pauline Chronology', *The Journal of Religion*, 16 (1936), 341–9.

—— 'The Preaching Mission Starts', *The Christian Century*, 53, 40 (30 Sept. 1936), 1288–90.

1938   'The Bible in College', *The Christian Century*, 55, 2 (12 Jan. 1938), 47–9.

    In response see: Chester Warren Quimby, letter to the editor, *ChristCent* 55, 4 (26 Jan. 1938), 117; Albion Roy King, 'Religion in the Colleges', *ChristCent* 55, 7 (16 Feb. 1938), 206–8; and Chester W. Quimby, 'Teach the Bible as Religion', *JournBibRel* 6 (1938), 70–2.

—— '"As Religion"—But in What Sense?' *The Journal of Bible and Religion*, 6 (1938), 72–4 [in reply to C. W. Quimby above].

    In response: Albion Roy King, 'Religion a By-Product in Education', *JournBibRel* 6 (1938), 74–6; and Chester W. Quimby, 'Mr. Quimby Comments', *JournBibRel* 6 (1938), 76.

—— 'Beauty and Religion', *Chicago Theological Seminary Register*, May 1938.

—— 'Our Knowledge of Jesus', *Christendom*, 3 (1938), 44–54.

—— 'Philemon and the Authenticity of Colossians', *The Journal of Religion*, 18 (1938), 144–60.

1938 'A Pastoral Prayer', *The Christian Century Pulpit*, 9, 6 (June 1938), 139.

1939 'The Pauline Chronology', *Journal of Biblical Literature*, 58 (1939), 15–29.

> For comment see: Werner Georg Kümmel, 'Das Urchristentum', *TheolRund* 17 (1948/9), 4, 48–9.

—— 'On the Vocabulary of Marcion's Gospel', *Journal of Biblical Literature*, 58 (1939), 193–201.

—— '"They Suffer from a Nothingness"', *The Christian Century*, 56, 43 (25 Oct. 1939), 1303–4.

1941 *The Man Christ Jesus*. Chicago: Willett, Clark and Company, 1941. Pp. 100. [Japanese edition, 1944; Korean edition, 1955; German edition, 1962.]

1942 *Marcion and the New Testament: An Essay in the Early History of the Canon*. Chicago: The University of Chicago Press, 1942. London: The Cambridge University Press, 1942. Pp. ix+ 195.

> For comment see: C. Leslie Mitton, *The Formation of the Pauline Corpus of Letters* (London: The Epworth Press, 1955), *passim*; C. F. D. Moule, *The Epistles of Paul the Apostle to the Colossians and to Philemon* ('Cambridge Greek Testament Commentary', ed. C. F. D. Moule; Cambridge: The University Press, 1957), pp. 14–18; and Walter Schmithals, 'Zur Abfassung und ältesten Sammlung der paulinischen Hauptbriefe', *ZeitNTWiss* 51 (1960), 225–45. [See also 'A Note on the Format of the Pauline Corpus' (1957) below.]

—— 'Re-examining Pacifism', in *Religion and the Present Crisis*, edited by John Knox ('Lecturers under the Charles R. Walgreen Foundation for the Study of American Institutions', The University of Chicago, 1941; Chicago: The University of Chicago Press, 1942), pp. 30–47.

1943 'We Are Divided', *The Christian Century*, 60, 1 (6 Jan. 1943), 13–14.

—— 'Can Evil Always Be Overcome With Good?' *Christianity and Crisis*, 3, 3 (8 March 1943), 2–4.

1944 'The Beginnings of Christianity', chapter 2 of *The Vitality of the Christian Tradition*, edited by George F. Thomas (New

York and London: Harper and Brothers Publishers, 1944), pp. 36–53.

1945 *Christ the Lord: The Meaning of Jesus in the Early Church.* ('The Ayer Lectures of the Colgate-Rochester Divinity School', 1944.) Chicago: Willett, Clark and Company, 1945. Pp. xiv+ 146.

—— *The Christian Church and Race.* 'Pamphlet Library on the Church and Minority Peoples.' New York: Distributed by the Commission on the Church and Minority Peoples of the Federal Council of the Churches of Christ in America, 1945. Pp. 24.

—— *The Fourth Gospel and the Later Epistles.* ('A Guide for Bible Readers', edited by H. F. Rall; NT iv.) New York: Abingdon-Cokesbury Press, paper, 1945. Pp. 157.

—— 'Christianity and the Christian', chapter 5 of *The Christian Answer*, edited by Henry P. van Dusen (New York: Charles Scribner's Sons, 1945), pp. 160–90.

1946 'The Revelation of God in Christ', chapter 1 of *The Gospel, the Church and the World*, edited by Kenneth S. LaTourette ('The Interseminary Series', vol. iii; New York: Harper and Brothers Publishers, 1946), pp. 3–26.

—— 'A Survey of Recent Theological Literature: The New Testament', *Union Seminary Quarterly Review*, 2, 1 (Nov. 1946), 26–7.

1947 *On the Meaning of Christ.* ('The William Belden Noble Lectures', Harvard University, 1947.) New York: Charles Scribner's Sons, 1947. Pp. xviii+ 117.

1950 *Chapters in a Life of Paul.* (An expansion of 'The Quillian Lectures', Emory University, 1949.) New York: Abingdon-Cokesbury Press, 1950. 'Apex edition', paper, 1964. London: Adam and Charles Black, 1954; paper, 1965. Pp. 168.

For comment see: Donald T. Rowlingson, 'The Jerusalem Conference and Jesus' Nazareth Visit: A Study in Pauline Chronology', *JournBibLit* 71 (1952), 69–74; George Ogg, 'A New Chronology of Saint Paul's Life', *Exp Times* 64 (1952/3), 120–3; S. Agourides, 'St. Paul after 1900 Years', *EcumRev* 5 (1952/3), 309–12; Thomas H. Campbell, 'Paul's "Missionary Journeys" as Reflected in His Letters', *JournBibLit* 74 (1955), 80–7; M. Jack

Suggs, 'Concerning the Date of Paul's Macedonian Ministry', *Nov Test* 4 (1960), 60–8; and John Coolidge Hurd, Jr., *The Origin of I Corinthians* (London: S.P.C.K.; New York: Seabury Press, 1965), pp. 6–42, 296.

1950   'The Peril in Thanksgiving', *Union Seminary Quarterly Review*, 5, 2 (Jan. 1950), 3–5.

1951   'A Note on Mark 14: 51–52', in *The Joy of Study: Papers on the New Testament and Related Subjects Presented to Honor Frederick Clifton Grant*, edited by Sherman E. Johnson (New York: The Macmillan Company, 1951), pp. 27–30.

1952   *Criticism and Faith.* ('The Jackson Lectures', Southern Methodist University, 1950, and 'The McFadin Lectures', Texas Christian University, 1952.) New York and Nashville: Abingdon-Cokesbury Press, 1952. Pp. 128. London: Hodder and Stoughton, 1953. Pp. 126.

——   'The Gospel According to St. Luke: Exposition of Chapters 7–12', in *The Interpreter's Bible*, edited by G. A. Buttrick *et al.* (12 vols.; New York and Nashville: Abingdon Press, 1951–7), VIII, 128–239.

——   'Christian Hope', *Christianity and Crisis*, 12, 5 (31 March 1952), 33–4.

1953   'Pliny and I Peter: A Note on I Peter 4: 14–16 and 3: 15', *Journal of Biblical Literature*, 72 (1953), 187–9.

——   'Authenticity and Relevance', *Union Seminary Quarterly Review*, 9, 1 (Nov. 1953), 3–9.

1954   'The Epistle to the Romans: Introduction and Exegesis', in *The Interpreter's Bible*, edited by G. A. Buttrick *et al.* (12 vols.; New York and Nashville: Abingdon Press, 1951–7), IX, 353–668.

——   'Ethical Obligations in the Realm of Grace' (Lectures delivered at the Butler University School of Religion), *The Shane Quarterly*, 15 (1954), 53–93.

1955   *The Early Church and the Coming Great Church.* (Contains 'The William Henry Hoover Lectureship on Christian Unity', The Disciples Divinity House of the University of Chicago, 1955.) New York and Nashville: Abingdon Press, 1955. London: Epworth Press, 1957. Pp. 160.

——   'The Mystery of God', in *Best Sermons, 1955 Edition*, edited by G. Paul Butler (New York: McGraw-Hill Book Co., 1955), pp. 181–6.

1955 'The Epistle to Philemon: Introduction and Exegesis', in *The Interpreter's Bible*, edited by G. A. Buttrick *et al.* (12 vols.; New York and Nashville: Abingdon Press, 1951–7), XI, 553–73.

1956 'The Ministry in the Primitive Church', chapter 1 of *The Ministry in Historical Perspectives*, edited by H. Richard Niebuhr and Daniel D. Williams (A Publication of 'The Survey of Theological Education in the United States and Canada'; New York: Harper and Brothers Publishers, 1956), pp. 1–26.

—— 'A Note on the Text of Romans', *New Testament Studies*, 2 (1955/6), 191–3.

1957 *The Integrity of Preaching.* ('The James A. Gray Lectures', The Divinity School of Duke University, 1956.) New York and Nashville: Abingdon Press, 1957. London: Epworth Press, 1965. Pp. 96. [Portuguese edition, 1964.]

—— 'Literary Chronology: The New Testament', in *The Interpreter's Bible*, edited by G. A. Buttrick *et al.* (12 vols.; New York and Nashville: Abingdon Press, 1951–7), XII, 669–72.

—— 'A Note on the Format of the Pauline Corpus', *Harvard Theological Review*, 50 (1957), 311–14 [a reply to J. Finegan, 'The Original Form of the Pauline Collection', *HarvTheolRev* 49 (1956), 85–103, which commented upon 'The Epistle to the Romans: Introduction' (1954), and *Marcion and the New Testament* (1942)].

1958 *The Death of Christ: The Cross in New Testament History and Faith.* (Contains material from 'The Shaffer Lectures', Yale Divinity School, 1956; 'The Carew Lectures', The Hartford Theological Seminary, 1957; and 'The Convocation Lectures', Eden Theological Seminary, 1957.) New York and Nashville: Abingdon Press, 1958. London: William Collins Sons and Co., Ltd, 1959. Pp. 190. [Japanese edition, 1963.]

For comment see: F. H. Cleobury, 'Jesus or Christ?' *ModChurch*, n.s. 2 (1958/9), 200–4; and Peter C. Hodgson, 'The Son of Man and the Problem of Historical Knowledge', *JournRel* 41 (1961), 91–108.

1958 *Jesus: Lord and Christ—A Trilogy Comprising 'The Man Christ Jesus', 'Christ the Lord', 'On the Meaning of Christ'.* New York: Harper and Brothers Publishers, 1958. Pp. x + 278. [See 1941, 1945, and 1947 above.]

For comment see: Richard R. Niebuhr, *Resurrection and Historical Reason: A Study of Theological Method* (New York: Charles Scribner's Sons, 1957), pp. 62–71, 94–6, 100–4; and Robert E. Cushman, 'Christology or Ecclesiology? A Critical Examination of the Christology of John Knox', *RelLife* 27 (1957/8), 515–26.

—— 'The Church *Is* Christ's Body', *Religion in Life*, 27 (1957/8), 54–62.

1959 *Philemon Among the Letters of Paul: A New View of Its Place and Importance.* Revised edition. New York and Nashville: Abingdon Press, 1959. Pp. 110. London: William Collins Sons and Co., Ltd, 1960; paper, 1963. Pp. 96. [See 1935 above.]

—— with J. Christiaan Beker, 'Bibliography for Ministers: The New Testament', *Union Seminary Quarterly Review*, 14, 2 (Jan. 1959), 51–7.

1960 with J. Christiaan Beker (NT eds.). *A Basic Bibliography for Ministers Selected & Annotated by the Faculty of Union Theological Seminary, New York City.* 2nd ed. New York: Union Theological Seminary Book Service, 1960. Pp. 139. [See 1959 above.]

—— *Christ and the Hope of Glory.* (Essay written in preparation for 'The Ingersoll Lecture on the Immortality of Man', Harvard University, 1960.) New York and Nashville: Abingdon Press, 1960. Pp. 63.

—— 'The Hope of Glory: The Ingersoll Lecture 1960', *Harvard Divinity Bulletin*, 24, 2 (April 1960), 9–19.

1961 *The Ethic of Jesus in the Teaching of the Church: Its Authority and Its Relevance.* (Draws on 'The Willson Lectures on Christian Education', Nashville, Tenn., 1960; and on addresses delivered at the United Theological Seminary, and the Wesley Theological Seminary; 'The C. I. Jones Memorial Lectures', Rayne Memorial Methodist Church, New Orleans, La.; and 'Ethical Obligations in the Realm of Grace' [see 1954 above].) New York and Nashville: Abingdon Press, 1961. Pp. 124. London: The Epworth Press, 1962. Pp. 160.

1961   *Life in Christ Jesus: Reflections on Romans 5–8.* Greenwich, Conn.: The Seabury Press, 1961; paper, 1966. Toronto, Canada: Oxford University Press, 1961. London: S.P.C.K., paper, 1963. Pp. 128.

1962   *The Church and the Reality of Christ.* (Contains 'The Bohlen Lectures', Philadelphia, Pennsylvania, 1962.) New York: Harper and Row, Publishers, 1962. London: William Collins Sons and Co., Ltd, 1963. Pp. 158.

> For comment see: E. Tilson, 'The Eclipse of Faith', *Interpretation* 17 (1963), 466–78.

——   'Introductions and Annotations to Romans, 1 and 2 Corinthians, and Philippians', in *The Oxford Annotated Bible: Revised Standard Version*, edited by Herbert G. May and Bruce M. Metzger (New York: Oxford University Press, 1962), pp. 1359–1407, 1421–5.

——   'Caesar', 'Letter to Diognetus', 'Docetism', 'Fulness of Time', 'Letter to the Galatians', 'Members', 'Minuscule', 'Muratorian Fragment', 'Martyrdom of Polycarp', 'Sibylline Oracles', 'Textus Receptus', 'Unical', in *The Interpreter's Dictionary of the Bible*, edited by George A. Buttrick *et al.* 4 vols. New York and Nashville: Abingdon Press, 1962.

——   'What I Believe About the Activity of the Holy Spirit', *Union Seminary Quarterly Review*, 17 (1961/2), 294–6.

1963   *A Guide for the Reader of the New Testament for Use with the New English Bible.* New York: The Oxford University Press and the Cambridge University Press, paper, 1963. Pp. 39.

——   'Archippus', 'Epistle to the Colossians', 'Demas', 'Epaphras', 'Epaphroditus', 'Epistle to the Ephesians', 'Onesimus', 'Philemon', 'Epistle to Philemon', 'First Epistle to the Thessalonians', 'Second Epistle to the Thessalonians', 'Tychicus', in *Dictionary of the Bible*, edited by James Hastings; revised edition by F. C. Grant and H. H. Rowley. New York: Charles Scribner's Sons, 1963.

——   'The Foolishness of God', *Union Seminary Quarterly Review*, 19 (1963/4), 1–4. [Reprinted: *Lutheran Woman*, March 1964.]

1964 *Myth and Truth: An Essay on the Language of Faith*. ('The James W. Richard Lectures in Christian Religion', The University of Virginia, 1963–4.) Charlottesville, Va.: The University of Virginia Press, 1964. Pp. 87.

—— 'Romans 15: 14–33 and Paul's Conception of His Apostolic Mission', *Journal of Biblical Literature*, 83 (1964), 1–11. [Presidential Address, Society of Biblical Literature, 1 Jan. 1964.]

—— 'The Greatest Missionary: Paul', *Life*, 57, 26 (25 Dec. 1964), 112–25. [Special issue of *Life*: 'The Bible'.]

1965 'The Humanity of Jesus in New Testament Thought', *The Alumni Bulletin of Bangor Theological Seminary*, 40, 2 (April 1965), 1–8. [The first of 'The Francis B. Denio Lectures on the Bible', Bangor Theological Seminary, 1965.]

—— *The Spirit in the Church*. 'Cathedral Papers.' Cincinnati, Ohio: Forward Movement Publications, 1965. Pp. 19. [A lecture delivered at the Cathedral of St John the Divine, New York.]

1966 'Paul's Mission to the Nations', *The Bible Today*, 24 (1965), 1571–7. [Cf. 'Romans 15: 14–33 . . .' (1964) above.]

—— 'A Few Memories and a Great Debt', *Criterion*, 5 (1966), 24–6.

—— 'The "Prophet" in New Testament Christology', in *Lux in Lumine: Essays to Honor W. Norman Pittenger*, edited by R. A. Norris, Jr. (New York: The Seabury Press, 1966), pp. 23–34.

—— 'Acts and the Pauline Letter Corpus', in *Studies in Luke-Acts: Essays Presented in Honor of Paul Schubert*, edited by Leander E. Keck and J. Louis Martyn (New York and Nashville: Abingdon Press, 1966), pp. 279–87.

1967 *The Humanity and Divinity of Christ: A Study of Pattern in Christology*. (Contains 'The Francis B. Denio Lectures on the Bible', Bangor Theological Seminary, 1965.) Cambridge and New York: The Cambridge University Press, 1967; paper, 1967. Pp. x + 118.

NOTE: The present compiler has deposited in the libraries of the Union Theological Seminary, New York, and of the Episcopal Theological Seminary of the Southwest, Austin, Texas, a fuller version of the above bibliography. The additional material consists of references to reviews written by Professor Knox and to reviews of his work written by other scholars. Also in New York is the following: Alexander Kee, 'Kerygma and Memory: Rudolf Bultmann and John Knox', unpublished S.T.M. thesis, Union Theological Seminary, 1962.

EDITORSHIPS

1936–8 Managing Editor, *Christendom*, 1, 5 (Autumn 1936) through 3, 4 (Autumn 1938).

—— Member, Editorial Staff, *The Christian Century*, 1936–8.

1939–43 Editor, *The Journal of Religion*, 19, 3 (July 1939) through 23 (1943).

1942 Editor, *Religion and the Present Crisis*. ('Lectures under the Charles R. Walgreen Foundation for the Study of American Institutions', The University of Chicago, 1941.) Chicago: The University of Chicago Press, 1942. Pp. xii + 1965.

1947– Member, Editorial Board, *Religion in Life*, 16, 2 (Spring 1947) and following.

1951–7 Associate Editor of New Testament Introduction and Exegesis, *The Interpreter's Bible*. 12 volumes. New York and Nashville: Abingdon Press, 1951–7.

1960– Member, The Standard Bible Committee, 1960 and following.

1962 Associate Editor for New Testament Articles, *The Interpreter's Dictionary of the Bible*. 4 volumes. New York and Nashville: Abingdon Press, 1962.

1964– Member, Bible Translation Committee of the Bishops' Committee of the Confraternity of Christian Doctrine, 1964 and following.

EDITORS' FOREWORD

The present volume of essays is a tribute to John Knox. Necessarily it constantly refers to the work that he has already given to the worlds of Christian faith, scholarship, and interpretation. But much of the pleasure which the contributors and editors have gained from the making of this *Festschrift* has come from the knowledge that John Knox's devotion to the understanding of the New Testament and to the strengthening of the Church continues to produce new findings and further extensions of his theology. Hence, what the reader will find here are testimonies of indebtedness to one man by many who are working with him.

Some of the essays are by men who began their professional lives under Knox's care, while others are by long time colleagues. Some are essays that directly assess issues and themes in Knox's books and articles, while others pursue topics more central to their authors' minds, perhaps, than to John Knox's, but which nevertheless show a direction or shape that owes much to the influence of his thinking. These essays contain a fair amount of criticism, but that is as it should be where the intention is to honour a man who has always subordinated himself to his subject-matter, the reality of Christ and the Church. This book is a meeting of minds under the auspices of a fine, generous, and fair mind. We hope that it contributes to the work to which John Knox has long given himself.

The volume has two divisions—not historical and theological, for no such division could accurately reflect John Knox's specific genius —one dealing principally with questions of history and faith focused on Jesus of Nazareth and the other dealing chiefly with the mind of Paul and problems of Pauline interpretation. The division, of course, is partly artificial, since the nature of history and Christian community and memory run as constant themes throughout the book, and of course Jesus Christ is the subject-matter of the whole. But inasmuch as John Knox has worked steadily on both the clarification of Paul's legacy to Christendom and on Christian faith's relation to the historical Jesus, it seemed appropriate to give the book a structure that would agree with the consistent twofold bearing of John Knox's thinking and research.

The editors have many thanks to express gladly, first of all to the contributors, and then on behalf of all who have had a part in this book to members of the editorial staff of the Cambridge University Press who have helped both as official representatives of the Press and as enthusiastic supporters of the project.

W. R. FARMER

C. F. D. MOULE

R. R. NIEBUHR

ABBREVIATIONS

Abbreviations of the titles of journals follow, so far as possible, those used by *New Testament Abstracts* (Weston, Mass.); other abbreviations are closely modelled on the system used in the Kittel-Friedrich *Theologisches Wörterbuch zum Neuen Testament* (Stuttgart).

Rabbinic references follow the system adopted by Marcus Jastrow in his *A Dictionary of the Targumim, the Talmud Babli and Yerushalmi, and the Midrashic Literature*, (New York, 1950).

PART I

PROBLEMS OF HISTORY
AND FAITH

1

SOME IMPLICATIONS, PHILOSOPHICAL AND THEOLOGICAL, IN JOHN KNOX'S WRITING

NORMAN PITTENGER

In the field of New Testament scholarship, the work of Professor John Knox is widely recognized and highly esteemed, but it is not often enough understood that the conclusions reached in Professor Knox's specifically biblical study both rest upon and result in a view of history, nature, and God and of man and his social relationships which in and of itself is both interesting and important. The double purpose of this brief essay, one of a number of tributes to John Knox, is to indicate some central aspects of this philosophical-theological position and to attempt an evaluation of its significance, in the hope that the attention of theologians may be given to one possible way of understanding the Christian reality.

At the outset, it should be said that in his writings Professor Knox does not set forth the scheme which this essay will suggest. He has proceeded with his work on the New Testament, developing his views in book after book and essay after essay, without feeling the need to present a statement of philosophical and theological pre-suppositions and without drawing out in any detail the implications of his work in these areas. Yet it is my conviction that for various reasons—probably not unconnected with his long association with the University of Chicago and his cooperation there with the faculty of the divinity school, with his equally long association with Union Theological Seminary in New York and his warm friendship with such theologians as Paul Tillich, and with his growing aware-ness in the past two decades of the importance of 'Christian tradi-tion' as a living reality in the present, an awareness which led him finally to his present affiliation with the Episcopal Church— Professor Knox has been working on the basis of certain general philosophical and theological ideas and has been directing our attention to certain conclusions in these fields—all of which are plain enough in his writing, even if they are not 'spelled out' in a precise and definite fashion.

The three points to which I shall ask the reader's attention may be stated in this way:

(1) Professor Knox holds a dynamic view of history and by implication a processive view of the world order. That is, he believes that both the world and human experience in it are best understood, not in terms of 'being', 'substance', or 'metaphysical essences', but in terms of movement, purposive change, 'becoming', and relationships.

(2) Professor Knox thinks of the several 'events' which occur in this processive world, not as fixed moments which can be given precise location and exact dating, but as richly complex occasions in which the preparations in the past, the happening and its reception in the present, and the consequences which follow from the happening and give it continuing significance for the future, are all seen as integral to any adequate description of what a given 'event' *really* is.

(3) Professor Knox is convinced that it is only by an engagement in faith that the revelatory and salvatory character of an 'event' can be grasped. Hence the necessary kind of historical inquiry which concerns itself primarily with what might be styled archaeological research must be supplemented, if the full religious import of the 'event' is to be known, by participation (either in actual fact or by some attempt at sympathetic identification) in the community which brings the story of the 'event' to the present-day believer and also enables him to respond in commitment, in faith. Then the event 'comes alive' in his own experience and has the deepest possible significance for his own life: he *knows* what it means.

We shall discuss briefly each of these points in the following section.

I

First, the dynamic and processive view of the world and of God in relation to that world. While Professor Knox makes no explicit avowal of his personal philosophical position, the line which he suggests throughout his writing is strongly reminiscent of the work of Charles Hartshorne, who for many years was a member of the faculty of the University of Chicago. Furthermore, some of the incidental comments which Knox has made, especially in his earlier essays and books, reflect something of the understanding of the nature of the world in process as marked by growing concretions of good—a view developed by Henry Nelson Wieman, who was also at Chicago during those years.

We may illustrate this dynamic view from Professor Knox's insistence on the interpretation of Jesus as 'an act of God' in human history. In the third volume of the famous trilogy, *Jesus Lord and Christ*, Knox writes that

the utmost, and inmost, it is given us to know of God's 'substance' is that he is love...and love is not a metaphysical essence but personal moral will and action...What we are trying to say is that (Jesus') supreme import-ance is best seen when he is viewed as the living creative centre of the supremely important event of human history, and also that the 'nature' of Christ is most truly known under that same category: God's action is the divine nature of Christ.[1]

And in *The Church and the Reality of Christ*, in a discussion of the early Church's Christological development, Knox speaks of 'the event of Christ' as 'nothing less than a "divine" Event (a locus of God's "acting" or "working")'. And again, 'the concrete meaning of what God did in Christ cannot be expressed in the definition of a hypostasis; it must be "told" as the story of an action'.[2]

It is apparent that we have here the rejection of the philosophical view that any entity may be described in substantial terms. And for such a description is substituted the concept of an activity running through history and—by a necessary extension of the principle, since Knox is quite clear about the impossibility of a dichotomy between the realm of historical occurrence and the total cosmic order—running also through the world as a whole, whose purpose is the reconciliation of the world to God through the provision of actual and concrete opportunities for a response which will establish focal centres of love. Obviously this kind of activity is most clearly revealed in the historical order, from which, however, it may be read back into the total created world. Supremely, the activity is disclosed at work in and through the complex occasion which we call by the name of its centre Jesus Christ. From this occasion, the drive in creation may be read and understood so far as men are able

[1] *Jesus Lord and Christ* (New York, 1958), p. 235.
[2] *The Church and the Reality of Christ* (New York, 1962), pp. 89 f., 98.

to do so, and to it may be given the responsive co-operation of human agents who are thus caught up into the ongoing purpose of good. This movement of love and faith brings into existence both an awareness of and a participation in love; and Christian talk of atonement, redemption, salvation, and the like is intended to describe and communicate this. Knox prefers to speak of *reconciliation*, the overcoming of man's alienation, deeply felt in experience, from his human brethren but more especially and terribly from the creative source of his being, from God. Through his response in continuing commitment, he is assured that the basic activity in the world is nothing other than the Love who may be addressed, in the word Jesus himself used, as 'Father'.

What is being emphasized then is that just as Jesus himself is best interpreted in terms of divine activity rather than in terms of 'substances' and 'essences', so also the work of Christ and the 'benefits of Christ' will be best understood when they, too, are seen in the context of a movement in history which enables a response—a response that itself establishes new foci of loving reconciliation in succeeding generations. The work of the Holy Spirit, released into the world through the total impact of Jesus in his coming and in his impression upon men, is a process into which men are caught up; and it is through that continuing Spirit that they can 'remember Jesus' (in the phrase that Knox has made famous) not only as an historical individual but also in his full significance as precisely an 'act of God' for the wholeness of men.

What sort of a world is it in which such a Christian drama can be said to have meaning? Surely it is a world which is in itself a *created* order, a world where things certainly have got out of hand, but a world where a purpose of love is at work to bring all things back to their intended character as instruments of the divine Charity. It is a world in which we have to do with living, vital, relational occasions, rather than a world in which we have to do with static entities, with entirely separate or discrete beings, or with ideal forms in some supernal realm. In other words, it is the kind of world which Whitehead, whom Knox obviously has read and appreciated, and which Knox's former colleagues Hartshorne and Wieman, each in his own way, have portrayed as a world 'in process'. And the God who is at work in this world is to be known as nothing other than 'the living

God'. Knox's profound sense of the biblical portrayal of God as indeed living, as purposive, as related to his world and most deeply affected by what goes on in that world, has led him to a view which (whatever may have been the conscious influences of the writers we mention) very closely resembles the position of contemporary American process-thought.

I believe that in such a context we can best approach our second point, which has to do with Professor Knox's way of thinking about the actual concrete 'event of Christ'. This event, like all other events but in its special way supremely and even uniquely, can never be seen in isolation from its setting and from its results. To attempt to speak of Jesus in any such fashion would be to commit what White-head called 'the fallacy of false abstraction'. Indeed, *no* occurrence can be isolated from other occurrences and especially from those which are intimately related to it as giving the historical occasion for its happening, the setting in which it did happen, and the results which its happening has brought about. In the 'event of Christ' we have a focus which brings together the long history of the Jewish people, in their hopes and aspirations, their failures and their sense of the divine forgiveness, their grasp of a divine purpose working through their past and their confidence in a divine fulfilment of that purpose in the future. Jesus was a Jew; into his teaching, but very much more significantly into the whole reality of his concrete exis-tence, all his Jewish past had entered to mould and shape him as the man he was. And there was also the setting for this coming of Jesus in the wider culture of the time. Not only the specifically Jewish but also the more general Graeco-Roman patterns played their part; and, behind all this, there was the given *situation*, as we might say 'cosmically', in which this occurrence took place.

But, Jesus was a particular historical individual. For in Knox's view we have to do with no imagined figure of religious fancy, but with an actual historical person, whatever may be the way in which we come to know about that person and are given the recollections of his teaching, his quality of life, his actions, and his relationships with those who companied with him. Jesus as such a particular historical individual is the centre of a group who responded to him, first in the simple discipleship of the early days of the ministry and increasingly with deepening awareness that there was 'more here than met the eye'. Nor was the death of Jesus, with all that it meant by way of disappointment and frustration to this company, the end of their loyalty and commitment. In fact, the Resurrection is the sign of the persistence of response through and beyond Jesus' death. This means that it is not only the historical figure who is at the heart of the matter, although indeed he is always 'remembered' as precisely such an historical figure. It is chiefly through the Spirit, who reproduces the reality of Jesus and thus makes him 'come alive' in the empowering and inspiring of his followers, that Jesus is affirmed to be Lord and that his life is taken to be that very activity of God which assures men of the divine Father's love, forgiveness, strengthening, and nourishing power, and which demonstrates and enacts in the historical experience of men his unfailing care for those who live in faith.

This brings us at once to the importance of the Christian fellowship, the Church. For as the first disciples, in the days of our Lord's historical human life and later in the days when he was known through the Spirit, 'received' him and made their response to him, so the continuing Christian believers were brought into the situation where reception of Jesus was made possible and were given the power to make response to him. There was established in the world a community which not only 'remembers Jesus' and is possessed by the Spirit which makes him present to them. The community which has been thus established, with its experience of reconciliation, its openness in greater or less degree to 'the love of God which was in Christ Jesus our Lord', and its possession of a deep sense of the divine purpose of love, is also itself the place in which the reconciling, love-creating, meaning-giving work of Christ goes on, even down to our own day. The Christian fellowship becomes the incarnating of the same one God who in Jesus and in the historical context of his life has inaugurated the process of reconciliation, the creation of love, and the giving of significance to the daily experience of men.

Such an interpretation of the 'Christ-event', derived from an analysis of the primitive Christian life in faith as recorded for us in the New Testament, requires a view of history which refuses to confine historical enquiry to a study of 'sources', documentary probabilities, and a search for bare and uninterpreted fact. Indeed it is implied that there is no such thing as a 'bare and uninterpreted fact';

and it is made clear that the purpose of the study of the 'sources' and the weighing of documentary probabilities is primarily to enable us to enter into and so far as may be to appropriate that which was being accomplished in the events which gave rise to the Christian community and which constitute its particular identity as 'the Body of Christ'. I have often quoted, in other contexts, a saying of an old teacher of mine, Dr Frank Gavin: 'History is really an understanding of "how we got this way".' It would seem that Professor Knox's whole work, in so far as it is directed to the New Testament material as historical data, could be described as an explication of that saying.

Whatever may have been the conscious influences upon Knox's thinking, one finds here remarkable parallels to the thought of the distinguished Chicago social philosopher, George H. Mead, with his insistence on the social nature of man's experience, the intimate relationship of individual and environment, the way in which even the 'mind' of a given individual can be seen only in that inescapable relationship, and consequently the necessity for a 'social psychology' if we are ever to grasp the meaning of 'individual psychology'. But let it be noted that no more than Mead does Knox feel that such an awareness diminishes or destroys the reality and integrity of the individual; rather, it is precisely *through* that awareness that one comes to appreciate the individual's reality and integrity. We are all bound together in 'a bundle of life' and we are never genuinely *ourselves* save in our total rich relatedness, with all that our social past, our present social environment, and the social consequences of individual achievement, whatever they may be, have brought to bear upon us or will have revealed to be the wider significance of what we are and what we have done.

We need give but a little space to our discussion of the third of our points—the central importance of commitment in faith; already we have commented indirectly on this point in our treatment of the preceding ones. It will suffice to say that Professor Knox is clear about the necessity for the engagement of the total self in the whole relationship with God. Especially is he clear about this necessity in respect to the relationship which is possible with Jesus understood as 'the act of God' in human history for the reconciliation of man with God and hence for the fulfilment of the divinely established intention of human existence. So far as I know, he has nowhere worked out schematically the relation of faith and knowledge, or faith and reason; but throughout his writing he has spoken of the essential role of faith in all response to God and has rejected that kind of 'natural theology' which would suppose that from strictly rational grounds and by strictly rational argument one can proceed to an awareness of the reality of God, his character as moral will, and his communication of himself to his children in love. For Professor Knox, indeed, commitment would seem to be a part of *all* knowledge which is other than theoretical; his analogies drawn from personal human relations and from the experience of life in a family group all presuppose a sort of awareness, a kind of knowledge, and a mode of understanding which while certainly not *irrational* must be recognized as deeper, more penetrating, and more *engaging* of the whole self than the use of man's ratiocinative powers alone.

But in what he has to say about this engagement of self, Professor Knox has more and more been ready to speak in terms which suggest that the commitment is the reflex side, so to say, of one's being grasped, or being engaged, by the reality of God which encounters one in the ordinary experiences of life and *a fortiori* in the encounter with Jesus as God's supreme action in human affairs. Once again, without assuming that there has been any consciously felt influence, it is clear that the line which Professor Knox has taken is closely parallel to the thought of Paul Tillich, with his emphatic assertion that the believer is grasped by, and feels himself possessed by, the divine in its various manifestations. Knox would lay special stress, however, on the way in which that kind of grasping by God, as he acts in the world, is enabled in the community of faith which is the Church. He would assert, I believe, that the Church is signally if not uniquely the place where this kind of experience is given a setting and is also made evocative for the believer. By this concern for the community, Professor Knox is delivered from the dangers of a too strictly individualistic view of faith. One might say that for him 'the faith of the Church' is prior to and establishes the possibility of 'the faith of the Christian believer'.

All that we have been arguing in this section finds its illustration in what Professor Knox has to say about the position of Jesus in Christian faith, the meaning of reconciliation as the clue to the nature of Christian life, and the necessity for the Christian fellowship as the context for both, which it expresses primarily in its proclamation of the gospel and its celebration of the Lord's Supper. In this complex Christian enterprise, the main emphasis is on the activity of God as loving purpose working through the world, an activity which is supremely focused in Jesus and all that he means as 'the event of Christ' and is brought home to contemporary believers in the community of faith and discipleship. Activity, event, engagement: these might be taken as key-words in Knox's understanding of the Christian reality—and all are set in a world of social relationships and organic mutuality.

2

If our analysis is correct, Professor Knox's study of Christian origins has developed itself along lines which both reflect and demand a metaphysic of process, with a view of history as social *anamnesis* and an insistence on the necessity for commitment as a precondition to the deepest awareness of the significance of events. As I have noted, this position is not explicitly stated in his writings and there is nowhere in his books a systematic discussion of the several points to which we have referred; yet it seems, at least to the writer, that there can be no doubt about its presence. There is a special interest in this fact to theologians like the present writer, in that the attempt to grasp what appear to be the implicit philosophical and theological ideas in Professor Knox's essays and books leads to a general position strikingly similar to that which in another place I have described as 'a contemporary movement in North American Theology'.[1] Indeed, one might say that consciously or unconsciously John Knox reveals clearly the way in which important contemporary tendencies in philosophical, theological, and *biblical* study in North America are converging towards a kind of reconception of Christian faith which differs in many ways from the popular and prevalent kind found in much European writing and also from the major emphases which have been dominant in Great Britain for the last few years.

The clue to this kind of reconception is perhaps the rediscovery of the significance of the later writings of Alfred North Whitehead for theological thought. However, it is not only Whitehead's philosophy of process, as developed (for example) by Charles Hartshorne in a

---

[1] *ExpT* 76 (1965), 268–73.

number of important books, and as expounded theologically by such experts as Bernard Loomer, Bernard Meland, Daniel D. Williams, Schubert Ogden, John B. Cobb, and others, which has been found helpful in preserving the specifically biblical insights concerning the nature and purpose of God, the dynamic quality of the created order, and the meaning of man as created 'in the image of God', as 'fallen', and as redeemed. The impact of existentialism has been felt very strongly in North America, to take but one example, yet it has been shown that this particular way of describing man's 'felt reality' in the world fits in with and receives a deeper philosophical importance from the metaphysical approach which process-thought offers. Such essays as Professor Hartshorne's discussion of Berdyaev and Whitehead[1] and Schubert Ogden's contribution to the Hartshorne *Festschrift*,[2] in which he discusses the relation of Heidegger and Hartshorne, have reflected this sense of convergence. Furthermore, Collingwood's study, *The Idea of History* (which is representative of a whole movement, both on the continent and in Britain, among writers on the philosophy of history) has been related to the American concern for *social* history with its roots in *social* psychology and its explication in *social* philosophy and in a view of 'mind as social'— most notably seen in Mead of Chicago, to whom reference has already been made—and this provides still another illustration of the convergence to which I have called attention. For this organic view of human thought and life is intimately related to the insistence of process-thinkers on the organic, inter-relational interpretation of the world as 'societal' in its basic nature, which is the main thrust of the work of Whitehead and those influenced by him in North America.

The kind of convergence to which we refer is all the more interesting because it offers an 'alternative way' to that which has been popular in theological circles in recent years. The latter has represented a combination of so-called 'biblical theology' with the more or less idealistic philosophy of Paul Tillich, or it has prescinded entirely from philosophical concerns and has assumed that the biblical world-view itself, when understood in its integrity, will satisfy all the requirements for a viable Christian theology in our time. But a

[1] *JR* 37 (1957), 71–84.
[2] *Process and Divinity* (Chicago, 1965), pp. 493–513.

centring of all attention in Scripture can very well lead to considerable difficulty; not only is there a *variety* of material in the Bible which cannot be brought under one set of categories without damage to the richness of the Scriptures themselves, but there is also the possibility—this writer would say the certainty—that it is only by the use of non-biblical categories that the essential biblical emphases can in fact be maintained. At another period in Christian history, the theologians who were most zealous for safeguarding the *total* biblical understanding of the significance of Jesus found themselves using a non-scriptural word (*homoousios*) as the best way in which that understanding could be preserved—and the thinkers who were simply 'biblicists' were the very ones whose position imperilled, if it did not undermine, that understanding. On the other hand, it is doubtful whether the idealistic philosophical orientation developed in the nineteenth century by, say, Schelling, is very happily married to the biblical conception (in all its rich variety) of the living God who acts in nature and history, who may indeed in one sense be described as 'the ground of being' but who is much more the dynamic 'sovereign ruler' about whom the New Testament finally comes to tell us that his 'nature and his name is love', in the great phrase of Wesley. It is only by a methodology which proceeds by 'symbols', taken seriously but somewhat ambiguously, that one is able in such a Tillichian theology to guarantee the basic Christian insights.

The convergence, then, to which we have called attention, has its peculiar value in that it begins with a dynamic universe, taken as including human experience with its full 'aesthetic' element; it is prepared to say, with Whitehead, that man's experience, thus understood, is so much organic to the totality of things that it must be taken with utmost seriousness. Furthermore, by building upon Whitehead's notion of 'importance', it can find a place for particular events as specially indicative not only of man's subjective feeling but also of the quality of the cosmic process itself. When to this initial conviction we add the existentialist analysis of what in fact it *means* to be a man, and couple this with the recognition of man's inescapable sociality, we are enabled to see a context for the general biblical story which is, so to say, 'natural' to it and appropriate for it. Nor does such a position make it impossible to assert the Christian claim for a certain finality—or better, decisiveness—in the 'event' of Jesus Christ. Of course the way in which Jesus' uniqueness is understood will differ from the way in which it was understood in another context; we are led to emphasize what Professor Moule has lately described as an 'inclusive uniqueness' rather than an 'exclusive uniqueness'. But it is here, precisely, that Professor Knox's understanding of the meaning of 'event', in its rich complexity, is of such great assistance. For here we have to do not with a simple kind of 'location', as if God were at work in the specific historical person of Jesus and nowhere else, but rather with a 'focusing' of God's ceaseless activity in that person—with the recognition that any such 'focusing' demands prior and succeeding activity as the preparation is made for the person and as the consequences of his appearance are seen for what they have shown themselves to be.

That this convergence is not simply a fancy of the present writer is demonstrated by the work of Professor Schubert Ogden in his *Christ without Myth*, where the final chapter works in precisely the direction which we have argued. Further, in a forthcoming book of Professor Knox's[1] (which the writer has been privileged to read in manuscript), the same line is taken, as Knox attempts to work from the varied New Testament portrayal of Jesus both as entirely human and also as 'act of God' towards a Christological statement that will be possible in our own day. The *story* of Jesus is to be preserved in its integrity, but the putting of that story in some coherent, intellectually viable pattern leads Professor Knox to write along the lines of process-thought, although here (as is usual with him) he does not find it necessary to go through a detailed philosophical analysis or engage in metaphysical discourse.

There are some possible dangers in this approach, dangers which need to be borne in mind. This is not to say that Professor Knox himself succumbs to these dangers, for he is too careful and judicious a thinker and writer to allow himself to be carried to perilous extremes. None the less, it may be useful in concluding this essay to speak briefly of the exaggerations into which those of us who take the general line found in Knox's work may be tempted to fall.

First, there is a possibility that in reaction from historicism the

[1] *The Humanity and the Divinity of Christ* (Cambridge, 1967).

necessity for Christian faith of a definite and specific rootage in the impact of one specific human life—that of Jesus—may be forgotten or seriously minimized. If we grant that Professor Knox's interpretation of the meaning of 'event' is correct and also that his description of the way in which such an 'event' continues to exert its influence on succeeding ages is true to the facts, there is still a danger that the actual historical career of Jesus will lose its centrality in the picture of Christian faith. For that historical career there may very well be substituted 'the Christ of faith'. This charge was often made—although, as I have shown elsewhere, it was made with less than justice[1]—in respect to the writing of Roman Catholic modernists, whose position Professor Knox's conclusions in many ways resemble. It should be said at once that Knox himself has demonstrated, over and over again, that he does not and cannot sit loose to the historical Jesus. But some who take his position here, without seeing the qualifications with which he works it out, may not be so cautious.[2]

A second danger is the possibility that the high place given to the Church, as the necessary carrier of Jesus and his gospel, may lead to an acceptance of development in a very uncritical fashion. As a friend of mine once remarked, 'If you let this view get in control, anything that has come down the road will be all right, provided the Church has found it useful'. Of course Professor Knox does not think in this way and he has guarded his discussion very carefully, especially in refusing to identify *any* particular institutional expression of the Christian tradition with the ongoing life of the fellowship itself. But those who follow his line need to remember always that there is false and distorting development as well as true and sound development. We need some criteria in terms of which any given development of the initiating Christian faith and the continuing Christian life may be tested for its fidelity to the essential Christian thing. Neither Professor Knox nor those who have carried on his kind of study seem so

[1] See my *The Word Incarnate* (Welwyn Garden City and New York, 1959), pp.76-8.
[2] For two of the many places where Knox demonstrates this concern for the historicity of Jesus and the impression made by the historical person, see *The Church and the Reality of Christ* (from which we have already quoted in a different context), pp. 50-8; and *Criticism and Faith* (Nashville, 1952), pp. 43-56. See also Part 1 of *Jesus Lord and Christ*, a book from which we have also quoted above. In Part 1, concerned with 'The Man Jesus', Knox lays his stress on the reality of the historical man, who in the Church is 'remembered' and in the Church's present experience is known as *also* 'the living Lord'.

far to have given enough thought to the working out in detail of these criteria. Nor is this essay the place to make suggestions about what the criteria might be. But there can be no doubt that serious attention must be given to the question.

Finally, Professor Knox's rejection of a philosophy of 'metaphysical essences' and his acceptance of a philosophy of 'moral will, and action'—in other words his preference for a philosophy of process rather than a philosophy of substance—is altogether right, at least in this writer's view. So also is his willingness to value and use the expressions of Christian belief, traditionally made in substantial terms, if it is granted that these expressions were the best attempts of Christian thinkers in given times and places to state the supreme importance of Jesus and the cruciality of the disclosure of God in action in and through him. Yet our time needs imperatively a new statement of this abiding importance and cruciality, made in the patterns of thought appropriate to such a processive world as Professor Knox sees our world to be. And while we can and must value, and indeed in the appropriate times and places use, the classical metaphysical statements of theology, we cannot rest content with this; we must go on, boldly, bravely, responsibly, to reconceive the Christian faith not only 'in other words' but also in a quite different perspective and with quite different presuppositions. Our peril is simply that we shall rest content in our reverence for the tradition we have received, employ its formulae in a purely 'allusive' fashion, and fail to concern ourselves seriously with the intellectual task of theological reconstruction.

But, as we have said, Professor Knox himself does not fall victim to these possible temptations. We owe him an enormous debt for having done what he has done. He has not only provided for us a convincing picture of the beginnings and early development of the faith to which we are committed, but also through the philosophical and theological ideas which both precede and follow from his study he has suggested to us the sort of Christian reconception which will indeed make sense in our time. When to these scholarly contributions we add his own vigorous Christian stance, his deep personal devotion, and his entire loyalty to the Christian community which is the Holy Catholic Church, we can only feel an enduring gratitude for the work and for the man who has done the work.

2

JOHN KNOX'S CONCEPTION
OF HISTORY

DANIEL DAY WILLIAMS

The Church has always been uniquely preoccupied with the idea of history, and it is hardly too much to say that it was in its life and thought that history first acquired full reality and universality.[1]

This sentence gives the key to John Knox's conception of the significance of history for Christian faith. As interpreter of the New Testament Knox accepts as his first obligation the understanding of the Christian faith from within the history of the Church. He gets at the meaning of history by asking what history is for the Church from within its perspective of faith as given in its primary documents and its tradition. Knox does not begin then with a general philosophy of history. He directs his attention to the Church's self-understanding as this is given in the New Testament. The clarity, penetration, and single-minded devotion with which Dr Knox has pursued this work has given us one of the outstanding achievements of biblical scholarship in our century.

At the same time, Dr Knox is concerned with the *idea* of history. He recognizes that the Christian faith speaks to man in his situation in the world, with his scientific understanding of nature, his variety of historical experience, his search for knowledge which includes the development of critical methods of historical research. Therefore the interpreter of Christian faith must consider the implications of what he says within the context of man's search for truth.

This double concern for history as understood from within Christian faith and for the relation of this understanding to all human experience and thought suggests the way in which I shall proceed in this chapter. First I shall try to state Dr Knox's conception of history as it develops within his explication of the nature of Christian faith with its source in the New Testament witness to Jesus Christ. Then

---

[1] John Knox, *The Church and the Reality of Christ* (New York, 1962), p. 43. (Hereinafter *Reality of Christ*.)

17

I shall try to analyse the way in which Dr Knox explicates the nature of Christian knowledge in relation to human experience, reason, and critical understanding. Here I shall try to remain faithful to what he explicitly says and to his intention, but I shall be drawing out the implications of his view for a systematic understanding of Christian knowledge. This leads to the raising of two primary issues which grow out of Knox's position. The first has to do with the relation of Christian knowledge of God to historical experience, and the other is the question of the Christian view of universal history, especially the relation of the salvation known in Christ to the totality of man's life in all times and cultures.

In thus approaching Dr Knox's thought I am raising systematic theological questions about the implications of his position. He has given us, I believe, the most adequate basis for a conception of the relation of Biblical witness to the faith of the Church in modern theology. I should like to draw out the implications of his view, perhaps in directions he would not altogether approve, but in ways which I believe he has made possible through his powerful analysis of the problem of historical knowledge in relation to faith.

I

Dr Knox seeks to say what history is as it is understood from within the Christian faith. There are innumerable conceptions of history and 'defining history is in its own way as difficult as defining myth'.[1] His own point of departure and court of appeal is clear: 'The task of the Christian theologian, as I understand it, is primarily a confessional and descriptive one. He is trying to say as accurately and adequately as possible what Christians—that is, sharers in the life of the Church—find true in their common experience.'[2] We are not then in the first instance to look for general categories of historical understanding, or a philosophy of history, but for that grasp of historical reality which is present in the experience of the Church.

This starting-point leads directly to a doctrine about what history is, for the Church is a community, a shared life in time and space which moves through history with memory and hopes, united by a

[1] John Knox, *Myth and Truth* (Charlottesville, 1964), p. 60.
[2] Knox, *Reality of Christ*, p. 11.

18

common spirit. Here is the clue to what historical existence is, the 'human thing' which Collingwood and others have helped us to see. Every human community has its own distinctive body, its distinctive spirit and its distinctive memory.[1]

To exist as a human individual therefore is to participate in some community of shared memory and spirit. 'A person simply as an individual is not a historical event.'[2] Man is a creature of history. He belongs to his cultural past and cannot permanently break with it.[3]

Real history is lived in this shared communal existence in a temporal process. We can say therefore that history is made up of events, but we mean by events not simply passing moments but processes of concrete life which move from the past through the present into the future. Events have temporal thickness. They are the concrete fullness of those processes which bring communities into being and give them their continuing identity and their shared memories and hopes.

The statements just made are indeed general statements about the nature of history; but their source as the Christian understands them is the life of the Church itself with its reference to the event which brought it into being. That is, if we would understand the relation of an historical event to a community which significantly remembers it, and lives by and in the event, we will look at the meaning of Jesus Christ for the Church.

It is here that Dr Knox not only makes his most important contribution to the understanding of Jesus Christ in Christian faith but establishes the terms in which a valid answer to the problem of our knowledge of the historical Jesus must be given.

The historical event which is the ground of our knowledge of Jesus Christ and of our knowledge of God is the coming into being of the Church. 'The community and the Event belong inseparably together. The Event *was* the community becoming its characteristic self. And the historical ground of the kerygma under all its aspects was the community's existence.'[4] Again, Knox says: 'The historical

---

[1] John Knox, *Myth and Truth*, p. 56; cf. *ibid.* p. 60; John Knox, *The Hope of Glory* (New York, 1960), p. 36.

[2] Knox, *Reality of Christ*, p. 28.

[3] John Knox, *The Early Church and the Coming Great Church* (New York, 1955), p. 137. (Hereinafter, *Coming Great Church*.)

[4] Knox, *Reality of Christ*, p. 34.

Event to which all distinctively Christian faith returns is not an event antedating the Church, or in any sense or degree prior to it, but is the coming into existence of the Church itself.'[1] Now the critical point is that the life of Jesus, what Jesus means in the faith of the Church, is not an event prior to the Church. He is within the event in which the Church knows God's revelation, his salvation, and the ground of its own existence. No arbitrary boundaries can be set to the event. One might plausibly argue that the event began with Israel's self-consciousness as the people of Yahweh. Perhaps no event ever strictly begins or ends except with the beginning and end of history itself, for, Knox says: 'Events are the stuff of history; and history is a living, organic process, in which every part participates in the whole and the whole is present in every part.'[2] We must keep our attention fixed here on the Christological basis of such a statement and its meaning for the Church's understanding of its relation to Jesus as remembered and as presently known in the Spirit. Here Knox sometimes speaks of the *continuation* of the event. Since an event has duration we can think of the event which the Church knows as God's saving action in Jesus Christ as continuing in time. But he also speaks of the event as recurring. 'The Church is thus more than the consequence of the event; in its life the event continually recurs.'[3] The ground of the Church's being is the reality of the event, which includes the present experience of the Spirit. The Spirit bears past, present, and future in its dynamic presence. For Paul: 'The Spirit was the past actually continuing and the future already beginning. The Spirit was the living present which united past with future by participating in both—the witness to our redemption as sons and the earnest of our inheritance.'[4]

There are three implications of the view of the meaning of history for Christian faith as it bears upon the Church's understanding of Jesus. The first is that the concrete reality in which God's saving action is to be seen is not something confined within the individual personality of Jesus but is involved in the personal historical relations of Jesus with the community in which he lived, preached, taught, died and was experienced as present after death. The 'deed of God' in Jesus, Knox says, 'took place in him in the midst of his own, and

[1] Knox, *Reality of Christ*, p. 22.   [2] *Ibid.* p. 24.
[3] Knox, *Coming Great Church*, p. 18.   [4] *Ibid.* p. 59.

involved action, reaction, and interaction, as all human existence does. It took place in the concrete body of relationships in which he stood to certain ones about him, and they to him and to one another in his presence.'[1] I may note in passing that the other contemporary theologian who has insisted most explicitly that the locus of the revelation of God is in the interactive process between Jesus and those around him is Henry Nelson Wieman.[2]

The second important consequence of this historical view of Jesus is that when the Church knows him as Jesus Christ it knows Jesus as he is in the total event of revelation. There is no prior knowledge of him as the Christ which precedes knowledge of him as the subject of the Church's confession. Dr Knox's insistence on this point is one of his most characteristic themes:

The career of Jesus of Nazareth, simply as a human career, was, for all its intrinsic greatness, a relatively unimportant incident in Jewish history. The event of Jesus Christ the Lord was historically the important thing; and this event happened only in the life of the Church.

In a word, except for its connection with the Church, the event of Jesus of Nazareth was hardly an event at all.[3]

In his discussion of the resurrection Knox shows how this view makes all attempts to base the faith of the Church upon the demonstration of a particular kind of happening as the resurrection of Jesus miss the point. The resurrection of Jesus as known in the Church is the coming into being of the Church itself and therefore can be no more a subject of debate or doubt than the existence of the Church. 'In this moment of recognition the Resurrection (whatever it may be conceived to have been in and of itself) became for the first time a historical fact, and the Church, which had been in process of ''becoming'' since Jesus' first disciples were gathered about him, came finally into actual being.'[4]

The third consequence of this view of the Christian faith is the recognition that the Christology of the Church is the product of the interpreting, remembering, and witnessing to the meaning of the

---

[1] Knox, *Reality of Christ*, p. 87; cf. John Knox, *On the Meaning of Christ* (New York, 1947), pp. 42–3.
[2] Cf. Henry Nelson Wieman, *The Source of Human Good* (Chicago, 1946).
[3] Knox, *Coming Great Church*, pp. 47, 46.
[4] Knox, *Reality of Christ*, p. 77.

event which has taken place in the life of the community. Here Dr Knox gives full weight to the results of biblical scholarship in describing the historical development in which the many Christological conceptions in the life of the early community expanded, clashed, were fused together, and led finally to the Church's elaboration of the Christological dogma.

Here Knox finds the real significance, and what is, for faith, the *only* significance, of the miracle stories, and the elaborated doctrines of Christ's pre-existence, his ascension, and his expected return. The miracle story may be the actual carrier of 'the ineffable concrete meaning of the Event'; but it is the event itself which is the miracle, the one great reality which can be given no naturalistic explanation. The elaborated Christologies of the Church, the miracle stories of the gospels, the high Christologies of Paul are the developments of the Community's way of understanding the meaning of what has brought it into being whatever the 'factual' origin of the stories may be.

We are here, however, raising the question of the *meaning* of the event. The Church declares that the meaning of the event is that it is God's action in history for our salvation. The language of faith describes the source and the outcome of the event in terms which express something which cannot be 'historically' defined or limited, that is, God's action. When the Church speaks of the life of Jesus, his death and resurrection, it is speaking about its memory of concrete history; but when it speaks of God taking the form of a servant, sending his son into the world, raising Jesus from the dead, judging the nations before his throne, it is speaking in a realm where history is not annulled but transcended.

For Knox, then, the meaning of history is not given in history itself, but transcends history, though it comes to us through the historical community, the Church. How we know, in Christian faith, is through our life in the community. What we know is not only this life but the action of God which has brought the community into being. The mode of this knowledge, and its expression is clearly something other than literal discourse. The word Dr Knox prefers for it is *myth*.

Knox's doctrine of truth involves the acceptance of a plurality of kinds of discourse. He holds that 'the tests of truth are various'.[1]

---

[1] Knox, *Myth and Truth*, p. 18.

For example, truth in an historical drama has a different meaning and different criteria from truth in an historical textbook. He is most concerned to keep the objective meaning of truth when that truth is of the kind which must be expressed in myth. Indeed, belief in the objective truth of myth is essential to its functioning as myth in a community. Knox accepts Eliade's category of 'mythical' time: to apply to those original happenings which the myth expresses. Myth is therefore an expression of a divine action which really asserts the truth of that action, but it cannot be literally true for 'no human narrative of a divine action could conceivably be literally true'.[1] This assertion of the impossibility of any literal language about God is so far as I know a presupposition in Dr Knox's thought. He nowhere argues for it or considers an alternative. For him language about God's acts points beyond history while it originates in the attempt to express the meaning of history: 'We have seen that a true myth cannot conflict with history for the reason that its essential action takes place outside history entirely—in another realm or at another level than the historical.'[2] But while myth refers to a realm beyond history, it may grow, and characteristically does grow, within history as the community's understanding grows. 'The developing story will inevitably find us moving further and further from the *time* of the original experience and perhaps from the bare facts of it, but it may be bringing us nearer and nearer to its meaning.'[3]

We recognize two ways in which this understanding of Christian faith and the truth it has to express is invulnerable to any historical critical research into the 'facts' of the life of Jesus or the rise of the Church. On one side the existence of the Church is indubitable, and everything in its memory of the event, its understanding of Jesus which belongs to that existential reality, is beyond any historical scepticism. The Church remembers its own existence, how it came into being. That is what it speaks about when it speaks of Jesus Christ. It is as impossible for the Church to doubt the existence of Jesus as it is to doubt its own existence, for these are aspects of the one event in which and by which the Church lives.

The language of faith about God is also invulnerable to criticism from an objectively rational standpoint independent of faith, for the

---

[1] Knox, *Myth and Truth*, p. 27.   [2] *Ibid.* p. 65.
[3] Knox, *Reality of Christ*, p. 88.

meaning of the event which constitutes the Church's origin and life transcends all historical experience. It is a meaning which God gives to history from beyond itself through his action within it.

The knowledge we have of God, then, we have only on the ground of our life in the Church, and that knowledge comes with a self-authenticating power. In characterizing the New Testament's view of knowledge Knox writes: 'The knowledge of the Spirit, like our knowledge of concrete things generally, was self-authenticating—the basis of inferences, not an inference itself.'[1] This analogy between knowledge of the Spirit and knowledge of all concrete things is important to Knox's position and I will develop my analysis of it in the next section.

We see here his conviction of the givenness of the character of revelation, and of the mythological expression which the Church gives to its grasp of the meaning of revelation. Only the indispensable myth, that which cannot be avoided, can survive.[2] Knox holds that the Church knows in whom it believes as indubitably as it knows its own existence. Hence to participate fully and personally in the history which is the life of the Church is to know the meaning of history itself and of what lies beyond it. It is to be given not only faith but hope.

We must conclude this characterization of the general perspective on history in Dr Knox's thought by noting what he says about the course of history and the life of the Church within it. Here again, he looks from within the Christian community out toward the world with its search for meaning and its variety of faiths. In the Christian faith we know that history has a centre, a purpose and a meaning. This purpose cannot be found in the secular ideals of progress and humanistic culture. These have been exposed in their limitations and ultimate inadequacy.[3] But in the Christian faith knowing that God is Creator and Redeemer we find an ineluctable hope. This eschatological dimension of Christian faith cannot be absorbed into a non-temporal eternity. It really points forward. I take this to be the force of Knox's statement, 'The eschatological expectation in some literal, temporal sense is implicit and essential'.[4] But whatever

---

[1] Knox, *Coming Great Church*, pp. 57–8.   [2] Knox, *Myth and Truth*, p. 38.
[3] Knox, *On the Meaning of Christ*, p. 112.
[4] Knox, *The Hope of Glory*, p. 32.

this temporal sense is, it points to the 'new eschatological order of the Spirit'. The Church is the embodiment of that order, and for all its imperfection it is 'a bit of heaven', an enclave within time and space of the 'ultimate eschatological order'.[1]

Thus history which has its origin in God's action, which cannot be understood in literal terms, has its end in the Kingdom of God, an order which transcends any meaning we can assign to time or space or existential reality. Yet these ultimate dimensions of the outlook of faith are there because they are present as the meaning of an historical reality we do experience, the Christian Church.

There is a further word to be said about the course of history. The direction of the life of the Church is, in principle, the key to the direction of God's purpose for humanity, that men should live together in the solidarity of fellowship. This is the real meaning of the ecumenical reality of the Church, and is the reason why the unity of the Church is of such fundamental importance. Dr Knox sees the Church as having always lived in a certain disunity. From the beginning it had to search for forms and modes for expressing the shared spirit and faith which brought it into being. The fulfilment of the Church's life in the visible embodiment of its unity is of the essence of the Church's being in history.

Knox does not look for any complete harmony and uniformity in the Church; but its organic union must be believed in, prayed for and worked for when it is seen from the perspective of his understanding of history and faith. There is a place for development of form and structure. In the early centuries the catholicizing tendency was the inevitable expression of the Church's call to be the one body of Christ. That unity must be one of an organic community in history and therefore Knox takes a conservative view of the grounds of Church union. The catholic elements of Canon, Liturgy, Creed, and Episcopacy belong to the concrete life of the Church in history, and he looks for no success for an ecumenical programme which does not take them all into the basis of the Church's life. He takes a similarly conservative view of the traditional creeds. They are not infallible oracles, but any tampering with them probably 'reflects... the assumption that the whole Event of Christ and the whole life of the Church can be described and explained in naturalistic or

[1] Knox, *The Hope of Glory*, p. 47.

humanistic terms'.[1] Certainly there is more in the Church's life than realizing its own unity. There is the life of love and service in the world. Dr Knox never slights the ethical obligation in the Christian life. But the Church bears within its life the healing of humanity and it is true to itself only when it seeks to make that concrete life of the community of faith and hope and love manifest in history.

For John Knox the Church comes to its understanding of history through its existence within the redeeming activity of God. The event in which God revealed himself has brought the Church into being, sustains it, and gives it its hope. History cannot be understood through some universal perspective which claims objectivity beyond all particular standpoints. History is known only from within particular histories. There is then in Knox an acceptance of cultural relativism. The Church believes that it knows what history is. It cannot see it in any other way. But it knows in the only way which is given to it through its own existence.[2]

2

While he holds this view that the Church speaks only from within its own perspective Dr Knox recognizes that what we say about history in the biblical outlook requires some expression in the ordinary categories of speech and knowledge. It is reality which the Church knows, and not just subjective appearance. Hence one finds Knox giving many suggestions which bear upon the nature of any human knowledge. It is this more general aspect of his position which I shall now try to explicate. Dr Knox would, I am sure, deny any intention to develop an epistemological and metaphysical position. Indeed he makes quite explicit criticism of the attempt to import philosophy into the religious way of knowing. Yet there are implicit philosophical elements in his view and it is useful to try to uncover these in arriving at a fuller statement of his conception of history. In what

---

[1] Knox, *Reality of Christ*, p. 75; cf. *Great Church*, chapter VI and *Myth and Truth*, chapter V.

[2] I find Knox's position closest perhaps to that of H. Richard Niebuhr in *The Meaning of Revelation* (New York, 1941), and Knox makes explicit acknowledgement of his relation to H. Richard Niebuhr's thought.

follows I believe I am stating what Dr Knox holds; but I am frankly interpreting certain statements in ways which he might not allow.

The question of how we know real things and especially how we know historical realities concerns Knox deeply. The primary distinction which runs all through his work is that between what is 'concrete' and our way of knowing the concrete as over against abstract concepts which we may find useful but which do not give us the concrete reality. For example, in speaking of the nature of love in the New Testament faith Knox writes: 'The quality of this love, as of all concrete things, cannot be defined; it must be felt, and it can be expressed only in the forms of life and art.'[1] He illustrates what he means by concrete knowledge in memory with reference to his experience of the impact of the American Civil War upon his family and upon himself. There is of course the knowledge of happenings of dates and places. But he says, 'I have knowledge of another, more concrete, kind. My father although he did not speak of it often, carried in his memory the grim, dark days of the South's defeat and prostration. And *I remember his memory.*'[2] Here the significance of memory consists in its 'effectiveness in preserving something of the concrete quality, the felt meaning, of an event in the past'.[3] Indeed, Knox even says that it is only persons and things and happenings that we remember. We do not 'remember' ideas or concepts or generalizations.[4]

Now our access to the concrete reality, which Knox frequently refers to as the 'inner substance' of the community's life, is given in *feeling*. All concrete things are 'immeasurably rich and complex', and Knox contrasts the direct knowledge of qualitative richness which we have in feeling with the mere abstractions of conceptual thought. 'We may speak of God as a mere object of thought, a mere term in a philosophical construction, without resort to this kind of [mythological] discourse...but any statement about God's relations with us, about his "presence" or "action" in nature or history, must needs be mythological in character.'[5] It is tempting to ask whether this statement just quoted is a philosophical or a mythological statement, but passing that query for the moment we see the basis for Dr Knox's view that philosophy cannot deal with the truth which religious

[1] Knox, *Coming Great Church*, p. 61.   [2] Knox, *Reality of Christ*, p. 39.
[3] *Ibid.* p. 42.   [4] *Ibid.* p. 45.   [5] *Ibid.* p. 89.

27

faith is concerned about: 'The truth is that religious faith is not a matter of accepting or rejecting facts with which the scientist is concerned or of believing or denying propositions with which the philosopher is dealing.'[1]

The question of what we mean by 'fact' is raised by this statement, and it is of course of crucial importance for the interpretation of history. Knox distinguishes between 'experienced or existential fact', and 'scientific or historical fact'.[2] It is important to understand his usage here to avoid confusion. Surely the concrete realities of history are existential fact, and Knox frequently uses the term fact in just this way to refer to the felt qualitative depth and meaning of history. But when he here contrasts 'historical fact' with 'existential fact' he means by the former the facts which can be established by scientific historical method. In so far as the historian seeks facts in this sense of what can be established in documentary analysis and critical discourse he is dealing with abstractions. The 'historical facts' thus understood are something less and other than the concrete personal realities which we know in direct experience.[3]

A further aspect of this doctrine of what is real in history is Knox's insistence on the organic character of the concrete. The whole is more than the sum of its parts. He appeals here again to the nature of the Church. He speaks of 'the Church as organic community, a living social whole, which could not exist without its parts but cannot be simply identified with the sum of them'.[4] It is interesting to see this characterization of the Church reflected in a more general doctrine of the organic category. In a discussion important for Knox's view of history he says:

Nothing organic can be explained; temporal occasions and sequences can be found, but not adequate causes. We know that when the seed, soil, and season meet, the plant will grow, but as to just why it does we do not know *and shall never know*. History is not different: we see the close connexion of event with event, but as to why a particular 'cause' issues in a particular 'effect' we do not know.[5]

---

[1] Knox, *Myth and Truth*, p. 9.   [2] *Ibid.* p. 73.
[3] On the general question of how far Knox regards secular history as restricted in principle to the 'facts' I am not clear, though he does say that probably all historical writing has a tendentious aspect. Cf. Knox, *Coming Great Church*, p. 31.
[4] Knox, *Reality of Christ*, p. 83.
[5] Knox, *On the Meaning of Christ*, pp. 102 f.

I have italicized the phrase 'and shall never know' in the above quotation because it sets forth emphatically Knox's doctrine of the transcendence of concrete knowledge over reason. While he certainly does not disparage scientific and philosophical knowledge when kept in their proper sphere of abstractions, he sees the knowledge of faith laying hold of truth which reason cannot grasp: 'Accepting the Cross does not mean understanding it; it means almost the contrary—recognizing a dimension and a potency in human life which defy our comprehension and all our little systems, whether of law or truth.'[1] Faith is knowledge for Knox, but it is the kind of knowledge which arises in 'empirical awareness and response'.[2] The term empirical here refers clearly not to sense observation alone; but to personal participation in the organic movement of life in communal history.

We cannot conclude this analysis without reference to one important implication which Knox draws for the Church's understanding of Jesus. That understanding is grounded in a memory of Jesus which is even more rich and more adequate than the written records concerning him. Knox believes that we see in the record attempts of the Church to shade or to qualify certain aspects of the memory which fit more nearly into later dogmatic structures; but the attempt fails. There is a concrete memory of Jesus' moral stature, and of the quality of love in his relationship to men which is deeper than the record itself expresses. Thus the Church bears in its concrete life a knowledge of its Lord which lies deeper than any words or formal testimony can convey.[3] This appeal to the concrete experience of the Church even against, or beyond, the text of the Canon is the most dramatic illustration in all Knox's writing of the confidence he places in the living memory of the Church as giving access to historical reality.

3

I have tried to set forth John Knox's understanding of history. In this concluding section I raise two questions which seem to me pertinent for further clarification and discussion. The first of these has to do with the relation of God to history and especially the bear-

---

[1] John Knox, *The Death of Christ* (Nashville, 1958), p. 168.
[2] Knox, *The Hope of Glory*, p. 22.   [3] Knox, *Reality of Christ*, pp. 53–7.

ing of this relationship upon our knowledge of God. The second concerns the relation of the Christian Church to other faiths and communities.

The question of the justification of our language about God, and the norms which govern such language is a perennial theme in Christian theology. Dr Knox proposes a solution of this problem which is very attractive; but it leaves some unresolved issues.

His solution is that our knowledge of God is grounded in history, and history is understood as the concrete life of the community of faith. What we say about God however is myth which points to a realm or plane above history. Hence language about God is that language which the Church uses to express its faith about the meaning of history; but what it refers to, the action of God, is not historical.

The attractiveness of this solution is apparent. It relieves us of any necessity to identify acts of God in an objective historical way. It puts language about God in a dimension where it does not come into conflict with other language. It is not subject to justification or judgment by the criteria which apply to our language about facts, or about concrete things in history.

Is this solution bought at too high a price for Christian faith which does make assertions about God's acts in history? This is my question. There is one level at which what Dr Knox says must surely be accepted. To speak of 'God raising Jesus from the dead' is to speak in a different way about reality from speaking let us say about Peter casting a net in the sea for fish. But that is not where the problem arises for theology. It arises where we make such statements about God as that he is 'actually working in and through nature and history'. Or again, when we say that God forgives sin. Or again, as Dr Knox writes:

When God's Spirit is given, his love is being poured out...The 'love of God' is not merely a loving attitude of God towards us, of which we could at best become persuaded or convinced; it is God himself giving *himself* to us, to be actually received and enjoyed, to be known even more intimately and surely than one can know the love of a friend.[1]

This leads me to ask whether *this* language about God is mythological. If God can be concretely experienced as present in history, as

[1] Knox, *Coming Great Church*, p. 60.

loving and forgiving, then there seems to be some language about God which is not simply mythological expression about another plane, but is language about God as present in history.

That God transcends history will be agreed in every Christian theology; but is there not also an immanence of God which gives us one of the dimensions for the control of our language about him? In other words are not our symbols for God grounded in actual experience in such a way that we can speak of some structural relationship between God's being and action and the categories of history? It seems to me that Dr Knox really asserts that history is not only made up of the acts and thoughts of men but is the field of divine activity. If our statements about God represent the true inwardness of historical fact then our statements about him are not only on another plane or in another realm but they are in some way grounded and justified in historical experience.[1] Dr Knox says quite rightly that if we are to speak of God's being we must make use of 'analogy'.[2] But the justification of analogy is a notoriously difficult problem in all human speech and certainly in theology. I will not conceal my conviction that here all theology becomes involved in the relation of the being of God to the being of the creatures. The problem becomes a metaphysical one, and Dr Knox is involved it seems to me whether he wishes to be or not in the problem of the 'analogy of being'. Which analogies are justified when we speak of God? And what are the limits of analogy? The questions about God as person, God's relation to time and space, to suffering and evil, to the order of nature and the forms of human experience are raised here.

While I believe that all theology has implicit metaphysical elements I do not wish to rest the case for an examination of our language about God with a plea for metaphysics. For even if metaphysics be disavowed the questions still arise from within faith's attempt at self-clarification. There are many things said about God in scripture, in tradition, in the language of devotion and the reports of mystical experience. Granted all such language is limited and inadequate, but is it all equally valid? What are our resources for purging 'God-talk' of irrelevancies, and errors? Evidently we cannot rely on revelation alone. Knox takes the view that revelation does not provide us with facts and concepts. 'In the moment of

---

[1] Knox, *Myth and Truth*, p. 63. [2] *Ibid.* p. 6.

revelation we are confronted by One of whom we dare not ask any questions.'[1] But surely it is necessary at times to reflect upon our interpretation of revelation. When questions have to be asked how do we go about answering them?

A brief comment on the relation of Knox's view to Bultmann's may help to sharpen the question I am raising. Dr Knox seems to me to give much more significance to historical existence as the context of faith than does Bultmann. Knox rightly puts the knowledge of God in the context of the life of the personal organic community in history. And Knox seems to me more adequate than Bultmann when he interprets revelation as God's act in history, that is in the concrete becoming of the Church, not simply as a flash of light from eternity stabbing into time. But should this not lead Dr Knox to a more unequivocal assertion that when we speak of God's acts in history we are asserting that God is in living interaction with the events in time, and that this does lead us to say some things about the being of God which are not myth but interpretations of God's being, however difficult and inadequate these interpretations may be? God is not only beyond history but is at work within it.

The other question I ask comes from the fact that there are many communities in history with their common memories, hopes and faiths. Where does Knox's position stand with respect to a Christian interpretation of life and salvation in history outside the empirical Church?

His position here again has a type of invulnerability. Accepting a cultural relativism he states his intention only to express from within the Christian community what its faith is. The knowledge of God with which he is concerned is that knowledge which the Christian Church has and no other. He says: 'The only "name" of God we know contains also the name of another. We worship not a private God, but the God of Christ and therefore the God of those who belong to him. Is there any conceivable way in which *that* God can be known except in and through the historical community?'[2] Knox does not absolutely deny knowledge of God outside the Christian Church. 'We may have some knowledge of God in our solitariness or through some such other social or cultural medium...'[3] But

---

[1] Knox, *Myth and Truth*, p. 12. [2] Knox, *The Meaning of Christ*, p. 101.
[3] Knox, *Reality of Christ*, p. 30.

he obviously is not concerned with this knowledge. It has no pertinence to the Christian way of knowing God. And he comes close to a rejection of any other knowledge when he says 'we could not have come to know him from observing either the starry heavens, or the human story, or the human heart'.[1]

What then about salvation and fulfilment for all men? Here Knox says clearly man cannot assert limits to God's reconciling action. It would be presumptuous to do so. He seems to identify his position with that of the writer to the Ephesians. 'God's action in Christ is finally to encompass all of heaven and all of earth in its healing, reconciling effect.'[2] In short Knox appears to be a universalist. All will be fulfilled. None is excluded from salvation. But do only Christians know that there is salvation?

On this point Knox seems to me to take an exclusivist view of our *knowledge* of salvation. It is only in the Church that the love of God 'has actually found and healed *us*'.[3] I have italicized 'us' here as the critical word. Has the love of God found and healed any one else? Knox says, 'unless the Church *is* the locus...of God's reconciling work in Christ, that work, so far as we can know, did not take place at all'.[4]

I am frankly puzzled as to how to construe these words in relation to the Christian view of other religions and faiths. Does it mean that God is not known truly at all anywhere outside Christian culture, or does it mean only that we speak solely from within the Christian community and we just do not have anything to say about God's working outside that community except that he must be working there since he is the Lord of all things?

Here Knox's position seems very close to Karl Barth's that God is really known only in Christian faith though I do not know that Knox would pass the judgment which Barth does on other religions, that they all represent nothing but man's sinful *hybris*. It solves many problems if we simply speak of God from within our community of faith and make no statements at all about God or salvation outside Christian history.

I question however whether in this time of the world's history we can maintain this position. Cultural relativism is a powerful fact, but

---

[1] Knox, *Reality of Christ*, p. 107.   [2] *Ibid.* p. 118.
[3] *Ibid.* p. 118.   [4] *Ibid.* p. 106.

so is the new meeting and discussion across the lines of many cultures and religions. If Christianity comes to mankind with the statement God is known as merciful, healing and saving only in Jesus Christ, the question of the relation of Christ to other religions becomes a critical one.

There is the pressing issue of the Christian interpretation of Judaism for example. Is God's mercy, his healing, his salvation known only as hope and not as fulfilment in the Old Testament? Or is Christ already present in the experience of the 103rd Psalm or the Servant of Deutero-Isaiah? This question forces us to some examination of the position that only in our community is God's salvation known. Whether that is Dr Knox's position I am not sure. I am not seeking to criticize his position so much as to understand it. But surely the relation of the Christian view of history to world history, and to God's cosmic action becomes more significant for the Church as human life takes cosmopolitan form in the twentieth century.

While I raise these questions I realize they move beyond the central focus of the problem to which Dr Knox has given his attention, that is how the Church understands its being, its origin in Jesus Christ, and its life in the Spirit. He has brought to that problem such powerful energies of thought and feeling, such a mastery of the historical critical method and its results, and such a painstaking capacity to say clearly what he means that he has given the Church a way of approaching its understanding of its Lord and its scriptural witness which is of permanent significance. He brings to the Church's self-understanding a perspective which is authentically catholic in the full sense of that great word.

3

THE ATONEMENT

F. W. DILLISTONE

Over a period of approximately forty years my major interest in the field of Christian theology has been the doctrine of atonement. Naturally during that time certain books have played an outstanding part in the development of my own thinking, and amongst them all I am aware of having responded most readily to those whose appeal has been not only to the mind but also to the heart. If an interpretation of the saving work of Christ has seemed capable not only of suggesting new lines of thought but also of stimulating new impulses of devotion, it has been doubly welcome and has found a permanent place amidst my small collection of most valued books.

Amongst these books of a double character I certainly include John Knox's *The Death of Christ*. I well remember my initial reaction to it. It was to feel that here was an author prepared to face every challenge of biblical and historical criticism with complete rigour and yet able to emerge with a confident faith in and warm devotion to the Christ of Calvary and the resurrection. Historical supports on which I had relied he evidently felt to be insecure. Yet there was no question about the way in which he regarded the cross. For him it was the means by which all life could be—indeed had been—redeemed and transformed.

Trying to think again about Knox's contribution to our understanding of the doctrine of the atonement, I have found myself returning in memory to other books which have played a somewhat similar role in my own continuing concern to interpret the significance of the cross. Three, in particular, made a strong impact upon me at successive stages and I purpose to speak of the importance of each of these before coming to Knox himself. As it happens, each author, like Knox, was primarily a New Testament scholar and I do not think that this is just a coincidence. The gospel of the saving work of Christ belongs to the very warp and woof of the New Testament. Here, if anywhere, the expert on New Testament

35

3-2

history, language and criticism can give help to the systematic theologian as he tries to perform his constructive task.

I

My first book is James Denney's *The Christian Doctrine of Reconciliation*. At an earlier stage I had read *The Death of Christ*—indeed it was one of the earliest full-scale treatments of the doctrine of the atonement that came into my hands—and had become aware not only of the strength of his scholarship but also of his passionate desire to communicate the central message of the New Testament to the modern world at the turn of the nineteenth century. Armed with the best linguistic and historical weapons of his time, he made a valiant attempt to show that there was one, and only one, theory of the atonement—the theory that Christ, by his death, had accomplished something final and utterly determinative for mankind by bearing the judgment that in the nature of things must fall upon human sin. 'He died for our sins', Denney believed, was written across the whole collection of books which we call the New Testament and in a sense influenced the writing of every page.

But it is his later book, actually published after his death, to which I owe my greatest debt. There was a trace of intolerance in *The Death of Christ*, a tendency to force the case by narrowing everything into one channel. *The Christian Doctrine of Reconciliation*, however, is in every way a big book, wide in its sympathies, open to the testimony of human experience, impressive in its grasp of history and related to the ways in which men of the twentieth century were beginning to think. Yet, when this has been said, it still is the case that Denney was first and foremost a New Testament exegete. The New Testament was 'the great witness to the gospel'. It was 'the primitive interpretation of the new life' in Christ—and in his view there was only one gospel in the New Testament. There may be relative contrasts within it, different emphases, but the whole bears witness to Christ as 'the redeemer of men from sin and their reconciler to God through his death on the cross'.

The chapter entitled 'The New Testament Doctrine of Reconciliation' is, I think, a masterly summary of constructive New Testament inquiry at that time. Denney is well enough aware of two

36

major difficulties which had been gathering strength during the
nineteenth century. First there was the question: Can the witness
of the gospels be regarded as entirely in harmony with, if not
identical in every respect with, the witness of the Pauline writings?
Obviously it is this which lies behind Denney's passionate affirmation of the unity of the New Testament. On the face of it the gospel
which Paul preached—the revelation of the righteousness and the
wrath of God over against the universal sinfulness of mankind, the
death of the Messiah for our sins and his rising again for our justification—seems to be set in a different key from the gospel attested by
Mark in which Jesus came preaching the Kingdom of God and
proclaiming free forgiveness to those who believed. Yet Denney
clung to his conviction that the difference was only apparent. Both
lines of witness converge on him who is the supreme reconciler. In
his examination of the synoptic gospels Denney focused attention
on the words and actions of Jesus directed towards the outcast and
the lost.

He received sinners. He declared, bestowed and embodied forgiveness.
He came to seek and to save that which was lost. Whatever else He did,
He came to men who were alienated from God by their sins...and He
brought them back to God and to the assurance of His fatherly love...
We may say that the reconciling virtue of His being was concentrated
in His death or that the reconciling virtue of His death pervaded His
being; in any case that the whole influence exerted upon sinners by
Jesus...is a reconciling influence cannot be denied.[1]

And, Denney would have said, it is to this central 'reconciling influence' that every writer of the New Testament bears witness.

Secondly, there was the question: How can historical events, i.e.
events occurring in time and space, reveal eternal truth and have
eternal value? How could the death of Christ, which few would have
difficulty in regarding as a climactic manifestation of human sin, be
also the final revelation of the love of God? How could history,
which is essentially relative, be at one single point transcended and
given an absolute significance? Clearly Denney feels the pressure of this
question keenly. He in a measure takes refuge by recalling what is
obviously true, that the New Testament writers did not feel the

[1] James Denney, *The Christian Doctrine of Reconciliation* (London, 1917), pp. 131 f.

perplexity in the same way that we are inclined to do. They even gloried in the paradox that an event surrounded by circumstances of squalor and perfidy and horror should have been the means chosen by God to reconcile the world to himself. 'They do not reason upon this, they seem, rather, to have had an instinctive sense of its truth. The assertion that the murdered Jesus is the Lamb of God who takes away the sin of the world is too great not to be true and the verification of it has been too wonderful to let us suppose it false.'[1] These are fine words but perhaps they do little more than cover up an underlying anxiety. To be fair to Denney it must be said that he did his best to wrestle with the problem of history but in his time it had not assumed its full proportions. Both of the difficulties that I have mentioned have remained with us and, as I shall try to show, more recent writers have helped us to grapple with them in ways which Denney could not foresee.

Denney stood firmly in the reformed tradition with its radical dependence upon holy scripture as the all-sufficient witness to what God had done in history for us men and for our salvation. He recognized the obligation to apply to scripture the new methods of critical historical investigation which nineteenth-century scholars had advocated. He shared the new emphasis on the place of the individual within the calling and purpose of God which had become more and more prominent from the eighteenth century onwards. There is little reference to the Church in his writings or to society or to the continuities of history. He sought to dwell in what he called 'the region of historical and moral reality', himself first standing under the judgment and salvation of God mediated through the Christ of the New Testament and then proclaiming as an evangelist, whether in lecture-room, in commentaries, or in the pulpit: 'We beseech you in Christ's name, Be ye reconciled to God.'

2

The Christian Doctrine of Reconciliation was in course of preparation during the early years of the First World War. It coincides therefore with the end of an era, an era in which the overall moral and social framework seemed utterly stable, even if many forces of a liberal

[1] James Denney, *The Christian Doctrine of Reconciliation*, p. 130.

and individualistic kind were operating within it. In the new era virtually everything would ultimately be questioned—historical traditions, moral standards, transcendent realities. And all this was bound to affect the theologian whose work was rooted in the New Testament and its interpretation. The two difficulties already mentioned were likely to become more and more acute. Could this collection of writings really be regarded as a unity, speaking with one heart and voice about God and his saving work for mankind? And in any case, could that which lay far back in history, subject to all kinds of historical relativities, really be a firm foundation for man's ultimate faith and commitment in all ages? Barth and his associates had their own ways of dealing with these questions but English scholarship at least persisted in seeking for less radical solutions. One of these was presented in the second book to which I shall refer.

It was in 1937 that Vincent Taylor's *Jesus and His Sacrifice* appeared. His preface began with these words:

After devoting something like twenty-five years to the study of the problems of literary and historical criticism in connexion with the Gospels, and especially to the minutiae of source criticism, I am conscious of a strong desire to investigate some more vital issue, arising out of these studies, which bears intimately upon Christian life and practice. For this reason during the last four years, in the intervals of a busy life spent in teaching and administration, I have endeavoured to make a careful investigation of the Passion sayings, with a view to discovering how Jesus interpreted His suffering and death. The results of this inquiry are published in the present volume.

As is well known, this volume was followed by two others—*The Atonement in New Testament Teaching* [1] and *Forgiveness and Reconciliation*,[2] the three together constituting a very impressive re-examination of the doctrine of the atonement in the light of the findings of New Testament scholarship as they stood at that time. But it was the first volume which I recall as the most exciting and original. It seemed to underpin the central superstructure of doctrinal formulation afresh with a firm New Testament foundation.

The plan of the work is easy to describe. The first part deals with the Old Testament background of the leading categories of the gospels—Kingdom of God, Messiah, Son of man, Servant of

---

[1] London, 1940. [2] London, 1941.

Yahweh, sacrifice. If we can be reasonably certain about the way these terms were being used and interpreted at the beginning of the Christian era we find ourselves in possession of valuable clues to Jesus' own understanding of his mission, an understanding which would at least in a measure have been shared by others. In other words, we discover one of the great unities of the New Testament in the use made of these Old Testament symbols. The second part discusses with immense care and attention to detail the references by Jesus to his own passion which are to be found in the gospels and in the Pauline narrative. Source-criticism and form-criticism are employed and the opinions of a wide range of New Testament scholars are sifted and judged. The whole purpose is to discover what lay in Jesus' own mind and consciousness. Are the sayings reported in the New Testament genuine? Can we place a firm reliance on them as having actually been spoken by Jesus and therefore as true revelations of his own self-consciousness? Does their context, general (Old Testament background) and specific (the development of a messianic vocation), enable us to interpret them with confidence and depth of understanding? If so what is the final result for doctrine and devotion?

It is the last question which leads on to the development of the third part of the book. Taylor believes first that the passion sayings viewed as a whole enable us to understand Jesus' own thoughts 'about the purpose of His sufferings, the end they were to fulfil and the manner in which they would prove effective'. The cross was the highway of 'conscious messianic purpose', a purpose interpreted not in terms of political and nationalistic redemption but rather in terms of representative and universal sacrifice. The source, further, of this interpretation of sacrifice is to be found not so much in the cultus of Israel as 'in the sublimated expression of the sacrificial principle which is found in the description of the Suffering Servant'. What is at the heart of the Christian doctrine of atonement is that Jesus consciously identified himself with sinners and in their name and on their behalf offered a perfect self-oblation to God. He willingly accepted the way of the cross in obedience to the Father's will and in identification with those whom he had come to save. In his offering the world of mankind is gathered up and reconciled to God.

In the detailed examination of categories and texts which Taylor makes, it is clear enough that a large body of opinion was opposed to his general interpretation. He seeks honestly to allow for these dissentient voices but still comes down firmly on the side of his own conviction. The question of the unity of the New Testament is answered, not so much, as by Denney, in terms of Jesus, mediator of reconciliation in word and action, but rather in terms of Jesus, offering the representative sacrifice consciously and willingly. The problem of the event in history having eternal significance is solved by fastening upon a universally valid '*principle*', the sacrificial principle, and by portraying Jesus as gathering together into his own consciousness and dedication all the inchoate fumblings and strivings towards the implementation of this principle out of the past history of mankind (and particularly the inspired picture of the servant of Yahweh in the Servant Songs): deliberately acting it out in and through his own passion and gathering into that action all the future generations of mankind who were destined to be united to him in faith and love.

In Taylor's writings we find a quite remarkable combination of painstaking, critical scholarship and warm, single-hearted devotion. His work is, we feel, in the context of the Church and on behalf of the Church. He is concerned that the Church should think rightly in order that it may live rightly and worship rightly. The crux of right thinking, he believes, is the sacrificial principle and this was *perfectly* manifested in the thinking and acting of Jesus. This was and is the atonement on behalf of mankind. By committing himself in faith to Christ, a man is conformed to the principle of sacrifice in thought and in life. It will regulate his private prayer and his worship within the fellowship of God's people: it will direct his life of service both to God and to the community at large. So we can almost hear Taylor saying: 'Jesus the Messiah-Servant of God, is the perfect Sacrifice; He through the eternal Spirit offered Himself without spot to God: I beseech you therefore brethren that ye present yourselves a living sacrifice, holy, acceptable to God which is your reasonable service.'

3

Taylor's interpretation was in harmony with a marked new emphasis upon the Church, community and society which received a signal expression in the Oxford ecumenical Conference on Life and Work in 1937. It was also related to new interests in the psychology of the self and in forms of sacramental worship which were gaining strength in the life of the Churches. But with all its impressiveness, his reconstruction was open to criticism. It depended precariously upon a single imaginative identification in the mind of Jesus—the figures of Messiah and Servant of Yahweh brought together creatively in his own self-consciousness. How far, it may well be asked, can we speak confidently about what is going on in the self-consciousness of another human being even in our own contemporary period? But this is as nothing compared with the self-consciousness of a messianic figure living in the midst of a remote community some two millennia ago. The words and acts attributed to him are, it is true, immensely significant and demand the most careful study. But the haunting feeling at the back of the mind constantly is that those words and stories *could* have been the adaptation or reorientation or even inexact rendering of the early Christian witnesses. Do the passion sayings recorded in the gospels and recalled in the Pauline narrative really cohere with interpretations of the significance of the death and resurrection of Jesus found in other parts of the New Testament? In particular does a theory framed almost exclusively in terms of the sacrificial principle do justice to Paul's leading categories and imaginative comparisons as found in his Epistles generally? What could help most at this juncture would be some access to new light on Paul and his environment of language and ideas. Fortunately such light was to be forthcoming in a book bearing the marks of meticulous scholarship, as well, it must be said, as of deep religious insight. I refer to W. D. Davies's *Paul and Rabbinic Judaism* (1948).

In the struggle to discover a firm historical basis on which the doctrine of atonement could be built it was above all desirable to identify another body of ideas, another cultural outlook outside the New Testament itself, with which the New Testament concepts and categories could be compared and contrasted. In a measure this had been done by appealing to the Old Testament, to the Apocrypha and Pseudepigrapha, to various Hellenistic writings and to the evidence of the papyri. But there was one area which could be more significant than any of these for the identification of controlling canons of interpretation. This was the area of rabbinic Judaism, an area in which much work had been done but whose results had not, I think, been applied in any comprehensive way to the exegesis of Pauline theology. Davies's exposition is not so dependent on single categories—Messiah, Kingdom of God, etc.—as was Vincent Taylor's book. It is more in the nature of a sociological interpretation of history with Paul acting as the catalyst to bring to fulfilment deep-seated longings and hopes in the life of his own people. In Taylor's exposition it often seems that Jesus is deliberately taking current ideas of, for example, Messiahship, sacrifice, the Kingdom, Son of Man, and rejecting all that they implied in order that he might create something entirely new in their place. For Davies the object seems rather to be to reveal the way in which Paul took the notable concepts of the culture to which he belonged—the hope of a new creation, a new humanity, a new obedience, a new resurrection-life—and sought to show how these hopes had been brought to fulfilment in and through the work of Jesus the Christ. Through fulfilment they had, of course, been transformed. But the discontinuity is less radical than Vincent Taylor seems to suggest.

In his chapter on the death of Jesus he deals at length with the theory *and* practice of sacrifice in first-century Judaism. The evidence is complex but it is obviously hazardous to assume, as Vincent Taylor tended to do, that a single 'principle' of sacrifice existed then or indeed at any other time. Sacrifice was integral to the ritual of the Passover: it was also integral to the ceremonies of the Day of Atonement. Yet the atmosphere and intentions associated with the first of these festivals differed enormously from those associated with the second. Probably the pattern of images belonging to each of these occasions was used by Paul to bring home a particular aspect of Christ's atoning work but neither was in itself sufficient to constitute a comprehensive instrument of comparison. If there is one category to be given pre-eminence beyond all others for the interpretation of the meaning of the death of Christ, this, Davies believes, is the category of *obedience*.

At the back of all Jewish thinking about the relationship between

43

man and God was the conviction that God had made a *covenant* with his people and that their welfare consisted above all in *obedience* to the requirements of the covenant. But the history of this people had been marked by constant disobedience in spite of the fact that they possessed a law which made the nature of their necessary obedience even more explicit. Over against this we see Jesus, perfectly obedient in his sonship, delighting to do the will of God even when it involved obedience to the death of a cross. Yet such a career was not foreign to the best thought of his own day for, according to Davies, 'the idea of obedience unto death' (and he has been referring particularly to the Maccabean martyrs), 'a passive acceptance of death out of loyalty to the revealed will of God as the crown of loyalty to the Torah, was in the air in first-century Judaism.'[1] Davies admits that there is a certain complexity in the notion that he who was in the totality of his being a new Torah should have been perfectly obedient to that new Torah. Yet this conjunction is not self-contradictory. The career of Jesus can be regarded as the perfect revelation of obedience to the mind and purpose of God; at the same time it can be regarded as in itself a new and unsurpassable revelation of what a true life of human obedience should be.

The total effect of Davies's work has been, I think, to enable us to see in a new way how the witness of Paul to Jesus' saving work and the witness of the Synoptists hold together and complement one another. The common background is the general outlook of rabbinic Judaism revealed in and through the large body of literature which is available to the modern student. At the heart of this literature is the ideal of obedience to the Torah, Torah being interpreted as the full revelation of God and of his will for man. All too often this ideal was envisaged in a dominantly literalistic and legalistic way. But Jesus was able to grasp it and embody it in dynamic *personal* terms. And Paul on his part was ultimately to see that the norm of obedience towards which he had himself been striving had in fact been realized to the full in the life and death of Jesus. Further, this total realization had been effectual not only for himself but for all those whom, as messianic deliverer, he gathered into his own perfect obedience. In other words, obedience in life, obedience unto death, had been freely accepted by Jesus as the controlling principle of his words and

---

[1] *Paul and Rabbinic Judaism*, p. 265.

activities: Paul, recognizing that such an obedience had been actually worked out in the fabric of a human career, yielded himself up in faith and allegiance to the one who had perfectly fulfilled the whole will and purpose of God on his behalf. Dying to himself and to his own efforts, he became indissolubly united with the Christ who had loved him and given himself for him.

Davies left many questions still open but he succeeded, it seems to me, in shedding fresh light on the formulation of early Christian doctrine by expounding the leading ideas and concepts of contemporary rabbinic Judaism. He laid hold of such categories as 'Torah', 'obedience', and 'community', and used them to forge vital links between the recorded ministry of Jesus and the writings of Paul himself. The result is a bracing new emphasis on the ethical realism of the New Testament with Davies in effect saying: 'Jesus is the full revelation of life in obedience to the will of God: living for others, he became obedient even unto death on their behalf: wherefore I beseech you yield yourselves to God as men who have been brought from death to life and yourselves as slaves of obedience which leads to righteousness.'

4

I have briefly examined two notable attempts since Denney's time to interpret the significance of the death of Jesus, the one by concentrating on the implications of Jesus' own words recorded in the various passion sayings, the other by seeking to point up the challenge of the teaching, both of Jesus and Paul, by setting it within the context of the ideas and categories of first-century rabbinic Judaism. But during the period of the gestation of these two books a powerful movement had been in progress amongst German scholars—and its influence was being strongly felt in America—towards a position in which the total concentration of the Christian mind would be upon man's existence-in-the-present as it is determined once-for-all by the saving event of Jesus' cross and resurrection. To seek assurance by relying upon some pattern of historical reconstruction—the sequence of events in Jesus' ministry, the march of ideas in his teaching, the unveiling of purpose and intention in his self-consciousness—is not a viable possibility. All these are the constructions of men writing at some considerable remove from that which they are describing.

There is the strong possibility that adaptations and adjustments were made to render these reconstructions relevant and meaningful for the solution of the problems of later generations. Only one event stands out unmistakably—it is the death of Jesus on Calvary. All else belongs to the realm of faith and interpretation.

As a typical example of this general outlook I will quote some words of its most distinguished representative.

Faith [Bultmann writes] does not relate itself to historical or cosmic processes that could be established as free from doubt, but rather to the *preaching* behind which faith cannot go and which says to man that he must understand the cross as God's act of salvation and believe in the resurrection—only in preaching is the cross God's saving act. Faith comes from preaching and God's act of salvation is the institution of the 'word' of reconciliation...This preaching of God's saving act, however, is not a communication about events that one can also establish outside of faith; rather in speaking of God's act of salvation, it at the same time addresses the conscience of the hearer and asks him whether he is willing to understand the occurrence that it proclaims as occurring to him himself and thereby to understand his existence in its light.[1]

This concentration on the word of reconciliation and man's response in faith is impressive. It avoids troublesome questions about what may or may not have been present in Jesus' own self-consciousness: it regards as secondary any inquiries about the character and motives of those who compassed Jesus' death: it dismisses as mythological and therefore peripheral the later attempts in the Church to bear witness to the meaning of the cross in terms drawn from general social experience. Instead, it confronts the cross in its nakedness and horror and says: 'God is there! There I see his judgment on man. All of man's boastings are at an end. I too am judged. My independent existence is negated. I am crucified with Christ.' But the very act of saying this brings liberation and redemption. 'This, I now realize, is no dead Christ. He is alive—for me and in me. The word of the gospel is death and resurrection through the one saving event of which Jesus is the substance and the sum. This is the only *meaning* of the cross that finally matters.'

But in spite of all that is attractive in such a concentration upon the individual and his existence, I have the uneasy feeling that it is an

---

[1] R. Bultmann, *Existence and Faith* (London, Fontana edition, 1964), pp. 163 f.

oversimplification, that it fails to do justice to man's life-in-history and life-in-community, that indeed it fails to give significance to Jesus' own career in history and in society. It is because this wider context is taken seriously, while at the same time the difficulties of establishing what precisely an individual, however exalted, said or did in history are taken equally seriously, that my fourth book, *The Death of Christ* by John Knox, seems to me so important. He is not prepared to rest content with a *word* of the cross to be proclaimed as judgment and salvation to human existence; nor with a *picture* of the cross disclosing a way of reconciliation in the midst of human estrangement: he wants to be able to set forth the meaning of the cross in such a way as to reveal its power to transform and redeem the *whole* of life.

So far as the historical circumstances of Jesus' death are concerned, Knox affirms that no clear picture can be drawn. We cannot discover its meaning in terms of any conjunction of human forces which can be accurately determined. Nor, he claims, can we discover it in terms of a convincing exposition of Jesus' own consciousness of the exact nature of his vocation. In both of these areas there are suggestive possibilities, even probabilities, to be derived from the documents which we possess, but of themselves they would not be sufficient to lead us to the heart of the reality which we seek. How then is the meaning of the cross, its significance both for the life of the Church and for the experience of the believer, to be found? The answer to this question constitutes Knox's major contribution to atonement-doctrine.

His basic appeal, as he seeks to work out his answer, is to *the memory of the Church*. We only know about the death of Jesus because of all that has been enshrined in the memory of the Church and this applies both to the event itself and to its interpretation. But the event of the death cannot be viewed in isolation. It is part of a larger event

which began (in the sense in which any event can be said to have a beginning) with the gathering of Jesus' disciples and ended (in the same approximate sense) with the creation of the Church, the new community of the Spirit, in which Jesus was remembered and was still known as the living Lord. The meaning of the Cross can be seen only in this context.[1]

[1] John Knox, *The Death of Christ* (London, 1959), p. 129.

For Knox it is the early Church 'rather than events lying behind it, with which the New Testament puts us directly in touch'. Therefore to recognize the radical significance of the early Church and to accept without reservation our continuity with it and dependence upon it—these attitudes are for him quite fundamental.

We need now to see that the Church's priority is not only epistemological, but actual; that the basic, objective, historical reality underneath, and presupposed in, all primitive confession—picture, kerygma, or whatever else—and the actual carrier of all the meanings being confessed was the early Church; and that, in consequence, the only adequate way to define the Event is to identify it with the Church's beginning. We need to see this meaning of the Church with our minds and to embrace it in our hearts. If God acted in history, as we affirm He did, He acted to bring this social community into being. The historical Event to which all distinctively Christian faith returns is not an event antedating the Church, or in any sense or degree prior to it, but is the coming into being of the Church itself.[1]

Nothing, I think, is more characteristic of Knox than his enthusiasm for the Church. He is fully aware of its weaknesses and its divisions. He knows that its necessary forms and structures may cramp the life of the Spirit. Yet he recognizes with overwhelming gratitude the knowledge of Jesus which has come to him through the Church's memory. He sees the supreme evidence of God's reconciling activity in the creation around Jesus of a community of faith and love. And he believes that the presence of Jesus, the risen Lord, is made constantly real to him and to others within the fellowship of the Church's continuing life. The meaning of the reconciling work of Jesus can therefore be found only by sharing as fully as possible both in the Church's memory of him and in its abiding experience of his presence.

With this as his controlling principle Knox proceeds with confidence to interpret the death of Christ in terms of *victory* and *sacrifice*. Through his death Christ gained the *victory* over the powers that held man in bondage and thereby delivered him from evil. At the same time he made the full, perfect and sufficient *sacrifice* and thereby reconciled man to the Good. In the New Testament these interpretations are expressed in dramatic form, the first setting Christ at the centre as conquering hero who brings to nought all the

[1] John Knox, *The Church and the Reality of Christ* (London, 1963), p. 22.

machinations of sin, law, death and demonic powers, the second giving him the central place as the sacrificial lamb who takes away guilt, estrangement, anxiety and despair. But they are not simply dramas of the individual imagination, created at a particular point in time. They are representations of realities within the life of the Church, realities which had actually come into human experience as the result of Jesus' death and resurrection. They are not arbitrary estimates of meaning which can be accepted or rejected at will. The Church would not be what it is and has always been apart from these realities at the heart of its life. The meanings could never have been expressed in this way had it not been that they are part of the life of the Church, God's new creation in Christ. Jesus was—in the two representations of His death, which the Church made no effort to keep apart—both 'saving Victim' and 'Redeemer King'. But both representations were concerned to set forth the heights and depths of a reconciliation which was one day to comprehend 'all things in heaven and on earth' and of which the Church, where alone it was embodied (however partially) in history, was the 'first fruits' and the promise.[1]

The supreme appeal of Knox's formulation of the doctrine of the atonement is surely to be found in the strong impression it gives that here is a man who has wrestled unflinchingly with the problems of historical fact which beset the New Testament scholar and yet has emerged with a ringing assurance that through the total event, of which Jesus' death on the cross was the centre and symbol, reconciliation between God and man, between man and man, has become a living reality within human experience. As a rough means of expressing my sense of indebtedness to him I shall try to enumerate some of the most valuable aspects of his exposition and then some of the problems which still remain.

A. POSITIVE EMPHASES

(1) Any convincing historical reconstruction must be written from within a tradition. The historian must identify himself as closely as possible with the ways of thinking and feeling and imagining and remembering which are manifested in the society whose historical experience he is seeking to describe.

[1] *Ibid.* p. 113.

F. W. Dillistone

(2) A historical account becomes alive and convincing when it bears some relationship at least to the world of present experience. If that which is recalled from the past has no connexion with present possibilities of experience it is incapable of becoming meaningful.

(3) Every event in history is part of a larger complex, every individual is part of a larger society. The historian who elects to deal with a cluster of events related to the experience of a definable social group is likely to achieve the greatest success in the exercise of his craft. Excessive limitation, either in regard to an event or to an individual, is beset with dangers of misinterpretation.

(4) To elucidate the *meaning* of an event in the past it is essential to view it in its wider context and to compare the whole cluster of events with dramatic sequences already familiar to the human imagination. The drama of conflict issuing in defeat and victory is for example widely, if not universally, familiar within human experience. To use a dramatic story drawn from such a context and to use it to bring meaning to a particular cluster of events in history is not only legitimate, it is essential. The only danger lies in assuming that one dramatic representation of this kind can exhaust the meaning of the event under consideration. Varying stories must be told if a rich fullness of meaning is to emerge.

Each of these affirmations, I believe, receives valuable illustration and confirmation in and through Knox's exposition.

B. SOME REMAINING PROBLEMS

(1) The term 'memory' occupies a key position in Knox's writings. How is the memory of a *society* brought to outward expression? How are the accuracy and faithfulness of social memory checked? If the New Testament represents the memory of the early Church (though Knox affirms that the Church's 'memory' contains both more and less than the New Testament itself) what are the criteria by which attention is to be directed to these elements within the memory which are of major importance for the construction of any particular Christian doctrine?

(2) Two other important concepts, 'continuity' and 'community', tend to recur in the course of his exposition. Are these two concepts

assumed too uncritically? It is true that Knox in an important passage[1] takes into account the element of *discontinuity* in our understanding of the meaning of the resurrection. Yet he makes it clear that he wants to lay the greater emphasis on the *continuity* between Jesus' earthly life and his resurrection life and it is this emphasis, I think, which governs his whole exposition of the nature of the Church, of the Church's doctrines and of the Church's ministry. Similarly in relation to community. Allowance is made for the creative contributions to thought and imagination made by individuals,[2] but again the greater emphasis is on the communal process which follows. It is what is remembered and experienced in the life of the community which takes precedence over whatever may have been put forward by individuals in moments of creative illumination. I recognize that there is a delicate balance or, to put it another way, a vigorous dialectic to be preserved here. Knox is doubtless conscious of too great attention having been paid in much of theological thought (particularly in the reformed Churches) to crises, discontinuities, individual genius, charismatic leadership, etc. But 'continuity' can easily imply an unchanging continuum, community can easily become a congealed mass. The perversions of 'continuity' and 'community' may be more dangerous than those of 'crisis' and 'the individual'.

(3) The tendency to underplay the part of the individual is perhaps at the root of the unease that I feel about the treatment of the Pauline theology in Knox's reconstruction. It is the immense strength of Denney's and Davies's interpretations that they seem to be measuring the heights and depths of Paul's imagination and to be showing how great was his contribution to the Church's understanding in every period of history. Whether this contribution really coincided with 'the memory' of the early Church or with the memory of the Church at any time, I find myself questioning and wondering. The vast implications of his concepts of righteousness and justification, of death to sin and life in the Spirit, and of the passing away of the old and the coming of the new, all these do not appear to me to stand out clearly when the emphasis is so strong on the continuity of memory and the common mind. Yet I fancy that it is these ideas which have constantly led to a revival of understanding of atonement in the course of the history of Christianity.

[1] *Death of Christ*, pp. 134 ff.   [2] *Ibid.* p. 45.

(4) This emphasis on the community and its two leading dramatic representations (victory and sacrifice) raises the further question in my mind about other dramatic comparisons which the New Testament contains. There is no doubt that the images of the great deliverer and the sacrificial lamb occupy a notable position in the early witness of the Church and this has been brought out beautifully and convincingly by Knox. But I question whether the sacrificial comparison is as frequent or as uniform as he seems to suggest and I believe that there are other comparisons—death to the old creation and life in the new, judgment under the law of righteousness and justification through grace, forgiveness and reconciliation within the structure of personal relationships—which are used symbolically to express the *double* effect of the cross–resurrection event which again Knox brings out so clearly.

(5) Fifthly, while appreciating immensely the concentration upon the meaning which comes to us through our membership in the body of Christ and our sharing in its memory, I still wonder whether fresh insights may not come to us through our identification with the world outside the Church, its interests, its insights, its conflicts. For example, does not a fresh understanding of the meaning of the cross begin to dawn on us through the whole theory and practice of modern psychotherapy? Is not the living Christ at work in the world as well as in the Church? Ever since *The Death of Christ* was written there has been a marked swing of concern among Christians away from the Church itself with the slogan 'Let the Church be the Church' to the world in which the Church must live and in whose life it must be involved. 'God was reconciling *the world* to himself in Christ.' 'Not for our sins only, but for the sins *of the whole world*.' What are the implications of affirmations such as these? Can the modern dramatist, poet, painter, whose imagination is deeply sensitive to the world's travail give us new insights into the meaning of the cross which have no obvious dependence on the Church's memory?

(6) Finally, in attempting to focus attention upon Knox's most distinctive contribution to atonement-theology I turn to sections III and IV of Chapter Seven in *The Death of Christ* (pp. 153–9). Having affirmed that the two conceptions—those of a victory won and of a sacrifice offered—belong to the very warp and woof of the New

Testament ('As Son of Man he has overcome our enemies and set us free; as Servant he has atoned for our guilt and reconciled us to God'), he goes on to state that these conceptions remain throughout history both true and illuminating, 'not as theories of the Atonement, not as rational explanations of the fact of Jesus' death, but being taken much more concretely, as dramatic ways of expressing meanings of the whole event of Christ, of which the death is...both the actual and symbolic centre' (153). Deliberately he chooses the language-terms 'conceptions', 'images', 'dramas' rather than the traditional 'theories', 'explanations', or even 'historical causes'. The two great New Testament 'conceptions' in his view have nothing to do with describing the historical factors which brought about the death of Jesus of Nazareth nor with constructing a metaphysical rationale of transactions within the divine being. Rather they are myths, stories, dramatic representations, images whose function it is to express the *meaning* of the whole event of Christ. And at the centre of the event itself stands the cross, acting as the symbol of the whole meaning of the whole event.

What strikes me immediately in these sections is the way in which Knox tries to grapple with matters which have become an urgent concern within the period in which we are now living. Denney was concerned with the impact of historical criticism and the question of whether one particular theory of atonement was common to all the writers of the New Testament. Vincent Taylor was concerned with the figure of Jesus himself in history—his consciousness of mission, his attitude to his impending passion, his acceptance of the sacrificial idea to define the nature of his work. Davies was concerned with the relation of Paul to the total activity of God in the history of his own people—the Exodus, the giving of the Law, the operations of the Spirit, the coming of the Messiah—and the reinterpretation which Paul constructed in the light of the life and death and resurrection of Jesus himself. But Knox, though himself a fine historian, is little concerned with *historical* or *rational* issues when it comes to discourse about atonement. Atonement for him is essentially an experience enjoyed within the fellowship of the Church. Myths, dramas, stories are the language-forms appropriate to represent this experience. Only through the use of such forms, Knox is—I think—claiming, can there be any hope of discovering the ultimate *meaning* of the event of Christ in relation to human existence. And it is *meaning* that men are seeking today.

The key-words are stories and dramas rather than theories or rationales: whole event rather than historical facts: whole meaning rather than particular explanation: the cross as symbol rather than as isolated action. Knox does not accept as a proper sequence:

(*a*) God acted in the cross.
(*b*) Chosen witnesses explained the cross as the victory and sacrifice of the Son of God.
(*c*) Men accepted this explanation and thereby entered into the enjoyment of reconciliation with God.

Rather he sets forth the sequence:

(*a*) The Church came into being as part of the total event—God's new creation in Christ.
(*b*) Within the Church men participate in the memory of Christ and through his Spirit enjoy redemption and forgiveness.
(*c*) They bear witness to this new experience by reciting dramas of victory and sacrifice.
(*d*) In these dramas the cross always occupies the central position as symbol of the whole meaning of the whole event.

Probably the following paragraph is the most forthright statement of his position.

The Church's knowledge of the victory and the forgiveness which God made available in Christ does not follow upon its acceptance of the truth, in any sense, of these images (i.e. the images of Christ as victor and Christ as lamb of God) although that knowledge is,...intrinsically and by a kind of necessity, bound up with them; rather the images depend upon the knowledge. The knowledge does not follow upon the belief that the ancient myths are true; rather we find the myths meaningful and true because the knowledge is given independently of them, although insepar-ably with them. The knowledge is given with membership in the Church, with participation in the memory and the Spirit which together constitute and distinguish the Church. It belongs—as the myths also do but in a prior sense—to God's new creation.[1]

I do not intend to quibble about the use of the word 'knowledge' though I am surprised that Knox does not employ the word 'ex-perience' in this context. My main concern is with the *sequence* which

[1] *Death of Christ*, pp. 158 f.

Knox regards as indispensable for any true statement. He is clearly critical of a long tradition of reformed theology which demanded the acceptance of a particular theory or formulation of atonement doctrine as a preliminary to the enjoyment of the experience of the reconciled life. Knox holds that this is contrary to what happened in the early Church and is untrue to the general pattern of human experience at any time. Only when we are brought within a society, sharing its memory and its living spirit, do we find ourselves liberated and integrated: and only then do we begin to express what we have experienced through the myths and dramas and symbolic forms which belong to the total experience of the society. 'The knowledge is given independently of them, although inseparably with them.' Such a statement approaches very near to contradiction or at least to an insoluble problem of priorities even though I have every sympathy with the author's desire to prevent any single model or theory or myth coming to be regarded as the essential gateway to the enjoyment of the Christian experience.

In the end however I wonder if Knox does not press the question of sequence too rigorously. He is ready to insist that there must be *two* dramas. Why could there not be *two* sequences? In some cases the recital of the story, the enacting of the drama, *precedes* the experience. In other cases the enjoyment of the experience *precedes* the rebirth of the images. I find it hard to accept an either/or. I find it difficult to reconstruct with any confidence the temporal stages within the total complex which Knox calls the whole Christ event. Throughout I see a dialectic of image and experience, drama and involvement, idea and enactment. I do not find it helpful to insist on priority one way or the other. All that finally matters, as it seems to me, is that each arm of the dialectic shall be directed towards *the centre* which, as Knox so firmly and so finely declares once and again, is the cross of Christ. There myth and history, subjective and objective, individual experience and corporate memory converge. At the still centre of the turning world we finally become silent. The death of the Son of God becomes the inexhaustible symbolic source of ineffable meaning.

It is because I admire John Knox's work so greatly that I have ventured to raise these questions and make these criticisms. The last three chapters of *The Death of Christ* constitute, I think, one of the finest constructive attempts to restate the doctrine of the atonement in a form capable of appealing to the heart and mind of the mid-twentieth-century Christian. In particular it moves beyond details of historical causation and rational explanation on to broader categories of dramatic representation and ultimate meaning. It stretches out in the direction of the philosophical and sociological questions which are under debate today. Yet the process of re-statement never ends. To be faithful to the Church's memory on the one hand, to be sensitive to the language and symbols which belong to a particular age on the other, and to bring all together within a creative relationship may be one form of the experience of recon-ciliation within the continuing life of the Church to which Knox bears such eloquent testimony.

4

THEOLOGICAL ARGUMENTS FOR CHRIST'S HISTORICITY: PARALLELS WITH THE THEISTIC PROOFS

A. DURWOOD FOSTER, JR

I

There are patterns of argument for Christ's historicity that parallel the traditional ontological, cosmological, teleological and moral proofs for the existence of God. The present essay undertakes to sketch the parallels and discuss them theologically. One may indeed question whether the historicity of Christ (as perhaps distinguishable from that of Jesus) can be argued, particularly as here contemplated. Or if such argument is feasible, one may ask what significance it has for faith or for historiography. These kinds of questions are also paralleled in the problematic of the theistic proofs. In both cases— the theistic and the christic (using this term instead of 'Christo-logical')—the arguments are complexly related to faith. But even if their effective function depends on faith, they are not meaningless either for faith or for unfaith. They offer themselves as an expressive structure for faith and as a means of framing the questions faith addresses. Historiography stands in this connexion in an interesting parallel with scientific investigation of the world. The research of the special sciences, including historiography, is methodically neutral toward affirmations of faith. Yet the inquiry ramified in these sciences is humanly dependent upon and significant for a motivating perspective that involves faith. Thus the same kind of relation that empirical natural science has to the understanding of God and the world, historiography has to the understanding of the historical Christ. In this relation the patterns of argument considered below can play for the theologian a heuristic and integrating role.

2

We may begin with the most controversial of the classic proofs since it is also, as Kant saw, the most basic. The ontological argument moves from essence to existence, from idea or concept to actuality. It would show that in a supreme case existence is implied in essence, that the concept of God entails his real being beyond his being merely in the concept. In St Anselm's formulation, God is that than which a greater cannot be conceived. Now if God were conceived merely as idea, a greater could be conceived, namely a really existing God. Another version of the argument uses geometric analogy. As triangularity implies three sides, so the idea of God implies existence. For Spinoza and Hegel the crux is the thought of that which is presupposed in all possible thought. Hartshorne stresses that the reality thus necessarily thought must be adequate to ground the world we know. To be sure, the ontological argument must concede that many fail to grasp clearly the idea of God. But its point is that if God be rightly thought, he must be thought as actually existing. The christic parallel is that if Christ be rightly thought, he must be thought as historically real.

Whatever the validity of the argument, a difficulty in the parallel at once suggests itself. More than the other arguments, the ontological may seem exclusively applicable to the theistic case. This could appear so on the ground that the argument has to do essentially with the concept of necessary being, whereas Christ belongs to the order of historical or contingent being. To contemplate a christic case of the argument might seem to repeat the mistake of Gaunilo, who proposed the *reductio ad absurdum* that, on St Anselm's showing, the concept of a perfect island would entail the island's existence. The reply to Gaunilo has usually sought to restrict the argument to the one supreme case of the *ens necessarium*, the absolute, or God.

Here, however, we confront different possibilities in the interpretation of the ontological argument. For whom, for what more precise object, and in what way is the argument supposed to function? Karl Barth has held that the argument functions in and for faith.[1] It exemplifies the process of *fides quaerens intellectum* in which

---

[1] Karl Barth, *Fides Quaerens Intellectum: Anselms Beweis der Existenz Gottes im Zusammenhang seines theologischen Programms* (Zollikon-Zürich, 1958).

faith seeks to unfold and illuminate itself in respect to and by the power of its object. So far as this is so, the parallel of the theistic and christic cases is certainly more apparent than it would otherwise be. For on this understanding 'that than which a greater cannot be conceived' is not an *ens necessarium* somehow certified from without faith, but is the self-certifying God of biblical revelation. The God who thus makes himself known becomes both the supreme object and the basis of faith's rational self-explication, i.e., of theology. However, if the referent of the ontological argument is the biblical God, the suggested reason for applying the argument solely to the theistic and not to the christic case disappears. More exactly, it disappears so far as the existence of the biblical God is no more grounded in an *a priori* certainty outside faith than is the existence of Christ. This holds true even though (as a rigorous Barthian would hardly admit) some kind of faith in God, in biblical purview and in human experience generally, is more widely distributed than faith in Christ. In any event, so far as God is known in Christ, there is a coalescence of the theistic and christic cases. In the order of knowing, God's existence is dependent on that of Christ, while the existence of Christ partakes of the primordial certainty of God's existence as reflected in the ontological argument. Epistemically the one is neither more necessary nor contingent than the other. God—but that means the God who is known in the historical Christ—becomes the prius of certainty from which faith thinks and lives.

To apply the ontological argument so understood to Christ would not imply its indefinite extensibility, as for instance to Gaunilo's island. One might agree that in order to be perfect an island must exist, without being led for that reason to posit the island's existence. For in the idea of an island, even a perfect one, there is no intrinsic reality claim. To say that the perfection of a hypothetical thing-in-question would entail existence is not to say that the thing actually occurs. On the other hand, in another person who addresses me, or most radically in whatever establishes my world, that is, in the prius of my being and thinking, I have to do with that which cannot be thought as mere idea. Its actuality, for those who think it, is not hypothetical but categorical. It would be wrong to say that such a prius is indubitable. It can be doubted, but the doubt must be of an ultimate kind, surmountable only by the power of the prius itself or by a new prius which, displacing the old, would constitute a conversion.

More specifically, then, how does the ontological argument so understood shape itself in relation to Christ? As in the theistic case too, the basic motif is capable of varied expression. In an intuitive-fragmentary form it occurs in the kind of statement, sometimes found in prefaces or conclusions to historical studies of Jesus, that in its fundaments no such figure could have been invented. That is, if one rightly apprehends the biblical portrait of Christ, he will perforce apprehend in or through it more than mere portrait. Akin to this is Herrmann's appeal to the self-evincing inner life of Jesus.[1] The logic is more clearly elaborated in Schleiermacher's assertion of Christ's indefeasible historicity as the archetype of the new humanity,[2] echoed in Tillich's use of the phrase 'real picture'.[3] If Christ functions as normative ground of the new humanity—or of the new being, as Tillich has it—then he is necessarily accorded, from the new humanity's own outlook, reality in at least the same measure as the new humanity. Since participation in the new humanity is faith, the logic can be expressed in terms of what faith requires of its ground. As Ebeling puts it, 'unless' faith were grounded in Jesus as historical reality, 'there would remain to us nothing but christological myth', which however would contradict 'the self-understanding of Christian faith'.[4]

One could give the christic application of the argument an Anselmian turn by formulating Christ, in some appropriate terms, as that than which a greater cannot be conceived. This is directly suggested in Schleiermacher's discussion of the archetype of the new humanity, where perhaps however the bond of the christic with the theistic is not sufficiently explicit. One could alternatively formulate that Christ is the supreme instance of divine saving action, or of divine self-manifestation. Now if the biblically pictured Christ be understood as only a product of faith, a greater Christ would be conceivable, a historically actual one. Then we should have to look

[1] Wilhelm Herrmann, *The Communion of the Christian with God* (London, 1930), pp. 72, 76 *passim*.
[2] Friedrich Schleiermacher, *The Christian Faith* (Edinburgh, 1928), pp. 373 f.
[3] Paul Tillich, *Systematic Theology*, 2 (Chicago, 1960), 116.
[4] Gerhard Ebeling, *Wort und Glaube* (Tübingen, 1963), pp. 207–8.

forward to one who had not yet come, and that, as Schleiermacher remarks, would signal the end of Christian faith.[1]

There are many ways of elaborating how Christian faith requires the existence of its ground. Beginning from the humanity of Christ, one may reason that if he were really a man he must have had a history as other men do. Or one may focus on the meaning of existence and/or historicity. Historical existence acknowledged in another means reality over against me, not originating in but impinging upon my own conceptuality. It means capacity to encounter my own existence in judgment and grace. Either term, existence or historicity, can include the meaning of the other. But if existence (of another) registers the primary note of encounter from without my own limits, historicity underlines the already-having-become-manifest of this encounter for a historical community. Now the conditions indicated are among those that must be fulfilled if there is to be a Lord and Saviour of my actual being and of the historical community. Hence the adequate idea of Christ includes that of his actual historicity. In this sense, contrary to the Kantian dictum, existence is most certainly a predicate, and a decisive one in Christian faith's explication of itself.

Here let us confront the possible objection that the so-called argument is tautological, since it simply expounds what is believed without offering reasons why this should be regarded as true. Thus one might judge the argument superfluous for those who already believe as well as pointless for those who do not. But what is a tautology? If it were a rhetorical redundancy, that could be left to the appraisal of homiletics. If however a tautology is the induction or deduction of a conclusion that is already *logically* implicit in its premises, then every logical operation is tautological. Plainly tautology *per se* is not worthless, though in a particular case it may be irrelevant. Now if a process of reasoning succeeds in unfolding a premiss, in framing corollaries and thus in illuminating the coherence of further terms within a perspective determined or co-determined by the premiss, then the process may be regarded as rationally fruitful. Much of philosophy as well as theology is such a reflective explication of meaning.

The kind of argumentation here considered would thus confirm

---

[1] Schleiermacher, *The Christian Faith*, p. 373.

dimensions of faith in terms of their consistency within the whole they mutually comprise, while the relevancy of a particular piece of argumentation would depend upon the confusion and debate prevailing at a given time. In its confirmatory function, such argumentation can also have heuristic or regulative and stimulative value for related areas of the theological enterprise. A propos the theistic case one thinks of the concern of Leibniz and others to show that the concept of God is possible, i.e., free of self-contradiction. If possible, then necessary! Today, in the effort to formulate a more adequate God-concept by including in it temporality and contingency, we may well see with Charles Hartshorne a crucial strengthening of the ontological argument.[1] The christic parallel to the theistic case is the effort to think through a coherent doctrine of Christ's person and work. This shows the possibility of the Christ-concept. Moreover, just as no God-concept would be adequate that lacked positive implications for the world of the sciences, so would no Christ-concept that failed to imply contact in particular with historical research. There is thus a sense in which the execution of the ontological argument, which pivots upon the intrinsic credibility of the concepts in question, both implies and depends upon everything that goes to make these concepts clear and adequate.

So far we have interpreted the ontological argument as from and for faith. Along these lines Karl Barth has expounded a meaningful function of the argument, even if he has over-clarified the intention of St Anselm. For the latter and for others before and since who used the argument, it has had at least partly the sense of corroborating faith, or some element of faith, in a structure of reason not construed as belonging to the faith thus corroborated. In this way one has assumed that the argument might serve as a bridge between faith and reason and therefore between faith and unfaith, so far as unfaith were able to reason clearly. There would then accrue to the argument an apologetic value, first for the man of faith himself, inasmuch as he must always still contend with his own unfaith, and further for the world of unfaith, in the manner of a natural theology.

Now these alternative interpretations of the argument, in their

[1] Charles Hartshorne, 'The Theistic Proofs', *Union Seminary Quarterly Review*, 20 (1965), 115–29.

positive intent, are not mutually exclusive, It is entirely feasible that it should function in the self-explication of faith and yet also actualize a point of contact with unfaith. In fact (as Barth early saw), when faith exhibits rational integrity and luminosity by virtue of its object, that in itself achieves the end of apologetics. But so far as there are two distinct undertakings—the self-explication of faith and the dialogue with worldly reason—one of these need not in principle suppress the other, nor in the history of theology has this happened. Accordingly it is appropriate to ponder whether there is a christic case of the ontological argument also in the distinct apologetic sense, that is, in a sense that utilizes rational grounds common to Christian believers and to unbelievers.

The classic theistic model for apologetic use of the ontological argument is the effort to establish, from the concept of such a being, that there is a necessary being. The christic parallel would show that the idea of Christ, construed as a general idea and not merely a Christian one, entails the existence of Christ. The theistic argument is that there is accessible to all men (who think clearly about the matter) the thought of a necessary being or ground of being, which we call God. In the christic case one can formulate that there is universally possible the thought of a positive relationship with the ground of being, and that the thought of this relationship (for all who clearly think it) necessarily implies an existing mediator.

As concerns the theistic case, Kant has been credited with showing that the necessity we may attribute to a supreme being is a matter of our own reason, not of the 'thing in itself'. That we may think a necessary being does not mean there must be such a being. There is always involved a leap from the order of our thought to that of reality (or of whatever may transcend our thought). Interestingly, Kant regarded the ontological as basic to the other classic proofs because it assumed the burden of executing, or (as he thought) of eliminating the leap, before which the cosmological and teleological proofs, however preliminarily successful, must finally halt. Kant denied the competency of the ontological argument and of all mere reason to bridge the chasm between thinking and being. Accordingly, he understood his work as limiting reason 'to make room for faith'.[1]

---

[1] Immanuel Kant, *The Critique of Pure Reason* (London, 1929), p. 29.

Kant's procedure is paradoxical, as Hegel and others saw. For it seems contradictory to admit a necessary being within the order of thought and yet to question the reality of this being beyond thought. How can a 'beyond thought' enter the horizon of thought? How am I permitted to doubt what my reason is able to register as necessary? Thus absolute idealism proposed to go beyond Kant and posit the rational as the real. Yet Kant's problematic expresses the human situation. Particularly in what matters most, we do doubt the reason that shares our frailty and corruption, and reason alone is not able to reassure us.

But where does this leave the ontological argument? Certainly not demolished, *if* the argument be construed as an undertaking of faith. Indeed, Kant's critique is quite congenial to that sense of the argument. But as distinct from its faith function, has the argument's apologetic value been undermined? Hardly, for what has happened is that reason, through its critique of itself, has made clear that it cannot guarantee its inner necessities without transcending its own limits. There then emerges the prospect of the kind of correlation between reason and faith (or revelation) which, for example, Paul Tillich took as the principle of his theological work. Reason formulates humanly fundamental questions which it acknowledges it cannot as mere reason answer. Such a question is that of God, the necessary prius of all being. Such a question is also that of Christ, the normative and healing manifestation of the prius of being. If anything, this post-Kantian way of understanding the role of the argument as formulative and questioning greatly enhances its apologetic value. For an apologetics that could do without faith would defeat its own end. In the last analysis the only feasible apologetics is one which employs reason to indicate the indispensability of faith.

We observed above that the parallel of the theistic and christic cases is more apparent when the ontological argument is viewed strictly as an explication of faith. Nevertheless, if it is possible and significant to view everyman as subject within the structure of his own reason to the question of God, the same is not less true of the question of Christ. The two questions do not completely correspond, since the God-question is already implicit in our finitude. That can hardly be claimed for the Christ-question, even though the religious consciousness projects its Christ figures into the creational act. But in *seeking an answer* to the God-question, the Christ-question is implicit. What the ontological argument would show is that the Christ involved in this question is necessarily an historically existent Christ. That would not mean that the actual Christ can be produced from the conceptually necessary one. It would mean only that any other Christ than an actual one is conceptually inadequate. A good example of such argument is Tillich's exposition of how the normative manifestation of the logos of being must combine universality with the maximum concreteness of an historical personal life.[1] If this life were not already there in history, the argument would be frustrated, or rather would never have arisen. Nevertheless the argument may help faith interpret responsibly to the world the so-called offence of particularity.

Any concrete faith can employ ontological argumentation (as well as the other types of argumentation considered below). The Maha-yanist can find implicit in his thinking the necessary prius of the Buddha-reality. In principle he could also maintain the necessary historicity of Gautama, though he may not characteristically do so. It does not annul the argument's apologetic function that it can be so used. That there are positive analogies between the religions tends to strengthen rather than weaken their common position. Further, any final revelation will surely embrace and fulfil, as well as transform, the anticipations and parallels of the history of religions. Thereto, common patterns of argumentation provide for significant encounter. The Buddhist and the Christian will better understand both their kinship and their distance when they discuss that the non-existence of which each holds inconceivable.

Suppose, however, that the Buddhist does not acquiesce in the christic case, i.e., that there must needs be an historically existent mediator. This remains then a question that promises to induce crucial exchange. For if there is an intrinsic implication of historicity in the adequate concept of mediation, the lack of such in a given religion is a definite point of contact for apologetics. But suppose on the other hand that the Buddhist does employ the christic case and thus does posit the historicity of Gautama or of another mediator. Then it will still be a decisive point of differentiation whether and to what degree the respective historical mediations can be unreservedly

---

[1] Paul Tillich, *Systematic Theology*, I (Chicago, 1959), 16–18.

opened to the test of critical research. For historicity that cannot be so opened is, to say the least, conceptually suspect. It does not really meet the requirements of the ontological argument.

3

While granting its validity for those already having the right God-concept, St Thomas held the ontological argument incompetent to establish the concept for others. He favoured the cosmological-type argument, which moves from the known reality of the world to God as its necessary ground or cause. Even one as congenial to ontological thinking as Tillich describes the ontological argument in terms of the possibility, the cosmological in terms of the necessity of the question of God.[1] Because the latter argument refers to something (at least to a degree) openly given, it more readily secures the common ground of human experience. And while it too is tautological, it seems less redundantly so than the ontological argument in that there is a more apparent distinction between its premises and its conclusion. Thus it may have more apologetic utility in the sense of arresting the attention of unbelief.

As the theistic cosmological argument leads from the world to God, the christic parallel leads from the New Testament witness and/or the church to Christ as necessary ground or cause. While the term 'cosmological' is incongruous here, the causal pattern of argument may be less problematic in the christic than in the theistic case. From Hume onward a standing objection to the latter has been that causality is a category not fitted to compass the world itself. Related to this is the difficulty of maintaining the conceptual necessity of the ostensible distinction between a cause of the world and the world itself. And in the third place, since there is both good and evil in it, the demurrer arises that no more can be concluded from the world than a duality of causes, or else a mixed cause both good and evil. Now these questions do not trouble the christic case. In line with all historical reasoning, it is perfectly feasible to distinguish hypothetically the New Testament witness and/or the Church from Christ or other factors as cause. It is within this frame of reference that critical research operates, whatever its results may indicate respecting the

---

[1] Tillich, *Systematic Theology*, 1, 204–10.

methodological and factual difficulty of disentangling the original happenings from the Church's witness. As for the third place, the New Testament and the Church are, like the world, mixed effects. But in their case there is no need to conclude a single cause. A diversity of co-operating factors is obvious, and all that the christic case requires is the presence within the total effect of an element pointing to the historical reality of Christ himself.

The crucial element, or elements, may be variously construed. Studies of the resurrection have often stressed the dramatic post-crucifixion rally of the disciples as an event explicable only by the historical reality of the resurrection itself. The originality of Christ's teaching, God-consciousness, self-understanding and/or existential posture are further points in the witness which require the grounding of a distinct commensurate reality preceding the witness itself. Or one may go on to say that the whole biblical picture of Christ, as it coalesces in and through the multiplicity of witness, evinces integrity and power not intelligibly derivable from causes other than a unique personal life. Or, focusing on the church, one will ask how it emerges into history not only with its failures but also with the norm which discloses them, not only with its ambiguities but with forgiveness and hope. One may ask this of the Church's historical origin two millennia ago, or of its continuous origination in the lives of believers today. In either instance the only possible answer centres in the figure of Christ. The biblical witness to this figure and the unconquered though fragmentary reality it calls forth as the essential life of the Church are, if anything, less self-explanatory than the cosmos. They point beyond themselves to the historicity of Christ himself.

The kind of examples just adduced range from the more public to the more inward of which only the believer would be cognizant. The unbelieving historian must acknowledge a phenomenon such as the post-crucifixion resurgence of faith, though he seeks other explanations than that which faith gives. He must also come to terms with singular features in the portrait of Christ. Yet the 'grace and truth' which faith 'beholds' (John 1:14) are by definition invisible to unbelief. (As they become visible to our existence, unbelief recedes, and vice versa.) Similarly an objective sociological analysis of the Church will not discern in it the reality of the new being, though it can record that a certain theologian used the phrase. One might challenge the proposed parallel with the cosmological argument on the ground that the christic case rests largely on intuitions not public in the sense the world is. Yet the datum of the theistic case is similarly ambiguous. The *Weltanschauungen* attest how differently the world is perceived. There for all is the space-time continuum. But the relative essentiality of good and evil, and the implicit finitude or aseity of the whole involve apperceptions inseparable from the question of faith.

One thus sees that, like the ontological, the cosmological-type argumentation is primarily a matter of faith. It helps to formulate faith's perception of the world or, in the christic case, of the crucial data of Bible and Church. However, that does not rule out, any more than in the instance of the ontological, an apologetic co-function for the argument. To be sure, the theistic case is confronted by the view that the cosmos derives from chance, or from we know not what. And there are those who find in Bible and Church only a mélange of socio-psychic needs compensated by an invented Christ. It would be foolish to think that any argument can infallibly sway unbelief. Nevertheless, in both the theistic cosmological argument and its christic parallel, there is a range of data wherein compelling questions for human existence are posed. As with the ontological argument, the theistic case—here the cosmic question—is wider. But for those encountered or enveloped by the biblical history, or those personally addressed by the Church's witness, the question of Christ is no less pressing.

The prospect has been entertained, in both the theistic and christic case, that the issues might be settled by the special sciences, in the one case by cosmology and in the other by historiography. However, it was not feasible to identify the world's dependence on God with a particular cosmogonic theory, nor could the historical Christ be equated with the Jesus of history certifiable by methodically neutral research. In both cases the wide recognition of the unfeasibility (which was already seen by Schleiermacher and Ritschl, as well as Kierkegaard) precipitated a reaction which would have held faith all too aloof from natural and historical science. Lately there are again signs of appreciation for the critical clarifications as well as positive analogies that emerge for Christian faith, cosmologically, for instance, from the work of Whitehead and Teilhard de Chardin, and in the christic case from those who continue or who pursue anew the question of the historical Jesus. From Barth and Bultmann one learned that cosmology and historiography can produce neither the God nor the Christ of faith. But it is also sensed today that Christian faith inescapably implies constructive relations with the scientific understanding of the world and history. In this context the cosmological-type argumentation has a heuristic and regulative role. By proposing God as the world's real cause and the historical Christ as decisive ground of the biblical-church witness, it stimulates and formulates interchange with the natural scientist and the historian.

Important in this regard is the kind of knowledge with which the argumentation has to do. In traditional terminology, when a cause is known only through the effect, and thus cannot be inspected in itself, it is known according to the analogy of causal relation. We thus know God analogically, as cause of the world.[1] In parallel, we know the historical Christ analogically as cause of the biblical picture and the essential life of the Church. This accords with the understanding achieved over the last decades regarding the Christ of faith and history. There has been general agreement that, while corroborative traces of the original Jesus are with high probability identifiable, Jesus Christ as ground of faith cannot be disentangled from the biblical witness. Indeed, no historical fact can be absolutely disentangled from the sources through which it is known. Nevertheless there has been firm theological consensus that Christian faith is grounded in historical fact and not simply in the projections of faith. Tillich sums up the situation by recognizing the indissoluble merger of 'fact and reception' in faith's foundation, by emphasizing however that 'both sides' are integral, and then by expressing our knowledge of the original fact as the 'analogy of the picture'.[2]

So understood, the theistic cosmological argument means that all knowledge of the world is potentially knowledge of God. Thus scientific findings are in principle relevant to our understanding of God, though most findings are not theologically crucial. Scientific discovery as such cannot establish or refute belief in God, but it can and inevitably does amplify and modify our conception of him as

[1] Of course this is not the most decisive way God is known by faith.
[2] Tillich, *Systematic Theology*, 2, 97–8, 114–15.

creator. The christic parallel is that what is known of the picture of Christ—and thus of the tradition that bears it—is in principle relevant to our knowledge of him. We remarked above that the christic case of the argumentation assumes plural causality and does not require Christ as sole cause of the New Testament and the Church. However, critical analysis of the sources can sharpen our knowledge of Christ also by disclosing the influence of other factors and thus differentiating a given feature (e.g. the touches of anti-Jewish polemic) from the direct causality of Christ himself.

What then does cosmological type argumentation add to the findings of research? Clearly it does not yield information co-ordinate with that gathered by cosmology and historiography. It is rather a logical transaction that frames and concludes the multifarious process of knowing for some dimensions of which the sciences are specialized organs. When I think God as cause of the world, or Christ as essential cause of the biblical picture and Church, I summarize innumerable preliminary observations and judgments in a conceptually decisive form. But the matter of my knowing includes not only the deliverances of objective empirical study, of which apologetics may and must take account, but also intuitions insusceptible of purely objective assessment. While objective study may fragmentarily render probable Jesus as referent of the biblical witness, the personal range of my experience is indispensable for the affirmation of Christ in his full meaning for faith. However, the meaning of Christ for faith implies also the more objective or public range of knowing, just as faith in God implies relation to cosmology. It would drastically contradict Christian faith if on the respective horizons of cosmology and historiography there was no logical or scientifically responsible place for the concepts of world ground and historical Jesus.

Thus, as it functions on the one hand for faith, the cosmological-type argumentation embraces the whole process of knowing. The deductive form of the argument does not bring to a halt the flux of knowledge that it subsumes. For, like faith altogether, its cogency is continuously in question. The argument rather motivates knowing. It is one way of ordering the innumerable possibilities and results of empirical inquiry in terms of relevance. Then, inversely, the argument is also a way in which my knowledge, in its situation at a given time, registers its upshot for my existence. This remains true, however it may be in that moment with my faith, which is never a static possession. Accordingly, whether or not I can unreservedly affirm the argument, it is integral to the standing problematic of my faith. On the other hand, the apologetic co-function selects from the argument's total range those more public data over which discussion with unbelief can be joined. A fixed agenda is not feasible here, since faith and unbelief are not nicely bounded terrains. It is a matter of beginning where conversation in fact proves possible and going on from there. Presumably along the way the inward and personal range of experience must be traversed. Otherwise apologetics would fail in its aim to mediate faith.

4

The last two major types of argument, the teleological and moral, may be more briefly considered, since much of what applies to them too has already been considered under the other types. The older and narrower sense of the teleological argument, which reasons from design in the world to a designer, can indeed be regarded as a special case of the cosmological argument. Instead of taking as its basis the world as such, it argues from a distinctive feature (purpose) in the world to a distinctive character (purposive intelligence) of the world ground. Parallel to this is the derivation of the distinctive character of Christ from traits otherwise inexplicable in the biblical picture and Church. But we have already had this kind of argumentation in view above. In the christic case there is no occasion, as perhaps there is in the theistic, to differentiate the sheer causality of the ground from its character as purposeful. Thus what might otherwise be treated as a christic parallel to the classic teleological argument has been pre-empted by the parallel to the cosmological.

On the other hand the wider and more recently favoured sense of the teleological argument is well suited to cover both theistic and christic case simultaneously. *In nuce* it maintains that the pattern of meaning which best comprehends the totality of man's experience and best resolves his predicament is one hinging on God's act in the historical Jesus Christ. What makes most sense of life is a 'Christocentric metaphysic' (William Temple). This type argument can be even more variously developed than those previously treated.

St Anselm employs it in his *Cur deus homo* when, bracketing for the moment the actual knowledge of Christ, he deduces the necessity of the God-man from the requirements of the divine purpose and the human predicament. Kierkegaard uses it when he argues that our world is meaningful only if its telos is that subjectivity maximalized by faith in the historicity of the God-man.[1] The logic of the argument appears in Ritschl's 'necessary concatenation' between man's dignity, plight of finitude and guilt, and the historical redeemer.[2] Tillich, Bultmann and Gogarten provide good examples in their depiction of existential distortion, inauthenticity and historical fate in ways that correspond to the solution manifest in Jesus Christ. Very many instances could be given because no attempt to state the case for the Christian faith—to interpret it convincingly to modern man—can avoid employing some kind and degree of teleological argumentation. Even theological irrationalism does so, in stressing the absurdity of the incarnation or the cross as appropriate to the way life is.

Most if not all of the theologians just mentioned are aware that their argumentation presupposes the historical impact of Christ. The question Christ answers—even in its pre-theological forms in a Kant or a Heidegger—arises within the history and existentiality that Christ has impregnated. This circularity does not render the argumentation apologetically pointless. It makes it all the more relevant at least to Western unfaith, which in its estrangement from traditional versions of the answer is still deeply involved in the question. That the historical Christ makes possible both question and answer—the whole pattern of the argument itself—does not weaken but rather in the last analysis strengthens its cogency. Nor does this mean that the pattern of argument must be incommunicative with human existence beyond the spheres of Christian culture. In India or the Far East apologetic discussion will use conceptual idioms different from those of the West. But the kinds of questions formulated in Christian apologetics (whether Western or Eastern) may be continuous with

---

[1] Søren Kierkegaard, *Concluding Unscientific Postscript* (Princeton, 1944), pp. 142, 178, 182, 185–9 *passim*.

[2] Albrecht Ritschl, *A Critical History of the Christian Doctrine of Justification and Reconciliation* (Edinburgh, 1872), p. 540; *The Christian Doctrine of Justification and Reconciliation* (Edinburgh, 1902), pp. 24–5, 530 *passim*.

and clarifying of man's situation universally, even though men at large do not yet clearly ask or know how to ask these questions. It is no weakness in an argument that it requires a preliminary clarification of the questions it proposes to answer.

Our presentation of the teleological argument is at points close to what also appeared under the ontological. Under both types mutual implication or coherency is determinative. A distinction in principle can be made by identifying the ontological argument as moving from the concepts of God and Christ to their existence, the teleological as moving from a meaningful pattern (usually anchored in exposition of the human question) to God's act in Christ as necessary solution. But these argumentations do indeed overlap. In the ontological the intrinsic existence claim of the key concepts cannot be divorced from the pattern of existential meaning in which they function. In the teleological argument the implication of God's act in Christ by the logic of the purposive pattern becomes a necessitation of the existence of Christ only through the implicit presence of what we have called the ontological argument. As Kant observed, the same is true of the cosmological argument at the point where it indicates that the cause logically implied in the effect must be an existent. On the other hand, neither is the ontological independent of the cosmological argument, since the concepts which exert an intrinsic existence claim are those which are grounding to our being and thinking. Thus the arguments are not neatly separate co-ordinates, but rather interpenetrating logical structures. When we turn to the last of the major types, this interpenetration is all the clearer.

There are two generally recognized forms of the moral argument, both of which stem from Kant and both of which are applicable to the christic case. In the one, certain truths—God, freedom, immortality—are postulated to guarantee the rationality of the moral law. Such reasoning can be regarded as an instance of the wider teleological type considered above, even though the focus now is exclusively on the moral consciousness. For in any case the moral is a species of the teleological; and if, as is plausible, it is understood so broadly as to compass the whole exercise of man's freedom, then its overlap with the teleological is much greater. To be sure, as introduced by Kant the argument makes a point of conceding that its case cannot be established by pure reason. The postulates are demanded only by man's practical interest as a moral being. But the distinction between pure and practical reason must be carefully analysed. If pure reason means the limitation of reason to the matter of the special, or ideally the physical sciences, thus leaving the dimension of the personal as well as all ultimate questions out of view, then clearly it cannot comprehend the tasks of philosophy and theology. The moral argument is obviously not a matter of pure reason, but neither is any of the other arguments. They all belong to the practical reason as envisaged by Kant. They are all, in a sense, moral arguments. But then the meaning of the moral argument needs expanding, so as to embrace not merely the moral consciousness narrowly conceived but also the ontological, cosmological, and teleological perspectives. Moreover, it needs to be clear that moral or practical reason is no separate and circumscribed organ beside pure reason. Actually the special sciences are methods and instruments of practical reason; in principle they presuppose and serve human purpose.

The christic application of the first form of the moral argument turns on man's inability or delinquency respecting the law or ought of his being. There are three key problems which may be understood either independently or in conjunction: the need for revelation of the ought, for objective atonement, and for subjective reconciliation. First, although the ought as practical reason belongs to man's essential nature, the prevailing state of forgetfulness and estrangement necessitates a vivid presentation of essential manhood—and that entails a real human person—as a condition of the fulfilment of the ought. Second, if man is required to fulfil the ought, but cannot or does not, a contradiction threatens the ought. The historical Christ is required through his obedience to make good the deficit and thus remove the contradiction. (The penal substitutionary theory is one attempt to express this theme but by no means the only one.) In the third place, if man is required to fulfil the ought, but finds himself so burdened with guilty alienation that he cannot, he needs the historical manifestation of God's reconciling will, the actual impartation of divine forgiveness.

The second form of the moral argument is not structured in terms of the implications of the fulfilment of the law. Rather the law itself is construed as immediately implying a lawgiver. In the first form of the argument God is postulated to insure the outworking of the law in an immortal life. In the second form, the moral ought, as the categorical requirement of our essential nature, is itself understood as divine imperative. For God as the ground of our being commands through the essential law of our being. The christic parallel to the theistic case puts in the place of the general moral law the claim and promise faith finds confronting itself in Christ. 'He taught them as one having authority...' (Mark 1:22) and still does. To faith Jesus authenticates himself as a personal reality entitled to unconditional commitment. Yet this commitment brings true freedom. It would be heteronomous (a contradiction of moral reason) if we submitted to anything other than the claim of our own essential nature—which posits Christ's perfect humanity. And, as for the divine presence in him, 'who can forgive sins but God alone?' (Mark 2:7). The intuitions here indicated as the basis of the reasoning are valid only for faith, or rather faith is the acknowledgment of their impinge-ment upon our human existence. In any case, they further spell out how faith posits the historicity of its Lord.

The second form of the moral argument brings us round again to what was said of the ontological argumentation in its first (for faith alone) interpretation. God-in-Christ is faith's self-authenticating ground of being and meaning. There is indeed a necessary merger of the moral and the ontological. For no moral authority could ulti-mately command and forgive which was not the ground of being and meaning. On the other hand, an essential mark of the way ultimacy reveals itself to biblical faith lies in the forgiveness of sins and the moral imperative.

5

Faith involves no single aspect of the self exclusively but the whole self in unison. Intuition and feeling, decision and experience have their place, and so does reason. In fact the separation, or even the sharp distinction of these modes of the self is an abstraction. In the living person they interlock and coalesce, though not absolutely and not identically in different individuals. Faith is ideally the union of these modes in that, while no person's faith actualizes all of them equally, the believer is nevertheless called to receive and serve Christ with his whole being. In this light the kind of argumentation we have considered is a way in which the rational mode of faith actualizes and expresses itself. It is not as though faith were already complete prior to the rational component. This component is rather actualized in and with the more inclusive act of faith. Hence the complex mutual relation in which argument and faith stand. The possible apologetic effectiveness of a rational argument for faith does not presuppose that faith is already there beforehand, but only that it will begin to be there as the larger personal context within which the argument, if effective, plays its part. Are we saying, then, that faith cannot occur without the reasoning structure, or in defiance of it? Certainly the other modes—feeling, intuition, decision—may dominate the rational. And obviously no outer form of apologetics can be prescribed. But in spite of assertions to the effect, it is hard to conceive how one would believe against his reason. What would he believe? Would he really affirm God-in-Christ as prius of his being and thinking, or only as prius of his emotions? In any case, unless his reason too believes surely the whole man does not yet believe.

The arguments or proofs we have discussed are patterns of reason wherein faith thinks and affirms its object. The same patterns clarify for unbelief what it does not believe. They also may establish rational connexions—which are important though not sufficient—through which unbelief may be drawn toward faith. The arguments do not usually (if ever) succeed in convincing opponents in open debate. But when was the other debater ever convinced in open debate? If the ground and object of faith must itself in the last analysis convince unbelief, the patterns of ontological, cosmological, teleological and moral reason serve as presentational forms in and through which the convincing is at stake. That the forms are indeed earthen vessels does not disqualify their service.

It is not surprising that the structure of what we have called the theistic and christic cases are congruent and interdependent. The traditional construction of the theistic case in complete separation from Christ has compartmentalized theological thought and brought discredit to rational theology in the name of faith as well as to mere faith in the name of reason. Over against a christless metaphysical theism it tends to engender an atheistic Christology. However the relation between the theistic and christic cases may best be developed, their bifurcation is surely untenable.

Also untenable is a rigid bifurcation between faith and the special sciences. The rational arguments for God and Christ do not obtrude *a priori* results into the work of cosmology and historiography. But they do comprehend the work of the sciences as a component element. Further, in the history of culture and in individual life their substance has energized scientific endeavour. As is true of the theistic arguments in respect to God, the patterns of affirming Christ's historicity require only the existence of the essence of Christ—that is, his fundamental meaning as framed in the ontological, cosmological, teleological, and moral patterns of reasoning. But while historiographical details are crucial only as they affect the essence of Christ, it belongs to his essence that he is a fully historical reality manifest through concrete detail. Moreover, as research into details proceeds, the overall picture of Christ is not impassive to the thrust of the results, as is shown in the history of Christology as well as in literature, hymnody and art. The affirmation of Christ's historical reality implies, though it cannot be derived from, the historiographical plausibility of those dimensions of the essential biblical picture which may in principle become objects of research. This forecloses no historiographical questions as such, since historiography operates under the canon of methodical openness. But it does mean that faith regards historiography not merely as a discipline to which it must stand open, but as one from which it expects and receives clarification of its own most essential concern.

5

ARCHEGOS

AN ESSAY ON THE RELATION BETWEEN THE BIBLICAL
JESUS CHRIST AND THE PRESENT-DAY READER

RICHARD R. NIEBUHR

I. READING THE NEW TESTAMENT

My purpose in this essay is to join in the discussion prompted by the familiar question: What is the personal connexion between the figure of Jesus Christ in the New Testament and the present-day reader or auditor of the gospels? Modern New Testament interpretation and theology have long dramatized the issues involved here—most recently as the issue of existential hermeneutics—and therefore the following paragraphs implicitly acknowledge and rely upon the validity of several of the prior responses to this query. But these in turn, I believe—including the formulations and categories of John Knox—presuppose the substance if not the specific language of what this essay advances.

Whoever takes up this question will perhaps first of all ask what kind of reader the question applies to. For it would seem that the connexion between the biblical Jesus and the New Testament scholar ought to be different from the connexion between the biblical Jesus and the person who is reading simply for edification. And no doubt there is a measure of indisputable difference between these two situations, a difference that is perceptible not only between the scholar and non-scholar reader but also between different occasions when one and the same person addresses himself to the scriptures, now in the mood of detached inquiry and now in the attitude of personal involvement in issues of human faith. Nevertheless, it is easy to make too much of this difference.[1] While we can and must distinguish between the theoretical and practical interests of the mind, we should

---

[1] It is also easy to make too much of the apparent difference between the situations of a Christian and a non-Christian reading the gospel. The similarities of these two situations are implied in the discussion that follows in the third and fourth sections of this essay.

not separate these interests or deny their influence upon each other. Indeed, if we attend closely enough to these situations of reading the New Testament accounts of Christ, we find one point in particular at which the theoretical, scientific investigation of the gospels converges—as we trace it back to its roots—with the frankly personal engagement with the gospel portraits. This point appears in the fundamental intuition that the reader of the New Testament has—be he scholar or preacher or Everyman—of the human meaning of the central actor in the history that the New Testament recounts.

By such an intuition I mean a perception of Jesus as a person, a perception in which the reader's imagination necessarily plays a large role. Certainly, this intuition is not identical for all men. But every kind of thinking about the content of the New Testament begins with some specific opinion or belief about the intentions of Jesus of Nazareth. Even critical description and analysis of this early Christian literature cannot direct itself unless it has such an impression that is capable of becoming a principle for interpreting the import of Jesus' conduct and the ends that it served. The great epoch of the lives of Jesus in the last century and in this followed on the realization by scholars that they had to ask about the meaning of Jesus on the basis of a fresh reading of the gospels without depending on the dogmatic formulae that had so long satisfied the mind of Christendom. To be sure, in any given instance of scholarly or of personal interpretation of the gospels subsequent reflexion, research, and experience may render the first fundamental intuition untenable; but then the reader must substitute another such impression, for some concrete image or other is always the starting point for thinking about Christ.

Hence, all reading, all attentive listening, and all inquiry concerning Jesus of Nazareth begin with at least an implicit answer to the question: What is Jesus about?[1] In order, however, for the necessary fundamental intuition to arise at all, it is evident that the appearances of Jesus in the gospel narratives must strike a chord in the inquirer's own experience. Understanding of a person, as Wilhelm Dilthey characterized it, is the rediscovery of the I in the thou. Or, as his forerunner Schleiermacher observed, whoever would rightly understand another man must be able to find traces of all the qualities and in-

---

[1] Even if the reader doubts that the historical Jesus is accessible, he asks what the meaning of the biblical figure is.

gredients of human nature in himself.[1] Therefore, when men ask, either as scientists or as private readers of the gospels: What is the meaning of Jesus of Nazareth? they are also asking: What is the connexion between him and ourselves?[2]

It is of course true that the historical scientist might not choose to call the perceived bond between the biblical Jesus and himself a personal bond, for the word personal can suggest that his reactions as a private person are one and the same with his obligations as a public scholar. Nevertheless, the public scholar does need to perceive and comprehend the religious intention of Jesus, viz. Jesus' very specific claimance of faith in God from each man. For Jesus' meaning and intentions as a man are inseparable from his religious vocation, and one cannot have an impression of the former without also having a perception of the latter. Therefore, even the scholar asks, in one way or another, What has this prophet or messiah to do with me? What is incumbent on the scholar then is not to deny his own involvement as a man with Jesus of Nazareth but rather to attempt to understand this connexion in an impartial, disinterested way.[3]

---

[1] Wilhelm Dilthey, *Gesammelte Schriften*, 7 (Stuttgart, 1958), 191. *The Life of Schleiermacher as unfolded in his Autobiography and Letters*, ed. F. Rowan, 1 (London, 1860), 330.

[2] This question is the one asked by the Gerasene demoniac: 'What have you to do with me, Jesus, Son of the Most High God?' (Mark 5: 7).

[3] The scholar (or any reader) does not have to make a formal confession of faith, as he approaches the business of understanding the biblical figure of Christ. But he does have to recognize a connexion between Christ and himself. A generation ago and more, some theologians deprecated this perceptible human relation between Christ and the individual. Barth, for example, argued that it had nothing to do with the revealing and healing works of Christ. There is no need, however, to reproduce here the train of Barth's thinking. His rejection of the importance of the perceptible human relation seems now to have been a gratuitous rather than necessary consequence of his central affirmation that Christ as the revelation of God utterly transcended all human history and human capacities. The generation between the wars, to the extent that Barth typified it, was intent upon presenting Christ as an *arche* of being and knowledge absolutely secured in its inviolate transcendence of all human frailty. But our times, since World War II, do not appear so much to yearn for an archimedian point outside history and human invention or perversion as to require a renewed sense of solidarity, of sympathy, of cohesion with what has gone before, especially with the pioneer of faith. A feeling of isolation in great spiritual distances afflicts men today, who see in the generation only just passed into death—not to mention the early Christians —men acting and suffering in a milieu astonishingly different from our own. But this sense of isolation has long been growing. Both the increasing turbulence of

Richard R. Niebuhr

John Knox has contributed greatly in our day to the understanding of the fact that Jesus of Nazareth does have a perceptible bond with the present, does display a quality of life which men recognize as having connexion with their own lives. Knox has done this work chiefly by calling attention to the Church's recollecting of the ministering, suffering, dying, and rising of Christ. Through his repeated investigations and critical elucidations of the ways in which this action takes place and in large part constitutes the life of the Christian Church, Knox has widened and deepened our appreciation of the fact and the significance of such remembering in all that the Church does and is: preaching, instructing, healing, celebrating the Lord's Supper, and caring for men. To be sure, his idea of memory (and the correlative category of event) requires close scrutiny, as do all interpretative concepts.[1] But clearly Knox has given to the world of New Testament theology and interpretation a renewed insight into the twentieth-century reader's relation to 'the pioneer and perfecter of faith', Jesus Christ. If I may freely paraphrase the thrust of much of Knox's writing, it seems to me that he has been saying something like the following: Here is a contemporary way in which to understand the historical and effective relation of Jesus to those who come after him. Here is an appropriate category by which we today may express what the ancient fathers of the Church meant in their assertion of the metaphysical union of the incarnate Logos with mankind. We participate in him and he in us not through our common inherence in the eternal essence of humanity but concretely through the Church's remembering of Christ's history. According to this theology of remembering, then, the Church is the organ of the living memory of Jesus Christ, and it endows the individual in the situation of reading or hearing the gospel with a compelling and urgent bond to Jesus. However, apart from the Church the individual in the situation of reading or hearing the gospel can have only an adventitious relation to Christ, for lacking the spirit of the community he cannot

modern political and social history and the rising intensity of historical studies have emphasized our estrangement from the past by the contrasts they yield between its reality and our own. The lives of Jesus written in the nineteenth and twentieth centuries show this sense of estrangement with respect to the historical Jesus and the primitive church.

[1] This writer's detailed critique of Knox's ideas of memory and history is set down in *Resurrection and Historical Reason* (New York, 1957).

perceive a significant connexion between Christ and his own existence.[1] But in the 'body of Christ' this relation becomes a determining part of his humanity. The Church's remembering now is his own, so that the story of Christ is also his story.[2]

This theme in Knox's books is a great theme. And to his description and criticism of the Church's remembering generations of his students and his colleagues are indebted. The argument that follows here does not deny what Knox affirms. Rather it affirms the importance of certain features both of Jesus' situation, as the gospels describe it, and of the present-day reader's situation, which the concept of remembering does not draw to our attention. What is affirmed here is that the twentieth-century reader is related to the biblical Jesus of Nazareth by a form of life at once more universal and more elusive than the Christian Church and its organs of memory, a form of life that defined Jesus' character and history with a peculiar force but that also defines men today. The reader shares with this Jesus a perception—perhaps quite obscured—of the manifestations of power that Jesus called the kingdom of God. Moreover, fully self-conscious faith today still focuses itself on Jesus of Nazareth and seeks to remember him clearly not only as the founder of the Church but also as *the* locus of the appearance of the power that, assailing our senses still, awakens in men today the passion of believing in a rule or government of God, as it did also among those who first listened to Jesus' parables and saw how he conducted himself.

[1] Apparently this is the case. To my knowledge, Knox does not really discuss the relation of Christ to those outside the Church. But in view of the role he does assign to the Church, I do not see how the individual's relation to Christ can be conceived on any other terms.

[2] Knox's thinking is Augustinian in its general theological outlines, although he draws much from other traditions also, particularly from the Whiteheadian. But in his great emphasis on memory and on the priority of the Church he follows the first father of medieval and modern Christian thought. Over against Knox stands Rudolf Bultmann, the foremost contemporary representative of Kantianism in biblical interpretation. Bultmann gives us a picture of man-before-the-scriptures or man-hearing-the-gospel in whom the action of willing rather than the action of participating in a collective memory is pre-eminent. Just as Kant believed that the universal moral law demands respect and repeated acts of allegiance from each man, so Bultmann shows Jesus as ever challenging each man to decide for God, despite the inclinations of his sensible nature. The interpretation of man-reading-the-Bible that this essay presents is meant to supplement Bultmann's as well as Knox's ideas of man in this situation.

The thesis, then, is that men belong to God before Christ belongs to them through the Church. God's power batters the mind and body before the faculties of memory and attention find meaning in the images of the New Testament. This original 'God-relation' shows itself in the phenomena of power assaulting and shaping men into persons and of men learning to suffer such power through the recognition that it is the working on and in them of God. Jesus Christ as the one who came into Galilee (and comes into the mind with each reading of the gospels) as a vanguard of God's rule interprets both power and suffering as moments in the action of God's ruling. His life and death are at once a new theatre and new presentation of God's dealing with men. As such, Jesus of Nazareth is the beginning-again, the pioneer, of a re-formed mind toward God. It is this intimate relation of Jesus to the kingdom or field of God's power—which all men endure, perhaps, without understanding or accepting—that makes him capable of being present and alive to today's reader of the gospels and of becoming an author of human faith and so the Lord of the Christian Church.

In order to place this argument in its setting, however, I must first indicate my own understanding of the basic impression to which the reading of the New Testament and particularly the synoptic gospels gives rise.

2. THE BEGINNING-AGAIN

The New Testament is a legally defined body of literature of heterogeneous forms, pertaining to the founding of the Christian Church. But of course to speak in this manner does not apprise us of the specific nature of the institution or movement these writings concern, and it is necessary to be more concrete. The gospels, then, concern events and personal deeds having as their unifying rationale Jesus of Nazareth's radical declaration, exhibition, and enactment of the ruling of the God of Abraham, of Isaac, and of Jacob. Such a characterization does not negate the formal definition of the New Testament as the records of the founding of a community and institution, but it does give a different nuance to the meaning of the history that the New Testament represents. And we may even extend this characterization to the events narrated in Acts and to those that occasioned the epistles to the various churches, regarding these chronicles and documents of the infant Christian movement as the graphic aftermath of the Messiah of the kingdom, as the literary deposit in the translation of the declaration of the kingdom of God into institutional forms.

Hence, the books and letters of the New Testament are the accounts and literary remains of a great beginning in human affairs, but this beginning is not an absolute beginning. For the men and women who appear here as speakers and agents, as spectators of wonderful transactions and as victims of the consequences of these transactions are, in large number, Jews and if not Jews then people who have been touched and deflected in their life courses by the faith and politics of Israel. So Mark and 'Q', Matthew, Luke, Paul, and John and the other authors of these scriptures are the tellers and agents of a history that began with Abraham, Isaac, and Moses as they entered into their prehistorical covenants with God. The New Testament authors present the actions and passions of Jesus and his people as happenings receiving much of their intelligibility from these earlier beginnings, not—to be sure—as inevitable, necessary consequences of those primordial meetings with God but as repetitions that resound and amplify the significance of the archetypal covenants and covenanting partners.

In this way, Jesus appears and acts in the gospel accounts as a concrete figure who makes Abraham and Moses and David and Elijah more real, not only because he is related to them by national religion and descent but also because he is related to them directly through the sovereign decrees of God. And so he brings into the present the archetypal figures of covenant, the personal reality of covenant faith, and the palpability of the steadfastness of God, making all these things experientially real and convincing. As Jesus stands among his disciples, indisputably present in his mission, the decrees, promises, and rule of God appear as equally concrete, and in this newly vivid field of vision the familiar and prescriptive agents and messengers of God—Moses, Elijah, the suffering servant—emerge from cultic memory and scriptural tradition with a fresh immediacy.[1]

---

[1] There is a consistent view of the reality of personal existence in these books and letters forming the New Testament, which does not express itself in philosophical language but nevertheless profoundly influences their portrayal of human nature. In the mind represented by these literary compositions, God is no respecter of persons. He chooses those through whom he will work and his choices have neither social nor legal rationale. The legendary and the humble, the heroes and

Consequently, we may say that Jesus is a commentary on these earlier authors of Jewish faith. He is a living gloss, a restatement of the intentions that the lives of Abraham and Moses and the others served. But by reason of the intensity of his own aliveness, he becomes more than that; he becomes a new embodiment of the covenant meetings of God and men. He lets his own life be so completely shaped by the steadfastness of God, that the scripture portraits of the fathers wrestling in faith with covenant promises of God become more credible and attain a new meaning for all who suspect what is happening to Jesus.

The New Testament authors narrate the ways in which Jesus acted as such a living commentary. Their pictures of him show him appearing to his hearers as a new beginning of all the great beginnings of faith between men and God from which their life and faith take their substance. Jesus is, accordingly, the summation and the breaking point of the law of Moses (Sermon on the Mount); he is the meaning and the reinterpretation of the sabbath (Luke 13 : 10 ff.; Matt. 12 : 1 ff.); he is the fulfilment of the promise of release to the captives (Luke 4: 16 ff.); he is the prophet who weeps anew for the city of David (Luke 19: 41 ff.); he is the one whose life is for the renewed life of others (Mark 14: 22 ff. and parallels); he is the stranger and traveller and prisoner whom to serve is to love as God loved Israel in its captivity and exodus (Matt. 25: 34 ff.).

In short, the Jesus of our evangelists, even of John, is the beginning again of the Abrahamic, Mosaic, and prophetic faith—a faith that is a turn of mind, a burning heart, a relish of life as gift and sign and part of God's good-pleasure. He is the beginning again of a faith that

the foot-soldiers, the wise and the presumptuous, the rich and the poor, the men of great and of little faith are alike the agents with and in whom he accomplishes his ends. Consequently men and women receive their determinate being in the world through the role that God gives them. In the language of patristic and medieval theology-philosophy, the men and women whom the New Testament describes are *personae* not by virtue of any property they own or social distinction they have acquired but by virtue of the God-ordained mission they have in the economy of history. In the non-technical language of contemporary speech, we should say that according to the view present in the New Testament a man is truly—in distinction from what his fellows may judge him to be— whatever God has intended to accomplish through and in him. Hence, the unity of personal existence, the identity we all assume to underlie our own and others' manifold acts and passions, is nothing else than God's act of intending that this or that be done in this or that way.

receives all blessings and woes as being for the sake of God's righteousness. And whatever else we have in the New Testament, especially in the letters of Paul, that endeavours to show Jesus as a man of universal qualities in whom all human aspirations culminate and by whom all human hopes and fears are transformed, the fact remains that Jesus presents himself to his disciples as the recapitulator of their inherited faith-history. He does not simply constrain men to have a new mind but constrains in them a new mind towards the God of Abraham. Nor does he stand for love but for love of 'the Lord thy God' (the Lord thy God of the Shema), nor for any righteousness but such righteousness as Elijah learned from the Baal-Destroyer. Jesus does not promise life eternal but promises the time of the kingdom of this God.

In these gospels Jesus is a Jew, and the resolution he embodies is the renewal of a human engagement with the God who showed and shows his government of men in cherishing and chastising Israel.

3. FAITH BEFORE FAITH

The Letter to the Hebrews calls Jesus Christ the *archēgos*, that is (in the language of our various translations), the captain, the author, the pioneer. He is 'the captain of salvation' (2: 10), 'the pioneer and perfecter of our faith' (12: 2). Of all the New Testament titles for Jesus, *archēgos* commends itself as the most descriptive, the most elastic, and the least metaphysical. And as we have seen, the relation in which Jesus stands to the tradition of Abraham and Moses, on the one hand, and to his contemporaries (so far as the evangelists represent them), on the other, is indeed that of a man whose life is a new beginning in the manifestation and acknowledgment of the rule of Abraham's God to Abraham's children.

However, the question we are considering concerns not merely the relation of Jesus to the contemporaries to whom he preached but his relation to the present-day reader or auditor of the gospels. What is the link between the Jesus of the gospels and ourselves and neighbours? Of what in our histories is he the recapitulator and new *archēgos*?

Christ is, to be sure, for all men in the western ecumene the *de facto* beginning of the long social, political and intellectual course of affairs that we call Christendom. But this position as author of an epoch, significant as it is, is not of the same order as the place he occupies in the writings of the New Testament. For there he is the living commentary on the still living faith between the patriarchs, prophets, and kings and their God. But of what faith is he the beginning again for those who come after him?

In one sense, the biblical Jesus is not and cannot be precisely the new *archēgos* of faith that he was for the Jews who were with him in his lifetime. For certainly the relation between Jesus and his fellow Jews was unique. No later generation can reproduce it or hope to enjoy what has irretrievably vanished. Yet in the experience of many men and women in after generations he has in fact been an author and captain of faith begun again. We think of all the 'twice-born men' from past and present whom we know. They were and are men and women whose conversions or—better—new minds would not be thinkable apart from the preaching and actions of the Christian Church. But the original relation of these reborn persons to Christ cannot be simply attributed to the sphere of the Church. For example, the remembering of Christ on the part of the Church is a salient feature of the personal world in which the Christ-formed mind of the latter-day reader of the gospels newly arises. But this remembering as such cannot be construed as the personal matrix out of which the faith-relation is born.[1] Neither, for that matter, can the instant of conscious decision on the part of the mature man be defined as the plasm of faith. To be sure both remembering and deciding are characteristic acts of the new-minded man. But they are more like sister moments *in* the complex new mind of Christ-hearers than names for the original connexion between the biblical Jesus and the reader/auditor. For to decide for God, forswearing historical, political, and scientific securities (as Rudolf Bultmann puts it) as the centre of one's life, one must first of all have been claimed by God. Again, to remember or recollect the story of the man Christ Jesus as a story about one's own destiny, one must first of all have such a mind as the

[1] Augustine's conversion illustrates the distinctness of the situation of the reader of the New Testament and the witnessing-remembering activity of the Church. Had it not been for his mother, for Ambrose, and numerous other members of the Christian community, Augustine would never have heard or understood the injunction: 'Take and read!' But what transpired in Augustine's reading is something else.

image and history of Christ can organize and collect. In short, to be born again, one must first of all be born into a human condition. Another way of stating the issue here is to say that the interestedness of the mind—what the Bible often calls the heart—precedes the determinate and specific acts of deciding and of remembering. Therefore, if a Christian is a man whose memory is possessed by the story of Christ, or a man whose freedom is energized by the call of the Messiah Jesus to be obedient only to God, then we have to search back in that man for the disposition or situation which makes such a remembering or obedient mind possible. We have to search for the 'faith' before this faith, the faith that in the individual parallels the faith of Israel and like the faith of Israel continues to supply the tension, the resonance, and the human timbre without which Christian preaching, teaching, and confession are easily flat and doctrinaire.

The problem therefore is to find an appropriate formulation of this original relation between Christ and the reader/auditor of the present or of any later generation than Christ's own, a formulation that will enable us to discern what so many have experienced and still experience in their entrance into a new mind.

The simplest response is this: the Jesus of the gospels is the beginning again of faithful life for those who share with him at least a common Jewishness, if not the actual background of first-century Judaic life and faith. Of course, it will not do to propose that men become Jewish in order to become Christians. For one thing, many men cannot; and for another, such insincerity toward Judaism (or any other religion) is no longer acceptable. But becoming Jewish *for the sake of* becoming Christian is not the issue at stake here. The issue is, rather, becoming—or discovering that as a human being one has already become—'Jewish' in a certain sense in so far as one has recognized a personal connexion betwen the Jesus of the gospels and himself. Whoever would perceive in Jesus the new *archēgos* of his own mind has to recognize in Abraham and Moses and the prophets metaphors of his own situation—not merely by searching the scriptures to see what is foretold there of the Christ but rather by searching himself to find there what is and remains the analogue of Israel's wrestling with God.

This analogue to Israel's history appears, I believe, in the common phenomenon of men suffering within themselves and also from without the assaults and shaping work of power, exercised today pre-eminently by institutions but also by individual agents, particularly those with forceful and charismatic personalities, and by the elements of nature. Such suffering qualifies as the 'faith before faith' for which we are looking, as the dispositional feature of human existence in our times that marks the personal situation of every potential reader/auditor of the gospels. Indeed, such 'faith' is itself a part of the manifestation of assaulting and shaping power, the interior pole, as it were, of the meeting with the energies that attack, coerce, and persuade men to give themselves to this or that way of life.[1] Hence, the faith that is the protoplasm of Christ-formed faith appears in the binary phenomenon of power and human pathos.

Today the greater part of theological discussion of human faith emphasizes the ability of men to will and to choose or to know the eternal God in some intuitive fashion. To compare human faith to human passion, however, is not much done.[2] Nevertheless, the capacity of human faith to affect the mind as a whole, indeed, our common use of the phrase to indicate cast of mind or quality of an orientation on life, calls for the direct comparison of human faith to passion, specifically to the dominant affection that the surrounding field of power awakens in the minds of men and of peoples, giving

[1] There was a time when to speak of faith before faith was to suggest a reduction of Christian faith to the status of an evolutionary product of inherent human tendencies. But such is no longer the case, for we can distinguish between historical sequence and relationships of efficient causality. What this way of speaking does mean is that Christian faith is a transformation of some pre-existing sentiment of faith, and it is as important to understand the latter as the former. In the light of any specific, self-consciously clarified faith, such as Christianity or Judaism, it is possible to recognize the elements of human nature and history that have been taken up and utilized by that specific faith, without supposing that these elements determine the transformation. John Knox recognizes this, in a way, in his use of the category event, which when applied to Christ can be extended backwards in time to include not only the history of Israel but also the history of human covenants with God, beginning with Adam.

[2] Kierkegaard is the last modern theologian to speak unequivocally of faith as a passion. He called it 'the happy passion' in *Philosophical Fragments*; see D. F. Swenson's translation (Princeton, 1946), chapter IV. However, human faith manifestly has a passional character in Whitehead's discussion of it in *Religion in the Making*. In general, wherever faith is understood to involve valuation there is some intimation of the affective dimension.

tension and release to the impulses of thought and action. Such suffering of power is the familiar 'religious situation'—to use Paul Tillich's phrase in a very specific application—that lies in the being of historical men and provides us with the crucial means of recognizing the distinctive spirit that informs their lives and influences all that they think and do by its character. Hence to perceive it is to perceive much of the heart of human existence in time.[1] For useful as it is to know and to apply the laws that reason adopts for its own work (logic) and also the physical and social laws of growth and decline (the biological, chemical, and economic patterns of human life) in our endeavours to understand persons, still their intentions and choices, their acts of creativity and self-destruction remain obscure to us until we grasp the passion that tempers their hearts and the cause or occasion that has brought the passion to birth in them. As Thomas Hobbes wrote, 'the thoughts are to the desires, as scouts, and spies, to range abroad, and find the way to the things desired'.[2] But what is true of thoughts and their public symbols is also true of deeds and every other revealment of the human mind. They can be understood only when the overwhelming desire or its opposite aversion and the thing desired or feared are perceived and recognized. Therefore, when we speak of discerning the religious situation in a man or a society, we mean recognition of the passion that collects, informs, and unifies the elements of his mind, inspires the voluntary motions of his body, and forms his chief bond of interest with his world.

The birth of this unifying passion is the process in the individual that is analogous to the history of Israel and the Jews. And so it is in the single person—in our potential reader/auditor of the gospels—that which furnishes the experience to which the gospel-Christ appeals and also the bond between him and the reader; just as the history of the covenant struggle from Abraham down through the millennia was the common experience out of which Jesus preached and the crowds in Galilee and Jerusalem listened. But this analogy between the individual and the history of Israel must be stated more carefully, if it is to be persuasive.

[1] There is no need to claim that faith in this sense is absolutely universal but only to observe that it is common to the generations accessible to our understanding, that is, to the generations of historical men.
[2] *Leviathan*, ed. M. Oakeshott (Oxford, 1960), p. 46.

Richard R. Niebuhr

First of all then let it be said that the argument here does not suggest that in the moral history[1] of the individual in our world there is a literal re-enactment of Israel's covenants and covenant defections. To be sure, ancient Christian preachers and exegetes long made use of the device of finding in the epics of the patriarchs, the chronicles of the kings, and the devotions of the psalmists figural explanations and foreordinations of the experiences of their present charges. But this method of reading history according to type and antetype has vanished. Nevertheless, one feature of human nature that made such a procedure possible remains as a common possession in human experience and affords a connexion or point of comparison between the histories of persons. This feature is the felt moral need for a clearly symbolized principle of internal or personal unity and of steadfastness in the human world. Both the need of such integrity and the struggle to appropriate it affect the personal history of men today, and it is this history in the individual of which Christ can be the new *archēgos*. For the shrewdest commentators on religion, politics, and human personality—from Augustine to Hobbes to Rauschenbusch to contemporary theorists of personality[2]—have discovered and rediscovered that the everlasting problem of human existence is moral birth: not the birth of the cell but the birth of nation or commonwealth from its regions, the birth of the city from its classes, and the birth of the person from his several powers of acting and many passions.

To be sure, the description of this process as a birth is not strictly accurate, since it is a lifelong affair for all human and social organisms rather than an event with a determinate beginning and end. Nevertheless, just as dying and death interpret aspects of the whole of human life, so can being born, especially when the genesis thus symbolized affects the very core of personal existence: the emergence of a ruling purpose out of a variety of inclinations and projects. For as the word *persona* meant, when the Latin fathers of the Church borrowed it, an actor's role and thence the part and character a man

---

[1] The word moral is used here to mean not right or good but ethically self-conscious, so that the moral history of the individual means the history of the agent who assumes responsibility both for his individual acts and the sum total of these acts, i.e. his life in society.

[2] See, for example, Gordon Allport, *Becoming* (New Haven, 1955) and Erik Erikson, *Childhood and Society* (Penguin Books, 1965), 'The Eight Ages of Man.'

sustains in the world at large, so for us a person is not merely an intelligent agent but one who can adopt and ultimately identify himself with his part in the world. And since human times are always changing, to be a person is to be destined to undergo not only one but many 'births', as Israel had to acknowledge its covenant many times. Personal existence involves the repeated reaffirmation and reidentification of one's part and character; it necessitates a continual submitting of ourselves to threatened dissipations in the stresses of new circumstances; it is a series of re-creations, always accompanied by the anticipation of further revolutions in inner and outer situation, through which alone human life maintains its moral identity.

It is evident, then—and this is the second qualification of the analogy between Israel and the individual—that such existence entails for men the unending task of maintaining an equilibrium of the many vital, psychic, and spiritual forces always at work in themselves. And this is the task that discloses most clearly, perhaps, the faith before faith in which the bond of the reader to the Christ of the gospels appears. Faith of this order is the perception and acknowledgment by a man of his dependence on that which is not himself for the personal unity and equilibrium he requires. It is the suffering that is evident wherever inchoate peoples, communities, and individuals show their intimate acquaintance with the poverty of trust, of mutual respect, and of concurrence among their own capacities and tendencies and with their impotence to engender such trust and cooperation in themselves. Theologians of modern times—particularly those whom Kierkegaard has influenced—have liked to call this felt poverty despair and to diagnose it as the necessary negative preparation for the gospel in the human mind. One need not reject this existentialist religious psychology out of hand because of its tendentious interpretation of the data to which it has called so much attention. But it is well to correct its one-sidedness by remembering that the perception of weakness calls for and presupposes the experience of strength all about, in others and in one's own faculties —but strength that one cannot use. Properly interpreted, despair is the experience of the presence of power visited on oneself on terms not of one's own choosing; it is the sense of not having oneself at one's own command; it is the awareness of being moved by forces one cannot regulate and of not being able to see how the motions of the mind and body have all one end. But these experiences are the desires and aversions of the mind, the movements of thought, volition, and sentiment, which philosophy long called the passions. They are passions not yet inspired and collected by a single affection illuminated by a living image of the unity and direction of human life in the world.

The reason for speaking of this state of mind, this consciousness of inhibited and inchoate personal unity and strength, as a faith before faith is that it contains within itself a prenotion of what is lacking. It is not an *a priori* prenotion but rather a surmise founded on past experience. The man who senses that he does not have himself at his own command, for example, is a man who simultaneously feels himself to be in the grasp of transient or partial elements of his nature. Hence, he also foreknows, however vaguely, that he can have self-command only as he receives it from an agency that affects and realigns him as a whole. He is like Israel in one of its times of forgetfulness and deafness to the prophets' calls to a renewed sense of the indefeasibility of God's covenant, suffering inner confusion under external threats. Israel's periodic reawakenings to the great covenant increased its sense of dependence for identity and purpose on God's steadfastness toward the whole people, while its lapses into lesser covenants with the local nature-gods sharpened its present sense of confusion and impotence. Thus the births of purpose and of internal collectedness came to the nation through the renewals of its 'heart' (whole mind) by fresh perceptions of the majesty, mercifulness, and righteousness of the creating-covenant of God. In this sense, the felt need of wholeness on the part of nation and of individual stands for the presence in both of a faith before faith.

The analogy between Israel and the individual reader/auditor of the gospels is, consequently, not a mystical relation or any other kind except the one which inheres in the common moral experience of coming to life as persons, that is, as beings who require confidence that something is being accomplished in and through themselves that is an augmentation of life at large.

A third point of correspondence in the general analogy between the individual and Israel, which now needs elaboration, is the fact that a sense of personal identity and collectedness can arise only together with confidence in the outer world of other human agents and natural forces. The first does not produce the second; nor, of course, is the opposite the case. It is difficult enough in our philosophical thinking to settle upon an adequate idea of the single 'cause' of all things. But the discerning of that in man's mind which has the inherent authority to govern the whole soul—discerning true virtue, in other words—is no less uncertain and perplexing. The discoveries of the principle(s) of these two collections, the person and the world, must transpire together. While, therefore, men undergo but cannot experience their first births or the conditions that made possible the space and occasion for their lives, afterwards in maturity they perennially look for appearances that display at one and the same time the character of the power that wells as human life within themselves and that forms their world without. And, to repeat our theme, the search for such an appearance on the part of the individual is analogous to the watching for signs of the kingdom of God on the part of Israel and Jesus' contemporaries.

Such an appearance of real authority, when it draws attention to itself and then assent, is not only the appearance of simple power but of power augmenting human life (the true meaning of authority), and of power as sublime, persuading men to offer a self-restraining admiration, and of power as generous, including all life and being in its sphere of work. The power that is capable of intensifying human pathos for stability and giving it a determinate character must be, in other words, not naked power (a notion as empty of content as that of pure matter) but power that works by ordering the individual in his world. Through the voices of the prophets, for example, the covenant not only called Israel back to a mindfulness of its collection in the desert into one people out of many tribes (the formative event corresponding to the organization of the individual's capabilities by a unifying passion); it also prompted the nation to look forward to the harmonious kingdom of peace between men and men, men and nature, men and God. In fact these two moments of personal and cosmic collection were parts of one continuing action of creation, in the prophetic faith. The God who delivered the members of Israel from enslavement by making of them a nation—one personal being destined to share in one land— was also the God whose beauty and glory would ultimately irradiate the whole universe. So Israel's genesis, when Israel began to understand it, contained promise not only for itself but for all being. Similarly, the reader of the gospels today can find promise and encouragement in the thought of his own births—both those already past and those to come—only if the rise of a ruling purpose in his own mind carries in itself a promise of relevance to the whole human age. Admittedly men today, especially the young, find such hope and sense of effective connexion between their own aspirations and the great world the most difficult of all passions to sustain. Yet, it must also have been difficult for Israel in its foreign captivity. And the fact remains that faith before faith, however rudimentary it may be, is a pathos for unity of purpose both within and without.

What Israel and the moral history of the individual show as a common experience, then, is the need to appropriate the suffering involved in personal existence—the distensions and distractions and even failures that the pressures of society and nature induce—as the signs and symptoms of the creating activity of God. Both Jesus' contemporaries and the present-day reader of the gospels exhibit a need of a visible and assimilable demonstration of the way in which a human being is born into full personhood in and through such suffering. Both are in need of being unified, not by some abstract doctrine of human nature—of the soul as a hierarchy of powers—but by a living example of actual personal unity in a tumultuous field of shaping and directing energies.

This way of understanding the faith before faith to which Jesus appeals, even in men of our own times, omits much that is important, and it cannot represent itself as an account of faith as such. What it is meant to do is interpret that in the human situation today which enables men to read the gospel accounts of Christ without forgetting either the differences or the similarities between themselves and those who were the first to hear and believe again, in a new way.

4. THE KINGDOM OF GOD

In this limited but valid sense, it is possible and helpful to speak of an analogy between the situation of the Jewish contemporaries of Jesus of Nazareth and the present-day reader/auditor of the gospels about Christ. What is common to the men in these two situations is the personal and communal experience of being in the process of birth into a new awareness of personal identity—an awareness mediated through the struggle to appropriate an organizing and energizing purpose into one's existence. There is, however, one great difference among many differences separating men of these two times, for the Jewish contemporary met the teachings and deeds of Jesus with a highly developed and articulated historical faith already present in his mind, in particular with a definite and sophisticated idea of God as the creator, covenant maker, and governor of all life; while no such cogent and intellectualized faith need be present today in the mind of the reader or auditor. Consequently, the comparison of these two types of men-in-the-presence-of-Christ would not suggest itself in the abstract. It is a possible comparison, only because history presents the man of today against the background of the faith of the man of the first century. The comparison suggests itself, because the act of reading or hearing naturally and inevitably raises the question of how the effort to understand Jesus in the present is similar to and different from the original efforts to understand him. Nevertheless, the things that men in these two situations have in common is significant and for the present-day reader potentially of great personal moment.

Jesus stood before his fellow Jews as a new beginning of the covenant faith of Israel. In his conduct he offered an intensified enactment of God's way with men, making the past covenant meetings of God and Israel (with all their attendant circumstances of human resistance, disorder, and willfulness and divine steadfastness and urgency) newly vivid and newly meaningful. All the aspects of Jesus' conduct, from his parables of the vineyard and words of forgiveness to his covenantal meals with his disciples and his acceptance of death, were symbols of God's steadfastness. At the same time, however, his life also called up an awareness of the resistance that the children of the covenant had always shown to the covenanting-God. In this latter capacity, Jesus dramatized, by personally suffering, the inhibitions and perversities that men inflicted on themselves by failing to perceive the rule of God in their single and corporate lives. Thus his life simultaneously exhibited the creating-redeeming activity of God towards men and the pathos of men needing and knowing and yet choosing to forget their author. The consequences of divine urgency towards and fidelity to men and of human suppression of responding faith both appear in his life 'writ large'. It is this last-named effect of his life and conduct as the gospels give them to the reader that in particular affects the reader's faith before faith. For in Jesus he can see a man sustaining the consequences of the suppressed faith—the consequences of the intensified and self-inhibited pathos—of other men, and in himself he can also recognize the same faith. The reader also is a man beset in a field of power by energies attacking, coercing, and persuading him in a score of different directions to dispose of his life in as many different ways. He too is a man under pressure, subject to distension, and like many of the disciples lacking a fully formed *persona*. With the biblical portrayal of Jesus before him and his own experience of distraction and imminent personal dissolution within him, he 'sees' two worlds in the same field of vision: the world of action that Jesus harmonizes in himself and the world of actions that threatens to destroy his own life-course. The reader then knows that he too is waiting to be born into the world of creative action—the world that affects him but to which he does not yet belong: the kingdom of God. Externally he sees the kingdom *in* Christ's actions and re-actions to his world; internally he feels the kingdom pressing him from without.

In a word, the reader attending to the history of Jesus is in a position to recognize himself as being so situated in life that he requires a pattern of action that will receive and harmonize the energies impinging on him from men and institutions and nature. As he first attempts to understand the import of Jesus' conduct, he may not recognize that this conduct itself is a pattern of a sort; but he is equipped to recognize that Jesus exists in a field of power qualitatively affecting him as it does the man of the present. At this point, then, the reader/auditor stands at the threshold of knowing that the direct bond between the biblical Jesus and himself is their common involvement in what Jesus called the kingdom of God. And, making his departure from that point, he can in time also come to see that Jesus' conduct in that government of God is a new beginning for all inchoate human faith.

Of course, such a conception of human faith as sketched here belongs to a wider understanding of the human world as a field of powers where Jesus of Nazareth is the manifestation of the tendency and character of the power that rules all powers. More than one article would be necessary to justify this wider understanding of the world, just as much more is really necessary to fill out the content of human faith of this order and to show in detail how Jesus begins such faith anew. Part of the material for this task lies in the further analysis of our own experience of the present times and part in the gospels' representation of human reality, and each of these sources interprets the other. For this conception of faith before faith and of Jesus corresponds particularly to the New Testament's account of Jesus as one who came preaching and pointing to the kingdom of God in parables that singled out the unpredictable, the abrupt, and the commonplace occurrences of life and interpreted them as the creating and conserving workings of God. This conception of human faith corresponds to Jesus' perception of the kingdom in himself, for he conceived himself, apparently, as 'the strong man' in whom this rule worked its purposes with directness and showed its intentions with graphic signs. This conception of faith corresponds above all with the gospel portrayal of Jesus as the man on whom God's way with men is stamped in an indelible character. So that when men ask: What or who is God and the rule of God? they may answer for themselves: God is the power that worked in that way (recounted in the gospels) on Jesus. When they ask: What does it mean to be a person? they may answer: It means to be shaped, unified, and used in something like that (Christ's) way by the power that displays its own consistency in the living unity of Jesus' life and death. When they ask: What is faith in such a government of God? they may then reply: It is the passionate recognition that in this being shaped, directed, and made a person there is movement of life, endowment of human life with a kind of definiteness or glory, and increase of human life with an appetite for generosity, such as we see exemplified in Jesus Christ. Christ is the personal theatre of all the powers of ordinary history—powers which men have been enduring without understanding.

Such a modest yet luminous history of the making and ruling of a man by God is something that transfixes the memories of the other men who are being made, in each successive generation, and so calls out and regulates their interest as to enlist them willingly in the government exhibited in Christ.

The question asked at the outset of this essay is: What is the personal connexion between the figure of Jesus Christ in the gospels and the present-day reader or auditor of the gospels? The answer that the foregoing pages have offered is that the immediate connexion between Christ and ourselves is what Jesus called the *basileia tou theou* and what we might call the experience of being made into persons, our lifelong experience. It is the recognition of this 'meaning' in Jesus' life, which also is latent in our own experience, that makes possible the new mind called repentance and faith, that makes the memory of Jesus thenceforth crucially important and obedience to his summons irresistible so far as men recognize what is happening in him.

The intuition on which the concepts of faith as decision and as remembering, on which the appeal of the fellowship of the Church, the sacraments, and preaching, the care of the poor are all founded is the perception of the kingdom of God in Christ and in ourselves.

6

AN HISTORICAL ESSAY ON THE
HUMANITY OF JESUS CHRIST

WILLIAM R. FARMER

INTRODUCTION

Jesus can be most adequately understood when his whole influence on history is kept in view. This was well understood in the nineteenth century, at least by Friedrich Schleiermacher and Ferdinand Christian Baur. These men refused to separate the historical study of Jesus from that of the Church, or from other speculative theological and philosophical disciplines. For Schleiermacher and Baur, Jesus was the founder of Christianity, not merely an historical presupposition of Christianity. Baur, although he understood well that the gospels bear witness to the early development of the Church, placed decisive importance, therefore, on the attempt to understand Jesus as he may be known through an historical-critical study of the gospels.

Where Schleiermacher had made the Fourth Gospel normative for understanding Jesus, Baur on historical-critical grounds gradually set John aside in his preference for the synoptics. Baur believed that it is in the human life of Jesus, as that may be known through the synoptic gospels (and above all through Matthew), that the divine-human relational quality of his person is to be perceived. And he was confirmed in this position by his understanding of Paul.[1] That it is in the humanity of Christ that his divinity is most truly perceived, was also the position of Luther, and has been implicitly basic to almost all modern Protestant theologies.

The confusion in our own day concerning whether Jesus of Nazareth really is the founder of Christianity, and whether the historical study of his human life is of decisive theological significance, is partly rooted in the failures, both apparent and real, of the nineteenth-century quest for the historical Jesus.

---

[1] In much that I say about Baur in this essay, I am indebted to the book *The Formation of Historical Theology, A Study of Ferdinand Christian Baur* (New York, 1966), and to correspondence with the author, Peter C. Hodgson.

This quest was dominated by the effort to reconstruct a convincing life of Jesus based upon the synoptic gospels and presupposed the essential historical trustworthiness of the story of his ministry as presented in those gospels. Significantly enough, Baur never attempted to write such a life. His interest in the historical Jesus was focused primarily upon Jesus' message and secondarily on his person—as revealed in his teaching, his words. Therefore, the subsequent collapse of the nineteenth-century quest through the discovery that the Marcan account is theologically rather than historically oriented would not have so decisively affected Baur (who knew that all three shared this orientation), as it did those who regarded the Marcan tradition as central for understanding Jesus. The enduring value of Baur's work at this point may be measured by the extent to which nearly one hundred years later Rudolf Bultmann's reconstruction of Jesus' message was in basic agreement with that of Baur.

Bultmann, coming after Johannes Weiss and Albert Schweitzer, has a greater appreciation for the importance of eschatology for Jesus than had Baur (though Baur was by no means ignorant of eschatology), and the availability to Bultmann of the form-critical method, unknown to Baur, results in certain other differences in their approach to reconstructing Jesus' message. Nevertheless, the most intriguing difference between Baur and Bultmann is not to be found in their understandings of this message, but in their respective understandings of the theological importance of Jesus as he may be known through historical study. For Baur, the teaching of Jesus, as studied historically-critically, and the person of Jesus, as revealed in his words, provide the decisive norm for Christian theology. For Bultmann, however, it seems that this norm tends rather to be discovered in the kerygma of the early Church—especially as that may be discovered in Paul and John.

But if Baur and Bultmann are in basic agreement on the message of Jesus, how can we understand their disagreement over the importance for Christian theology of the results of the historical study of Jesus? This question points to a fundamental problem for contemporary theology, the solution to which will not be known until we are better able to grasp the essential theological development of the past one hundred years. We are now witnessing a reassessment of the theological importance of Jesus in which, whatever allowances may be made for what is valid in the position of Bultmann, the decisive importance of the historical Jesus is being increasingly recognized. Whatever the outcome of the present debate, it may be anticipated that, on the point at issue (whether the study of Jesus as an historical figure can provide us with an adequate norm for Christian theology), the systematic theologian will be interested in having a clearer idea of what can be known at present about Jesus through historical study.

This essay includes the attempt to clarify the kind of knowledge about Jesus that can be made available through historical study and at the same time indicates some of the methodological presuppositions upon which such knowledge is based. It is assumed that, bearing as it does on the human life of Jesus, this knowledge will prove helpful to the modern theologian interested in the nature of historical existence and the person and work of Jesus Christ, and it is hoped that it will be of some importance in assisting him to develop a more adequate doctrine of the humanity of Christ.

In the course of this essay an attempt will be made to demonstrate that there is no reason to doubt that Jesus rebuked the attitude of self-righteousness on the part of those of his contemporaries who resented God's mercy toward repentant sinners. The importance of this fact will become clear once it is seen that this rebuke is what gave Jesus' preaching part of its cutting thrust. For it helps one to understand the basic twofold response to Jesus whereby the tax collector and sinner drew near to him, while others reacted negatively to his decision to receive these people into his intimate fellowship and thus provided the foundation for an historical rejection of Jesus by some of the religious authorities—a rejection which led eventually to his death. In this way it will be seen that Jesus' death is not to be separated from his life, or, to be more specific, from his basic attitude and behaviour in relation to a crucial problem in the religious and social life of his people. The complaint that Jesus ate with tax collectors and sinners cannot *by itself* be established as a cause for the opposition to him on the part of the authorities who were *directly* responsible for his death. This causal connexion can be made plausible, however, through a knowledge of the social, political, and religious realities in the life situation of Jesus as these may be understood through contemporary research in first-century Palestinian Judaism, once it *has* been established that in fact Jesus *did* rebuke the attitude of self-righteousness on the part of those Scribes and Pharisees who criticized him for receiving tax collectors and sinners into the intimacy of his table fellowship. The central aim of this essay is to establish only but exactly this latter point, and to establish it in such a way that the reader may justly feel that he has no reason to doubt it, and not be left with the haunting feeling that on this crucial matter he is 'indentured' for this understanding to some New Testament critic—or even to some consensus of New Testament scholarship.

This argument is advanced in such a way that it will become clear that, since the gospel materials which bear most directly upon this point stand in a complementary relationship to so large a body of the earliest tradition in the gospels, the only alternative to the view that they place us in authentic touch with Jesus is that they originated with some anonymous individual or group in the pre-Pauline Palestinian Church. That these materials are pre-Pauline is an important point, and we shall pause to consider briefly why, since the time of Baur, there has been so much confusion on this issue. As we shall see, Baur thought there was reason to question whether these materials were pre-Pauline. In any case, the point to note is that he did not make them basic to his reconstruction of Jesus' message. The failure of Baur and his generation to make these materials basic to their reconstruction of Jesus' message had a distorting effect on the subsequent development of nineteenth-century theology. It obscured the evidence of historical continuity between Jesus and the Church by which the later exaggeration and falsification of the theological differences between Jesus and Paul could have been best refuted, and it laid a plausible foundation for the denial of Jesus' historicity in the Christ-myth school, as well as for the notion that Paul rather than Jesus was the founder of Christianity.[1] The view that contemporary theology is basically a salvage operation made necessary by the havoc wrought by New Testament criticism is justified in so far as it draws attention to the confusion regarding what is central or normative in the message of Jesus which has prevailed since Baur.

Baur's fundamental methodological error was a consequence of what in retrospect is seen to have been an undue and in part uncritical

---

[1] This is a matter which deserves separate and extended elaboration.

reliance upon the Gospel of Matthew. Mark was then widely regarded as a very late gospel based on Matthew and Luke, and since the Gospel of Luke was written after Paul and could be understood as having been shaped by Pauline influence, Baur for this and other reasons concluded that one should go directly to Matthew in order to find the most authentic tradition about Jesus. Although he was prepared to date Matthew late (as late as the second quarter of the second century), and to acknowledge that it was influenced by Jewish-Christian interests, he believed it was based on the earlier Gospel of the Hebrews now lost, which gospel belonged to the eyewitness period and contained, Baur believed, an authentic historical account of Jesus' teaching. Therefore, Baur believed that if he utilized Matthew critically he could separate teaching for which Jesus was responsible and distinguish it from what was later in origin.

However, for reasons that are not absolutely clear, when Baur went to Matthew, he found his most authentic Jesus-tradition in one particular part of the gospel, namely in the Sermon on the Mount. More precisely, the Sermon on the Mount became for Baur the hermeneutical key to other Matthean texts including the parables. The normative character of the Sermon on the Mount for Baur may reflect the special interest in ethics characteristic of the enlightenment, or possibly even the direct influence of Kant. We know that Kant exercised a considerable influence on Baur and that his 'Categorical Imperative' did centre attention on the radical ethical demands of Jesus as these are set forward in the Sermon on the Mount, especially in the beatitudes and antitheses which come in the first third of the Sermon. Baur saw in this material the sharpest antithesis to the Jewish-Christian tendency of Matthew, and thus, on the basis of his understanding of Matthew, he considered this the material most likely to be authentic.

Today, however, especially in the light of form-criticism, one must proceed somewhat differently. In seeking to understand Jesus, the critic can no longer give to any particular gospel the place of importance Baur gave to Matthew, or for that matter the importance Schleiermacher gave to John, or that Emanuel Hirsch now gives to Mark. At present the critic looks for the earliest tradition preserved in all the gospels. When this is done, it is found that no one gospel is clearly superior to all others in its preservation of primitive tradition.

That is especially true when it comes to the parables of Jesus, which since Jülicher have more and more come to the fore as our most reliable tradition for understanding what Jesus had to say about God.

It is remarkable, however, to what degree contemporary New Testament critics have been willing to accept the authenticity of the parables of Jesus without making clear by what criteria they do so. It is sometimes pointed out that when the parables attributed to Jesus in the gospels are compared to the parables of the ancient world in general, including both Jewish and Hellenistic parables, his clearly belong with those which are Jewish and Palestinian. But that Jesus himself is responsible for these parables has never been convincingly argued. It is unlikely that Jesus originated all of the parables attributed to him in the gospels, and certainly no attempt will be made in this essay to deal with this question exhaustively. However, an effort will be made to give the reader adequate grounds for thinking that some, indeed most, of these parables do in fact put us in authentic touch with the preaching of Jesus.

With this introduction to what lies ahead, we shall now proceed according to the following outline: (1) Some presuppositions of this study. (2) The central importance of certain parables in Luke. (3) An argument for the authenticity of certain parables attributed to Jesus. (4) The complementary character of these and other Matthean and Lucan parables, and their close relationship to certain teachings of Jesus, found in the Sermon on the Mount and elsewhere in Matthew, Mark, and Luke. (5) Conclusions.

I. PRESUPPOSITIONS

The general presupposition of this study is that the life of Jesus is theologically important. In my student days, under the influence of Paul Tillich and others, I formulated for myself the following question: 'What place is to be given to the historical Jesus in any systematic expression of Christian faith?' During the intervening years this question has never been far from my mind. There was an interview with C. H. Dodd on the basis of which I decided to pursue in earnest a particular problem in Jewish history only after I had been given an affirmative answer to the question whether my research in this area would likely assist me eventually to come to terms with the question of the historical Jesus.

I also remember hearing John Knox say that he thought that more attention needed to be given to the humanity of Christ. I understood him at the time to mean that we ought to be concerning ourselves more with the question of the human life of Jesus Christ. This understanding of Knox's comment doubtless has had an abiding influence upon my thinking.

The reader should know that the results of my research to this date predispose me to think that, however much we may want to circumscribe the importance of the historical Jesus, it will be necessary in the future to give him a more rightful place than he has been accorded in some of the more dominant theologies of our time (Barth, Brunner, Bultmann and Tillich). What Jesus seems to have done and said in the life situation of his own flesh and blood existence has turned out to be too commensurate with what seems to me to be most decisive in these very theologies to warrant any other judgment, the tentativeness and subjectivity of all historical reconstruction notwithstanding.

In this connexion there is the common-sense assumption of continuity between Jesus and the community which bears and cherishes his memory. Jesus did do something with his life and did teach or preach something. Is it not reasonable to conclude that this something provided the Christian movement an initial impetus, that is, that authentic Christian life and faith, at one or more decisive points, is commensurate with the original intention of Jesus and the effect he had upon the life and faith of his disciples? Is it not reasonable to think that, however much our understanding of existence may have broadened, deepened, or changed, nothing has happened which sets aside, nullifies or contravenes the significance of the original event; and that this event was in part, if not altogether, historical?

In addition to this general pre-understanding there are several rather specific presuppositions or material assumptions that are important for this study.

The first is the *historical existence* of Jesus. The fact that some intelligent persons sincerely doubt whether Jesus ever existed as an historical personage, and that theologians like Paul Tillich have felt constrained to allow for this doubt, reminds us that in the intellectual history of the West this is still an item of unfinished business.[1]

The second is the *sanity* of Jesus. Jesus' sanity is hardly capable of competent definition or diagnosis. But the fact that it has been challenged deserves to be noted. There is no reason in principle why historical studies of Jesus presupposing that he was suffering from one or another mental illness should not be attempted. However, such studies as have been made seem incomplete and their results uncertain.[2]

The third is the *integrity* of Jesus. The point at issue here is primarily this: did Jesus intend to deceive his followers or did he allow them to be deceived? How complicated a question this can be is dramatically suggested by Sinclair Lewis in his characterization of Elmer Gantry (not that Elmer Gantry is a convincing parallel to Jesus, but that human motives can be so complex that one can never be absolutely certain, on the basis of what a man says or does, what his purpose may be). The attitude of the historian on this question must not be overly influenced by the faith of a man's disciples in their teacher's integrity. Therefore, when integrity on the part of Jesus is assumed by an historian, this assumption must not be made naïvely, but should be regarded as a presupposition, for it tends to limit the range of human experience by which the historian judges probabilities and improbabilities in his reconstruction of the past, by leaving out of consideration possibilities which might otherwise be entertained if the suggestion that Jesus may not have been a person of integrity were really taken seriously. To say that Jesus was a person of integrity does not rule out the possibility that he sometimes may have been conscious of failing to adhere to or wholeheartedly affirm what he preached. Such questions are virtually impossible to settle because of the

[1] See William Benjamin Smith, *The Birth of the Gospel. A Study of the Origin and Purport of the Primitive Allegory of the Jesus* (New York, 1957).
[2] See *The Psychiatric Study of Jesus, Exposition and Criticism* (Boston, 1948). This is a translation of Albert Schweitzer's doctoral thesis for his medical degree and was first published in German in 1913. The translator, Charles R. Joy, also provided a Prefatory Note and an Introduction. Winfred Overholser, M.D., President of the American Psychiatric Association in 1948, contributed a valuable foreword and presented a selected bibliography on the subject of paranoia up through 1940.

difficulties with which any investigation into the self-consciousness of Jesus is fraught. The materials we have for understanding Jesus do not afford us much if any of this kind of knowledge about him. The basic question is: did Jesus mean what he said; did he intend others to take his words seriously and did he himself take seriously the understanding of existence to which he gave expression in his teaching? It is an affirmative answer to this question which is presupposed in this essay. The degree to which the reader hesitates to agree that Jesus was in this sense a person of integrity should lead him to a corresponding degree of scepticism regarding the conclusions in the closing paragraphs of this essay, since these conclusions clearly presuppose such integrity on Jesus' part.

In the fourth place it is presupposed that within the primitive Church there were those who *remembered* Jesus. That Jesus was remembered in the Church by those who had known him is intrinsically probable from virtually every point of view, but since this is not argued here it should be listed as something assumed in the argument developed in this essay.

In the fifth place it is assumed that *all the gospels were written relatively late*, i.e. probably after A.D. 70, a full generation after the events described in the gospels. The evidence on which such dating is based is admittedly somewhat tenuous. Nonetheless, in balance such evidence as there is seems to weigh in favour of dating the gospels after rather than before A.D. 70.

The sixth matter that is presupposed or assumed is closely related to the fourth and fifth. It is, that *within the tradition preserved in the gospels, the memory of Jesus is preserved*. The alternative that, in the period between the time when Jesus was remembered in the primitive Church and the time the gospels were written, the memory of Jesus was completely or effectively lost is a real one. And although few would support this alternative, the fact that the contrary is assumed in this study deserves noting.

Finally this study presupposes that it is possible *to distinguish between what was remembered about Jesus and what has been added*. This analysis can be accomplished with the aid of contemporary knowledge of the relevant ancient languages; environmental research into the life situation of Jesus and of the first-century Church; literary and historical criticism (including source, form-critical and redactional analysis); and a reasonably perceptive understanding of human existence, informed by the humanities and social science disciplines.[1]

As a corollary of all this there is the further assumption that the humanity of Jesus Christ is a true humanity and that his uniqueness (or divinity) does not nullify his humanity or make of him a person unfit for historical study.

In the light of these preliminary considerations, we may now proceed to develop the main argument of the essay, beginning with certain important traditions preserved only in Luke.

2. LUCAN PARABLES

It is well known that the Gospel of Luke is especially rich in parables of Jesus. Few biblical texts are better known than the parables of the Good Samaritan (Luke 10: 30–7), the Prodigal Son (Luke 15: 11–32), and the Pharisee and the Publican (Luke 18: 9–14*a*). But these are only the better known of a much larger number of parables peculiar to Luke.

The theology of Luke's parables is of the greatest interest and may be outlined as follows:

(*a*) General theological presuppositions.

(1) Faith in the Covenant God of Israel who will faithfully fulfil his covenantal obligations, 11:5–8; 14:28–32; 18: 2–8*a*.

(2) God as heavenly father, 15: 11–32.

(3) Man as sinner, 15: 7, 10, 18, 21; 18: 13.

(4) Man's need for repentance, 13:9; 15: 7, 10, 17–19, 21.

(5) God's compassion toward the repentant sinner, 15: 20.

(6) God's joy over man's repentance, 15: 7, 10, 22–4, 32.

(*b*) Specific theological teaching concerning:

(1) Self-righteousness, and justification, 15: 7; 18: 9–14*a*.

---

[1] It is not presupposed that *all* the genuine remembrances can be identified, but that *in a significant number and variety of passages* in the gospels it is possible to distinguish between what has been remembered and what has been added. Some of the historical and literary grounds for making these critical judgments will be illustrated in sections 2, 3 and 4 of this essay.

(2) God's will for man in relation to other men.
  (i) Man should accept his brother's repentance and re-
    joice, because God has done so, 15: 32.
  (ii) Man should have compassion, and show his neigh-
    bour covenantal love (i.e. do *hesed* to his neighbour),
    10: 30–7.
(3) The folly of trusting in what one possesses, 12: 13–21;
  16: 19–31.
(4) God's impatience with man's excuses, 14: 16–24.
(5) The folly of postponing repentance, 13: 6–9.
(6) The faithfulness of God to his covenantal obligations.
  (i) That which he has begun, he will complete, 14: 28–32.
  (ii) God is mindful of the needs of his elect and their
    vindication is certain and imminent, 18: 2–8 *a*.
  (iii) God is mindful of his covenantal obligations and may
    be counted on to meet the exigencies of those who
    are persistent in pressing their claims upon him in
    faith, 11: 5–8.
(7) The futility of trusting in one's obedience to God's
  commands.
  (i) It excites man's impatience toward God, 17: 7–10.
  (ii) It provokes man's resentment against God's mercy
    toward repentant sinners, 15: 25–32.
  (iii) It blinds man to God's love, 15: 31.
  (iv) It subjects man to God's wrath, 18: 9–14 *a*.

The close affinity between the theology of these parables and
Pauline theology is quite apparent. For example, when we read
about the two men who went up into the temple to pray and hear
Jesus pronounce the judgment: 'This man went down to his house
justified (δικαιόω) rather than that one' (Luke 18: 14 *a*), we know as
clearly as it can be known what it means to be justified by faith and
not by the works of the law (cf. Rom. 3: 27–8; Gal. 2: 15–16). The
fact that for Paul justifying faith is bound up with the atoning death
of Jesus Christ, has not kept critics from noting the close kinship
between this parable in Luke and Pauline theology. On the surface,
it would appear that the view that this parable and perhaps others in
Luke may have been composed under Pauline influence is tenable.
This suggestion becomes all the more plausible to the degree that

one thinks in the traditional terms of identifying the author of Luke-Acts as an associate of Paul (cf. Col. 4: 14; Philem. 24). If, however, all or most of these parables in Luke originated with Jesus, it would be difficult to avoid the conclusion that these materials provide the theologian with a remarkably important avenue of historical access to *the mind and preaching of Jesus*, i.e. to that aspect of Jesus' thought which achieved communicable and abiding form through his words and action.

3. AUTHENTICITY

The question whether the parables in Luke may have been created by or developed under some kind of Pauline influence can best be explored by comparing them with their nearest counterparts among the parables peculiar to Matthew. Although there is a very close and interesting relationship between Paul and certain material in Matthew, critics do not usually think in terms of a Pauline influence upon that gospel. Certainly no critic has ever suggested that the parables in Matthew were created or developed under Pauline influence, and for good reason. There is no evidence for such a view. Therefore, the parables unique to Matthew afford a critical 'control' for evaluating possible Pauline influence on Lucan parables.

We may begin our comparison of Lucan and Matthean parables with a consideration of the Parable of the Labourers in the Vineyard (Matt. 20: 1–16). In interpreting any particular parable of Jesus the modern critic seeks to visualize how Jesus would have used it in his own life situation. Thus for the purpose of this essay which aims to be as critically self-contained as possible (i.e. where as much of the essential information as may be feasible is brought before the reader), it is necessary at this point to review those features of Jesus' life situation needful for understanding this and closely related parables.

Jesus was a Jew who lived in Palestine during the period of Roman occupation. The climax of his ministry came while the procurator of Judaea was Pontius Pilate, whose responsibilities included that of procuring supplies and funds from the local populace to defray costs of the occupation. Funds were procured through engaging Jewish tax collectors. As procurator, Pilate had at his disposal sufficient military forces to back the incumbent collaborating Jewish regime, to see that taxes were collected, and to police the normal rash of political discontent. It was seldom necessary to call for the help of the Governor who resided in Syria, and in whose hands was vested the real military power.

The Romans found the key to effective control of the situation through their influence within the high priestly families. Because of the strong place of the Temple cultus in Jewish law and piety, it was possible, by offering security to the temple authorities in Jerusalem, for Rome to maintain a basis for its hegemony over the population as a whole. Only such groups as rejected the authority of the incumbent high priestly families were free from some measure of effective collaboration with Rome and the price required for complete freedom was withdrawal from public life. Only a relatively small percentage of the population was either willing or able to pay this price. These included such groups living in the wilderness of Judaea as the Qumran community, and such para-military resistance elements as the Zealots.

The benefits of the Pax Romana were felt not only by the educated and privileged classes but by the general populace. But these benefits could not be enjoyed by the Jews with the same easy conscience as was possible with other nations within the empire. This was because of the peculiar heritage of the Jews, many of whose customs and laws needed to be set aside or liberally interpreted wherever and whenever the inevitable need for close contact with Gentiles arose.

Alongside the laws governing Jewish life and practice and inextricably bound up with them in the scriptures of the Jews were certain promises of God bearing upon the welfare of his covenanted people. These promises were conditional upon obedience to the law, and so the less privileged classes on the basis of these promises were always capable of envisioning a relative improvement in their welfare, if only more effective ways could be found to keep the law.

In this way conflict and tension were created within the common life by virtue, on the one hand, of the need to minimize or set aside the requirements of the law in order to facilitate the conditions favourable to a more effective integration within the Empire, and, on the other hand, of the need to maximize and strictly enforce these requirements in order to meet the conditions requisite for the fulfilment of divine promise.

Out of this conflict and tension and feeding upon the heterogeneous messianic materials preserved in Jewish writings, came the multifarious eschatological and apocalyptical hopes which excited the populace whenever the signs of the times could be interpreted so as to justify such expectations, or when an eschatological prophet like John the Baptist began to preach.

The collaborating elements of the Jewish population whose close co-operation was essential to the effectiveness of the Roman occupation and thereby to the prosperity and security of the Jewish people as a whole, included many who sought conscientiously to be observant of the Mosaic law, but also many others who were in this respect more or less lax. Those willing to be at times somewhat lax, especially in their attitude toward the dietary regulations and other Levitical cleanliness rules, were naturally preferred by persons in authority for some of the more important and lucrative positions in the complex fabric of Roman hegemony over Jewish life. By Jews who were strictly observant of the laws of Moses, these non-observant compatriots were derogatively referred to as 'tax collectors and sinners', but sympathetically as 'lost sons of Abraham'. To the degree that they were not observant, these Jews were regarded as having abandoned the covenant, and having sold their heritage for a mess of pottage. They were dead in trespasses. Observant Jews, on the other hand, were dependent upon the guidance and support of legal experts who could tell them what the law did and did not require under constantly varying circumstances. Prominent among those who were ready to provide such guidance and support were the Pharisees and the Scribes.

Therefore, at times when apocalyptic or messianic hopes were at a fever pitch, non-observant Jews, because of their fear of divine retribution, were in great numbers and in varying degrees seeking to return to the covenant. In principle this would always present a special problem for Jews who were already righteous before the law. For in this kind of situation they would naturally question any sudden or last minute repentance and object to any too ready acceptance of sinners on the part of religious authorities. (Most Jewish groups which covenanted together for the purpose of keeping the law insisted on from six months to two years probation for those who repented and wished to join them.) For even if the eschatological ful-

filment of God's long-standing promises were at last about to be
realized for *all* Israel, simple justice required the recognition of a real
difference between those who had suffered deprivation and injustice
because of their faithfulness to the law, in comparison with those who
had long held God's law in disregard, and had moreover profited
thereby.

The basic problem, therefore, conditioning the life situation of the
Jews in Palestine at this time was that of the law and of its adequacy as
a norm by which they could find a meaningful and satisfying mode
of existence within a life-affirming cosmopolitan culture which was
constantly calling the separatistic character of Jewish communal life
into question. For Jesus to receive tax collectors and sinners into the
intimacy of his own table fellowship at a time when this chronic
religious syndrome was being inflamed by the expectation of imminent divine judgment was for him to create a crisis within a crisis. It
is to this particular situation that Jesus addressed himself in several of
his most important parables.

The Parable of the Labourers in the Vineyard is one of these. A
parable by definition invites comparison. And when it is asked: To
whom in the life situation of Jesus are we to compare the labourers
who grumbled (γογγύзω) against the householder because he made
them equal to those who had worked only one hour, whereas they
had 'borne the burden of the day and the scorching heat'? the
answer is: The Pharisees and Scribes. And those who came at the
end of the day and 'worked only one hour' and yet were afforded
equal treatment with all the others, to whom are they to be compared? They are to be compared to 'the tax collectors and sinners'.
What then is the intention of Jesus in the parable? It is to rebuke the
attitude of self-righteousness on the part of those who resent God's
mercy to the repentant sinners. The words are unequivocal: 'Friend,
I am doing you no wrong; did you not agree with me for a denarius?
Take what belongs to you, and go; I choose to give to this last as I
give to you. Am I not allowed to do what I choose with what belongs
to me? Or do you begrudge my generosity?' (Matt. 20: 13–15).

With this parable from Matthew we must now compare one
from Luke, the so-called Parable of the Prodigal Son. In this parable
we are to compare the younger son with those sinners who had

abandoned the covenant and had been living like the Gentiles apart from the law, but now are returning to their true heritage in the covenant. And we are to compare the elder son, who for many years had served his father and never disobeyed his command, with the Pharisees and Scribes who stood outside the circle of Jesus' fellowship and criticized him for receiving the sinners at his table. Thus when the father reproves his elder son for not joining the joyous feasting occasioned by the return of his brother with the words: 'Son, you are always with me, and all that is mine is yours. It was fitting to make merry and be glad, for this your brother was dead and is alive; he was lost and is found', Jesus in effect is uttering a gracious word of rebuke to those Pharisees and Scribes who grumble (διαγογγύζω) and criticize him for receiving and eating with tax collectors and sinners.

The fact that the first part of the parable teaches the grace of God toward the sinner does not nullify the interpretation that is here offered, but rather serves to illuminate the inappropriateness of the self-righteous resentment of the elder son and thus to heighten the poignancy with which the rebuke is made, and to clarify its theological ground. That there is 'more joy in heaven over one sinner who repents than over ninety-nine righteous persons who need no repentance' (Luke 15: 7) serves to make the same point, namely the inappropriateness of the grumbling of the Pharisees and Scribes in the face of the altogether fitting accepting attitude of Jesus in response to the drawing near of the tax collectors and sinners.

In Luke 18: 9–14 a, the protagonists are explicitly identified within the parable; the one a Pharisee, and the other a tax collector. The self-righteous tendency of the Pharisee to trust in his goodness and despise the rest of men ('God, I thank you that I am not like the rest of men') is condemned, whereas the willingness of the tax collector to confess his sinfulness and place his trust in the mercy of God is set forth as the true ground for justification. It is abundantly clear, therefore, that Matt. 20: 1–16 contains teaching which is very closely related to that in Luke 15: 11–32 and 18: 9–14a. Since there is no reason to think that Matt. 20: 1–16 was created under Pauline influence, and it is clear that this parable has had a separate history of transmission from these two closely related parables in Luke, we are led to give serious consideration to the possibility that all three of these parables originated in some early pre-Pauline teaching in the Church.

But could not these parables have been taken over by the primitive Church from Judaism? We must give serious consideration to this question, for it is sometimes said that there is little that is distinctive about Jesus' teachings; that they can almost all be closely paralleled in the teachings of other Jewish rabbis.

So long as the Sermon on the Mount is regarded as the norm for what is distinctive in Jesus' teaching this view has some substance. We may consider for example the following:[1] 'Whoever calls another man "fool" will be cast into the fires of Gehennan' (Bab. B. Bath. 10*b*; cf. Matt. 5: 22*c*); 'It were good...that you vow not at all' (Sifre on Deut. 23: 23; cf. Matt. 5: 34); 'Whenever you have mercy on other creatures, they from heaven (i.e. God) have mercy on you' (Sifre on Deut. 13: 18; cf. Matt. 6: 14); 'As you withhold mercy, so they (i.e. God) withhold mercy from you' (Midr. Tannaim 15: 11; cf. Matt. 6: 15); '...my parents accumulated wealth upon earth, but I have put my treasures in heaven... my parents treasured up their money, but I have treasured up my soul...' (Bab. B. Bath. 11*a*; cf. Matt. 6: 19 ff.); 'Did you ever in your life see an animal or a bird which had a trade? And they support themselves without trouble. And were they not created only to serve me? And I was created to serve my maker. Does it not follow that I shall be supported without trouble?' (Kidd. Mish. 4:14 [Kidd. Tosef. 5:15 (343)]; cf. Matt. 6: 26); 'He who has what he will eat today and says "what shall I eat tomorrow?", behold, this man lacks faith' (Mekh. 16: 4 [Mekh. of R. Simon i.b.]; cf. Matt. 6: 30–4); 'In the measure in which a man metes it is measured to him' (Mekh. 13: 19 ff. [Sot. Mish. 1:7, Sot. Tosef. 3: 1 (295), Sifre on Num. 12: 15 ff.]; cf. Matt. 7: 2); 'Man sees

[1] In working with rabbinic materials I have been assisted by Morton Smith's indispensable *Tannaitic Parallels to the Gospels* (*JBL* Monograph Series 6, 1951), and by Jacob Neusner's fine study *A Life of Rabban Yohannan Ben Zakkai* (Leiden, 1962). With the exception of the two parables attributed to Ben Zakkai, which have been taken from Neusner's book as translated therein, all rabbinic materials cited below have been gleaned from Smith's work and follow his translations. In utilizing these discriminating secondary sources one enjoys the methodological advantage of working with rabbinic materials which on historical-critical grounds can be dated in the general period contemporary with the origin and development of the gospel tradition. Abbreviations of the titles of rabbinic sources have been conformed to the usage of Marcus Jastrow as given in 'The List of Abbreviations' in his *A Dictionary of the Targumim, the Talmud Babli and Yerushalmi, and the Midrashic Literature* (New York, 1950), pp. xvi–xvii.

the mote in his neighbour's eye, but knows not the beam in his own'
(Jerusalem Talmud, Arakh. 16*b*; cf. Matt. 7: 3–5); 'Whoever has
wisdom greater than his deeds, what is he like? He is like a tree with
many leaves and few roots; and the wind comes and uproots it and
overturns it on its face, for it is said...But whoever has deeds greater
than his wisdom, what is he like? He is like a tree with few leaves
and many roots; which, even if all the winds in the world come and
blow on it, they cannot move it from its place, for it is said...'
(Ab. 3: 17; cf. Matt. 7: 24 ff.)

Evidence of this kind makes it clear that although there is much in
the Sermon on the Mount that retains its own distinctive flavour
when compared to the closest parallels in rabbinic literature, there
is nonetheless a significant number of striking instances where the
intention of the sayings of other rabbis seems to be very similar to
their parallels in the Sermon on the Mount. The existence of these
parallels is by no means a negative consideration, however, for they
afford indisputable historical evidence for the true humanity of Jesus.
If we had no such historical evidence that Jesus was like other men,
especially that he was like other Jewish teachers who were his contemporaries, and that in his teaching he dealt with the same human
problems they dealt with and often in a very similar manner, the
Church could not refute those, like the Docetists and Gnostics, who
are disposed to doubt his true humanity, especially in view of the other
tendencies in the gospels to emphasize that he was not like other men.[1]

But what, we may ask, is the situation with regard to the parables
from Matthew and Luke with which we are immediately concerned (Matt. 20: 1–16; Luke 15: 11–32; 18: 9–14*a*)? Here the case is
quite different. For the teaching in these parables is not typical of the
teaching of any known rabbinic parables. Jewish rabbis contemporary
with Jesus did use parables. But the point is that these three parables
of Jesus are quite different in their intention from all known rabbinic
parables. This point is not made out of an interest in arguing for some
uniqueness for Jesus. It is simply made as an historical observation
which has no *immediate* theological purpose (although it may have
theological consequences) and it shows that there is no reason to
think that *these* parables were borrowed, either by Jesus or by his
followers, from some common stock of rabbinic parables.

[1] This christological insight was brought to my attention by Albert C. Outler.

The citation of a few rabbinic parables at this point will serve to enable the reader to form a more balanced view on this important question. We may begin with a parable attributed to Rabbi Yohanan ben Zakkai, a contemporary of Jesus; Ben Zakkai is addressing himself to the following question: 'Why were the first tablets made by God whereas the second by Moses?' He replies:

To what is the matter comparable? to a king who married a woman, and brought the paper, and the scribe, and the ink of his own, and brought her home. He caught her playing with a certain one of his servants, was angered, and divorced her. A friend of hers came to him and said, My Lord, do you not know from whence you took her? Was it not among the servants that she was brought up? And since she was brought up among servants, she shows no pride among them. He said to him, And what do you propose? That I take her back? Bring paper and a scribe of your own, and I shall sign the document. So Moses said to the Holy One (blessed be he) when Israel came to that deed. He said to him, Do you not know from which country you took them? From Egypt, a place of idolatry. The Holy One said to him, and what do you want, that I be appeased to them? Bring the tablets of your own, and behold my handwriting I shall inscribe on *your* tablets. (Deut. R. Ekev 3: 17; cf. also Yalk. Shimoni I, 397.)

There is no parallel to this parable in the gospels, yet a careful study of it and other rabbinic parables shows that such parables and the parables of Jesus belong to the same literary genre. There is the king (who is to be compared to God), and the interpersonal relationships of his family and/or servants, which serve to illustrate some teaching about God's attitude and action toward Israel.

There is, however, one rabbinic parable which is especially closely paralleled in the gospels, both in form and meaning. It also is a parable attributed to Ben Zakkai. Here he expounds the thesis that it is foolish to postpone repentance:

Said Rabbi Yohanan ben Zakkai, It is like the king who invited his servants to the banquet and did not name the exact time. The wise among them came and sat at the door of the palace, saying, Does the king's palace lack for anything? But the fools went about their business, saying, Was there ever a banquet without a set hour? All of a sudden, the king summoned them to his presence. The wise ones appeared all dressed and cleaned up for the occasion; while the fools appeared in their dirt. The king rejoiced to see the wise ones, and was angered at the appearance of the fools, and said, Those who have dressed themselves for the banquet, let them sit and eat and drink, while the ones who are unprepared may stand by and look at them (Bab. Sabb. 153 a).

It is possible that verses 11–14 of Matthew 22 were added to the Parable of the Marriage Feast under the influence of this parable, but otherwise the closely related parables attributed to Jesus which treat this same motif (Matt. 22: 1–10; 24: 45–51; 25: 1–12; Luke 12: 35–8; 13: 6–9; 14: 16–24) are best understood as quite independent creations affording distinctive variations upon a common theme. Considered by themselves in isolation from the other parables in Matthew and Luke, it would be difficult to decide whether these are authentic parables of Jesus or whether they have been borrowed from Judaism. But taken together with the entire corpus of synoptic parables there is, as we shall see, good reason to consider them along with others, among the probably authentic parables of Jesus.

The important point to recognize at this stage in the argument is that most rabbinic parables that have been preserved do *not* teach what is taught in the parables attributed to Jesus. In fact with rare exceptions (like the parable just considered) even when rabbinic parables closely parallel synoptic parables, they teach something quite different. In this regard we may consider the following:

(It is like) one to whom there fell in inheritance a residence in a sea-port city and he sold it for a small sum and the purchaser went and dug through it and found in it treasures of silver and treasures of gold and precious stones and pearls. The seller almost strangled (of rage and grief). So did Egypt because they sent away (Israel) and did not know what they sent away. (Mekh. 14: 5; cf. Matt. 13: 44–5.)

Evidence of this kind weighs against the notion that any great number of the parables attributed to Jesus were taken over by him or by the Church from contemporary Judaism.[1]

What may have been the case with respect to individual parables, of course, remains problematic. In order to settle the matter we need further evidence. With regard to the specific parables under consideration, i.e. Matt. 20: 1–16; Luke 15: 11–32 and 18: 9–14*a*, such

---

[1] But such evidence does not, of course, weigh against the notion that some of the parables attributed to Jesus may have been taken over—in the sense of familiar images and analogies—and transformed in their points and application. This use of familiar illustrative material is a normal and effective teaching device.

evidence is not lacking, for it is a most interesting fact that what may be regarded as the closest rabbinic parallel to these particular parables is a parable which serves only to highlight the differences. It reads as follows:

To make a comparison, what is this like? It is like a king who hired many labourers, and there was one labourer who worked for him a long while. The labourers came in to get their pay, and that labourer came in with them. The king said to him, 'My son, I shall be free for you (in a moment). These many (labourers) are those who did little work for me, and I am giving them little pay, but as for you, I have a large account to settle with you.' So Israel was asking their pay of God and the Gentiles also were asking their pay of God. And God says to Israel, 'My children, I shall be free for you (in a moment). These Gentiles did little work for me, and I am giving them little pay, but as for you, I have a large account to settle with you.' (Sifra 26: 9.)

This parable helps us to understand the point of view of the Pharisees and Scribes who criticized Jesus for receiving and eating with the tax collectors and sinners. From this perfectly understandable point of view, the tax collectors and sinners no more than the Gentiles deserve the equal treatment and non-discriminatory acceptance Jesus is according them by receiving them in his table fellowship.

But if there is no other known rabbinic parable which constitutes a closer parallel to the parables under immediate consideration, then the historian is left with the strong impression not only that these are authentic parables of Jesus, but that Jesus consciously formulated these parables to deal with the situation that was created by his decision to receive the tax collectors and sinners into his own fellowship and by the negative response this action evoked from the Pharisees and Scribes. Other rabbis may have shared Jesus' attitude in the matter, but we have no record or intimation of it.

4. THE TEST

The final test of the cogency of an argument bearing on the question of the authenticity of any particular teaching of Jesus is the degree to which that teaching can be shown to stand in a complementary relationship to a larger coherent corpus of teachings attributed to him. Therefore, at this point we turn to consider in outline form certain synoptic materials which, on form-critical grounds, are regarded as early units of tradition preserved in Matthew:[1]

A. Matt. 20: 1–16 (the Parable of the Labourers in the Vineyard). Jesus rebukes the attitude of self-righteousness and chides those who resent God's mercy toward sinners (cf. Luke 15: 1–32; 18: 9–14a; Matt. 9:9–13 ‖ Mark 2: 13–17 ‖ Luke 5: 27–32; Matt. 23: 13, 29–31).

B. Matt. 13: 24–30 (the Parable of the Weeds). No effort should be made by man to separate the sinners from the righteous, since this separation will more properly take place in the final judgment (cf. Matt. 13:47–50; Luke 18:9–14a; Matt. 7: 1–5; Luke 15: 1–32; Matt. 20: 1–16; Matt. 9: 9–13; Mark 2: 13–17; Luke 5: 27–32).

C. Matt. 21: 28–32 (the Parable of the Two Sons). He who more truly obeys the will of his father is not the man who quickly assents to the father's will and does not do it, but he who having said no, repents and does it (cf. Luke 15: 1–32; and Luke 18: 9–14a). Obedience rooted in faith and penitence, therefore, is the exemplary life for man, and best prepares him for the Kingdom of God.

D. Matt. 22: 1–10 (the Parable of the Marriage Feast). God is offended at the flagrant disregard of covenantal obligations and has opened his kingdom to those who have no claim upon him (cf. Luke 14: 16–24; Matt. 21: 28–32; Luke 18: 9–14a); Luke 15: 1–32; Matt. 20: 1–16; Matt. 9: 9–13; Mark 2: 13–17; Luke 5: 27–32).

E. Matt. 6: 1–6, 16–18 (on Almsgiving, Prayer and Fasting). We should not do our good works to be seen by men, i.e. we should not be motivated by the desire for recognition and the approval of men (cf. Matt. 23: 5–7), but by gratitude to God for his forgiveness (cf. Luke 18:9–14a; and Luke 7:41–3; and Matt. 18:21–33).

F. Matt. 18: 21–33 (on Reconciliation and the Parable of the Unmerciful Servant). We are obligated to forgive the brother because we have been forgiven by God. We cannot put our forgiveness of

---

[1] There is a critical consensus that the literary units from Matthew, A to L below, belong to the earliest strata of synoptic tradition. The manner in which secondary additions can be identified and separated from the earliest forms of this tradition can be found in Bultmann, *The History of the Synoptic Tradition* (Oxford, 1963) and Jeremias, *The Parables of Jesus* (London, 1963). There is also a critical consensus on the primitive character of most—perhaps all—the literary units referred to in parentheses in this section. To say that there is consensus on the primitive character of these literary units is not to say that there is critical consensus that all these literary units contain authentic sayings of Jesus. If there were such a consensus this particular essay would hardly be needed.

the brother on any calculating basis, since God has forgiven us an infinite debt of sin. We must therefore forgive our brother freely, i.e. from the heart (cf. Luke 7: 41–3; and Luke 15: 1–32).

G. Matt. 5: 43–8 (on Love of One's Enemies). God loves his enemies. Therefore, we should love our own enemies (cf. Luke 18: 9–14 *a*; Matt. 21: 28–32; Luke 15: 1–32; Matt. 20: 1–16; Matt. 22: 1–10; and Luke 14: 16–24; Matt. 9: 9–13; Mark 2: 13–17; Luke 5: 27–32).

H. Matt. 25: 1–12 (the Parable of the Ten Maidens). On the folly of postponing repentance (cf. Luke 12: 35–8; Luke 13: 1–9; Matt. 24: 45–51; Luke 16: 19–25; Matt. 25: 31–46; Matt. 22: 1–10; and Luke 14: 16–24).

I. Matt. 25: 14–30 (the Parable of the Talents). If God is not trustworthy, we will do well to placate him. If he is trustworthy, we offend him by our mistrust. In either case we have nothing to lose and much to gain by living out of our faith in God's faithfulness (cf. Luke 12: 16–20 where the rich fool's laying up treasure for himself is not unlike the man's taking the talent he has received and burying it. In both cases God's judgment separates a man from that which he has laid aside. Cf. also Matt. 6: 19–21).

J. Matt. 13: 44–6 (the Parables of the Hidden Treasure and of the Pearl). When a man enters into the sovereign love of God, everything that he possesses (i.e. his whole structure of worldly security) is joyfully placed at the disposal of that sovereign love (cf. Luke 19: 1–10).

K. Matt. 7: 7–11 (God's Answering of Prayer). We should expectantly trust God. For, if an earthly father is trustworthy, how much more so our Father in heaven! (cf. Luke 11: 5–8; Luke 18: 1–8; and Luke 14: 28–32. We can trust God, because he is trustworthy, cf. Luke 15: 1–32).

L. Matt. 13: 31–3 (the Parables of the Mustard Seed and of the Leaven). The beginnings of the reign of God among men are particular and unimpressive. But God's purpose is a large one and inclusive in design. Therefore, prior to its arrival, no man can discern its coming except from the vantage point of faith (cf. Luke 17: 20). That is, no sign shall be given except the sign of the prophet Jonah—*repentance at the gracious call of God, and self-righteous resentment against the acceptance of this repentance* (cf. Matt. 12: 38–9; Luke 11: 29; Matt. 16: 1–4; Mark 8: 11–12; Luke 15: 1–32; and Matt. 20: 1–16; Matt. 9:

9–13; Mark 2: 13–17; Luke 5: 27–32. Cf. also Luke 14: 28–32—that which God has begun he will complete!).

Four things can be verified by a careful study of this outline:

First, the parables found only in Luke, taken individually and as a whole, stand in a close and complementary relationship to this early tradition preserved in Matthew.

Second, this early Matthean tradition, while predominantly parabolic, is inclusive of logia found in the Sermon on the Mount (5:43–8; 6: 1–18; and 7: 7–11), and closely related to important biographical *Apophthegms* [*Chreiai*] (Matt. 9: 9–13 ‖ Mark 2: 13–17 ‖ Luke 5: 27–32; Matt. 12: 38–9 ‖ Luke 11: 29; Matt. 16: 1–4 ‖ Mark 8: 11–12), as well as some of the woes (cf. Matt. 23: 29–31).[1]

Third, the teaching represented in these materials taken as a whole has a highly integrated and organic character, i.e. it is coherent.

Fourth, Matt. 20: 1–16; Luke 15: 11–32 and 18: 9–14*a* are clearly organic to the corpus (cf. A, B, C, D, E, F, G, K, and L), and can be seen to be central to an important nucleus of this teaching (cf. A, B, C, D, E, F and G).

5. CONCLUSIONS

Our argument has led us to the following tentative conclusion: since these literary units in Matthew are independent of their Lucan parallels and have had a separate history of transmission, the close relationship between the parables in Luke and this early tradition in Matthew is best explained by positing some common origin. That is, taken as a whole, all these separable literary units from Matthew and Luke exhibit those characteristics of coherence and individuality that we would expect if we knew that with a reasonable number of possible exceptions they came from a single creative mind endowed with great imaginative powers. While it is possible that some unknown religious genius is responsible for the core of this corpus of teaching, there is no reason to think this to have been the case. And when the historian considers the range and difficulty of the historical

---

[1] The formal critical grounds for regarding some biographical *Apophthegms* (*Chreiai*) as tradition formulated during the eyewitness period is discussed by Bultmann, *op. cit.* pp. 27–69, and more recently by W. R. Farmer in 'Notes on a Literary and Form-Critical Analysis of Some of the Synoptic Material Peculiar to Luke', *NTS* 8 (1962), 307–13. N.b. Matt. 18: 21–2 is a *Chreia*.

problems that would be unnecessarily created by denying that Jesus formulated any of this teaching, he readily assents to the view that, while these sayings attributed to Jesus may include some that did not come from him, it is highly probable that they include many which did. After taking into consideration all such related questions, it is not difficult for the New Testament historian to conclude that Matt. 20: 1–16; Luke 15: 11–32; 18: 10–14*a* should be included in this latter group. For such reasons as these, we need not hesitate to affirm that Jesus *did* rebuke self-righteousness and *did* chide those who resented God's mercy toward the tax collectors and sinners.

If this historical conclusion is valid has it any importance for our understanding of Jesus? This is a legitimate concern because Jesus is not just the historically remote point of origin of Christianity but the present continuing historical centre of Christian faith. On the basis of what has been demonstrated in this essay, can we say something about the *character* of Jesus as well as his preaching?[1] In rebuking self-righteousness and chiding those who resented God's mercy toward sinners, does Jesus disclose to us something about the kind of man he was? Do we not see him in relationship to other men? Can we not understand this kind of human concern for others, and are we not moved by it? Do we see only love on a person to person basis? Do we not see more? Do we not see a concern for community? Self-righteousness on the part of individuals or groups is one of the most serious corrupting influences affecting the health and integrity of communal existence. Individual and collective self-righteousness is the cement with which outdated and unjust social, political and ecclesiastical structures are made defensible over against the storms

---

[1] To say anything about the character of Jesus is to presuppose some positive correspondence between his words and actions on the one hand, and his intentions on the other. However, it is not essential to explore the inner self-consciousness of a man in order to say something about his character. Character is something that is largely defined by objective criteria. It is something public more than something private (although there is of course a personal and private side to character). Character is the mark that a man makes or 'engraves' on his society. We can know something about the character of Jesus to the degree that the understanding of life which is expressed in the sayings attributed to Jesus was actually represented by Jesus in his own life situation, i.e. through his words and actions. (Thus the question whether we can in good conscience believe that Jesus actually used certain sayings becomes a matter of some importance.) The Church witnesses to the character of Jesus, in so far as it bears witness to, or keeps alive and renews the mark that he made on his own society.

of protest of those who wish to see economic, political and religious changes take place. The privileged person or class is secure only so long as it is possible to clothe the position of privilege with real or imagined garments of righteousness. When these garments are contritely recognized to be at best only like filthy rags, every real need for change then becomes a possibility for communal renewal. Therefore, for Jesus to rebuke the prideful self-righteousness of religious authorities was to strike at an important source of contra-redemptive influence in his own life situation and to encourage the continuation of the individual and covenantal renewal that was taking place in response to his preaching. The modern Christian who knows himself as a sinner dependent upon the unmerited grace of God is glad to know that Jesus not only received sinners, but defended this action when it was criticized; and in so far as it may be possible, he is moved to go and do likewise. And as a religious (righteous) man, subject to spiritual pride, the modern Christian finds it truly revolutionary to be caught up short by the realization that when he openly or secretly thanks God that he is not like the rest of men, not even like the elder son, he cuts himself off not only from his brother but from his heavenly Father as well.

Is there not then in this compassionate but disconcerting and re-volutionary stance of Jesus a dynamic source of redemptive power which works against sinful attempts to structure human existence on some exclusivistic ground? Is not this the main source of the redemptive power which provides the basis for that distinctively Christian style of life wherein men work joyfully for reconciling forms of human existence open to God's grace and open to a future conditioned not only by sin but much more by the unbounded sovereign love of God, and by that faith which leads men to submit to the judgment and trust themselves utterly to the mercy that is intrinsic to, and inherent in, that love?

Is not this stance, this personal structuring and restructuring of historical existence, this shaping of the realities of our human environ-ment, and the compassion and joy associated with this creative stance, that which lies behind and gives theological depth and direction to Christian soteriology and ethics? There is much more to the humanity of Christ than has here come to light. But does not this understanding carry us quite near, indeed right into, the very heart of the matter?

7

REFLEXIONS ON TRADITION:
THE ABOTH REVISITED

W. D. DAVIES

As a small token of the honour and friendship in which I hold Professor Knox, I had hoped to present a re-examination of a theme to
which he has devoted a great deal of creative thought—that of memory in the New Testament. Unfortunately circumstances conspired
against this. But during the last year I have been compelled to devote
myself to another, not wholly unrelated, theme. A recent re-reading
of the *Pirqê Aboth* (henceforward Aboth) raised again for me the
question of the nature of tradition in the Judaism within which Jesus
was born and from which the early Christians were largely drawn. I
shall here simply set forth certain significant aspects of Jewish tradition as it reveals itself in the Aboth. To recognize these, I suggest, is to
throw light on some elements at least in the tradition preserved in the
New Testament and to be warned against certain erroneous conclusions that might, at first encounter, be drawn from it.

On first reading the Aboth I felt

> ...like some watcher of the skies
> When a new planet swims into his ken...

To read the Aboth after being steeped in classical Greek and classical
Hebrew was at once to enter a new and strange world—that of the
rabbis. But the Aboth is a very singular work: it is utterly unlike the
rest of the Mishnah. All the other tractates of the Mishnah deal with
halakoth, minute points of law. But the Aboth contains no halakoth:
it is not concerned with the legal disputes and niceties of the rest of
the Mishnah and is, in some ways, like a miniature Book of Proverbs,
designed especially for rabbis and their students. But despite its
singularity within the Mishnah, the Aboth expresses the quintessence
of Pharisaism. Indeed, Herford has argued that the Aboth was designed as the epilogue to the Mishnah. All its contents were gathered
together in order to set forth the meaning or spirit of the completed

Mishnaic corpus.[1] It is uncertain whether we should follow Herford in this epilogic view of the Aboth,[2] but that it expresses the genius of the Mishnah and of the Pharisaism which gave it birth, in non-halakic terms, is clear. The Aboth is a document of Pharisaism. Here in the sharp, compact and memorable sayings of the forty rabbis mentioned, unliterary as they are, the central concepts of Pharisaism and the Pharisaic conviction that the purification of life comes by the halakah, the hedge built around the Torah, come to superb expression. Just as the New Testament, centring in Jesus Christ, reveals the nature of Christianity, so the Aboth, centring in the Torah, reveals the spirit of Pharisaism.[3] This was why to read the Aboth for the first time, even after being immersed in the Old Testament, was to enter a new world. And the significance of this new rabbinic world for the understanding of the New Testament became at once apparent. Here was the immediate mother-soil of the gospels and of much in all the rest of the New Testament. During the last thirty years there has been an increasing recognition of this fact: the corresponding shift in New Testament studies will need no documentation.[4] So marked has this shift been that some have been moved to protest against an incipient pro-Semitism in New Testament studies.[5]

But the recent re-reading of the Aboth has brought home to me again not only the relevance of this rabbinic tractate for the study of the New Testament, but its importance for the true understanding of Judaism itself. A closer attention to the Aboth would have helped us sooner to discover and appreciate the true nature of Judaism in

[1] R. T. Herford, *The Ethics of the Talmud* (New York, 1962), pp. 9 ff.

[2] However, the objection that it would be more natural, if its aim were such as Herford asserts, for Aboth to be the prologue to the Mishnah, is a Western one. Professor Heschel pointed out to me that haggadic materials often close tractates in the Mishnah, see, for example, the end of Mishnah Sotah: he finds in the inclusion of the Aboth in the Mishnah the recognition by Judah the Prince that Haggadah was as significant as Halakah. Herford refuses to regard Aboth as haggadic, *op. cit.*

[3] Strikingly enough the Aboth never mentions God directly, although it uses the circumlocution 'heaven'. But we cannot speak of any *Toraholatry* in the Aboth, because the Torah is God's gift, any more than we can speak of a Christolatry in the New Testament, because it was God who was 'in Christ'.

[4] See, for example, H. J. Cadbury, 'New Testament Scholarship: Fifty Years in Retrospect' in *JBR* 28 (1960), 144 ff.

[5] The late W. L. Knox once wrote to me about disreputable pro-Semitism in New Testament scholarship.

the New Testament period and delivered us from the simple—and false—antitheses in which we have previously too often indulged. I shall now deal briefly with a few of these antitheses which we have increasingly learnt to reject, but which a knowledge of the Aboth might have spared us from having accepted in the first place.

I

An antithesis familiar to all students of the Bible is that between priest and prophet, the former being the custodian and transmitter of law and tradition and the latter their critic. A classic example of the antithesis is that of R. H. Charles, who set prophecy and law over against each other in the Old Testament and carried over this anti- thesis into his interpretation of apocalyptic, the heir of prophecy, as opposed to Pharisaism, the heir of the law. His words deserve quota- tion.

But when prophecy became impossible owing to the claims of the Law, its place was taken, from the fourth century onwards, by apocalyptic... Essentially, therefore, prophecy and apocalyptic were identical...[1]

But the opening words of the Aboth are as follows:

Moses received the Law from Sinai and committed it to Joshua, and Joshua to the elders, and the elders to the Prophets; and the Prophets committed it to the men of the Great Synagogue...(Danby's translation).[2]

In the above quotation the prophets are listed among the transmitters of the law. The Hebrew text has no article before the term *torah*, so that Danby's translation might be misleading. By the term *torah* here is meant not only the Written Law and the Oral Law in all its mani- festations, but even the rules of hermeneutics, of grammar, syntax,

---

[1] *Religious Development between the Old and the New Testament* (London, 1925), p. 14, n. 1. Again recall the words of B. H. Streeter: 'Christianity began as a de-ossification, so to speak, of the emphatically monotheistic legalism of Pharisaic Judaism. It was as though the Lord, who spake of old by Amos and Isaiah, had awaked as one out of sleep, and like a giant refreshed with wine... John the Baptist...summons to righteousness against the background of that hope of a catastrophic world-redemption which had been generated by two centuries of Jewish apocalyptic...' (*Cambridge Ancient History*, 11 (Cambridge, 1936), 264).

[2] Translations from the Mishnah are from Danby unless otherwise stated.

punctuation and cantillation.[1] The fourth link in the transmitters of 'the Law', in this widest sense, were the prophets. The figures usually connected, in the scholarly mind, until very recently, and still certainly in the popular mind, with criticism and revolt against tradition here emerge as the transmitters of tradition. There can be little doubt that the canonical prophets are meant. On the other hand, the priests, who have usually been associated especially with the law,[2] are not mentioned at all.

The omission of 'the priests' is striking. Can we account for it? It cannot be due to any denigration of priests as such, because Simeon the Righteous, who is mentioned in Aboth 1 : 2, was a High Priest[3], and he includes the (Temple-)service, the special prerogative of priests, among the three pillars on which the world stands. Similarly, among the 'pairs', who transmitted tradition from Antigonus of Soko, the first mentioned, Jose b. Joezer of Zeredah, was a priest.[4] From an early date priest and prophet are recognized by Pharisaism as part of the chain of tradition. But the question remains why the priesthood as such, as opposed to individual priests, is not mentioned as a link in the chain as are the prophets. Was it because Pharisaism was essentially a lay movement which naturally tended to overlook the significance of the priesthood as a whole, although it could not but recognize the role of acknowledged priestly links in the tradition?[5] This may have been so. But on the other hand, the inclusion of the prophets, as a body, in the chain of tradition constitutes a problem when it is recognized that considerable criticism of a de-

---

[1] W. Bacher, *Tradition und Tradenten* (Leipzig, 1914), pp. 35 ff.

[2] See G. Östborn, *Tora in the Old Testament* (Lund, 1945), *ad rem*.

[3] This holds whatever view be taken of him. It is generally assumed that Simeon is either Simeon I, the high-priest from *c.* 300–270 B.C., who is called 'the just' in Josephus, *Antiquities*, 12. 2. 5, or Simeon II, probably a grandson of the former, the high-priest around 220–200 B.C. The majority of scholars favour the identification with Simeon II, who also seems to be the high priest, Simeon, praised by the author of Sirach at the end of his praise for his forefathers (50: 1–24).

[4] Mishnah Ḥagigah 2: 7. He is mentioned with Jose b. Johanan of Jerusalem in Sot. 9: 9. In Gen. R. 65: 22 Jakum of Zeroroth was a nephew of R. Jose b. Joezer of Zeredah. (Note that here Jose is a rabbi.) Since Jakum is usually identified with Alcimus, the High Priest at the time of the Maccabean revolt, we *may* draw the inference that, since Alcimus is a priest, his uncle is also a priest. My pupil T. J. Kitchen pointed this out to me. See *Jewish Encyclopedia*, 7 (New York and London, 1904), 242. But this cannot be certain.

[5] On the nature of Pharisaism, see L. Finkelstein, *The Pharisees* (Philadelphia, 1940).

generate prophecy had arisen. Prophets had fallen on evil days. By the third century A.D. it was explicitly maintained that the sages had replaced the prophets as the custodians of prophecy. R. Abdimi of Haifa (A.D. 279–320) said: 'From the day whereon the Temple was laid waste, Prophecy was taken from the prophets and given to the Sages.'[1] The inclusion of 'the prophets' and the exclusion of 'the priests' from the chain of Pharisaic tradition remains a puzzle. At least, it breaks down the familiar opposition of prophet to law and priesthood.[2]

The rabbinic sources connect the prophets with the tradition in two ways. First, they are regarded as bearers or transmitters of the tradition. In this connexion, the last of the prophets of the Old Testament, that is, Haggai, Zechariah, and Malachi were regarded as especially important. They were an indispensable link with the men of the Great Synagogue.[3] In the Aboth de Rabbi Nathan these three prophets are expressly mentioned as having come up from the Exile as they are also in the following:

Rabban b. Hanah (A.D. 320–75) said in R. Johanan's (A.D. 277–320) name: Three prophets went up with them from the Exile: one testified to them about (the dimensions of) the altar; another testified to them about the site of the altar; and the third testified to them that they could sacrifice even though there was no Temple.[4] In a Baraitha it was taught, R. Eleazer b. Jacob (A.D. 80–120 or 140–65) said: Three prophets went up with them from the Exile: one who testified to them about (the dimensions of) the altar, and the site of the altar; another who testified to them that they could sacrifice even though there was no Temple; and a third who testified to them that the Torah should be written in Assyrian characters. (Bab. Zeb. 62 a.)

---

[1] See W. D. Davies, *Paul and Rabbinic Judaism* (London, 1955), pp. 210 ff.

[2] It should be noted that Moses is both the mediator of Torah and the prophet; see Deut. 18: 15. In himself he breaks down the distinction between law and prophecy. Professor Heschel referred me to *Ex. R.* 42: 8, where Rabbi Joshua b. Levi (A.D. 219–79) says: 'Each one was fully occupied with his own prophecy, save Moses who delivered all the prophecies of others with his own, with the result that all who prophesied later were inspired by the prophecy of Moses...' See A. J. Heschel, *Torah min ha-Shamain* (London and New York, forthcoming), vol. 2, 262.

[3] For the various theories on this, see G. F. Moore, *Judaism*, 3 (Cambridge, Mass., 1930), 7–11.

[4] The editor of the passage in the Soncino translation takes these three prophets to be Haggai, Zechariah, Malachi. The reason why they could sacrifice even though there was no Temple was that the sanctity of the Temple had hallowed the spot for all time (Soncino translation, editor, p. 305, nn. 4, 5).

It is possible that Malachi should be identified with Ezra the architect of post-exilic Judaism.

It has been taught, R. Joshua b. Korha (A.D. 140–65) said: Malachi is the same as Ezra, and the Sages say that Malachi was his proper name. R. Nahman (A.D. 320–75) said: There is good ground for accepting the view that Malachi was the same as Ezra. (The grounds for this view are then given.) For it is written in the prophecy of Malachi: *Judah hath dealt treacherously and an abomination is committed in Israel and in Jerusalem, for Judah hath profaned the holiness of the Lord which he loveth and hath married the daughter of a strange God* (Mal. 2:11). And who was it that put away the strange women? Ezra, as it is written, *And Shechaniah, the son of Tehrel, and one of the sons of Elam answered and said unto Ezra: We have broken faith with our God and have married foreign women* (Ezra 10: 2). (Bab. Meg. 15 a.)

In Bab. Meg. 3 a it is stated that Jonathan ben Uzziel, the author of the Targum, a pupil of Hillel, received the tradition from the three prophets mentioned. What this means is that Jonathan ben Uzziel's work rested on an ancient tradition going back to the prophets, so that the interpretation of biblical texts in the School of Hillel may be presumed to have rested on the work of the prophets. The passage in Bab. Meg. reads:

R. Jeremiah—or some say R. Ḥiyya b. Abba—also said: The *Targum* of the Pentateuch was composed by Onkelos the proselyte under the guidance of R. Eleazer and R. Joshua. The *Targum* of the Prophets was composed by Jonathan ben Uzziel under the guidance of Haggai, Zechariah and Malachi...

The above passages place the prophets in the stream of transmitters of the tradition. They are placed after the elders. The significance of thus placing prophets in the chain of tradition must not be overlooked in another dimension. The reference in Aboth 1: 1 to the elders looks back to Josh. 24: 31; Judg. 2: 7. The former passage, which is re-peated in Judg. 2: 7, reads: 'And Israel served the Lord all the days of Joshua, and all the days of the elders who outlived Joshua and had known all the work which the Lord did for Israel.' But part of this work which the Lord had done for Israel had been the giving of the Spirit to the elders, as is clear from Num. 11: 16–17:

And the Lord said to Moses, 'Gather for me seventy men of the elders of Israel, whom you know to be the elders of the people and officers over them; and bring them to the tent of meeting, and let them take their stand there with you. And I will come down and talk with you there; and I will take some of the spirit which is upon you and put it upon them; and they shall bear the burden of the people with you, that you may not bear it yourself alone...'

Moses, the mediator of the Torah, is a man of the Spirit and the Spirit that was given to him was transmitted to the elders who accompanied him to Mount Sinai to receive the Torah. So far from there being any opposition between law and Spirit the opposite seems to have been the case: the transmitters of Torah are bearers of the Spirit.[1] But the Spirit is also *par excellence* the inspiration of prophecy. This assertion is so well attested that no details need be given in support of it. For Pharisaism, law, Spirit, prophecy belonged to-gether as part of one complex. And the figure of Joshua—the second link in the Pharisaic chain—is also marked by the Spirit (Num. 27: 17; Deut. 34: 9 ff.). In Num. the giving of the Spirit to the elders, which means that they are given the gift of prophecy, precedes the giving of it to Joshua, and in Midrash Rabbah much is made of the fact that, although Moses gives of his Spirit to the elders, it remains undi-minished, and he is still able to endow Joshua with it (see Num. R. on 11: 17, Soncino translation, p. 672).

But the prophets are not merely links in a chain of Pharisaic tradi-tion; they themselves are also the source of halakoth: they create 'tradition'. Bacher has collected the references to laws which were instigated by or transmitted through the prophets. The first-century Shammai himself rooted one of his halakoth in the prophets, as is clear from Bab. Kidd. 43 *a*. This contains a comment on Mish. Kidd. 2: 1, which reads:

A man may betroth a woman either by his own act or by that of his agent; and a woman may become betrothed either by her own act or by that of her agent. A man may give his daughter in betrothal while she is still in her girlhood either by his own act or by that of his agent.

The *gemara* to this is concerned with the principle of agency. Shammai bases one of his halakoth on the prophet Haggai. The House of Hillel and the House of Shammai differed on the question whether inten-

---

[1] In Num. R. on 11: 16–17 (Soncino translation, p. 660), the elders are identified by R. Tanhuma (A.D. 427–68) with teachers.

tion is to be taken as deed. Shammai held that intention is as deed. The pertinent words are as follows:

Now, when it is taught: If he says to his agent, 'Go forth and slay a soul', the latter is liable, and his sender is exempt. Shammai the Elder said on the authority of Haggai the prophet: His sender is liable, for it is said, thou hast slain with the sword of the children of Ammon (2 Sam. 12: 9).[1]

Shammai holds the sender liable to the severest penalty as if he were the actual murderer. Hillel allows a less severe penalty for the sender. (Is he here more removed from Jesus than Shammai? Jesus, like Shammai, emphasizes intention.)

Another example of strictly legal, teaching activity being ascribed to the prophets occurs in Bab. R. Hash. 19 b. The Mish. R. Hash. 1 : 2 reads as follows:

Because of six New Moons do messengers go forth (to proclaim the time of their appearing): because of Nisan, to determine the time of Passover, because of Ab, to determine the time of the Fast...and because of Adar, to determine the time of Purim (Adar 14th)...

The *gemara* on this Mishnah in Bab. R. Hash. 19 b reads:

R. Joshua b. Levi (A.D. 219–79) testified on behalf of the holy community of Jerusalem concerning the two Adars, that they are sanctified on the day of their prolongation [the thirtieth day is known as the day of prolongation as it is the day which is added to make the preceding month full, i.e. contain thirty days]. In the case of the two Adars, the thirtieth day of each is sanctified as the New Moon of the next month [so the editor of the Soncino translation, p. 81]. This is equivalent to saying that we make them defective, but we do not make them full, and excludes the statement made in a discourse by R. Nahman b. Hisda (A.D. 375–427); (for R. Nahman b. Hisda stated in a discourse): R. Semai (A.D. 200–20) testified in the name of Haggai, Zechariah and Malachi concerning the two Adars that if they [the Beth Din] desired, they could make both of them full, and if they desired they could make one full and the other defective; and such was their custom in the Diaspora. In the name of our teacher [Rab], however, they said: One is always to be full and the next defective, unless you have been informed that the New Moon has been fixed at its proper time [i.e. that the Beth Din in Jerusalem fixed the New Moon of Adar II

[1] Notice that, although Shammai rested the halakah on the prophet Haggai, he also gave reasons based on the text for his position. (See Soncino translation, p. 215.)

on the thirtieth day of the first Adar, the thirtieth day always being regarded as the 'proper time' of New Moon] (The Soncino translation, p. 81, n. 3).

It is striking that here Rab goes against a prophetic permission. Typically, on such a matter perhaps, the prophets are more lenient than Rab.

In Bab. Succ. 44 a, a ceremony connected with the Festival of Tabernacles was regarded by some as instituted by the prophets.

It was stated, R. Johanan (A.D. 279–320) and R. Joshua b. Levi (A.D. 219–79) differ. One holds that the rite of the willow-branch is an institution of the prophets [i.e. according to the editor of the Soncino translation, p. 203, Haggai, Zechariah and Malachi, the prophets of the Second Temple, to whom tradition ascribes many enactments], the other holds that the willow-branch is a usage of the prophets ['Sc. they had it only as a custom, and since it did not have the force of a law, no benediction over it is necessary' (Soncino translation, p. 203, n. 6)]. It can be concluded that it was R. Johanan who said, 'It is an institution of the prophets', since R. Abbahu stated in the name of R. Johanan, 'The rite of the willow-branch is an institution of the prophets'. This is conclusive.[1]

Again, in Bab. Pes. 117a, the commandment to recite the Hallel Psalms (Ps. 113–18) on every important occasion is traced to the prophets:

The prophets among them [in Israel at the Red Sea] ordained that Israel should recite it [the Hallel Psalms] at every important epoch and at every misfortune—may it not come upon them—and when they are redeemed they recite it [in gratitude] for their redemption.

This is given as what the 'Sages taught', that is, it is an old tradition. In the same way the division of the priests into twenty-four classes is traced to the prophets in Mish. Taan. 4: 1–2, which reads:

Three times in the year the priests four times lift up their hands during the day (at the Morning Prayer, at the Additional Prayer, at the Afternoon Prayer and at the Closing of the Gates): namely, on the days of fasting, at the *Maamads* and on the Day of Atonement. What are the *Maamads*? In that it is written, Command the children of Israel and say unto them, My oblation, my food for my offerings made by fire, of a sweet savour unto me, shall ye observe to offer unto me in their due season (Num. 28 : 2)

[1] See Soncino translation on Bab. Succ. 44 a, p. 203.

—how can a man's offering be offered while he does not stand by it? Therefore the first prophets (David and Solomon) ordained twenty-four Courses, and for every Course there was a *Maamad* in Jerusalem, made up of priests, and Levites and Israelites. When the time was come for a Course to go up, the priests and Levites thereof went up to Jerusalem, and the Israelites that were of the self-same Course came together unto their own cities to read the story of Creation, and the men of the *Maamad*[1] fasted four days in the week...

In the Jerusalem Talmud, Erub. 21. c.15, the celebration of the New Year festival on two days was traced to the first prophets. Schwab translates as follows: 'Les sages reconnaissent, comme R. Juda, que les 2 jours de fête du nouvel an ont été institués par les 1ers prophètes...' (*Talmud Jérusalem*, 3 (Paris, 1879), 236). From 1 Macc. 9: 54 it is clear that the Temple was regarded as having been built according to measurements supplied by the prophets.

Moreover in the hundred fifty and third year, in the second month, Alcimus commanded that the wall of the inner court of the sanctuary should be pulled down; he pulled down also the works of the prophets (τὰ ἔργα τῶν προφητῶν)...

For this Alcimus suffered great torment. Josephus, in the *Antiquities*, xii. 10. 6, makes it explicit that the wall taken down by Alcimus had been there of old and had been built by the prophets.

The view of the prophets which emerges from the above is that of men standing well within the cultic and legal tradition of Pharisaism. It is striking how the cultus and its activity are assumed to have interested the prophets, not in any simple, condemnatory sense, but as part of their living constructive concern. The antitheses prophet and priest, Spirit and law, which have played so great a part in theological interpretations of Christianity and Judaism, cannot have been so sharp as has been commonly held. Exaggeration must, however, be avoided. The passages showing a connexion between the pro-

[1] *Maamad*: lit. 'place of standing' is 'the name given to a group of representatives from outlying districts, corresponding to the four "courses of priests". Part of them went up to the Temple as witnesses of the offering of the sacrifices (Taan. 4: 2), and part came together in their own town, where they held prayers at fixed times during the day coinciding with the fixed times of sacrifice in the Temple. This is the origin of the Synagogue system, in which the various daily offices were called by the names made familiar in the routine of the Temple' (Danby, *The Mishnah*, p. 794).

phecy and the law which Bacher was able to gather within the sea of the rabbinic sources are few. It must also be recognized that the rabbis did consider that the age of prophecy and with it the age of the Spirit had ceased with the last of the prophets,[1] that is, Haggai, Zechariah and Malachi, although, as we have pointed out elsewhere, there were phenomena in Judaism which pointed to the continued presence of the Spirit after the last of the prophets.

The point to be made here is that re-reading the Aboth has suggested precisely what decades of work by scholars on the Old Testament have revealed, that prophet and priest, law and prophecy, belong together. Attention to rabbinic sources would have spared us many exaggerated notions of the opposition between law and prophecy, priest and prophet. Under the impact of the work of such scholars as Aubrey Johnson,[2] Zimmerli[3] and others, the traditional gulf between these has been gradually lessened. It has been claimed that for a time even Amos worked as a cultic prophet in Bethel.[4] The attempt to prove that the cultic prophets were all false prophets has broken down. Priest and prophet, law and prophecy were not antithetical or mutually exclusive. Prophecy as well as law, prophet as well as priest, are endemic in Judaism. So much the opening of the Aboth makes clear.[5]

[1] Bab. Yoma, 9 *b*; Bab. Sot. 48 *b*; Bab. Snh. 111 *a*.
[2] *The Cultic Prophet in Ancient Israel* (Cardiff, 1942).
[3] *Das Gesetz und die Propheten: zum Verständnis des Alten Testaments* (Göttingen, 1963). But see also R. E. Clements, *Prophecy and Covenant* (London, 1965), especially chapter 4, 'The Law in the Pre-Exilic Prophets'. He emphasizes the criticism of the cultus by the canonical prophets: for him Amos was never a cultic prophet.
[4] J. Lindblom, *Prophecy in Ancient Israel* (Philadelphia, 1962), pp. 183, 209.
[5] In view of the position taken by R. H. Charles, mentioned above, it is also important to note here that the rigid separation of Apocalyptic and Pharisaism is no longer possible, see my *Christian Origins and Judaism* (London, 1962), pp. 19–30, on 'Apocalyptic and Pharisaism'. To note only one point, not mentioned there, the *Shemoneh Esreh* in all its members shows the influence of apocalyptic ideas. Notice further that on the Day of Atonement itself portions of the Book of Daniel were read to the High Priest; see Mishnah Yoma 1: 6. To some extent all minds in Israel were coloured by Apocalyptic. And, finally, as Professor Heschel again reminded me, the mere fact that both the law and the prophets (the *Haphtaroth*) were already being read regularly in synagogue services in the first century meant that prophecy and law were not conceived of as opposed. But see D. Rössler, *Untersuchungen zur Theologie der jüdischen Apokalyptik und der pharisäischen Orthodoxie* (Neukirchen Kr Moers, 1960), for a different approach.

2

The next antithesis to which a re-reading of the Aboth is pertinent is one which is increasingly being held in truer perspective: it is that between Semitic or Palestinian Judaism and Hellenistic or Diaspora Judaism in the first century. This dichotomy has invaded synoptic, Pauline and Johannine studies. In synoptic studies the detection of Hellenistic elements in the tradition about Jesus was taken to point to a late date and an extra-Palestinian setting. In Pauline studies, it enabled Schweitzer to set a Paul, who, he thought, was dominated by Palestinian categories, over against John, who was dominated by Hellenistic ones. On the other hand, the same antithesis enabled Montefiore to interpret Paul as a Diaspora Jew who, had he known the superior Judaism of Palestine, would never have embraced the gospel. The dichotomy between Palestinian and Diaspora Judaism made it possible to localize Paul conveniently, according to one's approach, either within or without Palestinian Judaism. In Johannine studies the dichotomy has been evident in works ranging from Dean Inge's famous essay to the latest work by C. H. Dodd, who is aware of the alleged dichotomy, but does not allow it to tyrannize over his treatment.

I have elsewhere argued against such a dichotomy, and, as already indicated, it is increasingly being questioned.[1] Here I merely wish to

[1] See my article 'Paul and Judaism' in *The Bible in Modern Scholarship*, ed. J. Philip Hyatt (New York, Nashville, 1965), pp. 178–83, for bibliographical details. Add, to the details there supplied, the following: A. Schlatter, *Markus, Der Evangelist für die Griechen* (Stuttgart, 1935); *Der Evangelist Matthaeus, Seine Sprache, sein Ziel, seine Selbständigkeit* (Stuttgart, 1948), *ad rem;* B. Lifschitz, on 'L'hellénisation des Juifs de Palestine' in *RB* 4 (1965), 520–38. Following S. Lieberman he rejects the view propounded by G. Alon (who wrote in Hebrew) that only the maritime areas had been Hellenized. 'La langue grecque et la culture hellénique avaient pénétré dans toutes les communautés juives de l'Orient Grec' (p. 538). I have garnered in recent reading the following items to confirm this.

   (*a*) *On the educational side*, there was a considerable influence from Hellenism on the Jewish schools that evolved in the first century. See B. Gerhardsson, *Memory and Manuscript* (Uppsala, 1961), pp. 27, 56, 68, 88 f.; V. A. Tcherikover, *Hellenistic Civilization* (Eng. trans., Philadelphia, 1959), *ad rem.*

   (*b*) *On the literary side*, note that the Wisd. of Sol. is regarded by J. Reider and J. Fichtner as a Palestinian work. See J. Reider, *The Book of Wisdom* (New York, 1957), p. 18, n. 81; J. Fichtner, *Weisheit Salomos, Handbuch zum Alten Testament*, 6 (Tübingen, 1938), pp. 7–8, who recognizes Greek influence but holds that the work remains essentially Jewish. On the Servant Songs as a drama or tragedy

point out how a re-reading of the Aboth has provided many side-lights which make the falsity of the dichotomy still further clear.

patterned directly after Greek tragedy, with a distinct succession of speakers including a chorus and with easily recognizable dramatic progression of time and action, see Julian Morgenstern, 'The Suffering Servant—A New Solution', in *VetT* 11 (1961), 292–320 and 406–31; 13 (1963), 321–32. The Servant Songs—it is suggested—were written by a Galilean in touch with an Athenian garrison at Dor in South Galilee in 460–450 B.C., especially under the influence of Aeschylus. This view is merely mentioned here; I have not examined it. Again Philo has been claimed to know more about Palestinian Judaism than did Josephus; so S. Belkin, *Philo and the Oral Law* (Harvard University Press, 1940). See also T. F. Glasson, *Greek Influence in Jewish Eschatology* (London, 1961).

(c) *On the philosophical side*, one indirect cause of Aher's (Elisha b. Abuyha) apostasy was apparently his interest in Greek philosophy and literature. According to Bab. Ḥag. 15 b, Aher did not stop singing Greek songs and when he would get up in the academy many unworthy Greek books would drop from his lap.

For the view that Hillel betrays a Sophistic element, see I. Sonne, *Louis Ginsberg Jubilee Volume* (American Association for Jewish Research, New York, 1945), on 'The Schools of Shammai and Hillel seen from within'. On Platonism in the Old Testament, see E. Burrows, 'Some Cosmological Patterns in Babylonian Religion' in *The Labyrinth*, ed. by S. H. Hooke (London, 1935), pp. 59 ff. I discovered a Platonic note in connexion with the Torah in Gen.R. 17.5, which reads: 'The incomplete form of the heavenly wisdom is the Torah' (Soncino translation, p. 136, of *nwblt ḥkmh šl m'lh twrh*).

(d) *On the archaeological side:* G. E. Wright and L. E. Toombs, *BA* 2 (1957), 19 ff. and 92 ff. respectively, report Hellenistic influences in Shechem. W. F. Albright, *The Archaeology of Palestine* (Harmondsworth, Middlesex, 1949), shows that the names of the deceased were written on ossuaries in Hebrew, Aramaic and Greek. In an excavation conducted in 1945 by E. L. Sukenik a tomb was discovered in the suburbs of Jerusalem containing two casques bearing Greek inscriptions, see *AJA* 51 (Princeton, 1947), 351 ff.; A. Parrot, *Golgotha and the Church of the Holy Sepulchre* (Eng. trans., London, 1957), pp. 113 ff. The buildings of Herod the Great were in the Hellenistic tradition, see Josephus, *Bell.* 1.21.4. Samaria was renamed Sebaste by Herod in honour of Caesar; see G. E. Wright, *Biblical Archaeology* (Philadelphia and London, 1957), pp. 218 ff., for the magnificent temple dedicated to Caesar; G. A. Reisner, C. S. Fisher and D. G. Lyon, *Harvard Excavations at Samaria 1908–1910*, 1 (1924), 48 ff.; J. W. Crowfoot, K. M. Kenyon and E. L. Sukenik, *The Buildings at Samaria* (London, 1942), pp. 123 f. Caesarea also shows Hellenistic influences: Antonia in Jerusalem was built in honour of Mark Antony, Josephus, *Bell.* 5.4.4; 5.5.8. On a pavement near Antonia there is a representation of a play board by Roman soldiers, see *RB* 59 (Jerusalem, 1952), 413 ff. At Nazareth a slab of marble was found in 1878 containing a Greek inscription possibly from the time of Claudius (A.D. 41–54); for the text and bibliography on this see R. K. Harrison, *The Archaeology of the New Testament* (New York, 1964), pp. 32 and 107, n. 66.

Goodenough has recently been criticized by E. E. Urbach in *IEJ* 9 (1959), 150 ff., in an article entitled 'The Rabbinical Laws of Idolatry in the Second and Third Centuries in the Light of Archaeological and Historical Facts'. Good-

First, let us consider the purpose of the chain of tradition with which the Aboth opens. Here an article by Bickerman is very important. It is entitled 'La Chaîne de la Tradition Pharisienne'. Bickerman contrasts the lack of historical concern which prevailed in the Hellenistic world between the death of Alexander and the period of Augustus with the prevalence of such a concern from the beginning of the Roman Empire onwards.[1] At that time the Greeks began more and more to look back to classical Greece, its life, art and literature. And, at the same time, what happened in the Hellenistic world—the return to the past—also happened in Rome[2] and Jerusalem.

Connected with this is a development within the schools of philosophy. Greek philosophers founded 'schools' in which the teaching of the founder was transmitted from generation to generation by successive scholars.[3] There were Platonic, Aristotelian, Stoic, Epicurean 'schools' in which such transmission took place. For example, Plato's Academy continued to exist during more than eight centuries down to A.D. 529, the date when it was closed by Justinian. Aristotle had followed the example of Plato, and in 322 B.C. had delegated his school to Theophrastus. There emerged lists of the successors who headed these various schools. Already in 200 B.C., Sotion, an Alexandrian who wrote between 200 and 170 B.C., had gathered the lists of successors in these schools; in the Roman period a literature of succession had arisen. Suidas, for example, held that the Epicurean school lasted from 271 B.C. to 44 B.C., during which period there were fourteen successors.

What was the reason for this concern to establish the lists of succession in the philosophic schools? Apart from the general concern to return to the ancients, no purely historical factors can be held to account for it. The reason lay elsewhere and deeper. Bickerman

enough has been defended against Urbach by J. Neusner in *JR* 43, no. 4 (1963), 285–94, on 'Jewish Use of Pagan Symbols after 70 C.E.' See also *Judaism*, 15, no. 2 (1966), 231 ff. on 'Judaism in Late Antiquity'.

[1] *RB* 59 (1952), 44–54.
[2] A. D. Nock in the *Cambridge Ancient History*, 10 (Cambridge, 1934), 471, lists as the marks of the Augustan age, the wish for revival and restoration in religion, the value set on tradition and legend.
[3] See P. Boyance, *Le Culte des Muses chez les philosophes Grecs* (Paris, 1937), pp. 261–7, 299–327.

points out that, ever since the time of Socrates, philosophy had not been merely a kind of technical or theoretical knowledge; it had been rather a way of life, discovered and revealed by the founder of the school. The philosopher's way of life was not only to be learnt from his books, but from the faithful transmission of his successors who had 'lived' his doctrine. In this lay the importance of preserving a 'living' succession.

A further point is to be noted. Greek historians were concerned to establish not only the succession for Greek schools of philosophy, but for pagan or barbarian wisdom also. In turn, 'barbarians' showed the same concern and recorded the successions of their 'schools'. For example, in the second century A.D., Pomponius Sextus, a distinguished Roman jurist, set forth in his *Enchiridium* the succession of Roman jurists down to his time.[1]

What particularly interests us is that Jews also came to share in this concern with 'philosophic' succession. According to Eusebius (*P.E.* ix. 30. 447 *a*), in the second century B.C., Eupolemos, a Jew, conceived the idea of a succession of prophets from Moses to Joshua. Such a succession is presupposed in Aboth 1 : 1. Josephus is also aware of a prophetic succession, however broken (*Contra Apionem* 1. 8. 38 ff.).

It is in the light of all this concern of the Hellenistic world to establish the succession of philosophic schools, and, as a result, of the concern among Jews also with the idea of succession, that we are to understand the chain of tradition presented at the beginning of the Aboth. The Pharisees also—in order to be respectable and respected— wanted to establish their pedigree or spiritual ancestry. They traced what might be called a professorial succession for their school just as the Platonists did for theirs. True, if we follow Finkelstein, they gave to the succession a peculiar form governed by Hebraic notions of the mystic number 'fourteen'. But the pertinent point here is that strange as at first sight it might seem, the Pharisaic chain of tradition is, in part at least,[2] an expression of Hellenistic pressures on Judaism.

---

[1] For references, see E. Bickerman, *op. cit.* The date of Suidas, the lexicographer, is about A.D. 970, but his lexicon contains valuable early materials. For all these figures, see *Paulys Realencyclopädie der Classischen Altertumswissenschaft* (Stuttgart, 1927). Sotion's chief work was entitled *The Succession of the Philosophers*.

[2] It should be recalled that the use of genealogies is familiar in the Old Testament and in Judaism. For a discussion of the purpose of genealogies, see an unpublished

The very manifesto of Pharisaism begins with a Hellenistic convention which sets the Aboth in the stream of Hellenistic philosophical interests.

The Hellenistic colour of the chain of tradition in Aboth 1: 1 ff. is confirmed by a very simple fact. The chain reads as follows:

Moses received the Law from Sinai and committed it to Joshua, and Joshua to the elders, and the elders to the Prophets; and the Prophets committed it to the men of the Great Synagogue...Simeon the Just was of the remnants of the Great Synagogue...Antigonus of Soko received [the Law] from Simeon the Just...

There follows upon the above a list of the 'pairs' of authorities who transmitted the traditions down to Hillel and Shammai and, with interruptions, beyond to Johannan ben Zakkai.

At first sight the opening list in the Aboth seems to be thoroughly Jewish, typically Pharisaic or rabbinic. But we have already seen that its inspiration may well have been Hellenistic. And it agrees with this that a striking fact stares the reader in the face. Among the comparatively early transmitters of the tradition there is one who bears a Greek name. This is a more likely view than that 'Antigonus' represents some Hebrew name. Antigonus himself, of course, was a Jew, a pre-Tannaitic teacher of the third century B.C. or of the first decades of the second century B.C. It has been suggested that the description of him as 'of Soko' implies that he was a considerable figure in his city (see Judg. 7: 14). What is important here is that he bears a Greek name. He lived in a period when Hellenistic influences on Judaism were strong. One might expect such a situation to produce, among leading Jews at least, a reaction against Greek names. In a Pharisaic chain of tradition especially one would expect classical biblical and traditional Jewish names. But here in Aboth 1: 3, in the honoured chain of tradition, we meet a Greek name. And at once it is to be recognized that this could only be so if Pharisaism were

dissertation at Union Theological Seminary by my pupil Marshall Duane Johnson, *The Purpose of the Biblical Genealogies with Special Reference to the Setting of the Genealogies of Jesus* (1966). The chain of tradition gives a 'professorial' genealogy, as it were, and cannot be wholly subsumed under the categories of the biblical genealogies. The Hellenistic parallels drawn by Bickerman seem to be more pertinent for its understanding.

open to Hellenistic influences.[1] The teacher of the first 'pair',[2] who thus occupied a historic position in the development of Pharisaism, bore a Greek name. In all there are eight Greek names among the seventy-two names in the Aboth and a number of transliterated Greek words.[3]

The saying ascribed to Antigonus of Soko has also pointed to the pressure of Hellenism. It reads as follows:

Be not like slaves that minister to the master for the sake of receiving a bounty (*peras*), but be like slaves that minister to the master not for the sake of receiving a bounty (*peras*); and let the fear of Heaven be upon you.

Bickerman[4] characterizes the view that *peras* represents the Greek term φόρος as strange, and prefers to expound the verse in terms of the maintenance of slaves in the Ancient World. *Peras* stands for rations given to slaves in the Hellenistic and Roman periods. Anti-

---

[1] Incredulity that a Greek name could have been so early introduced as this would imply persuaded Krochmal that the Simeon the Righteous of Aboth 1:3 could not be Simeon b. Onias I (around 300 B.C.); he had to be Simeon b. Onias II (219–199 B.C.). On the former view a Greek word would have entered the chain of tradition shortly after Alexander the Great. See the Hebrew commentary on the Aboth by Krochmal. Professor Weiss of the Jewish Theological Seminary pointed this out to me. According to Mish. Ḥall. 4:11, a Ben Antigonus brought up firstlings from Babylon. But some manuscripts here read: Antinos. One of the disciples of the School of Shammai probably bore a Greek name—Dositheus of Kefar Yatmah; see Mish Orl. 2:5. On Antigonus, see G. F. Moore, *Judaism*, 3, 14.

[2] Even the term 'pairs', *zgwt*, has been given a Hellenistic derivation from the Greek ζεῦγος, but this is not necessary. The verbal form *zwg* lies behind the form *zgwt*.

[3] *'btlywn* = Πτολίων; *'ntygns* = 'Αντιγένης (*'ntygnws* = Antigonos); *dwsty* = Δοσίθεος; *hwrknws* = 'Υρκανός; *trpwn* = Τρύφων; *lwyts* = Λευίτης; *sndlr* = σανδαλάριος; *trdywn* = θηραδίων (?). The following terms have been suggested as transliterations of or borrowed Greek words: 3:19 *gymtry'* = γεωμετρία; 4:16 *trqlyn* = τρικλίνον; 6:2 *krz* = κῆρυξ; 6:9 *mrglyt* = μαργαρίτης; 4:11 *sndlr* = σανδαλάριος; 5:15 *spwg* = σπόγγος; 3:17 *pnqs* = πίναξ; 4:16 *przdwd* = προστάς; 1:3 *prs* = φόρος; 3:18 *prprt* = περιφορά; 4:11 *prglyt* = παράκλητος. 4:11 *qtyqwr* = κατήγορος. But not all these items are acceptable. Bickerman (*op. cit.*) does not take *peras* to be derived from φόρος. How risky the connecting of Hebrew with Greek words is appears from the fact that W. Bacher refused to connect *gymtry'* with γεωμετρία and does so instead with γράμμα and γραμματεία (see W. Bacher, *Die älteste Terminologie der jüdischen Schriftauslegung* (Leipzig, 1899), p. 127 under *Notarikon*).

[4] E. Bickerman in *HTR* 44 (1951), 153–65 on 'The Maxim of Antigonus of Soko'.

gonus contrasts two categories of slaves—those who receive *peras* from the owner and those who do not. The slave is a permanent hireling who is maintained by the master. There was much discussion as to whether a master was in duty bound to maintain a worthless slave. In such a case, could the master not refuse the maintenance (*peras*) of the slave? This discussion was found among the rabbis. Bickerman cites a passage from Mish. Gitt. 1:6, which refers to an ancient tradition. The passage is instructive:[1]

If a man said, 'Deliver this bill of divorce to my wife', or 'this writ of emancipation to my slave', and he wished in either case to retract, he may retract. So R. Meir. But the Sages say: [He may retract] if it was a bill of divorce but not if it was a writ of emancipation, since they may act to another's advantage in his absence but not to his disadvantage save in his presence; for if a man is minded not to provide for his slave, this is his right; but if he is minded not to provide for his wife, this is not his right. R. Meir said to them: Does he not thereby disqualify his slave from eating Heave-offering just as he disqualifies his wife? They answered: [He has the right to do so to his slave] because he is his chattel...

Bickerman further points to Bab. B. Kam. 87*a* where the view is referred to that a master could wash his hands entirely of any responsibility for a slave working for him. The view is made explicit in Bab. Gitt. 12*a*, though there was much difference of opinion, which is dealt with in the passage from Bab. Gitt. on the question. It is in the light of such ideas, that the saying of Antigonus is to be understood. A man's relation to God is that of a slave: God can maintain him or not as he chooses. And as Bickerman summarizes Antigonus' saying, it means 'there is no compensatory harmony between man's obedience and divine favour'. As in the Book of Job and in Jesus 'God is boldly compared to the unfair slave-driver whose conduct violated the unwritten law of the slave system.' (See Luke 17:10.)

What is of interest is that Antigonus' saying emerges in the large context of the problem of theodicy which became acute in Judaism in the Hellenistic age. Bickerman writes as follows:

(the) optimistic principle of harmony between the obedience to the divine Law and prosperity, which for centuries had formed the moral basis of Jewish society, began to be challenged seriously in the time of Antigonus.

[1] Translation from Danby, *The Mishnah*, p. 307.

One of the recurrent topics in Ecclesiastes written by an earlier contemporary of Antigonus is that of theodicy. Doubters denied that man's
success or failure correspond to his deserts. Sirach also aimed at vindicating
the ways of God with men. He advanced the usual arguments: misfortune
may be a blessing in disguise: God will reward right doing later and so on.
A classicist will remember that at the same time in Athens, Chrysippus
laboured to vindicate the dispensation of Providence and was rallied by
Epicureans and other unbelievers (Kohelet 9: 2).

The saying of Antigonus is part of the failure of nerve of the whole
Hellenistic age. Later, the Stoic, Epictetus (*c.* A.D. 50 to *c.* 130), a
Phrygian slave, was to meet the same problem in words whose purport is the same as that of those uttered by Antigonus: 'I came because it so pleased Him, and I leave, because it so pleases Him, and
as long as I live my task is to praise God' (Epictetus, III, 26. 29)
(Bickerman's translation).

It might be argued that no direct Hellenistic pressures necessarily
called forth Antigonus' saying: might it not have been purely
indigenous to Judaism? Is it not such as could normally be expected
to emerge wherever, in distinct areas, the problem of theodicy became acute? This possibility must be recognized. But the final words
of Antigonus' saying suggest a possible polemic reference: 'And let
the fear of Heaven be upon you.' Is this a direct rejection of the
Epicureans, who urged that there were no gods above to be feared,
because such as did exist did not interfere with the world? Despite
the brute facts of persecution and suffering in the time of Antiochus
Epiphanes, when the Epicureans taunted the pious, the fear of heaven,
piety, was to remain. Such are the forces that moulded the saying of
Antigonus: it comes out of the fire of the struggle against Hellenization; it bears a Hellenistic ring and carries a Jewish challenge to the
'atheism' that was raising its head so plausibly. In the light of this it
is fitting that he should be the teacher of the Pharisaic 'pairs'. His
Greek name is symbolic of the fact that the emergence and nature of
Pharisaism is inseparable from the process of Hellenization which
engaged Judaism.

    An anti-Epicurean motif has been discovered elsewhere in the
Aboth and has recently been emphasized by Goldin.[1] That the school

---

[1] *Traditio* (*Studies in Ancient and Medieval History, Thought and Religion*), 21
(Fordham University Press, N.Y., 1965), 1–21.

gathered around R. Johannan b. Zakkai was engaged not only in legal (halakic) discussions and in esoteric doctrine associated with mysticism and with what is now recognized as proto-Gnosticism within Judaism has long been recognized.[1] But Goldin goes further. The School of Rabbi Johannan b. Zakkai, one of the chief links in the chain of Pharisaic tradition as presented by the Aboth, was also engaged in discussion of a strictly philosophical kind, and, in particular, in the exploration of ethical problems which were characteristic of the Hellenistic philosophical schools. Goldin refers to the verse in Aboth 2: 14 which reads: 'R. Eleazer (b. Arak), a pupil of Rabbi Johannan b. Zakkai, said: Be alert to study the Law and know how to make answer to an unbeliever; and know before whom thou toilest and who is thy taskmaster who shall pay thee the reward of thy labour.' The Hebrew word translated 'unbeliever' here is literally: *Epicurean*. It occurs also in Mish. Snh. 10: 1, where we read: 'And these are they that have no share in the world to come: he that says that there is no resurrection of the dead prescribed in the Law,[and he that says] that the Law is not from Heaven, and an Epicurean...'
Under the term 'Epicurean' Danby understands 'gentiles and Jews opposed to the rabbinical teachings. It is in no way associated with teachings supposed by the Jews to emanate from the philosopher Epicurus. To Jewish ears it conveys the sense of the root *pakar*, "be free from restraint", and so licentious and sceptical.'[2] Is this view of 'epicurean', as signifying 'unbeliever' in a general sense, acceptable? In fact, in the whole of the Mishnah, the term 'epicurean' occurs only in the two places we have mentioned—Aboth 2: 14 and Mish. Snh. 10: 1.[3] Does it have the strict meaning of an Epicurean? Later the term came to be used very loosely, in a slovenly way; but Goldin insists that both in Aboth 2: 14 and Mish. Snh. 10: 1 the term is to be understood in its strictly philosophical sense; and there is no reason to disagree.

On this view, the verse in Aboth 2: 14 is a direct warning against Epicurean philosophy. Eleazer ben Arak has in mind the refutation of Jews who had succumbed to the philosophy of Epicurus. Among

[1] See Lam. R. 12; Bab. Hag. 14b.
[2] H. Danby, *The Mishnah*, p. 397, n. 4.
[3] There are untrustworthy instances of it in other places; see C. Y. Kasovsky, *Thesaurus Mishnae* (Hebrew) (Jerusalem, 1956), 1, 261.

other things, that philosophy argued against the conception of God as either creator or providence—at least as popularly held. Against this R. Eleazer ben Arak roundly asserts '...know before whom thou toilest and who is thy taskmaster who shall pay thee the reward of thy labour...' There *is* a God who watches and rewards. Here R. Eleazer ben Arak joins hands with the traditional opponents of the Epicureans, the Stoics.

And it is not only with the Epicureans that the Aboth is concerned: it also looks, so it has been asserted, to the Stoics. The evidence for the interaction of Stoicism and Judaism has yet to be gathered. Here we are concerned only with traces of this interaction in the Aboth. According to Goldin the section in Aboth 2:9 is patterned after Stoic usage. After listing the virtues of the various scholars who formed Rabbi Johannan b. Zakkai's school Aboth presents the following:

He [Rabban Johannan b. Zakkai] said to them: Go forth and see which is the good way to which a man should cleave.
  Rabbi Eliezer replied: A liberal eye.
  Rabbi Joshua replied: A good companion.
  Rabbi Jose replied: A good neighbour.
  Rabbi Simeon replied: Foresight.
  Rabbi Eleazer replied: Goodheartedness.
Said Rabban Johannan b. Zakkai to them: I prefer the answer of Eleazer ben 'Arak, for in his word your words are included.
  Rabban Johannan said to them: Go forth and see which is the evil way which a man should shun.
  Rabbi Eliezer replied: A grudging eye.
  Rabbi Joshua replied: An evil companion.
  Rabbi Jose replied: An evil neighbour.
  Rabbi Simeon replied: Borrowing and not repaying: for he that borrowth from man is as one who borrows from God, blessed be He, as it is said, 'The Wicked man borrows and does not repay, but the just man shows mercy and gives' (Ps. 36: 21, Heb. 37: 21).
  Rabbi Eleazer replied: Meanheartedness.
Said Rabban Johannan to them: I prefer the answer of Eleazer ben 'Arak, for in his words your words are included.

Goldin[1] points out certain characteristics of the above passage which are noteworthy. First, the scholars around Rabban Johannan

---

[1] *Traditio, ad rem.*

do not—as we should expect—discuss the Torah, which was for them, as for all Judaism, the central concern. Secondly, the question asked by Rabban Johannan b. Zakkai is of a peculiar import. He asks: '...which is the right way to which a man should cleave (*dabaq*)?' The verb *dabaq* connoted a fervour which—in the light of its use in the Old Testament, as in the rabbinic sources—is unmistakable. But the phrase 'cleaving to a way' occurs neither in the Old Testament nor in the DSS. Rather the fervour implied by the phrase is reminiscent of philosophical questions concerning the good life which were especially typical of the Hellenistic age. τί πράττων ἄριστα βιώσεται; asks Diogenes Laertius. It is this philosophical question that Rabban Johannan b. Zakkai set before his school. Thirdly, the 'form' which the discussion of Johannan's question took is Hellenistic. It corresponds to the summary of Stoic teaching drawn up by Diogenes Laertius 7: 92 ff. The summary of Stoic ethics there given (see footnote) first presents the matter positively and then negatively.[1] In Stoic circles this was the pattern of discussion. And it is this pattern that emerges in the school of Rabban Johannan ben Zakkai. Goldin suggests that in Aboth 2: 9 we have the transcript of an actual session in the school of Rabbi Johannan in which the nature of the good life was philosophically discussed in Stoic terms; hence the absence of any reference to the Torah. But, fourthly, in the reply of Simeon ben Nathanel to the second question, that is, 'What is the evil way which a man should shun?', Goldin finds an explicit reference to Plato (Republic 1: 331*d*). Simeon's reply reads: 'Borrowing and not repaying...' This recalls, so Goldin holds, the definition of Justice in Plato, that is 'truth-telling and paying back what one has received'.

It is difficult not to feel that Goldin has here outstripped the evidence. The structure of the passage from Diogenes Laertius seems too elaborate to be profitably compared with that cited from the Aboth. The concluding words after both sets of answers in the Aboth, that is, 'for in his words are your words included' (*šebiklal debarayw dibreykem*) are perfectly natural in Judaism and they have no parallel in Diogenes Laertius, so that the formal parallelism suggested by Goldin cannot be strong.

But, while the specific Stoic parallel urged by Goldin may not be

---

[1] Goldin prints the whole passage but it is too long to print here.

entirely convincing, it is difficult not to find in Aboth 3 : 1 the reflexion of Gnostic questions which became familiar to the Church,
as to Judaism, in the first and subsequent centuries of the Christian
era.[1] The words are from Akabya b. Mahalaleel, a pre-Tannaitic
rabbi according to some and an early Tanna according to others.
Herford prefers to place him in the time of Hillel. The questions with
which Gnostics were concerned have been clarified by Festugière.[2]
He summarizes the content of salvation in Hellenistic mysticism in
the following terms:

Le contenu de la gnôse peut se résumer en trois points. C'est une con-
naissance:

(1) de Dieu, particulièrement sous son aspect de Sauveur (γν. θεοῦ);

---

[1] The presence of Gnostic or proto-Gnostic currents in first century and even
earlier Judaism has now emerged clearly into scholarly discussion. For Gnostic
infiltrations into Judaism, see especially A. Altmann, 'Gnostic Themes in
Rabbinic Cosmology' in *Essays in Honour of J. H. Hertz* (London, 1942), pp. 19 ff.:
'The early stages of Tannaitic thought are already under the spell of Gnostic
ideas' (p. 20). See also H. J. Schoeps, *Urgemeinde, Judenchristentum, Gnosis*
(Tübingen, 1956); J. Daniélou, *Théologie du Judéo-Christianisme*, 1 (Tournai,
1958), 82 ff.; G. C. Scholem, *Jewish Gnosticism, Merkabah Mysticism and Talmudic
Tradition* (New York, 5720–1960), *passim*. Scholem's work is accepted by G.
Quispel, see his essay on 'Gnosticism in the New Testament' in *The Bible in
Modern Scholarship*, pp. 259 ff. He writes on p. 269: '...the Gnostics have been
influenced by a very specific current within Judaism, namely the esoteric traditions of Palestinian Pharisees. This should stop once and for all the idle talk of
dogmatic minds about Gnosticism having nothing in common with Judaism
proper.' R. McLachlan Wilson remains cautious on the Jewish origins of 'Gnosticism', see his essay in *The Bible in Modern Scholarship*, on 'Gnosticism and the
New Testament', p. 277. Writing on the same theme in the same volume, pp.
279–93, Hans Jonas, while admitting that Gnostics made liberal use of Jewish
material, points to an anti-Jewish animus in Gnosticism. He states three hypotheses: (1) Gnosticism as an evolving state of mind *reacted* against Judaism when
and where it encountered it. (2) Gnosticism *originated* out of a reaction (that is,
as a reaction) to Judaism. (3) It was so originated *by Jews*. The first hypothesis is
accepted by Jonas without question; the second is, in his view, possible but
perhaps too narrow; the third remains very questionable because we know of no
Hebrew Gnostic writings and the only Jewish name among the Samaritans is
Simon Magus the Samaritan—a simple fact which Jonas considers very significant. U. Bianchi in *Numen*, 12 (1965), 161–78, writing on 'Le problème des
origines du gnosticisme', recognizes the role of Judaism in its emergence, pp.
176 ff. R. M. Grant, in *Gnosticism and Early Christianity* (Columbia University
Press, 1964), traces the origins of Gnosticism to Jewish sources. See the review of
this work by J. Neusner, *Judaism, op. cit.*
[2] On 'Cadre de la mystique Hellénistique' in *Aux Sources de la Tradition Chrétienne,
Mélanges offerts à M. Maurice Goguel* (Paris, 1950), p. 78.

(2) de soi, en tant qu'issu de Dieu et susceptible de retourner à Dieu (γν. ἑαυτοῦ);

(3) des moyens de remonter à Dieu et du mode de cette remontée (γν. ὁδοῦ).

In a rough way the saying of R. Akabya in Aboth 3 : 1 sets forth 'a gnosis'—simple, as opposed to the complex artificialities of Gnosticism, but none the less providing what the Gnostic looked for in a Pharisaic mould, purified and sobered by biblical realism. The passage reads:

Akabya b. Mahalaleel said: Consider three things and thou wilt not fall into the hands of transgression. Know whence thou art come and whither thou art going (2 and 3 in Festugière's list) and before whom thou art about to give account and reckoning (1 in Festugière's list). 'Whence thou art come'—from a putrid drop; 'and whither thou art going'—to the place of dust, worm and maggot; 'and before whom thou art about to give account and reckoning'—before the King of kings, the Holy One, blessed is he.

It is difficult not to see in the above a Pharisaic statement set over against Gnosticism—of however incipient a kind. It is not inconsistent with the point of view expressed in Mish. Ḥag. 2 : 1:

Whoever gives his mind to four things, it were better for him if he had not come into the world—what is above? what is beneath? what was beforetime? and what will be hereafter? And whosoever takes no thought for the honour of his Maker, it were better for him if he had not come into the world.

In this passage from Ḥagigah, uncontrolled speculation is condemned: in Aboth 3 : 1 the sober recognition of man's nature, not reflexion upon it, is urged. It is also to be noted that Akabya's designation of God as King of kings, the Holy One, blessed be he, may have been evoked by the necessity to assert the utter supremacy of the Holy One over all intermediaries. But this remains a mere conjecture.[1] Moreover the Gnosticism to which Akabya offers an alternative was not necessarily Hellenistic, but may have been native to Judaism. In Gnostic

---

[1] See J. G. Weiss in *JJS* 10 (1959), 169–71, 'On the formula melekh ha-'olam as anti-Gnostic protest', and E. J. Weisenberg, *JJS* 15 (1964), 1–56, on 'The Liturgical term Melekh Ha-'Olam', and J. Heinemann, *JJS* 15 (1964), 149–54, on 'Once again Melekh Ha-'Olam'.

studies, as in others, the fluidity between Judaism and Hellenism is increasingly recognized but cannot be pursued here (see above, p. 138, n. 1).

There is one other minor detail to note. The phrase 'and make a fence around the law' has been taken to reflect Hellenistic ideas in which truth is surrounded by a 'fence'. Clement of Alexandria[1] makes philosophy a φραγμός to the truth, as was pointed out by Taylor long since. Recently the view that the image of a fence around the Torah has been directly derived from Hellenism has been propounded by Professor Stern of London. This view would have increased probability if the term fence included exegetical activity, and if, as Daube[2] long since urged, the rabbinic methods of exegesis were based on Aristotelian models. Unfortunately, Professor Stern's lecture is not available to me, but the concept expressed in terms of 'a fence' might surely easily arise in different and independent cultures. No specifically Hellenistic origin for it need be postulated. Moreover, if Frankel be right in tracing the whole triadic saying in Aboth 1: 1 to the Persian period,[3] then the emergence of the idea of a 'fence' in Judaism precedes the Hellenistic period.

To conclude this section at this point, it can be claimed that, although doubts have been expressed on particular points brought forward above, enough has been written to show that a re-reading of the Aboth confirms remarkably the emphasis made by Daube, Lieberman, Morton Smith and others on the falsity of the traditional antithesis placed between Hellenism and Judaism in the first century. Their mutual interaction is attested in this most Pharisaic of documents.

3

The last item referred to in the previous section suggested that Judaism needed a fence to protect itself. Did it need to protect itself against Christianity? This brings us to the last antithesis with which we shall be concerned—that between Judaism and its daughter faith. To judge

[1] Stromateis 1: 20. See C. Taylor, *The Sayings of the Jewish Fathers*[2] (Cambridge, 1897), *ad rem.*

[2] *HUCA* 22 (1949), 239 ff.; also in *Festschrift Hans Lewald* (Basel, 1953), pp. 27 ff.

[3] Cited by J. Israelstam, Soncino translation of the Talmud, 8 (1935), 1. But we have seen that there is considerable uncertainty about the precise reference in the words of the Great Synagogue.

from the New Testament we should expect such an antithesis. Paul's epistles reveal the apostle in dialogue with Judaism, and so too does Matthew's gospel. I have pointed out elsewhere that the prologue of Matthew may even cast a side glance at the succession list or chain of tradition in Aboth 1: 1.[1]

But it is difficult to trace any anti-Christian polemic in the Aboth. Certain passages have been urged to point to Christian claims. First, Aboth 3: 6 which reads:

R. Halafta b. Dosa of Kefar Hanania (A.D. 80–120) said: If ten men sit together and occupy themselves in the Law, the Divine Presence rests among them, for it is written, *God standeth in the congregation of God.* And whence (do we learn this) even of five? Because it is written, *And hath founded his group upon the earth.* And whence even of three? Because it is written, *He judgeth among the judges.* And whence even of two? Because it is written, *Then they that feared the Lord spake with one another: and the Lord hearkened and heard.* And whence even of one? Because it is written, *In every place where I record my name I will come unto thee and I will bless thee.*

R. Halafta b. Dosa (A.D. 80–120, although Danby places him in the latter half of the second century) was a disciple of R. Meir. Was his saying prompted by the parallel one in Matth. 18: 20? Did he intend to set the 'study of the Torah' over against 'the gathering in the Name of Jesus' as the place where the Shekinah was present? This is not impossible; R. Halafta was a Galilean as the name of Kefar Hananiah suggests: but the thought expressed by him may be spontaneous: it need not have been evoked by Christianity.

Secondly, an attack on Paul has been detected in Aboth 3: 4 in the saying by R. Eleazer of Modiim, who lived at the time of the Bar Kokba revolt. It reads:

If a man profanes the Hallowed Things (1) and despises the set feasts (2) and puts his fellow to shame publicly (3) and makes void the covenant of Abraham our father (4), and discloses meanings in the Law which are not according to the Halakah (5), even though a knowledge of the Law and good works are his, he has no share in the world to come (6).

[1] *The Setting of the Sermon on the Mount* (Cambridge, 1964), p. 303, where I refer to the work of L. Finkelstein, *Mabo le Massekot Abot ve Abot al Rabbi Nathan* (New York, 1950), *ad rem.*

Item 3 above may have reference to Gnostics who made it their practice to put Jews into awkward predicaments.[1] Item 5 is omitted by
some manuscripts, but Geiger, who retains it, understands the phrase
to refer 'to allegorical interpretations of the Torah not in accordance
with the Halakah (i.e. the authoritative rulings of the law), with
special reference to the Christians who taught that it is only the ideas
symbolized by the precepts that mattered, but not their actual observance'.[2] Others find here a critical reference to Alexandrian allegorists.
Item 6 is referred by Israelstam to Jewish Gnostics. It is not impossible to hear echoes in R. Eleazer's words of charges made against
Paul in Acts.[3] But that Paul was explicitly in his mind cannot be
asserted. In addition, a document which was deliberately anti-Pauline
can hardly have included Aboth 3: 16 without some caution. This
reads according to one text: 'All is foreseen, but freedom is given; and
the world is judged by grace, and not according to works.' Danby
accepts the following text: '...and the word is judged by grace, yet
all is according to the excess of works (that be good or evil)'. But the
change of this text to the more 'orthodox' one given in Danby's
translation is understandable.[4] The detection of anti-Paulinism, however, must be carried on with the utmost caution: Taylor favours
the reading followed by Danby.[5]

But is there not a direct glance at the teaching of Paul in Aboth 6:
2? It reads:

R. Joshua b. Levi (A.D. 179–219) said: Every day a divine voice goes
forth from Mt Horeb, proclaiming and saying, 'Woe to mankind for
their contempt of the Law!' For he that occupies himself not in the study

[1] See the reference to Friedlander in J. Israelstam, The Soncino translation of the
Talmud, 8, 34, *ad rem.*
[2] J. Israelstam, *ibid.*
[3] Acts 24: 5 f.; 25: 8. It should be noted that R. Eleazer of Modiim was aware of
the Christian movement because he was a contemporary of Johannan b. Zakkai
and was at Jamnia when the *Birkath ha-Minim* was introduced into the Eighteen
Benedictions; see K. Marti and G. Beer, 'Aboth (Giessen, 1927), p. 76. Certainly
among those whom R. Eleazer had in mind were Jews who had become Christians, that is, Jewish Christians whose good works he could not deny.
[4] For textual details, see Taylor, *Sayings, ad rem.* Herford, *Ethics of the Talmud,*
p. 89, attempts to reconcile the two texts by affirming that the first form refers
to the works of man, the judgment of the individual. The other, negative form of
the text deals with the judgment of the world as a whole, the human race in
general. But this is subtle to a degree.
[5] *Sayings, p. 59.*

of the Law is called 'reprobate' (NaZuF), as it is written, *As a golden ring in the snout* (Nezem Zahab b'aF) *of a swine, so is a fair woman without discretion.* And it is written, *And the tables were the work of God, and the writing was the writing of God, graven* (haruth) *upon the tables.* Read not *haruth* but *heruth* (freedom), for thou findest no freeman excepting him that occupies himself in the study of the Law; and he that occupies himself in the study of the Law shall be exalted, for it is written, *From Mattanah to Nahaliel, and from Nahaliel to Banroth.*

It is difficult not to see here a rebuttal of a claim that there could be a freedom apart from the law. Was that claim the one made by Paul in Gal. 5: 1: 'For freedom Christ has set us free; stand fast therefore, and do not submit again to a yoke of slavery'? Or is R. Joshua b. Levi too late to be directly concerned with Paul? All the dicta in Aboth 6, except that of R. Joshua b. Levi, are *baraithas*, that is, dicta of Tannaitic authorship not included in the Mishnah. The date of R. Joshua makes it unlikely that he had Paul in mind. Similarly the last saying in Aboth 6: 11 *b* by Hananiah b. Akashya (A.D. 140–65), which is also found at the end of Mish. Makk. 3: 16, while it might be used in discussions against Pauline arguments about the law, is hardly likely to be directed against Paul, but is a natural expression of Pharisaic sentiment (see Isa. 42: 21). Aboth 6: 11 *b* reads:

R. Hananiah b. Akashya (A.D. 140–65) said: The Holy One, blessed is he, was minded to grant merit to Israel; therefore hath he multiplied for them the Law and commandments, as it is written, *It pleased the Lord for his righteousness' sake to magnify the Law and make it honourable.*

The translation of the last words in Aboth 2: 13—'And be not wicked in thine own sight'—might suggest a dismissal of such thoughts as are expressed, for example, in Rom. 7: 18. But, again, apart from the precise meaning of the words so rendered by Danby, there were others besides Paul who expressed despair.[1]

We are now in a position to assess the degree to which the Aboth reveals an anti-Christian concern. If anti-Paulinism be present at all in the passages indicated above, it is so by implication only. It is certainly safe to emphasize the absence of any *explicit* anti-Paulinism and anti-Christianity in the Aboth. Pharisaism was aware of the danger of Christianity to its own life, but in the Aboth, where Pharisaism

---

[1] On this, see *Paul and Rabbinic Judaism*, p. 13.

reflects upon itself, this awareness does not obviously intrude. Pharisaism had its own life to live, its own inner dialogue and concern that the Aboth testifies. But, as we have seen, this very concern involved it, if not in explicit anti-Christian polemic, in adaptations to change and especially to Hellenism and the vicissitudes of its own history. And before we turn to the relevance of what has been written above for New Testament studies, it is well to consider what light the Aboth throws on the way in which the tradition responded to challenge.

Exigencies of space make it impossible to deal with this at length; the briefest statement must suffice. Two things stand out.

First, the tradition did change to meet challenge. New occasions taught new duties and the most basic of statements were modified to meet new circumstances. The best example of this is supplied by the very first maxim given in Aboth 1: 1: 'The men of the Great Synagogue said three things: Be deliberate in judgment, raise up many disciples and make a fence around the Torah.' By a comparison of Aboth de Rabbi Nathan I and II Finkelstein shows that the original form of the maxim probably was: 'Be deliberate in judgment; make a hedge about your words; and *appoint many Sages*.' 'This was addressed not to a supreme legislative body like the Sanhedrin which in later times claimed authority to add restrictions to those mentioned in Scripture. It is addressed to individual scholars.' It is 'the directions of the Great Assembly to local scholars and judges'. But 'Rabbi Judah the Patriarch or one of his predecessors, seeking authority for the claim of the Sanhedrin that it could add new prohibitions as "hedges" to the Law transformed the original maxim into its current form. It was no longer a command to "make a hedge about your words"; it became a command to "make a hedge about the Law".'[1] This explains both the change in the order of the maxim and of its content.

The above example must suffice here to indicate how flexible was even the most honoured maxim: the tradition was pliable.[2]

---

[1] *JBL* 59 (1940), 463, on 'The Maxim of the Anshe Keneset ha-Gedolah'. For change in rabbinic tradition, see B. Gerhardsson, *Memory and Manuscript*, p. 98.

[2] The different forms which the various traditions took in different texts also bear witness to this pliability: an example of this has already been dealt with above in Aboth 3: 16. On the other hand, unlike Finkelstein, other Jewish scholars with whom I have discussed this matter find it exceedingly difficult, if not impossible,

W. D. Davies

But, secondly, this pliability must be carefully distinguished from a free creativity. Along with this readiness to change the law as time demanded, there was also a tenacity in holding on to the deposit of the tradition. The scholar who was most praised was the one who held best to the tradition in its exact form.[1] There is no suggestion of an emergent tradition, that is, a newly created tradition, which could be foisted on to a rabbi or introduced by a rabbi at will. Rather, words uttered by authorities are very carefully treasured, although they could be modified to suit new conditions. But such modification was always a reinterpretation of a given tradition, not the creation of a new tradition. Fixity and pliability are the mark of the tradition in the Aboth.

In the above, three antitheses, often assumed, have been found to be absent in the Aboth. This has a bearing on the understanding of tradition—the written memory of the Church—in the New Testament. Our study evokes the following reflexions.

First, the antithesis between law and prophet imposed on the Old Testament and Judaism with which we have dealt above was sometimes carried over *mutatis mutandis* into New Testament studies in several ways. The spirit-filled communities of the Pauline missions have been contrasted with the more legalistic churches of the Jerusalem wing.[2] Or, again, various ministries in the Churches of the New

to believe that Judah the Prince would have *deliberately* changed a given maxim. Is it not better to consider that he had a variant tradition which had developed unconsciously, that is, not by deliberate change, but by slow adaptation? (So Heschel and Weiss in private conversation). On the other hand, the Aboth de Rabbi Nathan does show how the maxim of Simeon the Righteous ('On three things the world stands—on the Torah, on the Temple Service, and on acts of loving kindness') came to be deliberately reinterpreted under the impact of the fall of Jerusalem. See especially J. Goldin in *Proceedings of the American Academy for Jewish Research*, 27 (1958), 52 ff. The theme of the 'adaptation' or 'change' of tradition would demand the lifetime study of many. I have sought to do justice to both continuity and adaptation or change in the above.

[1] Aboth 2: 8 '...Eliezer b. Hyrcanus is "a plastered cistern which loses not a drop...If all the Sages of Israel were in one scale of the balance and Eliezer b. Hyrcanus in the other, he would outweigh them all"'.

[2] See R. N. Flew, *Jesus and His Church* (London, 1938), pp. 185 f., for a convenient statement of Karl Holl's views and a critique of them. A. N. Wilder has emphasized recently the role of prophecy and charismatic authority in early Christian tradition in 'Form-History and the Oldest Tradition' in *Neotestamentica et Patristica, Freundesgabe O. Cullmann*, ed. W. C. van Unnik (Leiden, 1962).

156

Testament have been set over against each other. Harnack,[1] for
example, distinguished between a charismatic ministry belonging to
the whole of the primitive Church, consisting of apostles, prophets,
teachers, who were of direct divine appointment, and the localized,
administrative ministry of bishops and deacons. The tradition in
Judaism holds such oppositions—prophecy and law—together in a
living tension: it reminds us not to succumb to convenient antitheses
which are neat on paper but deny the rich variety of life in the early
Christian movement also.

Secondly, the breakdown of the old rigid antithesis between the
Hellenistic and rabbinic has its relevance for New Testament studies
in which the separation of Hellenistic and Semitic elements has often
been indulged too freely. The presence of Hellenistic elements in a
tradition was almost automatically held to point to a non-Palestinian
and late milieu.[2] The Aboth witnesses, as does so much else, to the
Hellenization of Judaism itself and, therefore, to the extreme difficulty,
if not impossibility, of drawing any certain conclusions about the
date and provenance of tradition in terms of its Hellenistic features or
of the absence of such.

And, thirdly, the combination of a rigid adherence to the deposit
of tradition together with readiness to adapt it has an important
bearing on our understanding of the tradition preserved in the gospels.
It has been frequently asserted that the early Christian communities
had a role not only in the transmission of the tradition, but in its
formulation, and, indeed, its creation. *If it be legitimate to understand
the tradition in the gospels at all in the light of that found in the Aboth*,
then greater weight should be given to the preservation of a given
deposit of tradition which was adapted and modified by the Church
as it faced new challenges rather than to a creating of 'tradition'
de novo by the communities. The Aboth would lead us to expect,
not that there was a wholesale creation of sayings by the primitive
communities, which were foisted on to the earthly Jesus, but that the
Church inherited and preserved sayings of Jesus which floated in the
tradition, modified them for its own purposes, and, again, ascribed

---

[1] *Constitution and Law of the Church in the First Two Centuries* (English trans.,
London, 1919).
[2] See a discussion of this by my pupil Ed P. Sanders, *The Tendencies of the Synoptic
Tradition* (Union Theological Seminary Dissertation: unpublished, 1966),
chapter IV, 'Semitisms', pp. 315 ff. The pertinent literature is cited there.

them to Jesus in their new form. The recognition of the original form may not be easy, but it is not always impossible.[1]

The Aboth, if its evidence be allowed as pertinent, would, then, predispose us to a certain degree of conservatism in the approach to the tradition of the sayings of Jesus. But it also reveals something else. Modern scholars in their approach to the gospels have been much exercised by the difficulty of treating them as historical documents, so overlaid do they seem to be with interpretation, the 'historical' data being subordinated to theological interests. But to a reader coming to the gospels from the Aboth, the exact opposite is the case. Apart from the chain of tradition in Aboth 1 and a very brief section dealing with Rabbi Johannan b. Zakkai and his disciples in 2: 8, the interest in the Aboth centres *entirely* on what individual rabbis *said*. There is no biographical or historical interest. The Aboth concentrates on *sayings*. To turn to the gospels is at once to recognize their 'historical', 'biographical' orientation. Here what Jesus *did* counts, not only what he said. The differentia of the synoptic gospels and of John now appears to lie precisely in their historical dimension. The early Christians not only remembered what Jesus

[1] I have underlined the regulative condition for all the above paragraph. How legitimate it is to pass from rabbinic methods of the transmission of tradition to that of Christian tradition is now a matter of acute debate spurred particularly by Birger Gerhardsson in his book *Memory and Manuscript*, and his later reply to his critics in *Tradition and Transmission in Early Christianity* (Lund, 1964). The matter is succinctly dealt with by Ed P. Sanders, *op. cit.* pp. 35 ff. Sanders points out: (1) the necessity to study the early Christian tradition in its own right; and (2) the many factors which differentiate the Christian tradition from the rabbinic —its belief in the living Lord, fostering a greater creativity; the brevity of its period of growth as compared with Old Testament and rabbinic tradition; its passage from one language to another, introducing increased possibilities of change; its transmission by untrained people. For our assessment of Gerhardsson we refer to *The Setting of the Sermon on the Mount*, Appendix xv, pp. 464–80. The necessity to study the early Christian tradition in its own right is reinforced by our study of the Aboth which is concerned with Pharisaism in its own right, the polemic elements in it, such as they are, being secondary. Both Pharisaic and Christian tradition are best understood, first of all, in their own light. But there is one aspect of Gerhardsson's treatment which should not be passed by easily and with which I find myself in agreement: it is that 'All historical probability is in favour of Jesus' disciples, and the whole of early Christianity, having accorded the sayings of one whom they believed to be the Messiah at least the same degree of respect as the pupils of a rabbi accorded to the words of *their* master' (*Memory and Manuscript*, p. 258). Given this, the force of what we have written in the body of the text above remains.

said but what he did: they concentrated on his works as much as on his words. It is this personal, historical reference in the gospels that a re-reading of the Aboth again unmistakably brings forth. The memory of him—not only of his words—informs the tradition and sets it apart from the rabbinic. The significance of this fact for the understanding of the tradition cannot be pursued here, but it is not to be overlooked.[1]

[1] Recent studies of Jesus have sometimes concentrated on his words (Bornkamm) or on his deeds (Fuchs). Truly to divine the tradition is to hold words and deeds together.

ADDENDA

To section 1, p. 129: In Mishnah Peah 4: 2 the pairs receive the tradition directly from the prophets. The prophets are interpreters of the Law in IQS 8: 14–16; and in Josephus, *Bell.* 2. 10. 12 there are prophets among the Essenes; part of their task is to read sacred books. Halakic activity is ascribed to prophets in Mishnah Yadaim 3: 4. Moore, *Judaism* 1, 6, points out that Ezra was a student of the Law in Babylon under Baruch, the son of Neriah, the disciple and amanuensis of Jeremiah. Ezra 9: 11 f. puts the prohibition of intermarriage into the mouth of the prophets.

To p. 138, n. 1: For a priest and ruler of a Synagogue before 70 A.D. bearing a Greek name, Theodotus, see A. Deissman, *Light from the Ancient East* (London, 1910), Appendix xv, p. 440.

To p. 143, n. 1: Note that the name of the chief power in Palestine after the death of Alexander (323 B.C.), from 315–306 B.C., was Antigonos Monophthalmos.

To p. 155, n. 2: See further J. Goldin on 'The End of Ecclesiastes: Literal Exegesis and its Transformation' in *Studies and Texts*, 3, *Biblical Motifs*, ed. A. Altmann (Harvard University Press, 1966), pp. 135–8. Compare with p. 158 remarks by E. Käsemann, *Exegetische Versuche und Besinnungen*, 2 (Göttingen, 1964), p. 95, in an essay entitled, 'Die Anfänge christliche Theologie.'

8

SAYINGS OF THE RISEN JESUS IN THE SYNOPTIC TRADITION: AN INQUIRY INTO THEIR ORIGIN AND SIGNIFICANCE

F. W. BEARE

Among the sayings which are attributed to Jesus in the synoptic gospels and given a setting in his public ministry there are a number which so clearly presuppose a post-resurrection situation that they must be seen as sayings of the risen Lord or formulations of the Church of the apostolic age. That the facts so stand is admitted by critics of all schools, not by radicals alone, though there would be wide differences of opinion about the amount of sayings-material which must be so regarded. The purpose of this paper is to ask how such sayings may have originated in the first place, and how they came to be so completely accepted as authentic sayings of Jesus that they could eventually be incorporated into what are ostensibly reports of words spoken by him during his earthly career. The possibility must of course be entertained that in some instances they were not found by the evangelist in any source available to him, either written or oral, but were coined by him and inserted into the record by him in full awareness of the fact that Jesus had never spoken them. We shall then go on to ask what significance is to be attached to such sayings. Are they to be dismissed as fabrications to which no value should be attached, once we grant that they were never spoken by the Jesus of history? Or are sayings which cannot be regarded as belonging to the strictly historical record of what Jesus in actual fact said at some time during his life on this earth to be accorded an authority equal to that which we acknowledge in utterances of unquestioned authenticity?

11

161

FCH

F. W. Beare

I

Although our primary concern is with sayings which have been given a setting in the story of the earthly life of Jesus, we may begin with a brief examination of the sayings which are reported as spoken by the Lord after his resurrection. The gospel of Mark offers us no examples, except in the 'longer ending' which is not part of the true text and is not found in any manuscript earlier than the fifth century (Mark 16: 9–20 in the received text and in the authorized version); along with this we may notice the 'Freer logion', which appears in the Washington codex as a secondary supplement to verse 14. This ending, without the Freer interpolation, appears in nearly all Old Latin manuscripts,[1] is mentioned by Irenaeus, and is included in the Arabic Diatessaron; it must therefore have been framed and attached to some copies of Mark by the middle of the second century. It offers a brief list of appearances of the risen Jesus; third among these is an appearance to the Eleven as they sat at table, where 'he upbraided them for their unbelief and hardness of heart, because they had not believed those who saw him after he had risen'. Then follows the mission charge: 'Go into all the world and preach the gospel to the whole creation. He who believes and is baptized will be saved; but he who does not believe will be condemned. And these signs will accompany those who believe: in my name they will cast out demons; they will speak in new tongues; they will pick up serpents, and if they drink any deadly thing, it will not hurt them; they will lay their hands on the sick; and they will recover' (16: 15–17 RSV, foot). The 'Freer logion', which is not found in any Greek witness except W, is cited in part by St Jerome (*Adv. Pelag.* II. 15). It reads as follows:

And they said in defence of themselves, 'This age of lawlessness and unbelief is under Satan, who by the agency of the unclean spirits does not allow the truth and power (*or*, the true power) of God to be apprehended. Therefore do you now reveal your righteousness.' Thus they spoke to Christ. And Christ declared to them, 'The limit of the years of Satan's authority is fulfilled, but other terrible things are at hand. And for the

[1] St Jerome, however, remarks that it is found in only a few Latin witnesses (*in raris fertur evangeliis*) and is lacking in practically all Greek books (*Epist.* 120. 3).

sake of men who had sinned I was delivered to death, to the end that they might return to the truth and sin no more, that they might inherit the spiritual and incorruptible glory of righteousness in heaven.'[1]

The longer ending in itself is little more than a pastiche of bits and pieces from other gospels and the book of Acts. The words of Jesus, with which we are alone concerned, echo (1) the commission of Matt. 28: 19 combined with Mark 13: 10; (2) John 3: 18 (faith as the decisive matter, without explicit mention of the baptism which is in the Matthaean passage); (3) the exorcism of demons 'in the name' of Jesus mentioned in Mark 9: 38–9; (4) speaking with [new] tongues, discussed above all in 1 Cor. 12 and 14 (the variant readings need not concern us here; see Klostermann's note, *ad loc.*); (5) the viper which bites Paul in Acts 28: 3–5; and (6) the healing of the sick by laying on of hands, recounted in Acts 28: 8. Direct literary dependence need not be postulated for the 'signs', especially as we have to wait for later writings to find references to the drinking of deadly potions without being harmed; all these 'signs' were the matter of experience, or of current report, in the early churches (cf. 2 Cor. 12: 12). But the sayings are in any case a literary patchwork, and we cannot postulate any kind of audition of a heavenly voice behind them.

It might be observed that these verses cannot be dismissed from consideration simply by reason of the fact that they were not part of the original text of this gospel. They were accepted as part of the canonical scriptures in virtually all parts of the Church for most of its history, and they have, in fact, much wider and better attestation than the *pericope adulterae* (John 7: 53–8: 11 in TR and AV). More important, they reflect a tendency in the history of the tradition which is already in evidence within the gospel text proper—a readiness to supplement the tradition as transmitted, by the more or less free composition of sayings which will be attributed not only to the risen Lord (as here) but even more often to the historical Jesus.

The Freer logion is a different matter; it survives only by a kind of

---

[1] The text of W is corrupt, and the translation requires a measure of conjecture; see Klostermann's note, *Das Markusevangelium* (Tübingen, 3rd revised ed. 1936), *ad loc.* and Aland, *Synopsis Quattuor Evangeliorum* (Stuttgart, 1964), p. 508. A slightly different rendering is given by Streeter in *The Four Gospels* (Macmillan, revised ed. 1930), pp. 337–8, but the substance is not affected.

11-2

freak of transmission. It would be futile to speculate about its origin, and it has in any case little significance.

The gospel of Matthew contains three sayings of Jesus as the risen one. Two occur in the little supplement to the story of the empty tomb: the greeting to the women, 'Hail', and the repetition of the charge that has already been delivered by the angel: 'Do not be afraid; go and tell my brethren to go to Galilee, and there they will see me' (28: 9, 10). It scarcely needs to be argued that what we have here is not an independent tradition but Matthew's own attempt to remedy what he felt to be the incongruity of the Marcan ending, that the women fled from the tomb terrified and 'said nothing to anyone, for they were afraid' (Mark 16: 8). In any case, the words have no significance apart from what has already been conveyed by the message of the angel; they simply confirm that Matthew (unlike Luke and John) is working with a tradition which reports that the appearances of the risen Jesus to his disciples did not take place until they had returned to Galilee.

The third saying is of a totally different character and is quite independent of any other written source known to us. The eleven disciples have returned to Galilee, and are gathered together on 'the mountain to which Jesus directed them'. Nothing is said of the nature of this manifestation of the risen Jesus, but there is the strange note that it was not of a kind to *compel* faith. 'When they saw him,' we are told, 'they worshipped him, but some doubted.' This is not like the story of the doubts of Thomas (John 20: 24 ff.), for there the whole incident is based upon the fact that Thomas is not present when the Lord first appears. He will not believe until he can see and touch the risen one, but when he sees, he does not hesitate to confess his faith; and the culmination comes in the saying: 'Blessed are those who have not seen, and yet believe.' There is no thought, as in Matthew, that doubt could be possible for those who had seen whatever the others had seen. The saying of Jesus, however, is given a setting independent of this introduction. 'Jesus came to them', we read—as if he were not already present among them, to be met with the faith of some, the doubts of others. Then we have the saying: 'All authority in heaven and on earth has been given to me. Go therefore and make disciples of all nations, baptising them in the name of the Father and of the Son and of the Holy Spirit, teaching them to observe all that I have commanded you: and lo, I am with you always, to the close of the age.'

Certain passages in Eusebius suggest that he was acquainted with a form of this saying which omitted the command to baptize and the triple formula, reading instead: 'Make disciples of all nations in my name.'[1] But the testimony of the manuscripts and the versions lends no support to the thesis that this could have been the original text. It cannot be seriously doubted that the command to baptize and the triple form of the name were in the text as it left the hand of the evangelist. This does not mean that it rests upon any early tradition. Nowhere else in the New Testament is there any evidence of any kind for the use of the threefold name in baptism; on the other side, there are numerous indications that in the early days baptism was administered 'in the name of Christ' (1 Cor. 1: 13 ff.) or 'in the name of Jesus Christ' (Acts 2: 38) or 'in the name of the Lord Jesus' (Acts 8: 16; 19: 5). And even the command to 'make disciples of all the nations' is not conceivable as an *early* tradition of a word of the risen Lord; for it is made unmistakably clear by the narrative of Acts that the disciples had no thought of carrying the gospel beyond the ranks of Judaism until after the persecution that arose around Stephen, and it was a matter of astonishment to the whole Jerusalem church when Peter reported the results of his mission to the household of the Roman centurion Cornelius (Acts 10: 45; 11: 18). Even after they have recognized that St Paul has been entrusted with a divine commission to carry the gospel to the Gentiles, the Jerusalem apostles still are persuaded that their own task is limited to the circumcised (Gal. 2: 9). Plainly enough, none of them had ever heard of a commission to 'make disciples of all the nations' as a command of Jesus. It follows that the saying as a whole was constructed some years after the resurrection, after the gentile mission was an accepted enterprise of the Church; and there is no reason to attribute its construction to anyone else than the evangelist himself. McNeile thus holds that 'the section must be regarded as the expression by the evang. of truths which the Church had learnt as a result of the resurrection, and on which it still rests its faith'.[2]

---

[1] Evidence is presented by F. C. Conybeare in *ZNW* 2 (1901), 275 ff.

[2] *The Gospel according to St Matthew* (London, 1915 [reprint of 1961]), p. 435. He adds: 'The universality of the Christian message was soon learnt, largely by the

In this instance, then, we have before us a saying attributed to the risen Jesus which has in all probability been composed by Matthew the Evangelist, and we take note that he has not felt himself inhibited from putting into the mouth of the risen Lord words which express the mind of the apostolic Church. The commission to carry the gospel to all mankind was accepted by the Church in the first instance without any direct instruction from Jesus,[1] except in so far as we may hold that the Church acted under the guidance of the Spirit of God in embarking on the gentile mission, and that the guidance of the Spirit was in substance the same thing as the direction of the living Christ. But the word of command was not the source of the inspiration to enlarge the field of the mission; on the contrary, the fact of the mission, accepted as the will of Christ for his church, gave rise to the formulation of the word of command.

The gospel of Luke and its sequel, the Acts of the Apostles, provide us with a much larger number of sayings of the risen Jesus. Several of these are set in the framework of the resurrection-narratives of Luke 24 and Acts 1: 1–8; others occur in stories of the apostolic mission, chiefly in connexion with the conversion of St Paul. The sayings of the second group are not at all like the first, either in their substance or in the manner in which the Lord's converse with his followers is conceived. They are specific revelations, usually commands to individuals, and they are given in dreams, visions or trances. In Luke, all the resurrection-appearances proper are vouchsafed in Jerusalem and its immediate environs; the tradition of the return to Galilee appears to be deliberately excised from the record, probably for reasons which may be termed theological—

spiritual experiences of S. Paul, which were authoritative for the Church. And once learnt, they were early assigned to a direct command of Christ. *It is impossible to maintain that everything which goes to constitute the essence of Christianity must necessarily be traceable to explicit words of Jesus*' (my italics). In an interesting concordance with this are the remarks of John Knox (on John 14:25; 16:12–15): 'The truth that breaks through such utterances as these is that many sayings attributed to Christ in this gospel were recognized by the author as being not remembered words of Jesus of Nazareth at all, but words of the Spirit—that is, they embody truths disclosed within the experience of the community where the living Christ is known', *Criticism and Faith* (New York, 1952), p. 53.

[1] In Matt. 10: 5 we have a command attributed to Jesus in his Galilean ministry which actually forbids the disciples to undertake a gentile mission: 'Go nowhere among the Gentiles.' The difficulties of this saying will be discussed below.

the word of the Lord must go forth from Jerusalem. The appearances of the first Easter day are but the beginnings of a new period of earthly fellowship between Jesus and his disciples which continues for forty days, and is depicted as a resumption of their life together under much the same conditions as before.[1] Jesus amplifies his teaching about the kingdom of God, imparts a new understanding of the scriptures, charges them to undertake a universal mission, and assures them that they will shortly receive the gift of the Holy Spirit as the 'power from on high' which the Father has promised, to equip them for the task.

The theme of instruction in the true understanding of the ancient scriptures is introduced first in the story of the walk to Emmaus (Luke 24: 13–27). Jesus, as yet unrecognized, rebukes the despair and incredulity of the disciples who have seen nothing in the crucifixion but the collapse of their hopes, and have given little credence to the reports of the women who found the tomb empty. 'And he said to them, "O foolish men, and slow of heart to believe all that the prophets have spoken! Was it not necessary that the Christ should suffer these things and enter into his glory?" And beginning with Moses and all the prophets, he interpreted to them in all the scriptures the things concerning himself' (verses 25–7). The sayings included in the pericope of verses 36–43 are of interest only as reflexions of a material conception of the resurrection-body (the risen Jesus is not a phantom, but a being of flesh and bones that can be seen and handled, and will even eat a piece of broiled fish). With verse 44, the risen Lord resumes his instructions in the interpretation of the Old Testament as bearing upon him and his destiny. 'Then he said to them,

---

[1] It is not clear whether Luke thinks of sporadic appearances and periods of instruction which took place from time to time over the forty days, or of uninterrupted converse. The participle συναλιζόμενος (Acts 1: 4) is of uncertain meaning—'being assembled together' (AV), or 'while staying' (RSV), or 'while eating' (RSV margin); 'while camping out with them' (taking it as a variant of συναυλιζόμενος) has also been suggested. In one of his stories, Luke tells of Jesus eating a piece of broiled fish in their company (Luke 24: 43); and even though this is a grotesquely naïve insistence on the materiality of the resurrection-body (Luke wants to make it unmistakably clear that the Jesus who appeared to them was no phantom), it is shown to be a settled aspect of Luke's conception by the words of Peter to Cornelius about the manifestation 'to us who were chosen by God as witnesses, who ate and drank with him after he rose from the dead' (Acts 10: 41).

"These are my words which I spoke to you, while I was still with you, that everything written about me in the law of Moses and the prophets and the psalms must be fulfilled." Then he opened their minds to understand the scriptures, and said to them, "Thus it is written, that the Christ should suffer and on the third day rise from the dead".'

This instruction is now supplemented by the charge to undertake the universal mission as 'witnesses' of all that has taken place; and by the promise of the Spirit. That which is written includes also the revelation of the divine will 'that repentance and forgiveness of sins should be preached in [Christ's] name to all nations' (verse 47). The mission is to begin from Jerusalem, but is not to be undertaken until the disciples have received the 'power from on high' which the Father has promised, and which the risen Lord will bestow. 'Beginning from Jerusalem, you are witnesses of these things. And behold, I send the promise of my Father upon you; but stay in the city, until you are clothed with power from on high' (verses 47b–49). The 'promise' is identified in the opening verses of Acts; it is the baptism with the Holy Spirit. And the commission to carry their testimony abroad is renewed. The disciples are forbidden to speculate about 'times and seasons' for the restoring of the kingdom to Israel (Acts 1: 7); the power to be given and the responsibility to be entrusted to them are for the world mission. 'You shall receive power when the Holy Spirit has come upon you; and you shall be my witnesses in Jerusalem and in all Judaea and Samaria and to the end of the earth' (verse 8).

None of this can reasonably be regarded as a deposit of spiritual experience of early days, even if we think of the instructions in less distinct terms than the articulate speech which Luke has framed for them. They 'reflect the theology and the historical perspective of the gentile Church in the later decades of the century' (J. M. Creed, *The Gospel according to St Luke* (London, 1930), *ad* Luke 24: 44 f.). It would be impossible in such matters to distinguish between the theology of the evangelist and that of the circles in which he moves and for which he is writing. He is not in any case drawing upon any deposit of tradition which goes back to the first days after the resurrection or to any time before the Church was fully embarked upon the gentile mission and had no doubt that it was directed by the Lord;

it also presupposes the Church's developed messianic understanding
of the Old Testament and the specifically Lucan doctrine of the
necessity of the passion, not as a sacrifice for sins or a victory over
Satan and the demons, but as the fulfilment of the revealed will of
God as *written* in the scriptures. We have evidence here of the
tendency which we have already noted in the ending of St Matthew's
gospel—the tendency to trace back to some command or instruction of Jesus things which in fact developed in the life of the
Church after, and as a result of, the resurrection of Jesus and the
experience of life in the Spirit. This means, of course, that we
must regard such sayings of the risen Jesus as literary creations of the
evangelist.[1]

We must return for a moment to the phrase of Luke 24: 44,
'while I was still with you.' This is a somewhat incongruous way of
indicating the difference between the post-resurrection setting and the
situation of the days of public ministry. Is Jesus not still with them?
All the rest of the context seems meant to convey that he is materially,
physically present in these resurrection-appearances just as he was
before the crucifixion. The phrase looks like an unwary retention of
words that properly belong in the context of a more spiritual conception of the resurrection-presence. (There is also a striking difference of outlook from that which is conveyed by the Matthaean phrase:
'lo, I am with you always'.) But apart from that, they suggest that
in Luke's view Jesus had taught the new understanding of the
scriptures to his disciples during his ministry, 'while he was still with
them', and that they were unable to grasp his meaning. Enlightenment
and understanding came after the resurrection; what had been taught
by their master in the former days was only now apprehended. This is
in keeping with the way in which Luke has described their response
to the prophecies of the passion, 'He said to his disciples ,"Let these
words sink into your ears, for the Son of man must be delivered into
the hands of men." But they did not understand this saying, and it

[1] It is of course conceivable that he found the work already done for him by some
earlier writer whose work he employed as a source, but this makes little difference.
In one way or another, Luke represents the latest stage in a relatively long process
of literary and pre-literary gestation which cannot be analysed with any precision.
The main point is that we have before us the literary deposit of a long spiritual
and intellectual effort, not the report of an early tradition of visions and auditions
of the risen Lord.

was concealed from them, that they should not perceive it; and they were afraid to ask him about this saying' (Luke 9: 43–5); and still more explicitly in 18: 31–4, 'And taking the twelve, he said to them, "Behold, we are going up to Jerusalem, and everything that is written of the Son of man by the prophets will be accomplished. For he will be delivered to the Gentiles, and will be mocked and shamefully treated and spit upon; they will scourge him and kill him, and on the third day he will rise." But they understood none of these things; this saying was hid from them, and they did not grasp what was said.' The teaching of the risen Jesus about the testimony of the scriptures is thus taken to be identical with what he had taught 'while he was still with them'; the difference is only in the capacity of the disciples to understand what was taught. This points to the further development in the formation of the tradition; it will be no long step for such a writer to attribute to the historical Jesus sayings which were first framed as words of the risen Lord. We shall now turn to examine sayings of this category which have actually received a setting in the period of the public ministry.

2

Every one of the gospels, and every one of the sources which have been employed in their construction, offer instances of sayings which are set in some context of the public ministry of Jesus, although they imply a situation or an outlook which cannot have arisen until after the resurrection. The most conspicuous examples are perhaps to be found in the materials peculiar to Matthew, but there are some in Mark and in Q and in the materials peculiar to Luke. We have here evidence of a tendency which has been widely operative in the tradition from a very early period. It is doubtful if any Christian of the first or second century would have been interested in making a clear distinction between words spoken by the historical Jesus in the days of his flesh, and words of the risen Lord—who was, after all, the same person.

We may begin with sayings which most obviously indicate a post-resurrection origin. In the gospel of Mark, our first example will be the little saying about the 'Strange Exorcist'. 'John said to him, "Teacher, we saw a man casting out demons in your name, and we forbade him, because he was not following us". But Jesus said, "Do not forbid him; for no one who does a mighty work in my name will be able soon after to speak evil of me. For he that is not against us is for us"' (9: 38–40; cf. Luke 9: 49–50; omitted by Matthew). Now the gospels report that Jesus sent out his disciples on a mission of preaching and healing, and gave them authority to cast out demons (Mark 3: 14–15; 6: 7, 13; Matt. 10: 1; Luke 9: 1), but in none of these passages is it suggested that they are to invoke the name of Jesus to overcome the evil spirits. This notion occurs elsewhere in the gospel story only in Luke 10: 17, where the Seventy(-Two) on the return from their mission exclaim with joy: 'Lord, even the demons are subject to us in your name!' But this is hardly sufficient to justify us in holding that the name of Jesus was invoked against the demons during his lifetime by his own disciples,[1] let alone by outsiders. Such a practice could arise only out of the belief that the name of Jesus was a divine name, and it is clear that the recognition of divinity in Jesus dawned upon his followers only after, and as a consequence of, the resurrection. He was 'designated Son of God in power...by his resurrection from the dead' (Rom. 1: 4). The invocation of his name in exorcisms and healings is a mark of the activity of the apostolic Church; and its adoption by non-Christians will arise only some time afterwards (cf. Acts 19: 11–16, with a very different attitude to exorcists who were not themselves Christians).

Our second example from Mark will be the entire 'interpretation' of the parable of the sower (4: 13–20). As Professor C. H. Dodd tells us: 'It is not necessary, after Jülicher, to show once again that the interpretation is not consistent with itself, and does not really fit the parable.'[2] Professor J. Jeremias adduces linguistic grounds as sufficient in themselves to demonstrate that 'this interpretation must be ascribed to the primitive Church'; and sums up his whole discussion with the conclusion that it is 'a product of the primitive Church which regarded the parable as an allegory, and interpreted each detail in it allegorically'.[3] There is good ground for holding that the

---

[1] It is rather to be taken as an indication that the words of the disciples have been reshaped, if not initially formulated, within the apostolic Church.

[2] *The Parables of the Kingdom*, revised edition (New York, 1961), p. 145.

[3] *The Parables of Jesus*, revised [English] edition (London, 1963), pp. 77, 79; cf. pp. 149 ff.

passage is a pre-Marcan construction.[1] The conditions envisaged reflect a time when the Church has not only experienced afflictions and
persecutions for the sake of the word, but has seen some of its
members enticed from the faith by 'the cares of the world, and the
delight in riches, and the desire for other things' (4: 11); that is to
say, it could not have been produced until some years of experience
had taught the apostles and other Christian leaders what disappoint-
ments they must expect. It cannot be said, however, that such a
passage was first conceived as a deliverance of the risen Lord. Rather,
we must suppose that it began as an exposition of the parable by
some later teacher, and was transmitted along with the parable in the
tradition received by Mark, in which it was already taken to be the
interpretation furnished by Jesus himself. But there can be no doubt
that it originated in the post-resurrection Church and was accepted
because it bore effectively upon the contemporary situation. It was
the word of Christ for the times, and the Church was justified in
giving it a place among the teachings of its master, adding it to the
store of its remembrances.[2]

A strangely assorted mass of material which bears marks of a post-
resurrection construction is to be found in the 'Synoptic Apocalypse'
of Mark 13. It is probable that some sayings of Jesus, based (with
some modification) on actual reminiscence, are embedded in the
discourse, but much of it consists of commonplaces of Jewish
apocalyptic imagery, and some of it is really inexplicable except as
reflexions of events in Judaea which took place years after the
crucifixion. It is held by many investigators that there is at the heart
of it a Jewish apocalypse composed at the time of Caligula's threat
to profane the Temple (A.D. 40), which was afterwards worked over
into a Christian apocalypse in the early stages of the Jewish revolt
against Rome (A.D. 66–70). No analysis is entirely convincing;[3] a
number of scholars do not accept the view that a Jewish apocalyptic

[1] Jeremias, *The Parables of Jesus*, p. 14, n. 11.
[2] We may take note here of some remarks of John Knox which are decidedly
pertinent to the matter in hand. 'If Christ still lives,' he tells us, 'we have no
right to limit his authentic utterances to words spoken by human lips in Galilee
or Judea', *Criticism and Faith*, p. 52.
[3] Cf. E. Klostermann's summation: 'Was dabei älter und jünger, jüdisch, christlich
und Herrnwort ist, kann der Natur dieser Literaturgattung nach nicht sicher
ausgemacht werden', *Das Marcukevangelium*, p. 132.

writing has been employed, and some even deny that the passage is properly classified as apocalyptic at all.[1] But all attempts to vindicate the substantial authenticity of the discourse as a whole have signally failed. There is no getting around the glaring lack of concord between the question of the disciples (verse 4), which bears upon the time at which the destruction of the Temple is to be expected, and the discourse, which (as Matthew has perceived, and changed the question accordingly—Matt. 24: 3) speaks of the end of the age and the *parousia* of the Son of Man, with mention of an anticipated *profanation* of the Temple, not its destruction.[2] And the whole extraordinary interweaving of pictures of cosmic catastrophe with scenes of panic in the face of invasion, warnings of the persecutions that await the disciples and of false Christs and false prophets—all this is so far removed from anything else that we find in the teaching of Jesus that it is impossible to regard it as emanating from him. Even the elements which may reasonably be regarded as originating in utterances of Jesus have been transformed in the transmission and surcharged with later Christian ideas. That Jesus should warn his disciples of the hostility and harsh treatment that they must expect at the hands of the synagogue authorities—this is comprehensible enough; but that he should prepare them for the preaching of the gospel to all nations, and for appearances before governors and kings—this, as we have shown in connexion with the commission of Matt. 28: 19–20, must be attributed to the expansion abroad of the apostolic mission.[3] For

[1] See G. R. Beasley-Murray, *Jesus and the Future* (London, 1954), p. 100, where C. H. Dodd is quoted for the view: 'For the most part I do not think it is an apocalypse at all. It is a *Mahnrede* in apocalyptic terms.' See also his account of C. C. Torrey's views, pp. 153 ff., and much else in his chapter 4, 'Attempts to Vindicate the Eschatological Discourse'.

[2] Klostermann (*loc. cit.*) cites the acute comment of one of the Greek Fathers (Victor of Antioch?): ἄλλο τοίνυν ἠρώτησαν, καὶ ἄλλο ἀποκρίνεται (from Cramer's *Catenae*, vol. I, p. 408).

[3] So Josef Schmid remarks (*ad* the Matthaean passage): 'Es gibt nur ein Wort aus der Zeit vor der Auferstehung in dem ausdrücklich und klar gesagt wird: " unter allen Völkern muss zuerst (ehe das Weltende kommt) das Evangelium verkündigt werden" (Mk 13, 10 = Mt 24, 14; vgl. auch Mk 14, 9 = Mt 26, 13). Weil dieses aber den Zusammenhang, in dem es steht, deutlich unterbricht, so kann die Möglichkeit nicht ausgeschlossen werden, dass es ein Wort des Auferstandenen ist, das erst Markus in die Wiederkunftsrede eingefügt hat', *Das Evangelium nach Matthäus*, 5th rev. ed. (Regensburg, 1965), p. 396. Cf. the note of McNeile on Matt. 24: 14 (*Commentary, ad loc.*): 'Had the words been a genuine utterance of

the parables of the fig-tree and of the doorkeeper (verses 28–9; 34–6), we may refer to the analysis of Jeremias (*Parables*, pp. 53 ff., 119 ff.), with his conclusion: 'It was the primitive church which first interpreted the [five] parables in a christological sense, and as addressed to the community, warning them not to become slack because of the delayed *parousia*' (*ibid.* p. 63; he includes three other crisis-parables in his discussion).

In the gospel according to St Matthew, we find to begin with that he has taken over from Mark the interpretation of the parable of the sower, and most of the apocalypse (transferred in part to the Mission Charge of Matt. 10). More remarkable is the fact that he has composed an allegorical interpretation for the parable of the tares, which he has then attributed to Jesus; and has even, it would seem, added some rather incongruous touches to the parable itself to make it fit the allegory. The examination of Jeremias leaves no possibility of doubting that the interpretation (Matt. 13: 37–43) is a composition of the evangelist himself (*Parables*, pp. 81–5);[1] and the same must be said of the interpretation of the parable of the seine-net (13: 49–50), which is obviously secondary to the former composition (the bundles of weeds may serve for fuel, but this is hardly an apt figure for the disposal of bad fish). It has even been held by some good scholars of generally conservative views that the entire parable of the tares is a free re-writing of the Marcan parable of the seed growing secretly (Mark 4: 26–9). T. W. Manson, for instance, felt that the only question was 'whether the Evangelist himself produced the new version...or whether the work had already been done'; in his opinion, 'there is little evidence in favour of the former alternative' (*The Sayings of Jesus* (London, 1949), p. 192). He sums up his study of the parable with the flat verdict: 'It is now clear what Mt. 13: 24–30 is. It is an allegory constructed out of material supplied by Mk.'s parable (4: 26–9) combined with the eschatological teaching of John the Baptist. The story, as it stands, is an allegory composed for the sake of the explanation which is to follow. It is not to be regarded as a genuine parable of Jesus' (*loc. cit.* p. 193). But even when

Jesus Himself, it is difficult to think that S. Peter and the other apostles could have acted as they did; see Gal. ii. 7 ff., Acts x.–xi. 18.'

[1] See also his article, 'Die Deutung des Gleichnisses vom Unkraut unter dem Weizen', in *Neotestamentica et Patristica* (Leiden, 1962), pp. 59 ff.

the parable is accepted as itself a genuine work of Jesus, the interpretation is seen as a product of the developed eschatology of the early Church. This is the view of C. H. Dodd, who goes on to tell us that 'we shall do well to forget this interpretation as completely as possible' (*Parables of the Kingdom*, pp. 147 f.). But is it simply a matter of consigning the passage to oblivion, once we recognize that it is not possible to attribute it to the historical Jesus? Matthew has given us an interpretation which misses the central point of the parable (the warning against premature judgments); but is it not true that the lesson which he does draw from the parable (the warning against false security) was needed by the Church of his day and by the Church of all subsequent ages? Is there a sense in which we may hold that the risen Lord here speaks to his Church through the evangelist?

The issue is much clearer when we come to the treasured saying of Matt. 18:20, 'Where two or three are gathered together in my name, there am I in the midst of them'. For it is perfectly clear that during the lifetime of Jesus, there were no small (or large) groups meeting 'in his name', and that if there were, he could not be present with them. So long as he was living the life of man on earth, he was subject to the same limitations of place as anyone else. At any given moment, he was in a particular locality—a house in Capernaum, a roadside in Galilee, a porch of the Temple, a boat on the lake. He could not be present wherever his followers should meet in his name until after the resurrection. Not this one verse alone, but the whole passage from verse 15 to verse 20, and in a certain degree the entire chapter, presupposes the organized Church of the apostolic age, exercising discipline over its members, provided with a ministry which is charged to use all diligence in regaining one who has gone astray, authorized to take measures that will be ratified in heaven (verse 18), and bound to grant unlimited forgiveness. No one will doubt that it is Jesus who has taught his disciples these principles of life; but it is equally beyond doubt that he speaks here as the ever-present Lord. In the words of T. W. Manson, 'The speaker is the risen and glorified Christ whose presence is a reality in the community of his followers' (*Sayings of Jesus*, p. 211).

Much the same may be said of the saying from the Sermon on the Mount: 'Not every one who says to me "Lord, Lord" shall enter the kingdom of heaven, but he who does the will of my Father who is in heaven' (Matt. 7: 21). The same saying is found also in a variant form in Luke 6: 46, 'Why do you call me "Lord, Lord", and not do what I tell you?' In both forms, but especially in that given in Matthew, it is implied that the address 'Lord' carries the *religious* force which it came to have in the worshipping church of the apostolic age; but in fact, 'Lord' (*Kyrie*) is in itself no more than a vocative of courtesy, equivalent to our 'Sir'. The rebuke as it stands is addressed to those who profess faith in Jesus as Lord but do not give effect to his lordship in their lives—members of the Church whose conduct is inconsistent with their profession. T. W. Manson took the Lucan form for the more original, and held that the Matthaean version 'has been given an anti-Pauline turn', with the suggestion that 'the saying has been shaped by the controversy between Jewish and Pauline Christianity, the same controversy that appears in the Epistle of James.'[1] McNeile goes too far in saying that during the lifetime of Jesus it is probable that he was addressed by his own disciples as well as by the Jews 'only as διδάσκαλε, i.e. rabbi... Κύριε was the later title of worship, adopted in consequence of the resurrection' (*Commentary, ad loc.*); but he perceives correctly that the saying here implies the post-resurrection content of the title *Kyrios*. It is the risen Lord who speaks these words to his Church.

An unusually difficult problem is set by the words which open the Mission Charge: 'Go nowhere among the Gentiles, and enter no town of the Samaritans' (10: 5). It is generally assumed that these words must be an authentic bit of tradition, since they correspond to the actual practice of Jesus and his earliest followers, and are the direct antithesis of the policy of the Matthaean Church, which is undoubtedly committed to the gentile mission. On the other hand, have we any indication that the disciples ever had any notion of going to the Gentiles or the Samaritans during the lifetime of Jesus or in the first years of the mission after his death?[2] Prohibitions are not

---

[1] *Sayings of Jesus*, p. 176. It must be remarked that the so-called 'anti-Paulinism' of Matthew requires to be taken with reserve. See the careful discussion of W. D. Davies in *The Setting of the Sermon on the Mount* (Cambridge, 1964), chapter v, 'The Setting in the Early Church', 1. 'Anti-Paulinism', pp. 316 ff.

[2] 'When we read the Acts of the Apostles it would seem as if the apostolic or missionary task was forced upon the primitive church...It is probably only when Paul went up to Jerusalem and started talking about foreign missions to the leaders

thrown into the air; they almost always reflect an action that has already been taken or is at least contemplated. It would seem likely, then, that this saying reflects one side of the conflict that arose in the early Church over the gentile mission.[1] The party hostile to the mission will have held that the risen Jesus charged his church still to go only to 'the lost sheep of the house of Israel'. Such a saying might even have been delivered by one of the Christian prophets 'in the Spirit'. If it has been given a place in the gospel by Matthew, that can only be because the evangelist found it in an ancient and highly-respected source.[2]

3

If space permitted, we might adduce examples of sayings from Q and from the special Lucan materials which likewise presuppose a post-resurrection situation and can hardly have originated except as sayings of the risen Jesus, even though they have now been given a setting within the historical ministry. But we have not in any case set out to examine all the sayings-material with a view to determining how much of it is of this description and how much may reasonably be regarded as authentic reminiscence of the words actually spoken by Jesus in the days of his flesh. It is sufficient for our purposes to have established that a certain proportion—be it greater or smaller, it is by no means insignificant—of the sayings attributed to the historical Jesus in the synoptic tradition were first formulated after his death and resurrection. They originated in different ways. We have seen reason to believe that some of them were conscious literary creations of the evangelists or of other teachers who preceded them. Some may have taken shape in popular story-telling; as John Knox has reminded us,[3] stories of Jesus are coined to this

of the Jerusalem Church that they decided to make some arrangements for carrying them on', T. W. Manson, *Ethics and the Gospel* (London, 1960), p. 92.
[1] So Julius Wellhausen, *Das Evangelium Matthaei*, 2nd ed. (Berlin, 1914), *ad loc.*
[2] Cf. C. F. D. Moule, 'St Matthew's Gospel: Some Neglected Features', in *Studia Evangelica*, 2 (Berlin, 1964), 96.
[3] 'In spite of the fact that for us the gospel has been given definite written form and has even been canonized, we still do not hesitate to create words for Jesus, not only in drama, novel, and poetry, but also in preaching...In the primitive period before the tradition had assumed either fixed or authoritative form, it was inevitable that some of these imaginatively created utterances should have become a part of it', *The Death of Christ* (New York, 1958), pp. 43 f.

day in preaching and teaching, with appropriate sayings included in them; and it would be all but inevitable that some of those which were thus created in the first generation would be cherished and repeated and would finally be taken up into the notebooks of an evangelist. Others may have originated as utterances of a prophet, prompted by the Spirit; there are many sayings of the glorious lord in the Apocalypse of John, for instance, which the ordinary Christian reader of today would assume to be drawn from one of the gospels, if they were read to him out of context. He would seldom be concerned about the strictly historical authenticity of such sayings as: 'Be faithful unto death, and I will give you the crown of life' (Rev. 2: 10), or 'Behold, I stand at the door and knock; if any one hears my voice and opens the door, I will come in to him and eat with him, and he with me' (Rev. 3: 20). If we now turn to such a saying as 'Come to me, all you that labour and are heavy-laden, and I will give you rest' (Matt. 11: 28), can we feel that it is radically different in character from these; and would it be any the less compelling if we were convinced that it was no part of the strictly historical tradition of the sayings of Jesus, but originated in the proclamation of the apostolic Church?

But over and above all attempts to distinguish between sayings which originated as words of the risen Jesus and those which were actually spoken by him during his earthly ministry is the recognition that *the whole of the tradition as transmitted* is conceived by the evangelists as instruction given to and for the Church, and as conveying the will of the risen Jesus for the community of his followers. It would be hard to maintain that any single saying was preserved out of pure detached historical concern. The things that Jesus once spoke as a Jewish prophet in a Jewish environment have been transposed into things which are still spoken by the risen Lord and Saviour to his Church. In this sense, all the sayings of Jesus—whether spoken in the days of his flesh, or formulated in the life of his community of faith after his resurrection—are preserved and heard as instructions of the ever-living Lord.

Such transposition has not always required any changing of the words of the strictly historical tradition. Many of the sayings which Matthew has woven into the Sermon on the Mount are probably accurate enough Greek renderings of words which Jesus spoke in his native Palestinian Aramaic. But when they are read in the gospel according to St Matthew, as part of a document intended for the instruction of Christian believers, the reader is not particularly concerned with what they meant to the Jews who first heard them spoken. His primary concern is to learn what the Lord requires of him. 'You are the salt of the earth...you are the light of the world' (Matt. 5: 13, 14)—these words were addressed to Jews and they cut the roots of the kind of conscious superiority that is scathingly depicted by St Paul in Rom. 2: 17–20. Jesus is not paying a compliment to his own disciples, any more than St Paul is joining in a chorus of complacency and self-congratulation with the Jew who boasts of his relation to God and is sure that he is 'a guide to the blind, a light to those who are in darkness'. Jesus is challenging this spirit of superiority *in his Jewish hearers*, in much the same way as Ezekiel turns the proud thought that Israel is the 'vine' of the Lord into burning rebukes and warnings of destruction (Ezek. 15). But the Christian who reads the words in Matthew does not read them as rebukes and challenges to *Jewish* pride. He transposes them into a challenge to Christians—to himself—and learns from them to guard himself against the same kind of religious complacency. Not a word of the original needs to be changed, but in the context of Christian discipleship the whole saying acquires a new and different force. The interest does not lie in the historical question of what Jesus of Nazareth once upon a time said to his Jewish hearers, but in what the risen Lord of the Church now says to those who profess to follow him.

For a substantial part of the tradition, however, this broad transposition has issued in changes in the form and even in the substance of the sayings themselves. The work of C. H. Dodd and of J. Jeremias has made us all aware of how profoundly the parables in particular have been modified in transmission to meet the changed circumstances of the Church as it emerged from its Jewish chrysalis to undertake the great gentile mission, and as it adjusted its outlook to the delay of the *parousia*, which was at first so ardently expected. But the 'laws of transformation' which Jeremias has sought to elaborate in connexion with the parables have operated with no less effectiveness in other areas of the tradition. We may, for instance, notice the remarks of T. W. Manson in his posthumously published lectures on *Ethics and the Gospel* (London, 1960): 'We must also realize that the five great discourses in Matthew, of which the Sermon on the Mount is the first, are not shorthand records of actual addresses delivered by the Prophet of Nazareth on specified dates at specified places. *They are systematic presentations of the mind of Christ on various matters of great moment to his Church'* (p. 46, my italics). And he goes on, in a comment on the position of M. Dibelius that 'these sayings, combined by St Matthew or his source, no longer proclaim a heavenly kingdom, but describe a Christian life on earth', to make his own acknowledgment that 'we have a good deal of evidence outside the Sermon on the Mount that parables and sayings, which originally were warnings to the man in the street to flee from the wrath to come, have been adapted by the early Church and have become pieces of good advice for those within the Christian community' (p. 47). Manson qualified this admission by claiming that there is little more involved than a shift of emphasis. 'It is not possible to make a complete distinction between a heavenly kingdom and life on earth. What we may observe is a certain shifting of emphasis, and I think that Dibelius is right in pointing out that the main emphasis has shifted from the future consummation to the present realization. But I should hold that both elements are part of the authentic teaching of Jesus' (p. 48). But there is far more involved than a mere shifting of emphasis, and Manson himself is prepared to go very much farther when he throws out the startling statement that 'if we think in terms of strict historical documentation these early Christians were guilty of tampering with the evidence' (!). He is prepared therefore to reject an approach 'in terms of strict historical documentation', and he tells us that 'they did not regard themselves as bound to store up archives for the investigation of historians nineteen centuries later. They saw themselves as the messianic community, and the words of Jesus their Master as full of instruction for them. They were prepared to take his sayings and apply them to their own case, and if in the process sayings which had originally been intended to serve other purposes were diverted, that did not appear to them to be a serious matter' (*ibid.* pp. 92 f.).

When the problem of the intrusion of manifestly post-resurrection sayings into the story of the pre-resurrection ministry is reviewed in the light of these considerations, it surely shrinks in importance. If the whole record is transposed into a second or third generation setting, with changes of context and shifts of emphasis, to shape it into more or less 'systematic presentations of the mind of Christ on various matters of great moment to his Church', it is no great matter if new insights into the mind of Christ and his will for his followers in the new age should find expression in words that are then attributed to him and read back into the days of his earthly ministry. Such words cannot claim authenticity in the strict sense of belonging to the store of reminiscences of the first followers of Jesus, who had known him in Galilee or Judaea; but they have the no less significant authenticity of expressions of the mind of Christ, as he came to be known in his continuing life in the Church which is his body, the extension of his incarnation.

We are led, accordingly, to the conclusion that there is no radical distinction to be made, in the matter of authority, between sayings of the most unimpeachable authenticity—words which can be accepted without cavil as uttered by Jesus in the days of his flesh—and sayings which were shaped by apostles, prophets, or evangelists in the years after the resurrection, as the Church was directed by the Spirit into new channels of activity and of thought. If we seek to distinguish sayings which belong to the strictly historical nucleus of words spoken by Jesus of Nazareth during his ministry on earth from sayings which originated in the minds and spirits of his followers after his resurrection, it will not be done with any feeling that we are separating gold from dross. The revelation of God in Christ did not come to an end with the crucifixion and the question of historicity is not ultimate.

9

THE PORTRAIT OF JESUS IN JOHN
AND IN THE SYNOPTICS

C. H. DODD

The distinguished scholar and theologian to whom this volume is offered, in his book *The Church and the Reality of Christ* (London, 1963), has an illuminating chapter on 'The Church and its memory'. In this chapter there is a passage to which I have found my mind coming back again and again since I first read it. He is making the point that the Church 'has always known more of Jesus than the Gospels tell us', and he instances 'the relation in which he stood to his disciples and friends and they to him'. In this connexion he observes, 'One reason why the Church has always cherished the Fourth Gospel, and has been unable to believe that it does not contain historical truth about Jesus, is that one can read there, and there only, such words as "Having loved his own...he loved them to the end".' That is finely observed. The implication would seem to be that the Church is right in its belief that the Fourth Gospel contains 'historical truth', in some sense. But 'historical truth' is nowadays a rather elusive concept.[1] I shall take leave, for my present purpose, to understand it as it would be understood by (shall we say?) the average juryman listening to evidence in a British court of justice. I ask myself: have we reason to believe that Jesus was, *as a matter of fact*, attached to his disciples, and they to him, somewhat in the way described in the Fourth Gospel? Any evidence that would justify such belief must come, Dr Knox would rightly say, from the 'memory' of the Church. 'This memory', he adds, 'is first reflected in the Epistles'—especially, of course, in the Epistles of Paul. Now Paul 'remembered' Jesus (if that is the right term) as one 'who loved me and gave himself for me'. If that were taken, quite literally, as a statement of alleged historical fact (in the ordinary sense of that term),

---

[1] At this point our German colleagues would introduce the distinction between *historisch* and *geschichtlich*. The English language does not possess this convenient resource. How much the poorer for that we really are, I am not quite sure.

183

then it would be an improbable one; we have no reason to suppose that Jesus ever in his life had any contact with Saul of Tarsus. The statement is, primarily at least, a theological one, interpreting Christian experience. Then is John's statement, 'Having loved his own he loved them to the end', on the same level as that of Paul? If it is, in what sense would it add to our knowledge of 'historical truth about Jesus'?

This opens up the general question of the historical value of the Johannine presentation as a contribution to the portrait of Jesus in his actual human condition. It has long been an accepted commonplace of criticism that the Fourth Gospel is an interpretation rather than a record. But it is pertinent to ask, an interpretation of what? Is it an interpretation of Christian experience (or of *Existenz*, as they say in Germany), or is it an interpretation of a real historical character? In other words, is the Johannine picture of Jesus essentially a theological construction based on the experience of the Church long after his death, and given dramatic reality by the powerful imagination of the author (and he *had* a powerful imagination), or does it give, in terms of a sophisticated theology, a rendering of a credible historical figure? This is a question in itself, apart from the question whether this or that story may be accepted as factual, this or that saying as authentic.

One way of approach to an answer to our question would be comparison with other interpretations—much as historians have tried to obtain a credible picture of the 'Socrates of history' by comparing the divergent representations of that enigmatic figure in Plato, Xenophon, Aristophanes and others. Among documents available for this purpose we have the epistles, whose importance Dr Knox emphasizes, and we cannot afford to neglect the less favourable interpretations in Tacitus, the Talmud, and (just possibly) Josephus. And we have the synoptic gospels, which for this purpose may be treated as interpretations of the personality and work of Jesus, for no one now regards them as factual record pure and simple. If we compare the Fourth Gospel with them, we are not comparing (as it were) a painting with a photograph, to see whether it is 'a good likeness'. We are comparing two paintings by different artists who work in different media, within different artistic conventions, each with his own individual technique, and we are asking whether characteristic traits which suggest a single personality come through in both.

The portrait of Jesus in John and in the Synoptics

If they do, then we learn something not only about the artists but about the sitter—more than we could learn from a single portrait. That John and the synoptics are in fact working in different media, within different conventions, and with different techniques, is evident, even though the difference can be exaggerated.[1] John is a highly individual artist, using his own idiom, which needs to be understood if we are not to be misled. To take a very obvious example, the Johannine picture, on the face of it, represents Jesus as one who persistently talks about himself and his claims, and this, it has often been pointed out, conflicts with the picture in the other gospels. But in fact John is simply following a convention employed by other Greek writers, in making his hero the mouthpiece of statements which he himself believes to be true about him. The method itself, no less than the style of writing, is part of the idiosyncrasy of the writer, which we must take in our stride in inquiring how far, using this method, he has succeeded in conveying the impression of a personality, and further, of the same personality that meets us in the synoptic gospels.

In attempting to arrive at an answer to this question, I propose to take a specimen passage in the Fourth Gospel and scrutinize it in comparison with material drawn from the other gospels. For this purpose I choose a passage which is admittedly a *locus classicus* of Johannine Christology: the great discourse of chapter 5: 19–30, which from its setting is clearly designed to be programmatic.

Jesus is here replying to the charge of making himself ἴσον τῷ θεῷ, in that he has appeared to claim that his work is parallel with that of the Almighty (ὁ πατήρ μου ἕως ἄρτι ἐργάζεται κἀγὼ ἐργάζομαι, 5: 17). He admits that he is indeed doing the works of God, which are ζωοποιεῖν and κρίνειν, but he is not doing so in independence of God

[1] To describe one aspect of the difference, one might offer (*exempli gratia*) some such rough approximation as this: while both artists (to keep up this way of speaking) depict the basic figure of a rabbi and prophet who shared many assumptions with other Jewish teachers of his time, but broke with them on some important issues and fell foul of the authorities, neither finds it possible to accommodate the *whole* character of the sitter within that pattern. John borrows (directly or indirectly) from the stereotype of the Hellenistic θεῖος ἄνθρωπος, the divine sage who offers initiation into γνῶσις, while the synoptics colour their picture from the palette of Jewish apocalypse. What is the 'extra' that the two are trying to show us in their contrasting styles? The question is vital to an understanding of the 'Jesus of history'.

185

the Father, or even (as it were) in rivalry with him—not as a δεύτερος θεός. On the contrary, in his whole activity he is completely dependent on the Father and completely subordinate to him, deriving from him both the power to give life and the authority to judge. But, this granted, yes, Jesus *is* the judge and the giver of life, and these *are* functions of deity.

In some such terms we might roughly sum up the argument of the discourse. It is a highly theological argument. It starts with a simple parable, similar in character to those of the synoptics—the parable of the Son as Apprentice[1]—and the aphorism with which it ends (verse 30) corresponds with the 'application' which is often appended to parables in the other gospels; and here, it may be, we are in touch with earlier tradition. But in verses 20b–29 we have a typical piece of Johannine exposition, in which the terms of the parable are treated allegorically, the working father standing for God the Father, the apprentice son for Christ, and the trade which is taught and learnt for the work of ζωοποίησις and κρίσις.

To begin with, then, the discourse sets forth the Johannine form of the doctrine of Christ as judge of men. The doctrine is not absent from other parts of the New Testament, though John has given it a distinctive form and emphasis. Among kerygmatic passages in Acts there is one (and only one) which affirms that Christ is κριτὴς ζώντων καὶ νεκρῶν (10: 42). Similarly in 2 Tim. 4: 1 he is ὁ μέλλων κρίνειν ζῶντας καὶ νεκρούς, and in 4: 8 he is the δίκαιος κριτής who will reward the faithful ἐν ἐκείνῃ τῇ ἡμέρᾳ. In the accepted epistles of Paul there is one quite explicit passage, 2 Cor. 5: 10, which speaks of the βῆμα τοῦ Χριστοῦ. Rom. 14: 10, on the other hand, has τὸ βῆμα τοῦ θεοῦ; and in Rom. 2: 16 God judges the secrets of men on the Last Day διὰ Ἰησοῦ Χριστοῦ (cf. Acts. 17: 31). Similarly in 2 Thess. 1: 5 f. the just judgment of God is to be manifested at the παρουσία of Christ, and in 1 Cor. 4: 5 each will receive his meed of praise ἀπὸ τοῦ θεοῦ when the Lord comes. Meanwhile there is a current 'judgment' of Christians of which the Lord is the agent, and this may be regarded as a kind of prolepsis of doomsday (1 Cor. 4: 4; 11: 29–32). In Hebrews God is judge (10: 30–1; 12: 23; 13: 4), and so in 1 Pet. (1: 17; 4: 5).

[1] See C. H. Dodd, 'Une parabole cachée dans le quatrième Évangile', in *RHPR* (1962), pp. 107–15.

The portrait of Jesus in John and in the Synoptics

In the synoptic gospels it is perhaps only Matt. 13: 41–3; 25: 31 ff. that explicitly represent Christ as judge of all men, unless we add Matt. 16: 27, where, however, it is possible (in view of the context) to understand the judgment as pronounced on Christ's own professed followers, rather than on mankind in general. This is clearly so in Matt. 7: 21–3, since the rejected are those who have called him 'Lord', without obeying his teaching. Similarly in such parables as those of the talents and the waiting servants (as these are understood by the evangelists) it is a matter of a κύριος taking a reckoning with his own household—i.e. of the lordship of Christ over his Church, rather than of a general judgment of quick and dead (to that extent like 1 Cor. 4: 4;· 11: 29–32). In Mark 8: 38 and parallels Christ appears rather as the advocate of his own at the judgment than as judge.

Without, therefore, professing to have made an exhaustive survey of the idea of judgment by Christ throughout the New Testament, we may, it appears, fairly conclude that this idea is less prominent than might have been expected, and certainly less prominent than it is in the Fourth Gospel. In this gospel God the Father is never said to be judge; we even find the bald statement, 'The Father does not judge anyone: he has committed all judgment to the Son' (5: 22). Like some others of John's rhetorical antitheses, this need not be taken strictly *au pied de la lettre*, but certainly this is the trend of his thought, and it is doubtful if any other New Testament writer would have gone so far. But what is most noteworthy is that whereas, outside this gospel, wherever the idea of Christ as judge appears, it is always the last judgment that is in view, in John the judgment of Christ takes place within his historical ministry, with its consummation in his death on the cross: νῦν κρίσις ἐστὶν τοῦ κόσμου τούτου (12: 31). Thus, while the common creed of the Church says, 'He *will come* in glory to judge', John makes Christ say, 'For judgment I *came* into this world' (9: 39). The incarnation, not the second advent, is the pre-condition for the judgment of the world by Christ. How is this related to the more usual, or conventional, conception of Christ as judge?

The easy answer, and the apparently obvious one, is that John has here reinterpreted the current eschatology of the Church, bringing the future into the present. He has done so elsewhere, and this might be the answer here. But it is perhaps not so obvious as it looks. For we have to consider the highly original way in which John understands the judgment of Christ. The *locus classicus* is 3 : 16–21, which contains the definition: 'This is the judgment, that light came into the world and men preferred darkness to light.' For this writer, the incarnation of the Word is the coming of light into the world, as it is also the coming of life; life and light being aspects of the same divine reality. The judgment of the world by Christ, therefore, in the Johannine sense, has the character of human reaction to his presence in the world, and primarily his presence as incarnate, that is, as an historical person. It is, in some sort, a self-judgment of men provoked by their encounter with Jesus. That is why the Johannine Christ can say, without more than formal contradiction, 'I did *not* come into the world to judge the world' (12: 47), 'I judge no one' (8: 15); for 'God did *not* send his son into the world to judge the world, but with the intention that the world should be saved through him' (3: 17). The master purpose of the incarnation is the salvation of the world, or, in other words, eternal life for mankind, but it carries with it, inevitably, automatically, judgment upon those who refuse the gift of life and light. This is an idea which it would be difficult indeed to derive from a mere transposition of doomsday into the historic tense.

The affirmation, then, that Christ came into the world to judge interprets the character of his historic ministry. Whether or not it is a credible interpretation we are not at the moment considering, but John certainly meant it seriously as such, for it provides a key to the structure of his gospel. The story he tells is the story of encounters between Jesus and representative persons and groups, as a result of which some are initiated into eternal life, while others are shown up as belonging to τὰ κάτω—the world of darkness and death.[1] It is a process of sifting, and the word κρίνειν in this gospel is often haunted by the shadow of its primitive meaning, 'to separate', 'discriminate'. Thus the conception of the ministry as judgment of men is a 'built-in' feature of the portrait of Jesus as it appears in the Fourth Gospel.

The question, whether such a feature has any basis in the actual

---

[1] Significantly, the presence of Jesus is repeatedly said to produce a σχίσμα among his hearers (7: 43; 9: 16; 10: 19).

facts of a career which ended tragically in or about A.D. 30, *sub Pontio Pilato*, we now approach by way of a comparison with the other portrait, that which is contained in the synoptic gospels. I ask, does any idea of the ministry of Jesus as a sifting and a judgment show through the synoptic account, which, so far as it speaks of judgment at all, is interested in it only in the context of doomsday? Let us examine some key passages.

In Mark 10: 17–27 we have a dialogue in which the question is raised, how to gain eternal life, or in other words, to enter the kingdom of God. (The terms alternate, as virtual equivalents. Such they are also in John, who prefers the term '(eternal) life', while the synoptics usually prefer the alternative expression.) Jesus offers the inquirer entrance into life, or into the Kingdom, in the words, 'Follow me'. John perhaps would have said, 'Believe in me', but the meaning would not be different: to be attached to Jesus, to be identified with him, is the way to life; he is, in Johannine phrase, the ζωοποιῶν. The man refuses the invitation, and the disciples comment, 'Then who can be saved?' They assume, rightly in Mark's intention, that he is *not* saved, has *not* gained eternal life.[1] He is outside the Kingdom; he has put himself there by rejecting the invitation of Jesus; and this is judgment, a judgment passed by the man himself on himself, in response to the challenge of Jesus. In that sense, which is John's sense, it is judgment by Jesus. The essential relatedness of judgment and the offer of life is as clear in this vivacious dialogue as it is in John's carefully formulated dogmatic propositions about κρίσις and ζωοποίησις.

There are other encounters, touched on more lightly, where the same idea is implicit. The three candidates for discipleship in Luke 9: 57–62 (two of them also in Matt. 8: 19–22) are offered the same kind of challenge as the man of great possessions in Mark, but their response is not recorded. The situation is open-ended, perhaps because the readers (or before them the hearers) were meant to see that they themselves were faced by a like open choice. But that a judgment (in the Johannine sense) is implied is clear, though we are not told how it went.

[1] Mark, it is true, admits an 'escape clause': for men, impossible, but for God everything is possible. John does not deal in qualifications, but perhaps the πάντας of 12: 32 should be allowed to qualify some of his black-and-white absolutes.

The theme, that in the encounter with Jesus a man is confronted with the kingdom of God, and is judged by his response, here exemplified in individual instances, is stated in more generalized terms in the *Missionsrede*. The disciples, sent out on their mission, are instructed to say, ἤγγικεν ἐφ᾽ ὑμᾶς ἡ βασιλεία τοῦ θεοῦ. If their message is rejected, they are to say, 'The very dust of your town that clings to our feet we wipe off to your shame. Only take note of this: ἤγγικεν ἡ βασιλεία τοῦ θεοῦ', to which Jesus adds, 'It will be more bearable for Sodom on the great Day than for that town' (Luke 10: 9–12). That is to say, the verdict has already been pronounced; the unbelieving towns have passed judgment on themselves by rejecting the offer of the kingdom of God and the judgment is sealed by a symbolic action; it remains only for it to be put into effect.

In the sayings about the Ninevites and the Queen of the South (Matt. 12: 39–42; Luke 11: 29–32) the standpoint is somewhat different, but there is no substantial difference of meaning. These characters out of ancient history are to be called as witnesses for the prosecution at the last judgment, and will secure the condemnation of an unbelieving generation. For their responsiveness to the prophet and the wise king will convincingly expose the obduracy of those who were confronted in the ministry of Jesus with the very presence of the kingdom of God, which prophets and kings longed to see but never saw (Luke 10: 24). Dramatically, the *venue* of the judgment is doomsday, but in fact Jesus is putting into words the judgment which the unbelieving generation has already passed upon itself by its refusal of the kingdom (or of eternal life).

Matthew has given a somewhat similar turn to his account of the interview with the centurion (8: 5–13); for he has appended the saying, 'Many will come from east and west to feast with Abraham, Isaac and Jacob in the kingdom of Heaven. But those who were born to the Kingdom will be driven out into the dark.' The faith of a Gentile (like the repentance of the Ninevites) is a foil to the unbelief of Israel, 'born to the Kingdom', but self-excluded from the messianic banquet.

In all such passages it is presupposed that men have been brought face to face with the reality of the kingdom of God, which is present in the actions of Jesus and in his words. Thus, his 'mighty works' have become a medium of judgment upon the unrepentant

Galilaean towns: 'Alas for you, Bethsaida! Alas for you, Chorazin! If the miracles that were performed in you had been performed in Tyre and Sidon, they would long ago have repented in sackcloth and ashes. But it will be more bearable for Tyre and Sidon on the Day of Judgment than for you' (Matt. 11: 21–2; Luke 10: 13–14). In the saying about the Ninevites, which we have just considered, there is more than a hint that it is the *words* of Jesus that convey the fateful challenge. The Ninevites paid heed to the κήρυγμα of Jonah; the Galilaeans have ignored the κήρυγμα of Jesus—his proclamation of the kingdom of God—and this is their judgment and condemnation. Perhaps we might also understand that the σοφία of Jesus, expressed in his teaching (cf. Mark 6: 2; Matt. 13: 54), has failed to command the response which the wisdom of Solomon drew from the Queen, and that this is the condemnation of his hearers. More explicitly the words of Jesus are the medium of judgment in the parable of the two builders (Matt. 7: 24–7; Luke 6: 47–9): 'What of the man who hears these words of mine and does not act upon them? He is like a man who was foolish enough to build his house on sand' —with disastrous results. John makes the same point: 'If anyone hears my words and pays no regard to them, I am not his judge... There is a judge for the man who rejects me and does not accept my words: the word that I spoke (ἐλάλησα: historic tense) will be his judge on the Last Day' (John 12: 47–8).

The twofold impact, in judgment, of the words and the actions of Jesus is stated by John with his usual dogmatic precision in a passage of the farewell discourses: 'If I had not come and spoken to them, they would not be guilty of sin; but now they have no excuse for their sin...If I had not worked among them and accomplished what no other man has done, they would not be guilty of sin; but now they have both seen and hated both me and my Father' (15: 22–4). For all their judicial objectivity, the words are unmistakably suffused with emotion; and it is the same emotion that comes to expression in synoptic sayings which speak of the doom of the unrepentant city: 'O Jerusalem, Jerusalem, how often...!' (Matt. 23: 37–9; Luke 13: 34–5); 'If only you had known...!' (Luke 19: 42–4). It is a feature of the portrait in both renderings.

The synoptic gospels, to sum up, in poetry, parable and vivid dialogue, yield a picture of Jesus as one whose impact on the situation brought men to judgment. Its finality is emphasized through the symbolism of doomsday, but in fact we see the judgment taking place before our eyes. John's method of presentation, in abstract general propositions, is widely different, but the picture lying behind it is essentially the same.

We pass to a further point. The discourse before us deals also with the theme of Christ's *authority* to judge. He is represented as claiming to have been invested with such authority by God the Father: 'The Father does not judge anyone; he has committed all judgment to the Son...He has given him authority (ἐξουσία) to pass judgment' (5: 22, 27). In the synoptic gospels there is one passage where Jesus (without using the term κρίνειν or κρίσις) claims, as he does here, to possess judicial authority: ἐξουσίαν ἔχει ὁ υἱὸς τοῦ ἀνθρώπου ἀφιέναι ἁμαρτίας ἐπὶ τῆς γῆς (Mark 2: 10 and parallels). (Acquittal as well as condemnation is within the province of a judge.) This authority, we observe, is exercised ἐπὶ τῆς γῆς. It is in his historic ministry, and not at the End, that Jesus exercises the authority to forgive sins. The claim to authority, therefore, in Mark 2: 10 is distinct from that in Matt. 28: 18, ἐδόθη μοι πᾶσα ἐξουσία ἐν οὐρανῷ καὶ ἐπὶ τῆς γῆς. The Johannine parallel to this is in 17: 2, ἔδωκας αὐτῷ ἐξουσίαν πάσης σαρκός—for the farewell discourses are in intention (like Matt. 28: 18) utterances of the Christ who has already passed through death and is 'glorified'. Thus there is only one passage in the Fourth Gospel and one in the synoptics where Jesus expressly claims to possess authority, and specifically authority to judge 'on earth', that is, in his historic ministry. It may (or may not) be that those critics are right who hold that in these two passages we have a reading-back of the Church's belief about its risen and glorified Lord. It may be that Jesus never expressly put forward a claim to such authority. He may have exercised it without troubling to formulate a claim. But the whole presentation, in the synoptics particularly, is governed by the concept of his authority. It is not simply that the evangelists remark on his teaching ὡς ἐξουσίαν ἔχων, or place comments to the same effect in the mouths of his auditors. What is more significant is that the actual shape of the sayings is determined by it. It is presupposed not only in such sayings as those we have already reviewed, but in the air of judicial finality with which, in dialogues and 'pronouncement-stories', the matter is brought to a conclusion, as well as in the ἐγὼ δὲ λέγω ὑμῖν of many sayings. It is presupposed no less in stories which turn upon his power to kindle faith, or to inspire his followers to stake their lives upon an enterprise whose purpose they only imperfectly understood. And indeed it becomes clear that the conflict in which he met his death was a conflict of authority, and he died as a defeated king. Here is a trait which cannot be eliminated from the portrait of Jesus in the synoptics, and it is the same trait that is delineated in the Fourth Gospel in formal dogmatic statement.

In one synoptic passage (Mark 11: 27–33 and parallels) the question is raised of the nature and the source of this authority: ἐν ποίᾳ ἐξουσίᾳ ταῦτα ποιεῖς ἢ τίς ἔδωκέν σοι τὴν ἐξουσίαν ταύτην; It is this double-barrelled question that John is answering in the passage before us. In the synoptics, significantly, Jesus refuses to answer directly. He gives an answer which implies that his critics ought to see for themselves whether or not his authority is ἐξ οὐρανοῦ, i.e. conferred by God, but further than that he will not go. Such reserve is characteristic of the synoptic portrait. But there is another passage which sharpens the conception of an authority ἐξ οὐρανοῦ. It is in the story of the centurion of Capernaum who asked for the help of Jesus for his sick boy (Matt. 8: 5–13; Luke 7: 1–10). In urging the point that Jesus *must* be in a position to do what he is asked to do, he uses the argument: 'You need only say the word, and the boy will be cured. I know, for I am myself ὑπ' ἐξουσίαν, with soldiers under me. I say to one "Go" and he goes, to another "Come here" and he comes.' That is to say, the officer is aware that in his comparatively humble rank he is able to exercise authority just because he is himself under superior authority. He is responsible to his tribune, the tribune, we may suppose, to Antipas, and Antipas, in the last resort, to Tiberius. Because he is himself loyal to his commanding officer, he can give orders to his men with all the authority of the Empire behind him. Therefore, he argues, Jesus can similarly exercise effective authority. It is indeed a remarkable argument; and, still more remarkably, Jesus accepts it. By implication, therefore, as the centurion exercises an authority which is that of Caesar himself, so Jesus exercises an authority which is that of almighty God; and he can do so because (like the centurion) he is himself completely subject to that authority. Now this is precisely what John says, using the simple analogy of the apprentice son instead of that of the army officer.

A consideration of the allegorized parable will disclose something of the manner in which John conceives divine authority to reside in Jesus. First, it is not only ἐξ οὐρανοῦ, God-given; it is held and exercised solely in continuous dependence on the Father: 'the Son can do nothing by himself...I cannot act by myself' (5: 19, 30). Secondly, it arises from a perfect confidence between Father and Son. In terms of the parable, the working father shows his son the secrets of the craft, and the son sees what he is doing and does likewise. That is to say, Jesus has been granted immediate apprehension of the mind of God (he has 'seen' the Father, 6: 46), and directs his life accordingly. This is put most succinctly in terms of mutual 'knowledge': γινώσκει με ὁ πατὴρ κἀγὼ γινώσκω τὸν πατέρα (10: 15), the verb having the pregnant sense which it owes largely to its Hebraic background. This appears in expanded form in the synoptic gospels: 'Everything is entrusted to me by my Father; and no one knows the Son but the Father, and no one knows the Father but the Son, and those to whom the Son may choose to reveal him' (Matt. 11: 27; Luke 10: 22). The first clause, πάντα μοι παρεδόθη ὑπὸ τοῦ πατρός μου, combines the sense of two Johannine expressions: πάντα δείκνυσιν αὐτῷ (5: 20) and ἐξουσίαν ἔδωκεν αὐτῷ (5: 27). The last clause, ᾧ ἐὰν βούληται ὁ υἱὸς ἀποκαλύψαι, has its counterpart in the Johannine ὁ υἱὸς οὓς θέλει 3ωοποιεῖ (5: 21). Thirdly, the authority of Jesus is grounded in an absolute obedience to the Father amounting to identity of will: οὐ 3ητῶ τὸ θέλημα τὸ ἐμὸν ἀλλὰ τὸ θέλημα τοῦ πέμψαντός με (5: 30). Here we need only recall the prayer in Gethsemane, πάτερ...μὴ τὸ θέλημά μου ἀλλὰ τὸ σὸν γινέσθω (Luke 22: 42; cf. Matt. 26: 42; Mark 14: 36), which is the simplest possible expression for a trait which is inseparable from the whole story of the ministry, in all gospels.

In this passage, then, which lays down comprehensively the main lines of Johannine Christology, we have before us, in theological guise, a picture of the personality and work of Jesus which corresponds, in point after point, with the picture offered by the synoptics in a very different idiom. When we have allowed for this difference, the character of the sitter comes through unmistakably in both portraits. The discourse is, then, not a purely doctrinal construction, based solely upon the evangelist's peculiar theology; the parallels show that it was constructed with reference to a conception of what Jesus was like which is attested also in the synoptic gospels. It may be that John arrived at it through reflexion on these gospels (if all three were known, or could have been known, to him). But it would not be plausible to suggest (for example) that his conception of Christ as judge, as we have it here, arose *either* out of a transposition of the future judgment (as known to the synoptics) into terms of present or past, *or* out of an induction from the comparatively numerous acts and words of Jesus recorded in the synoptics which can be seen to have a judicial character, though the evangelists have not noted them as such. Still less plausible would it be to derive the Johannine doctrine of the authority of Jesus from a combination of various passages in the synoptics referring to ἐξουσία, together with other parallels we have noted. It is not a patchwork of borrowings that we have here. The originality of this remarkable presentation of the ministry of Jesus is not less conspicuous than its far-reaching affinity with that which we find in the other gospels. I have elsewhere tried to show reason for believing that John worked from an early tradition independent of the synoptics but having much in common with the tradition they followed.[1] If that hypothesis might here be admitted, *argumenti gratia*, it would, as it seems to me, most readily account for the phenomena we have been observing. In that case, John's rendering of the portrait of Jesus will be neither his own invention nor the re-colouring of another artist's sketch. He will have had, through memories or traditions available to him, access to the sitter, and the similarities we have noted will go far to assure us that behind the two renderings of the portrait there stands a real historical person.

These conclusions, drawn from the study of a single passage in the Fourth Gospel (though one which might rank as *instantia praerogativa*), remain precarious until they are tested through the application of a similar process of analysis to other passages, with an attempt to envisage each of the two renderings of the portrait as a whole, and to institute a comparison on broad lines between them. This is no place for any such extended treatment of the question, and to offer a summary impression without supporting evidence would be *nihil ad rem*. But one observation may be offered. In any such comparison

[1] C. H. Dodd, *Historical Tradition in the Fourth Gospel* (Cambridge, 1963).

we should be on the look-out not only for features in which the two renderings of the portrait appear to corroborate one another but also for features in which they may be complementary. I will suggest two examples.

First, in the synoptic gospels one of the outstanding features of the personality and the ministry of Jesus is his association with disreputable characters, and the censure to which it exposed him. It has frequently been observed that this feature is conspicuously absent from the Fourth Gospel. But it is not entirely absent. In the highly wrought Johannine dialogue at Jacob's Well (4: 4–26) Jesus is in conversation with a woman. That in itself is something at which the disciples are taken aback (4: 27), as indeed they would be, on ample evidence from Jewish sources. Not only so, it turns out that she is a woman of loose morals, and, worst of all, a Samaritan.[1] Thus the woman from Sychar is as truly representative of a class neither morally approved nor socially accepted as the woman in Luke's story of the anointing in the Pharisee's house, and the 'publicans and sinners' who figure so largely in the synoptic narrative. John lays no stress on this aspect of the encounter, but there is enough to show that he was aware of Jesus as the kind of person who would brave the censure of public opinion to befriend 'the sick' who 'need a physician'. The synoptics complement with ample reports of his sayings and actions the slight allusion in the Fourth Gospel.

Secondly, on the other side—and here I come back to the point at which Dr Knox himself started me on this train of thought—John alone has much to say of the human relations of friendship between Jesus and his disciples. It is surprising how little of this there is in the other gospels, which lay stress rather on the severity with which he called them to order and the unsparing demands he made of them. Is this, possibly, because the synoptic evangelists here followed a tradition handed down in a *milieu* where the Church was most keenly aware that it was 'militant here on earth' and must always remember the stringent conditions of the service, while the tradition followed by John came from a *milieu* in which the Church was most conscious of the profound significance of its own κοινωνία? However that may be, the absence of these traits from the synoptics is not

[1] For rabbinic views on Samaritan women see D. Daube, *The New Testament and Rabbinic Judaism* (London, 1956), pp. 373–4.

total. They can be discerned in the conversations said to have taken place on 'the night in which he was betrayed'. Much recent criticism tends to deprecate treatment of these conversations as if they reflected in any way the human attitudes and relations of Jesus and his disciples in their historical situation, preferring to regard them as edifying *paraenesis* for the Church under trial. Undoubtedly we have here material which in its nature must have been rehearsed constantly over the years in the worship and the teaching of the Church, and such rehearsal cannot but have affected the shaping of the tradition before it was written down. But in any case these passages are an integral, and a very important, part of the synoptic portrait of Jesus; and in comparing the two renderings of the portrait we recognize that the idiosyncrasy of the artist plays its part in both; yet even so the comparison may bring to light, for all the different colouring of the picture, some traits of the sitter whom both purport to delineate. 'You are the men', says Jesus to the Twelve, 'who have stood firmly by me in my times of trial' (Luke 22: 28), and to his three intimates a little later, 'Could none of you stay awake with me one hour?' (Matt. 26: 40). At the supper itself and afterwards Jesus expresses his forebodings of desertion, denial and betrayal, and the reader is made to feel the shock and strain with which they were received (Mark 14: 17–21, 27–31, and parallels). All this is laden with an emotion that could have been felt only within a group closely united by ties of friendship and affection. It was because Jesus loved his disciples that he was so deeply moved; it was because he knew they loved him that he was hurt, but not alienated, by their defection. Though the synoptics do not say so, the implicit background of it all is the mutual love of Jesus and his disciples. John makes it explicit.

In the context of the last supper, where the synoptics have placed these pregnant sayings, John also gives variant versions of some of them (13: 21, 38; 16: 32), but they are here incorporated into the elaborate structure of the farewell discourses, in which the mutual love of Jesus and his disciples is a dominant and recurrent theme: 'As the Father has loved me, so I have loved you. Dwell in my love...There is no love greater than this, that a man should lay down his life for his friends. You are my friends' (John 15: 9, 13–15). There is indeed a difference. In the Fourth Gospel the weight rests on the affirmation that Jesus loved his disciples. In the synoptics he is, by implication, appealing to their love for him. This appeal is more oblique in John, but it is not absent: 'If you love me, you will obey my commands' (14: 15). The form is obviously more adapted to the situation of the Church in the world than to the passing and critical moment to which the synoptic sayings are addressed; but there is a common basic element. And we must not forget the simple and poignant 'Simon son of John, do you love me?' of John 21: 16. This has always been felt to be in some sort complementary to the story of Peter's denial, which in Mark 14: 30–1 is casting its shadow before.

In the farewell discourses our author's power of dramatic composition is at a peculiarly high level of accomplishment. Into the making of them, we cannot doubt, has gone long experience of that κοινωνία of the Church 'with the Father and with his Son Jesus Christ' which is the theme of the First Epistle of John (1 John 1: 3). But he has succeeded in depicting a system of personal relationships within which the synoptic sayings are entirely at home, and disclose their fulness of meaning. Here, then, it seems, the Fourth Gospel complements the comparatively meagre data of the synoptics. Here, as elsewhere, the same figure stands behind both, and the portrait is the more living because, being drawn from more than one angle, it can be viewed in depth.

10

...*ET HOC GENUS OMNE*—AN EXAMINATION OF DR A. T. HANSON'S STRICTURES ON SOME RECENT GOSPEL STUDY

D. E. NINEHAM

Dr A. T. Hanson, professor of theology in the University of Hull, concludes his contribution to a composite volume of essays he has recently edited,[1] with the words: 'the present position is intolerable.' Since the position to which he refers is that in the present debate about the historicity of the gospel records, it will no doubt be agreed that his judgment deserves the most careful examination, especially as it appears to be shared, at least in part, by other contributors to the volume; and since at one point in his essay[2] Professor Hanson lays the responsibility for the situation he deplores on a group whom he designates 'John Knox, and Professor Nineham, *et hoc genus omne*', perhaps it will be allowed that the present contribution to this volume is a suitable place for such an examination to begin.

Dr Hanson's statement is more complex than might at first appear, and for purposes of discussion it will be necessary to isolate several distinct questions:

(i) Is the factual part of Dr Hanson's essay accurate? Is the position he outlines and dubs 'intolerable' a position in fact held by the scholars he names, or any others?

(ii) Whatever the answer to that may be, is the position which in fact obtains with regard to this matter 'intolerable', and if so to whom, in what sense and for what reasons?

Obviously the first question calls for treatment first, and most of this paper will have to be devoted to the discussion of it.[3] This

---

[1] *Vindications* (London, 1966), pp. 74-102.
[2] P. 100.
[3] The other questions I hope to discuss in due course; I have already broached some of them briefly in the Gore Memorial Lecture for 1966, 'History and the Gospel', published in the *London Quarterly and Holborn Review*, April, 1967, pp. 93 ff., and later to appear as a pamphlet.

carries the consequence that the writer will be involved in a pro-
longed discussion of his own writings, especially his commentary on
St Mark.[1] However, Professor Hanson's remarks on Professor Knox's
views will also be discussed, and in extenuation of my procedure I
may perhaps be allowed to remind readers that virtually the only
evidence Professor Hanson produces for his general judgment is a
long series of passages from various writings of my own and a much
briefer selection from those of Professor Knox. Since these are the
only data we are given for assessing the meaning and justification of
Professor Hanson's judgment, they must inevitably be scrutinized in
detail. It is possible of course that even if Professor Hanson has misunderstood them and they do not support his conclusion, there may
be other evidence that does. In that case, however, the onus will lie on
Professor Hanson to produce such evidence. In default of it, the
presumption would have to be that if he has misconceived the
tendency of the only writings he quotes as representative of a movement, he misconceives the movement as a whole.

Probably, however, that already concedes too much to Professor
Hanson. We must ask, what are this movement and this *genus* of
scholars of which he speaks? One of the first questions that must be
raised about his essay concerns the way in which he groups scholars
and assimilates their views without offering any justification for his
procedure.[2] The point is important because on the basis of such
grouping he feels justified in using the assumptions of one scholar to
interpret the plain statements of another. This, as we shall see, is his
method throughout his essay. The dangers of it will be obvious but,
in case they need emphasizing, a clear example occurs on his very
first page (H 74), where he describes my commentary on St Mark
as 'deliberately following the methods and conclusions of Rudolf

---

[1] *St Mark* (London, Penguin Books, 1963). Since Professor Hanson's essay and
this commentary will have to be referred to very frequently, I shall save
space by referring to them as H and M respectively, following the letter
immediately with the number of the page(s) referred to, e.g. H91 or M200–2.

[2] For example, the wide variety of opinion among scholars who espouse the form-
critical method has often been pointed out, and indeed is often used as one of the
principal reasons for rejecting their method. Yet Professor Hanson feels free
not only to refer to these scholars as a more or less homogeneous group ('*the*
Form Critics') but to attribute to them corporate opinions, e.g. H 75 'The Form
Critics have always maintained...', or H 95 'the Form Critics are much less
confident about the historicity of the Gospels than they were...'

Bultmann'. As it stands, it can be said authoritatively that this statement is false; *deliberately*, at any rate, I made no attempt 'to follow the methods and conclusions of Bultmann'. Professor Hanson offers no justification for his statement and it is the more strange because the index to M shows that every one of the following scholars is quoted more frequently than Bultmann, some of them four or five times as often: Branscomb, Dibelius, Dodd, Jeremias, R. H. Lightfoot, Montefiore, Rawlinson, Taylor and Wellhausen.[1] The references to Bultmann in M are as a matter of fact comparatively few; and of those most are purely informative, and at least one is critical. In fact my attitude to Bultmann is very far from being one of unqualified agreement;[2] much though I admire some aspects of his achievement, no one who knows his work well will suppose that he would regard my commentary as exemplifying either his methods or his conclusions in any other than a very partial way. Perhaps, however, the reference to Bultmann is simply a *pars pro toto* construction, and Professor Hanson intends only to signify that my commentary is generally based on the form-critical method. As we have already seen, a wide variety of views exists among those who acknowledge legitimacy in the form-critical method, and if this is what Professor Hanson means, it is not only a very inexact, but a very unfortunate way of making the point. As we shall see, it seems to have misled Professor Hanson himself; and since in some circles Bultmann is highly suspect as an unnecessarily radical and negative practitioner of the form-critical method, to assimilate a work to his position is to prejudice many readers against it in advance.

On his second page (H 75) Professor Hanson goes on to say that behind the commentary as a whole there lies the 'unexamined assumption' that (and the italics are his own): '*virtually no trustworthy historical information can have survived the period of oral transmission*'. As it happens, this question is explicitly treated in the Introduction to M (50-1), where, under the heading 'Historicity of the Gospel', the following sentences occur:

[1] If a misprint is allowed for, Lohmeyer and T. W. Manson can be added to the list.
[2] Professor Hanson himself points out one of my divergences from Bultmann on H 93, though I must make clear that the ground of my criticism in the passage in question was not, as Professor Hanson says, Bultmann's 'indebtedness to Heidegger', but the fact that, as I put it, he 'absolutises the theories of Martin Heidegger'. It is wrong to attribute absolute validity to *anyone's* thought.

D. E. Nineham

We know a good deal now about the life and conditions of Palestine in the time of Our Lord, and, as the commentary will show, the general picture presented by St Mark fits very well into that background. Whatever qualifications have to be made, the Jesus of Mark, with the language he uses, the traditional parabolic method of teaching he employs, the claims he makes, and the hostilities he arouses, is beyond any doubt basically a figure of early first-century Palestine and not an invention of late first-century Rome.

...when we bear in mind the wonderfully retentive memory of the Oriental, who, being unable to read and write, had perforce to cultivate accuracy of memory, it will not seem surprising that we can often be virtually sure that what the tradition is offering us are the authentic deeds, and especially the authentic words, of the historic Jesus.

Professor Hanson makes no allusion to these statements and gives no hint how he reconciles them with his own statement. Presumably —and hints of this occur more than once in his essay—he feels he can detect what I 'really' believe despite what I say and indeed believe I believe. This in itself is not an unreasonable claim; 'outsiders often see most of the game', and it is sometimes possible to show that a writer's presuppositions are different from what he himself supposes. However, when statements are as definite and explicit as those just quoted from M, anyone who seeks to show that they do not express the writer's real views must expect to have the *onus probandi* placed fairly and squarely on his shoulders. Let us see how Professor Hanson bears the burden.

He starts from the proposition that, according to 'the Form-Critics', 'no detail about Jesus could have been preserved by the early Church unless it had some significance for the early Church'. While I should not myself want to put the point in that absolute way—the claim to know what *could* not have happened should always be made with great caution—I should broadly assent. If, with the majority of scholars, we assume that most of the material in the gospels was handed down in the context of the public preaching and teaching of the early churches, the point will be more or less obvious; but even if not, it is surely difficult to imagine that the early Christians, with their intense evangelistic and pastoral preoccupations, very often found it worth while to relate things about Jesus which, however well authenticated, seemed to them to have no moral, doctrinal or edificatory value of any sort. If that is what Professor Hanson means when he says: 'No historical fact can possibly have been preserved for its own sake by the earliest Christians' (H 75), his statement is broadly correct.[1] The same cannot be said, however, for the deductions he makes from it, and it is most important to be clear just how much— or rather, how little—is implied in what has so far been said.

No story about Jesus, and generally speaking—though here we must be more cautious—no detail in a story, is likely to have been preserved for very long unless religious significance or value of some sort was found in it. It is only to put the same point positively to say that the Church may be presumed to have found some significance in all the stories, and in many, at any rate, of the details, recorded in the gospels, or these stories would not have survived long enough to find their way into the gospels. And since the gospels, whatever else they may be, are undoubtedly theological works, it is surely the duty of the commentator to make clear the theological message of each evangelist by showing what religious significance he and his contemporaries found in the various sayings and incidents he reports. By so doing, a commentator implies no judgment, one way or the other, about the *historicity* of the incident in question, and certainly his procedure implies no negative judgment, as we can see from the case of the Church Fathers, who were often zealous to a fault in finding theological significance in the evangelists' reports without breathing so much as a hint of any doubt about their complete historical accuracy.

All this needs emphasizing because at this point Professor Hanson seems to be guilty of a serious fallacy which underlies and undermines most of what he says subsequently. He poses a false dilemma between the religious significance of a gospel story and its historical authenticity. He claims that since, according to the form-critics, 'no historical fact can possibly have been preserved for its own sake by the earliest Christians; *therefore* when we encounter in Mark what looks like an historical fact some alternative explanation for it must be found' (H 75; italics mine). But why *alternative*? The early Christians undoubtedly preserved the stories they did because they believed them to be *both* religiously significant *and* historically authentic. Indeed in their view they could only be the first because they were

---

[1] Though once again it is cast in too absolute a form.

also the second. Sometimes, no doubt, they were at least partly wrong about the historical accuracy of a story, just as we may sometimes feel they were wrong about a story's religious significance. But each case must be judged on its own merits; and a scholar who suggests that the early Christians saw religious significance in a story certainly is not *eo ipso* involved in denying that they also believed it to be historically authentic or indeed that they may well have been right in that belief. Professor Hanson himself recognizes this on p. 78, and still more on p. 91. On the latter page he asks, pertinently enough, 'why does a theological motive rule out the possibility of Mark relaying actual history? The motive may have influenced the selection of details; why must it be assumed to have created them?' Why indeed? And who makes this assumption? But in the very next sentence he is under the influence of his false dilemma again. 'On what compulsion', he asks, 'must we always choose the explanation that is *incompatible* with an historical origin for the detail?'[1] What is more, he attributes the same confusion to the *genus* of scholars he criticizes, and so when they attempt to find religious significance in any detail, he assumes that they are, at least implicitly, denying to it any historical basis. He writes, apropos my commentary on St Mark (H 75): 'the desire to find some theological significance in every detail supplied by Mark leads imperceptibly into the conclusion that Mark (or his predecessors) have invented the detail'. If that is true, I have been guilty of a serious and glaring logical error[2] to which my general position as such does not commit me. Professor Hanson allows that I have nowhere explicitly formulated such a step (H 75)—what of his evidence that I have nevertheless constantly taken it unawares?

It would not be practicable to discuss all the passages to which Professor Hanson points in support of his contention, and, since the

[1] Italics mine. He means an explanation in terms of the religious significance of the incident.
[2] The full enormity of the fallacy is evident when Professor Hanson restates it on H 89: 'If you believe that nothing whatever was reproduced by the earliest disciples merely because it happened, naturally you will conclude that the ensuing narrative will contain nothing whatever that happened.' So far from this being a 'natural' conclusion, it appears to me a complete *non sequitur*. Indeed, the inference seems to me so totally devoid of force that I wonder if I have understood Professor Hanson.

evidence is so readily accessible, it is not necessary. A few examples may however be discussed.

Professor Hanson begins by referring to M 204, where it is suggested that in the story of the cure of the deaf mute one of the reasons why details of the Lord's technique have been preserved so fully may have been because Mark had seen Christian healers employ the same technique successfully and wished to give guidance to other Christians who also wanted to copy the Lord's methods. The discussion is entirely about the *preservation* of the material and nothing is said about its origin. Professor Hanson, however, goes on: 'Notice the conclusion: this is not a description of what actually happened. It is a description of what Christian healers normally did in Mark's day' (H 76). So far from this being my 'conclusion', the very next words in M (which Professor Hanson does not quote) show that my view is precisely the opposite: 'For the general significance of the fact [*fact*, notice] that Jesus [Jesus himself, notice] used such techniques see Introduction p. 49.' Bultmann might well regard that as an unjustifiably dogmatic affirmation of historical authenticity!

Professor Hanson's second piece of evidence also deserves discussion. It is the section (M 216 ff.) dealing with the healing of the blind man of Bethsaida, in which I point out, as all other commentators do, the fact that the Lord's technique, as here described, can be closely paralleled in various Hellenistic healing stories. I then go on to say, in words taken from B. H. Branscomb, that these pagan parallels are taken by most scholars as suggesting that this story and that in 7: 31-7 'were developed, if not originated, in the syncretistic atmosphere of the Hellenistic world'. Professor Hanson gives this quotation (without making clear that it *is* a quotation), but fails to point out that I also quote Dr Vincent Taylor to the effect that one trait in the story 'strongly suggests the historical character of the incident', and that I deliberately refrain from judging between the two views. Despite that, Professor Hanson 'suspects' that my own sympathies are with the former view;[1] his reason is revealing. I agree with Lightfoot's contention that Mark saw in the story symbolic significance;

[1] He writes, 'It is not clear whether this is Nineham's view, though I suspect it is'. Five pages later he writes *of the same passage*, 'Nineham *obviously believes* that this story originated in the "syncretistic atmosphere of the Hellenistic world".' He does not tell us how what was only a suspicion on p. 76 has become obvious by p. 81.

if it is 'explained' in terms of such significance, it cannot also be 'explained' historically!¹ We see what serious consequences follow from Professor Hanson's original false dilemma.

This case and the next to which Professor Hanson refers, also exemplify another unjustified assumption he repeatedly makes, namely that the citation of parallels is taken as ruling out historical authenticity. He speaks here of the 'accusation' (H 76) that Jesus' healing technique resembled that of other healers, and on p. 77 he refers to my discussion of the healing of Peter's mother-in-law (Mark 1: 29–31), where I point out that some of the terms in which Mark describes the incident are 'known' (not 'drawn'; Professor Hanson misquotes) from contemporary narratives of healing. In both cases the existence of the parallels seems to me interesting,² but in neither do I suggest any implication with regard to historicity; and Professor Hanson's statement (H 77), 'The implication here is that the story is not a real one, but a conventional one inserted by Mark', is wholly without foundation in anything I have said in the commentary or indeed elsewhere.

The same sort of thing must be said about the passage later on the same page (H 77) where Professor Hanson refers to a note in the Introduction to M (28 n.), where I wrote: 'Some stories, it is true, contain specific notes of time or place…but it will almost always be found that in such cases the reference serves a *practical* purpose.' The point I was making is that, given the practical preoccupations of the early Church and the fact that the tradition was for the most part handed down in the essentially practical context of worship and religious instruction, it is unlikely that details of place and time, however well authenticated, will often have survived except where

¹ Failure to distinguish different senses of the word 'explain' and its cognates may well underlie a good deal of what Professor Hanson says in his essay. A passage may be 'explained' in terms of other passages or of various facts and customs, in the sense that these latter throw light on the author's meaning; or they may 'explain' the passage in the sense that it is made up exclusively on the basis of them and has no root in historical fact. See further, p. 210 below.

² E.g. the second passage provides support for the view that in their desire to celebrate the mighty deeds of holy men, different religious cultures in various parts of the world have been led to use more or less stereotyped forms and formulas of a very similar kind; and that similar motives have led to similar results in Christian accounts of Jesus. The importance of this in connexion with the form-critical method is well known.

they were essential to the appreciation of the religious truth the early preachers and teachers found in the stories. Of course the fact that some details *were* essential in this way, and so were preserved, implies nothing whatever about their lack of historicity. In fact the point under discussion in the note had nothing to do with the question of historicity at all and carried no historical implications. Yet Professor Hanson writes: 'The conclusion is therefore, that Mark made them (i.e. the details) up', and he goes on 'and the conclusion is extended to cover far more than details of time or place; it covers pretty nearly every detail that is given.' The casual reader might well be forgiven for failing to realize that not only did I draw no such conclusion, but that no such conclusion can possibly be drawn by any rules of logic from the point I was making.

In the light of this discussion readers are asked to assess the rest of the evidence in this part of Professor Hanson's paper for themselves. The samples I have discussed are, I believe, a fair selection; and will perhaps suffice to support the general point I wish to make in this connexion. One of Professor Hanson's main theses is the twofold one that:

(i) the scholars he criticizes take an excessively sceptical view of the historicity of the gospel stories, and

(ii) they do so because they insist on 'explaining' the stories in terms of their religious significance, to the exclusion of 'explanations' in terms of their historical authenticity.

We can now see:

(i) that at any rate on the evidence brought forward, these scholars are by no means as sceptical as Professor Hanson maintains, and

(ii) that since they do not accept Professor Hanson's unfounded disjunction between 'explanations' in terms of significance and 'explanations' in terms of historical accuracy, their historical conclusions, whatever they may be, are not vitiated by the arbitrary and fallacious presupposition Professor Hanson fathers upon them.

The use of the last phrase can be justified by an extremely revealing passage on H 78, where Professor Hanson is discussing the treatment of Mark 1: 20 in M, and making his usual unfounded assumption about it. The question asked in M, he says, 'is a perfectly legitimate question to ask if Nineham is merely speculating [as in fact I was] as to why this detail rather than that out of the historical material available was chosen'. 'But by now', he goes on, 'we can read between the lines (which it is necessary to do throughout this Commentary) and we know that what he means is...'—something which I did not mean at all. 'Reading between the lines' is sometimes a useful, but always a dangerous, occupation, and we can now see that what Professor Hanson means by the phrase here is interpreting a writer's statements on the arbitrary assumption that he holds to a false disjunction which you have yourself attributed to him. It is by the use of this procedure that he manages to extract the conclusion he does from most of the passages he discusses.

This ties up with another point to which, as will appear later, I attach considerable importance. One of the reasons[1] why Professor Hanson is able to find what he does in M is because *he will never allow a genuine suspense of judgment on the question of historicity*. In the case of many of Mark's narratives, and still more of details in the narratives, the evidence does not seem to me to justify a dogmatic verdict on historicity one way or the other. Sometimes a *probable* verdict is possible, one way or the other, but often the evidence is so scanty or finely balanced that I do not feel justified in pronouncing judgment at all. In such cases I tried in the commentary to indicate my own position and to provide the reader, so far as space allowed, with such materials as there are for making his own decisions. This course, however, Professor Hanson either does not understand or does not allow. A few examples from passages he refers to will make the point clear. It is quite true, as he says (H 79–80), that I share Lightfoot's uncertainty whether, and how far, Old Testament passages may at some points have coloured Mark's narrative.[2] But it is an uncertainty, and not a dogmatic scepticism, that I share, as I tried to make clear in M. For example, on 15: 24 I wrote: '*divided his garments* etc.: In the light of what was said in the last note, this is entirely plausible; but for the early Church its significance lay in its fulfilment of Ps. 22: 18, and it is impossible to say how far that passage has influenced the

---

[1] Another, as we have seen, is his *a priori* assumption that he will find in M 'the methods and conclusions of Rudolf Bultmann'.

[2] I gave grounds for thinking that if such 'colouring' has occurred, it was not due to lack of historical concern on the part of the early Christians, but to a belief that the Old Testament was, in its way, a trustworthy historical source for the events of Jesus' life. See M 367.

Gospel tradition at this point.' Or again, in the case of Mark 4: 35–41 (H 81) I certainly point out the relevance of various Old Testament motifs to the way the story is told and understood by Mark, and conclude by saying (M 148) *'without needing to be excessively sceptical about the historical basis of the story*, we may agree with Rawlinson that: "the precise historical basis, whatever it may have been, is now irrecoverable"'. By this I meant that I do not at present see my way to any decisive judgment on the historical question one way or another, and the same goes for my statement about the Cleansing of the Temple (M 301, H 80): 'Perhaps the most we can say is that while some definite historical incident may well underlie the story, St Mark's account is too brief and imprecise to enable us to be sure what it was.'[1] Yet on the basis of these statements Professor Hanson accuses me of holding that 'the Temple. . .probably was not cleansed by Jesus', and he 'gains the impression that, if only some Old Testament connexion, no matter how remote, can be found for some phrase or detail out it goes; it is a sign that there we have pious invention and not historical fact' (H 80).

Perhaps it is simply that being an Irishman, Professor Hanson has never heard of the good old Scottish verdict of *non liquet*; but probably there is more to it than that. One is reminded of how R. H. Lightfoot was often to be heard lamenting: 'If only they would say "we do not know".' New Testament scholars, he suspected, tend to have a false sense of obligation to decide definitely one way or the other even when the evidence does not really permit of such a decision. Professor Hanson's attitude gives some colour to this suspicion. We have already seen examples[2] of how he will not allow me to declare uncertainty, and a further example occurs on H 82–3. The historical questions to which the stories of Jesus' designation of twelve special apostles give rise seem to me so complex and difficult that I do not at present see my way to answering them definitely. Accordingly, in discussing Mark 3: 13–19 I tried to set out both the main positions which have been held on the matter and confined myself to hinting (as Professor Hanson correctly divines) that on balance I find rather more probability in the view that the incident is historical, though

---

[1] Cf. also M 411 with reference to the trial: 'the detailed historical facts are beyond precise reconstruction', though 'some such meeting as this there must have been'.
[2] E.g. H 76 and 81 discussed on p. 205.

I did not feel justified in venturing any definite statement. When discussing the last supper on M 380 I pointed out, without comment, that those who deny the historicity of 3: 13–19 are compelled to take a certain view of this passage.[1] Professor Hanson, having brought me down definitely on one side in the first passage (my 'characteristically indirect' statement is only a way of 'conceding' the point, H 82), now makes me come down equally definitely on the side of the other view in the second passage—merely because I mention it—and so accuses me of inconsistency. Given interpretation of this sort, it is virtually impossible to find a way of registering a *non liquet* verdict.

In the last resort the whole matter probably goes back to a large extent to a difference of conception, or at least of emphasis, between us over the function of a gospel commentator. In my view a gospel, however authentic its contents, was intended to provide edification and theological instruction. Accordingly, the prime duty of a commentator on a gospel is to make clear to contemporary readers the religious message the evangelist intended his various narratives to convey, whether as independent items or as collected together in the particular arrangement he gave them. To do this it is often necessary to refer to Old Testament passages and a number of other passages and facts which the earliest readers could be expected to have in their minds, but which would not form any part of the interpretative framework of a modern reader unless the commentator brought them to his notice. It was principally with this in mind that the various passages and parallels and so on were cited in M, and it is in this sense only that they can be said to 'explain' Mark's narratives. But Professor Hanson, with his intense historical preoccupation, sees them as intended to 'explain' the narratives in quite another sense. He thinks they were cited in order to suggest that Mark's narratives were simply edifying tales made up on the basis of them without any justification in history.[2]

[1] It is true that to some extent I am inclined to share their view; but I hoped I had made clear that this is on other grounds, the use of characteristically Johannine language.

[2] A good example occurs on H 77 where he points out that a number of such passages and facts are cited in M in connexion with 5: 21–43, and concludes: 'at every step the remoteness of the story from historical fact is emphasized'. It is to be hoped that the baselessness of this conclusion will now be apparent.

It is no doubt true that some of Mark's narratives, and of the details in them, do to some extent partake of this character, and I have sometimes quoted independent accounts of an event which suggest that in that particular case it is so; but Professor Hanson has (and gives) no justification for saying that in my view 'any evidence is better than St Mark's evidence' (H 80).[1]

It may also be true that I believe this sort of process[2] to have occurred more frequently in the course of the handing down of the Gospel material than Professor Hanson does; but if so, it is on the basis of a careful assessment of the evidence relating to each individual narrative. The point to be emphasized here is that in itself the citing of the various passages and parallels was not intended to imply sceptical conclusions, or indeed historical conclusions of any kind, and cannot properly be made to do so.[3]

This last point may be generalized. M was not in fact concerned with historical questions to anything like the extent that Professor Hanson's essay might lead one to suppose. One of the difficulties about his essay is that it constantly addresses to M a type of question it was not primarily intended to answer. The reasons for my comparative lack of emphasis on historical questions in the commentary are too many to be fully discussed here, but it may be instructive to consider a few of them.

(i) I have already explained, as I tried to do in the Introduction to M (15–17), that in my view the primary task of a gospel commentator is not historical but expository—to make clear the religious teaching of the gospel under consideration.

(ii) A full discussion of the historical problems raised by each narrative would in my opinion require so much space that it would be impracticable in a popular paperback commentary, and in any case would scarcely be justified by the rather meagre conclusions

---

[1] For example, with regard to rabbinic evidence, which Professor Hanson here and on p. 86 accuses me of using uncritically, I wrote in M 189 n.: 'The first formulation of the [rabbinic] code *in writing*, the *Mishnah*, dates from the latter part of the second century, which means that the *Mishnah* can be used only with great caution as evidence for. . .the time of Jesus.' And see M 190.

[2] For a more precise description of it see below, pp. 212–13.

[3] Professor Hanson's importation of 'demythologization' terminology into the argument on H 81–2 surely involves a misuse of a term already used loosely enough, and seems a clear case of *obscurum per obscurius*.

which are all that I should expect it to yield. This leads on to a more significant point.

(iii) The reason why I should expect such historical discussion to be so lengthy and comparatively abortive is because I take a different view from Professor Hanson about the nature of the historical problem involved. His view appears to be the simple—or *simpliste*—one that either an incident happened as St Mark relates or else he (or his predecessors) 'invented' it (e.g. H 78 and 81), or 'made it up' (e.g. H 77). To many scholars such language seems quite inappropriate. It does not describe at all accurately the process which in fact took place, and it carries with it moral and other connotations which are totally out of place.

When Matthew or Luke reproduce a passage from Mark they never do so in exactly the form in which he gives it. Sometimes their deviations are slight, at others they are considerable, and in most cases they can be shown to be connected in some way with the evangelists' general purpose and religious outlook. Presumably Mark is related in the same sort of way to his sources and they in turn to theirs and so on back to the period of the Lord's own lifetime. On the basis of such evidence as we have,[1] we can hardly suppose that the material was ever passed on without some modification; so what we have to envisage is the passing of the material through many intermediaries and its undergoing some modification, greater or smaller, each time it changed hands, the modification usually being connected with the religious significance that was seen in it.

Sometimes it is possible tentatively to pinpoint such a modification, for example if one element in a gospel narrative, which can be identified as later, clearly fails to harmonize with an earlier stratum. A possible case in point is the story of the paralytic in Mark 2: 1–12 (see M 90 ff.); but as that example shows, even when the evidence for modification is relatively clear, it is often very difficult to evaluate, and there are many cases where the indications of modification are so slight as to allow of a wide variety of interpretation. In other cases, for example Mark 4: 35–5: 43 (see esp. M 147) there may be signs that a story has received various interpretations, but no means of tracing whether they are late or early or how they de-

---

[1] According to most scholars a lot of the 'Q' material existed in different divergent recensions.

veloped. Even if a story in its present form shows no outward signs of having undergone modification, it is still unlikely that it passed through the whole period of transmission without being modified in some ways, though in the nature of the case the modifications will be virtually impossible to trace.[1] Even a story in which we can trace some modifications with a certain amount of confidence may have undergone further modifications which have left no clear traces. It will thus be apparent why the tracing of the historical basis behind each narrative seemed to me a proceeding too complicated and speculative to be suitable for a non-specialist commentary.

Accordingly, in the Introduction to M (50–1) I gave the reader reasons for thinking that the overall picture presented by Mark deserves a considerable measure of confidence, but warned him that when we come to the individual narratives 'it is important not to claim too much. What the Gospels give us, inextricably fused together in a single picture, is the historic Jesus and the Church's reactions to, and understanding of, him as they developed over half a century and more. Seldom, if ever, can we distinguish with certainty and say: "This is pure history" and "that is pure invention or interpretation".'[2] What I went on to say next brings us to a fourth point.

(iv) I do not think the question of historicity matters to the extent

[1] I recognize that that statement would be regarded by some scholars as too strongly worded. One of the too little known gems in Professor Knox's writings is his account in the second chapter of *The Death of Christ* of how New Testament scholars can be divided into two groups according as they hold that every gospel narrative can, and should, be accepted as historically accurate unless there is specific evidence to the contrary, or on the other hand, recognizing that 'the Gospels are primarily and prima facie church books', hold that 'the burden of proof rests with any attempt to establish a particular item as historically accurate' (*op. cit.* p. 38). He freely acknowledges 'that in many cases this burden can easily be carried' and in any case confesses that he has 'defined these positions more sharply than is appropriate'. Probably neither attitude, as so defined, is entirely defensible, but if on the whole I find myself, as he does, belonging to the second group, that is not only because of the evidence of Matthew, Luke and 'Q' discussed above, but on the grounds, among others, of general psychological probability. It is undeniable that no one ever repeats a story exactly as he heard it, especially if questions of emphasis and nuance are taken into account, and the possibility of a story's being handed down for any length of time completely unchanged, even in detail, appears to me extremely remote.
[2] The last, incidentally, is exactly what Professor Hanson accuses me of saying continually.

that, or rather perhaps in the way that, Professor Hanson appears to do. This leads naturally to the discussion of the third main section of Professor Hanson's essay, but before I discuss it I must explain briefly why I have decided to say nothing in detail about his second section (H 83–90).

That section comprises something of a *jeu d'esprit* in which Professor Hanson seeks to 'reduce my principles of interpretation to the absurd' by showing that impossible results would follow from their application to certain passages in Josephus. Since we have now seen that Professor Hanson basically misconceives my principles, there is little point in examining his application of his version of them to Josephus. Suffice it to say two things. First, that the nature of Josephus' writings and the character and history of his sources are so different from those of the gospels that it is in any case highly unlikely that any argument would lie from the one to the other.[1] Secondly it must be confessed that Professor Hanson is perhaps somewhat unduly complacent about the historical trustworthiness of Josephus' narratives. To take only one, comparatively trivial, example, he regards it as so preposterous to suppose that Tacitus' evidence about Ventidius Cumanus could possibly be superior to that of Josephus in any respect that he makes such a supposition the basis of a *reductio ad absurdum* argument. In fact, however, many of the most competent authorities on Josephus suppose precisely that.[2]

In his third section Professor Hanson advances two theses:

(i) that the attitude to historicity which underlies M cannot be made to provide a basis for preaching the gospel and that my attempts to show that it can are unsatisfactory; and

[1] The same sort of thing must be said, if anything more emphatically, about the attempt on H 99–100 to use Tacitus' *Agricola* as the basis of a *reductio ad absurdum* of Professor John Knox's position. Tacitus did not write as a member of a community which claimed that Agricola had been raised from the dead and that it was now living in the power of his resurrection!

[2] It is certainly true that Schürer (*Gesch. d. jüd. Volkes* 1[3] (Leipzig, 1898), 570, n. 14) agrees with Professor Hanson in strongly asserting the superiority of Josephus' testimony at this point, and gives an impressive list of authorities who take the same view; but he also cites a number of others who take the opposite view and to them can be added such scholars as Sir William Ramsey (in Smith's *Dictionary of Greek and Roman Biography and Mythology* 2 (1846), 143 a (*sub nom.* Antonius Felix) and now Rudolf Hanslik in *Pauly-Wissowa* (*sub nom.* Ventidius Cumanus).

(ii) that I show an unconscious awareness of this by implicitly adopting in my preaching and more devotional writings a more positive position on the historical question, inconsistent with that presupposed in M and elsewhere (H 92–3). My heart, he says, is better than my head (H 91).

It is difficult to deal satisfactorily with the first of Professor Hanson's theses until I have had the opportunity on some other occasion of setting out my real position on the historical question and my view of its implications for preaching and practical religion. So in this paper I shall for the most part confine myself to the charge of inconsistency, pausing only to note certain misunderstandings to which this section of Professor Hanson's essay suggests I have laid myself open.

On p. 91, as earlier on p. 81, Professor Hanson discusses my attitude to various details in Mark (e.g. in 3: 5 or 4: 38) which are often advanced as evidence that at these points the evangelist was reproducing direct eye-witness evidence. The argument of those who take this view is essentially as follows: these traits serve no edificatory or apologetic purpose, so they cannot have been introduced into the tradition for that reason; on the other hand, no one could have known about them unless he had been present at the scene. Therefore these details *prove* that for some of his material the evangelist could rely on original eye-witness testimony and also that he sometimes reproduced incidents without thinking that they had any religious significance, simply because he believed them to have happened. If so, certain conclusions about the general character of the gospels follow. As I said in the passage to which Professor Hanson refers[1] and have said frequently elsewhere, 'These and similar comments may well be justified'. But as against the *probative* force of this type of argument I have felt bound to point out that in some of the passages concerned it *is* possible to discern apologetic or edificatory motives for the inclusion of these traits, and in others (e.g. 4: 38) the detail is so commonplace that it would not be at all necessary to have been an eye-witness to know that it must have occurred. These considerations do not, and were not meant to, demonstrate that the traits in question do *not* go back to eye-witness testimony, but they do seriously undermine the contention that they

[1] *JTS* 9 (1958), 22.

must be explained in that way. And when we remember that the late, and historically untrustworthy, apocryphal gospels are specially rich in such traits, there seems full justification for my studiedly cautious conclusion (*JTS, ibid.*). 'This, of course, is far from showing that an argument can never lie from the presence of vivid detail to the presence of eye-witnesses, but it does suggest that the matter is by no means simple and that great discrimination is needed in the use of this argument.' It will be seen how far I am from dogmatically asserting that 'Mark invented these details', as Professor Hanson alleges (H 81).

In support of his charge of inconsistency Professor Hanson quotes something I said in a broadcast talk about two passages from St John's Gospel: 'St John may not have been reporting exact words, but the general picture is true enough.' 'If in his works of scholarship', he says, 'he could say even this about St Mark, let alone St John, there would have been no occasion for this essay.' I had supposed that in the passages from *St Mark* quoted on p. 200 and discussed on p. 213 above, that was very much what I was saying about St Mark.

Only one detailed example of the alleged inconsistency is quoted; Professor Hanson compares p. 41 (not p. 40 as he says) of the broadcast talks referred to above[1] and p. 100 of an article in *Theology* for March 1956. So far as the former is concerned, it simply does not say, as Professor Hanson alleges, 'that Jesus saw the necessity for his own death as stemming from the Old Testament', and specially from Isa. 53. On p. 41 I quoted a passage from Isa. 53 and then said: 'it is possible that it influenced Our Lord himself in his thinking about his task, *though that is by no means certain*'. In *Theology*, where I was reviewing a book by Dr Vincent Taylor, I described his reconstruction of the Lord's ministry based on the assumption that he was deeply influenced by Isa. 53 and then wrote:

This construction has much to commend it, yet it must be pointed out that at every point it is very largely speculative...Dr Taylor himself points out that Is. 53 is never quoted in Mark or Q...and it may be added that the Servant Songs as a whole are quoted only four times by the Evangelists, although they cite the Old Testament in all something like 400 times. It is probably true, as Dr Taylor argues, that an allusion to

[1] *A New Way of Looking at the Gospels* (London, 1962).

Is. 53 lies behind some Gospel passages which do not expressly quote it, but as many of these passages contain allusions as clear, or clearer, to other Old Testament passages as well...they do not provide any very strong evidence that the Servant Songs were as central to our Lord's mind as Dr Taylor's reconstruction suggests.

Is this 'scouting the idea that Jesus had any thought of fulfilling the role of the servant' (H 92), and is it in any way inconsistent with what was said in the broadcast talks?

Of the only other two passages Professor Hanson cites in this connexion suffice it to say that the degree of historicity I discover in them is only incompatible with what I have written in my 'works of scholarship' if one accepts Professor Hanson's interpretation of the latter discussed above.[1]

One other point from this section perhaps just deserves clearing up. On H 96 Professor Hanson refers to p. 10 of *Historicity and Chronology in the New Testament*[2] (London, 1965), where I suggest that patristic writers on occasion modified the historical data of the gospels in a theological interest. 'Nineham', he says, 'seems to suggest that they did so consciously', and goes on to point out that that would have been inconsistent with their known views about history. It is therefore worth recalling that in fact I made clear that the process was *not* conscious. Cf. p. 8 'though it was not fully realised at the time', and p. 9 'earlier generations, though they may not have explicitly formulated the principle...based their action upon it...'

We must now turn to Professor Hanson's treatment of Professor John Knox's views in the final section of his essay. So many different sorts of question are raised in these few pages (H 98–102) that it is difficult to know what to choose for discussion in the space available. Probably it will be best to proceed as before, leaving Professor Knox's positive position, and its implications for preaching and devotion, to another occasion and concentrating here on Professor Hanson's exposition and criticisms of him.

---

[1] In fairness I should perhaps add that, for reasons I shall give elsewhere, I regard the 'Christ of faith' as in certain circumstances a proper basis for preaching and do not therefore feel obliged always to discriminate nicely in sermons between 'Jesus' and 'Jesus as represented in the Gospels' etc., any more than I feel obliged to alter the introduction to the third of the 'comfortable words' in the Holy Communion Service to: 'Hear also what deutero-Paul saith.'

[2] The correct form of the title; Professor Hanson cites it incorrectly.

Professor Hanson clearly classifies Professor Knox among those who are radical sceptics about gospel historicity, and the first thing to note is that if he is right, this is another case of his knowing what a writer really thinks despite what he says and thinks he thinks. For this is certainly not Dr Knox's own understanding of his position. To quote one statement out of many,[1] in a note on p. 15 of his book *The Church and the Reality of Christ*, he writes:

...whether we are more 'conservative' or more 'radical' in our assessment of the historical trustworthiness of the Gospels. I have always felt that I belong at this point among the 'conservatives'—that is, I have found myself, as among the Form Critics, nearer in this regard to Dibelius than to Bultmann. I see no reason to doubt that the Gospels bring us a great deal of authentic information about Jesus. I have said this in other books. I...say it again...I believe that the picture of an actual historical person emerges in the Gospels and that this picture is to a large extent trustworthy.

It is true, as we have seen, that Professor Hanson takes no account of such varieties of opinion among '*the* Form-Critics', but in the face of so definite a statement we might have expected him to substantiate his very different assessment of Professor Knox's position. The only passage where he attempts to do so hardly carries conviction (H 101). He first of all states that in the matter of Jesus' resurrection 'John Knox goes beyond Nineham...Knox has the lowest opinion of all the resurrection narratives...he is anxious to explain *all* the resurrection appearances on...other grounds than that there was anything corresponding to them in the actual event'. In the passage on which Professor Hanson relies[2] here Professor Knox writes: 'I do not mean that visual experiences of the risen Jesus[3] did not occur... Nor am I denying that in the Providence of God these experiences served to open the way to that knowledge of the actual living reality of God in Christ which was the only effective ground of the Resurrec-

---

[1] Cf., for example, the passage quoted from him on p. 213, n. 1 above. 'In many cases the burden [of proving themselves historically trustworthy] can easily be carried' by gospel passages.

[2] Knox *op. cit.* p. 68.

[3] For better or worse, this is the expression Professor Knox uses to designate the phenomena described by St Paul at the beginning of 1 Cor. 15 and by the evangelists.

tion faith, whether among the few who had the experiences or among the multitudes who had not.'[1]

Professor Hanson's other piece of evidence is that on page 126 Knox argues that without the Church there would have been no resurrection, and 'comes within an ace of saying that the Church invented the resurrection'. It cannot be said too emphatically that this is a complete misunderstanding of Professor Knox's meaning. His real point is not easy to state briefly out of its context in his overall argument, but essentially it is something like this. Whatever exactly the historical events behind the New Testament accounts of the resurrection, they probably would not have been remembered, and certainly would never have been the saving event we know within the Church, unless they had met with a response of understanding and faith from the first Christians and, through them, from their successors. 'Something would have happened under this hypothesis, but not the Event. Jesus would have been born but not the Christ. . .He might even have been miraculously resuscitated after his death, but the Lord Christ would not have risen.' Only in this very special sense is it fair to say[2] that 'without the Church there would have been no Resurrection' and Professor Knox makes it clear that he would want to add with equal emphasis 'without the Resurrection there would be no Church' (see p. 125). So far from suggesting that the Church invented the resurrection, he is careful to add: 'to recognize this inextricable interdependence between Event and Church does not mean denying the reality of the distinction between them and the importance of our maintaining it'.[3]

To judge from such evidence as he provides, it would thus appear that Professor Hanson has misunderstood Professor Knox's position as much as he has misunderstood mine. It remains to comment on two other points he makes in this final section of his essay.

Dr Knox's position in this matter, as I understand it, is something like this. What the New Testament, including the gospels, *directly* reveals to us is a community, newly arisen in the first and early

[1] The last phrase makes clear that Professor Knox is referring to what Professor Hanson calls 'the resurrection appearances' and not to experiences of the risen Christ such as are open to all believers.
[2] The phrase is Hanson's not Knox's.
[3] P. 126; the remainder of the paragraph in Knox deserves to be consulted.

second centuries, whose members claim to enjoy a continuing dynamic communion with a supernatural being (called by them Christ, Lord and Son of God), as a result of which their lives evince a quite new quality. They assert that the immediate origins of this new community and its life lay in the activity of one Jesus, who had lived and died in Palestine in the earlier part of the first century but had been raised from the dead and was to be identified with the Christ with whom they were now in communion. Accordingly, they record some of their memories of the 'days of his flesh', mainly in the belief that a knowledge of his relationships and activities then would help to clarify and deepen relations with him in the present.

If down the centuries people have joined, and so perpetuated, this community, that is essentially because they have accepted the invitation to participate in the Church's experience of communion with the heavenly Christ and have found it as real for them as it was for the first Christians. Once inside the community, it is possible to find the recorded memories of the earthly Jesus as edifying and illuminating for faith as they were intended to be; but integrity demands that *modern* members of the community should apply to these memories all the refined historical techniques now available.[1] As a consequence they are led to recognize that in some cases the memories have been more or less coloured by experience of the risen Christ, and otherwise modified in the course of transmission.[2] In the case of a group of uneducated people intent on evangelism and not accustomed even to the highest standards of historical accuracy current in their area in the first century, there is nothing in the least surprising about that.

Against such a position it is no argument to say that if we cannot trust the precise accuracy of the early Christians' historical narratives, we cannot trust their experience at all (H 100). Communion with Christ and narratives about Jesus are phenomena of very different

[1] Failure to take adequate account of the implications of the modern 'historical revolution' surely invalidates Professor Hanson's appeal (H 100) to what 'never occurred to any Christian during the first nineteen centuries of the Church's history'.
[2] Professor Knox has repeatedly pointed out that (and why) the result is by no means always a net loss. 'Modified' memories may from some points of view be 'truer' than a bare recording would have been.

kinds and require validation of quite different sorts.[1] Nor does such a position involve any built-in historical scepticism of the kind Professor Hanson seems to suggest. Outside the Communist countries, the days of the Christ-myth school appear to be over, and the most rigorous modern investigator may well be convinced that the community which speaks to us in the New Testament owed its origin to events centring on the ministry of Jesus broadly corresponding to the gospel accounts. The exact degree of correspondence will be a matter for detailed discussion of individual passages, and no doubt competent authorities will continue to disagree considerably about it.[2] Dr Knox himself, as we have seen, occupies a comparatively conservative position on this matter, but as he himself repeatedly says, if he is right, it is not a matter of life or death, and a radical position with regard to it would be by no means 'intolerable',[3] especially as we can learn a great deal from 'memories' which have been modified, and even in certain cases created, by the faith of the early Church.

Secondly, it is not easy to see the relevance here of Professor Hanson's repeated insistence[4] that the New Testament writers believed themselves to be reporting sober historical fact. No one denies that; but medieval chroniclers believed the same thing— does that oblige us to accept all their accounts of miracles, however bizarre? Professor Hanson is the last person to be in a position to argue that writers are always doing what they believe themselves to be doing; and in view of what was said earlier about the membership of the earliest Church, and the way the gospel tradition was transmitted, it is perfectly possible to hold that the early Christians'

[1] An analogy which I have sometimes given to students may help to illustrate this. If we think back to the time when the insulin treatment for diabetes was first discovered, we can imagine that the sufferers who first benefited by the discovery may have developed a positively missionary attitude in the matter. They may well have sought out others still suffering from the disease, told them of their experience and urged them to avail themselves likewise of what the scientists had discovered. If they were not experts, their account of the historical and scientific facts relating to the discovery and its working may well have been sketchy and not entirely accurate; but that would have been a poor reason for refusing to recognize either the fact of their changed condition or the general truth of their account of how it had been brought about.
[2] Cf. the discussion by Professor Knox referred to on p. 213, n. 1.
[3] See p. 220, n. 2 above.   [4] See H 100–2.

accounts were in certain respects progressively modified without implying any accusation that they 'invented' or 'made up' what they tell us with any dishonest intent.

In conclusion it must be repeated that the scope of this essay is strictly limited. Professor Hanson claims that the present position with regard to gospel historicity is intolerable and he says this is due to the arbitrary assumptions and radically, but needlessly, sceptical conclusions of a whole *genus* of scholars of whom he singles out two for detailed discussion. The aim here has been to show that in the case of the two he names and discusses, both their assumptions and conclusions are quite different from what he suggests. Whether they are nonetheless intolerable is a question I hope to discuss elsewhere. It is of course possible that the views Professor Hanson wrongly attributes to these two are in fact held by the other members of the *genus* and that for that reason the present position is intolerable. About that, however, we cannot decide until Professor Hanson names them and we have had a chance to evaluate his account of their views and his justification for grouping them together.

PART II

CHAPTERS IN PAUL'S LIFE
AND THOUGHT

11

PAULINE CHRONOLOGY AND
PAULINE THEOLOGY

JOHN COOLIDGE HURD, JR

I. THE 'TRUTH IN PRINCIPLE'

In a recent article in a *Festschrift* to a fellow student from Chicago days John Knox mentioned with gratitude his indebtedness to his teachers at that university, particularly to Edgar J. Goodspeed.[1] Since in his paper Professor Knox was examining only one problem of New Testament study, he did not have occasion to speak generally about what may well be the most important legacy of that gifted faculty. It was their particular strength—and they passed this virtue on to their students—that to a special degree they allowed the New Testament documents to speak for themselves. To say this is to sum up three observations which can be made about the work of these scholars. In the first place they were especially sensitive to the historical circumstances reflected in each document. They interested themselves in the social, economic, political, and religious background of the sources. Secondly, these men were exceptionally free from traditional interpretations of the material. Thirdly, and as a result of the foregoing, they produced a brood of new and stimulating hypotheses.

However, of these three areas, the third has probably been the least influential. As Professor Knox himself noted, for example, the theory concerning the collection of the Pauline corpus and the writing of Ephesians which Dr Goodspeed considered his most important discovery has had little effect on the course of modern New Testament study, although Professor Knox himself is convinced of its value.[2] By and large, scholars have not accepted many of the particular hypotheses produced by this group of scholars. It is

---

[1] 'Acts and the Pauline Letter Corpus', in *Studies in Luke-Acts: Essays Presented in Honor of Paul Schubert*, edited by L. E. Keck and J. L. Martyn (Nashville, 1966), pp. 279–87.
[2] *Ibid.* pp. 279–80.

in the other two areas that their more important contribution was made. Here, as in other fields, the development of sound methods has been of more value than any particular set of results.

One methodological principle which these scholars' lively sense of history has put before us concerns the relationship which they perceived between Paul's letters and the book of Acts. As Donald W. Riddle, one of John Knox's teachers, wrote in 1940 in opening his book, *Paul, Man of Conflict*:

> The time is ripe for a new life of Paul...A major difficulty to be met... involves the use of the sources. If it be true that the biographer's prime necessity is to understand Paul's letters correctly, it is also incumbent upon him to follow the fundamental rule of biography, and determine the relative use to be made of primary and secondary source materials... Almost all biographies of Paul proceed by making a synthesis of... [Paul's letters and the data in Acts], thus confusing primary and secondary sources.[1]

Riddle himself took the other path and commented, 'The superiority of the method of following the primary sources needs little argument'.[2]

On the subject of Pauline chronology Riddle cited two papers which he considered to be 'of the highest importance'.[3] They were John Knox's first two articles on the subject: '"Fourteen Years Later": A Note on the Pauline Chronology' (1936)[4] and 'The Pauline Chronology' (1939).[5] Part of Riddle's admiration for these two papers was undoubtedly due to the methodology adopted by their author. The opening words of the earlier article are:

> It does not need to be said that our principal sources for the life of Paul are the letters generally esteemed authentic and the several sections of Luke-Acts that deal with his career. It is equally unnecessary to add that of these the letters are by all odds the more important and in cases of conflict with Acts, whether explicit or implied, are always to be followed. This is probably obvious enough and yet is often ignored.

Speaking on the same point in 1949 in the lectures published as *Chapters in a Life of Paul*, Professor Knox said again, 'Of our two sources the letters of Paul are obviously and incomparably the more

[1] *Paul, Man of Conflict: A Modern Biographical Sketch* (Nashville, 1940), pp. 13–15.
[2] *Ibid.* p. 78.   [3] *Ibid.* pp. 225–6.
[4] *JR* 16 (1936), 341–9.   [5] *JBL* 58 (1939), 15–29.

trustworthy. The truth in principle of this...statement no serious student of Paul's life is likely to deny, but its meaning in practice is not so widely or so clearly seen.'[1] On this occasion, although he added 'incomparably' to his earlier 'obvious', he took the precaution of prefacing the remark with a separate lecture on the historical and extra-historical purposes of the author of Acts. Moreover, he was candid enough to note that the 'meaning in practice' of this—to him obvious—principle had not been 'clearly seen'.

Nor has it been. In general, there have been three reactions to the proposal to rely primarily on Paul's letters. A small number of scholars have adopted both the principle and the use made of it by Professor Knox. Thus, for example, Frederic R. Crownfield in his *A Historical Approach to the New Testament* presents Knox's chronology without apology and with only a minor modification.[2] Again, M. Jack Suggs supports Knox's chronology 'based on the evidence of the letters, rather than Acts' by offering additional evidence for an early dating of Paul's ministry in Macedonia.[3]

More scholars, however, have responded to the proposals of Riddle and Knox merely by becoming more guarded in their statements about the dates and sequence of events in Paul's life. Donald J. Selby, for example, discussed the chronology of Paul's career in an appendix to his recent book, *Toward the Understanding of St. Paul*, mainly by listing the problems faced by anyone who would propose answers in this area. And he concluded, 'Fortunately, we need not decide all of these chronological questions in order to understand him'.[4] It is perhaps fair to say of scholars in this category that the extent to which they are willing to leave chronological and biographical questions uninvestigated is a measure of their conviction that these considerations really do not matter in the study of Paul's thought.

Probably the majority of scholars have rejected the chronological conclusions which Knox has reached. The grounds for this rejection are usually expressed with the word 'radical'. Thus, for example, Dieter Georgi said in a note at the close of his monograph, *Die*

---

[1] *Chapters in a Life of Paul* (Nashville, 1950), p. 31.
[2] *A Historical Approach to the New Testament* (New York, 1960), p. 259.
[3] 'Concerning the Date of Paul's Macedonian Ministry', *NovT* 4 (1960), 60–8. (Quotation, p. 60.)
[4] *Toward the Understanding of St. Paul* (Englewood Cliffs, N.J., 1962), p. 338.

John Coolidge Hurd, Jr

Geschichte der Kollekte des Paulus für Jerusalem, 'Die vorstehende Analyse zeigt, dass ich mich ausserstande sehe, den radikalen Vorschlägen, die J. Knox bezüglich der Chronologie des Paulus macht, zu folgen'.[1] Interestingly, in his second article Knox himself said that he intended to present 'a chronology radically different from that ordinarily adopted'.[2] Clearly many scholars believe that he succeeded. In general, Knox's reconstruction of Paul's ministry is viewed as a radical departure from established positions, and he has been characterized as one who puts a low estimate on the historical value of Acts. As G. B. Caird said in commenting on Knox's proposal concerning the relationship of Acts 15 and Galatians 2, 'This theory naturally avoids all the difficulties which beset those who take Acts more seriously'.[3] Since taking historical evidence seriously is ordinarily understood as a virtue in scholarly circles, Caird's comment is to be understood as a criticism of more or less severity. Again, Werner Georg Kümmel said flatly of Riddle, Knox, and Suggs that they had 'completely disregarded the statements of Acts about the journeys of Paul as historically useless'.[4] This seems a hard verdict, especially since Knox had specifically tried to meet this sort of criticism with his 1939 article. There he pointed out that his proposed chronology involved only two points of conflict with Acts beyond the adjustments which most scholars already make in the Acts account in order to accommodate the letters.[5]

While numerous scholars have taken exception to the dates which Professor Knox has proposed, very few have acknowledged that the basic issue is the methodology. One of the few is Thomas H. Campbell.[6] Writing in reaction to *Chapters in a Life of Paul*, Campbell undertook both to shift the methodological premise of Knox's work and to show that it need not lead where Knox has followed it. He began by attempting to qualify Knox's premise: 'Certainly Paul's

[1] *Die Geschichte der Kollekte des Paulus für Jerusalem* ('Theologische Forschung', 38; Hamburg-Bergstedt, 1965), p. 96, n. 23.
[2] 'Pauline Chronology', p. 18.
[3] 'The Chronology of the NT', in *The Interpreter's Dictionary of the Bible* (Nashville, 1962), 1, 606.
[4] *Introduction to the New Testament* (Nashville, 1966), p. 179.
[5] 'Pauline Chronology', pp. 23–6, 29.
[6] 'Paul's "Missionary Journeys" as Reflected in His Letters', *JBL* 74 (1955), 80–7.

letters are our primary sources for a reconstruction of his career, whereas Acts is at best a secondary source *except* at those points where the author is writing as an eye-witness or using the journal of an eye-witness'.[1] Campbell next admitted both that Acts was written for a number of reasons besides a strictly historical interest and that Acts is by no means a complete account of Paul's ministry. He then turned to the letters to see how much evidence could be found in them to support the reliability of Acts. In this endeavour his opening questions were: 'Are we compelled to assume that definite stages in Paul's missionary work cannot be discovered? And must we assume in advance that these stages cannot be the same, in their main outlines, as those which are so clearly marked out in Acts?'[2]

Apparently from the way these surprising questions are introduced, Campbell believed that Knox began with some such assumptions. What is clear, however, is that Campbell himself has begun with the opposite pair of assumptions and that it is his, and not Knox's, work which is marred by *a priori* considerations. In his argument he examined a series of quotations from Paul's letters in order to show that the general progress of Paul's ministry reflected in the letters corresponds to some of the sequences in Acts. He concluded that he had indeed found correspondences and that, although admittedly the Acts account is incomplete, it may be trusted at points where Paul's letters are not explicit. His final words are more sweeping, however: 'The traditional view of Paul's "missionary journeys" is not in any essentials foreign to the facts.'[3]

If 'not in any essentials foreign to the facts' means 'not untrue', then presumably he meant that the traditional view is in large measure true. The course of his argument indicates that by 'facts' he meant the evidence of the letters and that by 'tradition' he meant the evidence of Acts. Passing over for the moment the question of whether he has used the letters thoroughly and disinterestedly, we may notice that his method is to use the factual evidence of the letters to test the veracity of Acts. It should be observed that no amount of cataloguing of parallels will convert the secondary source into a primary witness. Campbell should not be misunderstood to have established Acts as an independent source which can be used to help

[1] 'Paul's "Missionary Journeys"', p. 81.
[2] *Ibid.*   [3] *Ibid.* p. 86.

229

in the interpretation of Paul's letters. Despite his criticisms of Knox, his conclusion is actually a restatement of Knox's premise. There are two types of material which are sources for our knowledge of Paul's life: (i) 'tradition' (Acts), which must be checked against (ii) the 'facts' (Paul's letters). However much these two types of sources may agree, they nevertheless lie on two different levels. The nearest that Campbell comes to modifying this basic distinction is his mention of the possibility that the author of Acts may have been an eye-witness, or may have used eye-witness evidence. This suggestion is the strongest claim that can be made for the reliability of Acts. Campbell has, however, given us no reason for supposing that the eye-witness hypothesis carries the same order of probability as the conviction that in the letters we have Paul's actual words at first hand.

Of course, secondary witnesses have varying degrees of trust-worthiness. If it could be shown that Acts agrees in some sections with a chronology derived by a thorough study of the letters alone, then we would have reason for increasing our respect for at least some of the source material used in Acts. It need hardly be said, however, that the four pages which Campbell has devoted to the evidence of the letters do not constitute an adequate basis of comparison. His use of the letters has been highly selective. He has not asked the question that Knox and Riddle propose: What do the letters tell us about Paul's career? Instead he has asked: What can I find in the letters which is similar to the picture of Paul's missionary activity as described by Acts? His question is admissible only if it is paired with its opposite: What are the differences between the biographical material in the letters and the account in Acts?

For all these reasons it is unfortunate, to say the least, that Kümmel in his exceedingly valuable *Introduction to the New Testament* should say, 'Campbell has convincingly demonstrated that the sequence of Paul's missionary activity to be inferred from his epistles so excellently agrees with the statements of Acts that we have every reason to infer the relative chronology of Paul's activity from the combination of both sources'.[1] In other words, Kümmel here reaffirms the traditional method of harmonizing the letters with the Acts account, so that, in spite of Campbell's witness to the distinction between

[1] *Introduction*, p. 179.

these two sources, Kümmel commends them as having the same order of authority. The fact, however, that Campbell believed that his survey of the evidence confirmed at some points the narrative of Acts is not, of course, grounds for shifting the initial methodological assumption which assigns different orders of authority to these two sources.

Another scholar who has weighed the methodological problem is W. D. Davies. In his recent book, *Invitation to the New Testament*, he discussed the method by which Acts may be approached, and he concluded:

Three positions can be taken: (1) We may regard Acts as so unreliable historically that we have to depend entirely, or almost entirely, on the Epistles. (2) We may take the Epistles as primary but take Acts with utmost seriousness as containing reliable information which must be reconciled with the Epistles. This is the position taken by British scholars usually. (3) We may take a mediating position. The Epistles are primary, but while we should not twist their evidence to fit that of Acts, Acts does provide valuable information which deserves to be considered as historically significant. This position is held by J. Munck.[1]

Davies himself chose the second position. Since he was writing for non-specialists, he did not go further in assigning scholars to his three categories.

We may, however, try to fill these categories for ourselves. When we consider Knox and Riddle, it is clear that they belong in the third category. While Riddle in particular emphasized caution in the use of Acts, both Riddle and Knox have maintained that, properly used, Acts contains 'valuable information which deserves to be considered as historically significant'.[2] When we do make this assignment, we are then faced with the problem of filling the first category. Davies did describe radical scholars who claim 'that Acts is a very unreliable document'. Some of them, he said, even 'regard it as written in the first quarter of the second century'.[3] But it is difficult to think

[1] *Invitation to the New Testament: A Guide to its Main Witnesses* (Garden City, N.Y., 1966), p. 240.
[2] Riddle, *Conflict*, pp. 185–200 (especially p. 199); Knox, *Chapters*, pp. 22–3 ('Excellent primitive sources...used...carefully and faithfully').
[3] *Invitation*, p. 238.

of scholars of this sort who have written on Paul's life in addition to their work on Acts. Thus there is a shortage of candidates for the first category.

Basically, the shortage arises from the manner in which Davies described this alternative. In the first place, he speaks as though scholars could be thought of as having a single, uniform attitude toward Acts. It is, however, an oversimplification to suggest that scholars can be classified adequately simply by asking whether they believe Acts to be (1) unreliable, (2) reliable, or (3) somewhat reliable. Acts is an exceedingly complicated document. It appears to be constructed from various types of source material, as, of course, are the synoptic gospels. For a scholar to say, for example, that the author of Acts may have the sequence of two of his traditions inverted, or may have arranged his material for theological, apologetic, or other reasons, is very far from saying that Acts does not give valuable historical information.

The second difficulty with Professor Davies's method of classification is that it does not take account of the methodological distinction urged by Riddle and Knox. It sounds fair and judicious to say that one will at every point consider the evidence both of the letters and of Acts. However, as our discussion of Campbell's article emphasized, the distinction between primary and secondary historical sources points to a difference in kind rather than degree. Simply relying more on one type of source than on another does not adequately put this principle into practice.

In his book, *The Historian and the Believer*, Van A. Harvey has made fruitful use of the analogy of the law court in his discussion of the processes leading to historical judgments.[1] The same analogy sheds light on our present problem. When we consider the use of sources to reconstruct Paul's career, we are faced by a problem similar to that governed by the rules of evidence in a legal proceeding: What evidence is admissible? In most types of court hearing secondhand information—hearsay, inference, supposition, and the like— is excluded, even though it frequently offers a more definite solution to the problem under litigation than the rather bare facts which are admissible. The reason for its exclusion is, of course,

[1] *The Historian and the Believer: The Morality of Historical Knowledge and Christian Belief* (New York, 1966), pp. 58–62, 77.

that information which has been interpreted by one or more minds to form a clearer picture is by the same token likely to have been misinterpreted, at least to some degree. The courts thus exercise close control over the type of information which is presented as evidence.

The historian, on the other hand, is not so well supplied with information that he can afford to exclude any crumb of evidence. But he can neither examine his witnesses without asking for their credentials nor entertain them in a random order. He must separate the firsthand from the secondhand witnesses, and he must place them on an agenda in such a way that the primary witnesses will give their evidence first, so that the evidence of the secondary witnesses will then be interpreted by it. The difference in kind between the witnesses results, therefore, in a difference in the time at which each type should properly give its evidence.

Furthermore, it should be observed that the simultaneous use of Acts and the letters, even if it were justified, is not a procedure which allows each to be heard with equal impartiality. The strong and unambiguous witness of Acts almost always overpowers all but the clearest evidence from the letters. The narrative of Acts seems far better suited to answer questions about Paul's biography than the letters. The latter rarely concern themselves with biographical matters directly. Even when such considerations come to the fore, the information which is provided is, like Melchizedek, without genealogy. The letters as separated pieces of evidence cannot hold their own beside the connected account in Acts.

We conclude, therefore, that the distinction between primary and secondary sources to which Riddle and Knox have very properly drawn attention means not just a difference in the degree of reliance that is to be placed on each type of source, but also involves necessarily the order in which these sources are to be consulted. Thus the basic first step in the reconstruction of Paul's career is the examination of his letters entirely apart from Acts. This step is necessary, not because Acts is or is not considered reliable, but because Acts is a secondary witness. The call for reliance on the letters by no means implies that Acts is judged a poor historical source. It is simply as a matter of historical discipline that we should begin the study of Paul's life with his letters. With respect to Acts, on the other hand, we should try to live ὡς μή. In the next section we shall consider the manner in which Riddle and Knox have put their distinction into practice.

2. THE 'MEANING IN PRACTICE'

In analysing the work of Donald Riddle and John Knox it will be convenient to keep three distinctions in mind. The first is, of course, the basic distinction between primary and secondary sources, which these scholars have done so much to recommend. To this distinction Knox adds a second. He distinguishes between the use of the sources to ascertain, on the one hand, the sequence of events in Paul's life, and, on the other hand, their use to give a picture of Paul's beliefs and character.[1] The former area he calls the outer or 'external' sphere; the latter, the inner or 'internal' sphere. He distinguishes, that is, between Paul's public and his private life, between his chronology and his theology. Using these terms he restates with admirable clarity his objection to the usual way in which Paul's life is reconstructed: 'While we tend to harmonize Acts with the letters as regards the inner facts of Paul's life, we tend to harmonize the letters with Acts as regards the outer. Neither instance of harmonization, of course, can be justified.'[2] Both types of harmonization are unjustified because of the difference in kind between the sources. The letters and Acts should be used successively, not harmonized by simultaneous use. Actually, Knox said, this misuse of the sources is not very distorting with regard to Paul's thought, 'since the letters are given their true importance in the process'.[3] In fact, Acts is practically ignored by most scholars as a source for a knowledge of Paul's thought. It is harmonization in the other direction which Knox called 'seriously distorting'. To avoid this distortion, the primary sources, that is, the letters, must be depended upon as the primary evidence for both spheres—for the 'ordinary biographical data' of Paul's life, as well as for his theology.

To the distinction urged by both Riddle and Knox, and to the further distinction proposed by the latter, it will be useful to suggest at this point yet another. It is the distinction between the use of a source independently of its historical context, and, by contrast, the

[1] *Chapters*, pp. 14, 15, 31–3, 89.   [2] *Ibid.* p. 32.
[3] *Ibid.*

observance of and dependence on such context. By 'historical context' we mean more than the general background in history of the source; we mean specifically the immediate set of circumstances which led up to the production of the document, circumstances which, because of the nature of our material, are reconstructed mainly from the source itself. The distinction which we are making contrasts, on the one hand, the acceptance of *what* a document says and, on the other, the attempt to understand what is said in the light of *why* or *how* it came to be said at all. For this distinction we shall in this paper use the rather awkward terms 'non-sequential' and 'sequential'. These are chosen for two reasons: (*a*) to avoid pairs like 'historical' and 'non-historical', 'in context' and 'out of context', or 'dynamic' and 'static', any of which tend to imply a value judgment, and (*b*) to emphasize with respect to Paul's letters that the close study of the immediate background of any single letter leads inevitably to the consideration of the circumstances which led to the production of one or more of the other letters. Thus the reconstruction of the historical sequence behind each letter evolves into the study of the sequence behind all the letters and therefore into a proposal for a sequence of the letters themselves.

The insight on which this distinction depends is, of course, axiomatic among historians, and, although not formally stated, underlies much of the work of Riddle and Knox. For example, in their discussions of the proper use of sources they both condemn what we may call the 'non-sequential' use of Acts and they urge that Acts be used only in the light of the purposes of its author. As Riddle says, 'Correct interpretation of the data in which Paul figures thus requires that each item be interrogated with reference to the plan, the object, and the purpose of Luke-Acts as a whole'.[1] Both Riddle and Knox, that is, reinforce their methodological objection to the usual dependence of scholars on Acts with the plea that Acts be used, when it is appropriate to use it, in the light of its historical context by taking into consideration the historical process behind it.

The distinction applies also to Paul's letters. On many points it is entirely possible to quarry information from one of them without regard for the circumstances which produced it. Particularly is this

---

[1] *Conflict*, p. 188; see in general pp. 185–200. For Knox see *Chapters*, pp. 15, 22–9.

permissible with Paul's statements about his past. For example, one can ask: How many times had Paul been to Jerusalem before his visit described in Gal. 2: 1–10? Here Galatians can give its evidence without being itself assigned a specific place in the sequence of events in Paul's life. Similar questions are: How was Paul educated? or, What was the nature of Paul's conversion experience? In answering these questions the letters can be used without the need for examining the immediate circumstances which evoked them. Here the letters need not be related to one another chronologically. Thus, in these instances the letters can be used non-sequentially.

On the other hand, such questions as, Had Paul heard about the situation in Galatia before he wrote to the Romans? or, What happened between the writing of 1 Corinthians and 2 Corinthians 1–9, and did it affect Paul's thought? or, Did Paul's teaching about the second coming of the Lord change during the period of the letters? all require that one relate the letters to the circumstances of Paul's life and to each other. There the letters must be used sequentially. In analysing a scholar's work on a Pauline letter we may notice whether he interprets the letter as a part of a historical sequence which includes perhaps one or more other letters, or whether he omits such a reconstruction. We may also observe whether or not the scholar makes a correlation between Paul's thought and his circumstances. The sequential use of the letters, as we shall discuss further, frequently involves such a correlation.

With these three distinctions in mind let us examine the reconstructions by Riddle and Knox of Paul's biography on the basis of the letters.

Although Riddle credited Knox's article, '"Fourteen Years Later"', with being the stimulus for his own work in this area,[1] we may conveniently begin with Riddle's book, *Paul, Man of Conflict*, since it preceded *Chapters in a Life of Paul* by ten years. The traditional procedure, according to Riddle, by which scholars have reconstructed Paul's career is to take the data of the letters and to fit them into the narrative of Acts.[2] The result is 'that general uniformity in harmonizing "lives" of Paul'.[3] Riddle, on the other hand, proposed

[1] *Conflict*, p. 9.   [2] *Ibid.* pp. 18, 77, 180.
[3] *Ibid.* p. 18.

to use the methods of 'scientific' historical biography. As he put it: 'Certainly one should give preference to the primary sources, and work out from them inductively the chronological and sequential relationships.'[1] This statement sounds very much as though he had in mind what we have termed the 'sequential' use of the letters. Indeed, he complained of the traditional biographies of Paul that their 'conventionality is a result of an almost uniform following of a traditional sequence of Paul's letters'.[2] Riddle himself urged 'that the whole question of sequence should be reconsidered'. Here again he sounds as though he had undertaken to study the letters sequentially.

On the other hand, Riddle spoke of the incompleteness of the sources and of the many unexplained hints in the letters, and he said, 'The task of working out the chronology of Paul's life as an apostle and letter writer is impossible'.[3] Thus he actually rejected the possibility of producing a connected sequence for Paul's life. Further, when he turned to the letters and listed the passages from which 'the chronological and sequential relationships' are to be derived 'inductively', he reveals that he had only four sections of the letters in mind: Gal. 1: 13 – 2: 14; 2 Cor. 11: 23 – 12: 9; Phil. 3: 3–16; and Rom. 15: 9–33.[4] Of these, only the first and the last give evidence about the sequence of events in Paul's life. The other two are valuable for their personal statements and for the information provided about Paul's background.

Riddle proposed that there is one crucial index by which the letters can be grouped into chronological periods. This index is the crisis Paul experienced shortly after the Jerusalem visit of Gal. 2: 1–10. At this conference Paul had thought that the problem of the relationship of the Jewish and gentile Christians had been settled.[5] The events which followed, however, showed him that he had been mistaken. Paul then was faced with a crisis almost simultaneously in Galatia and Corinth. 'The suddenness of its occurrence is difficult to appreciate.'[6] The letters which date from this period are, of course, Galatians and 2 Cor. 10–13. To these Riddle added Phil. 3: 2–16. Two other letters regard this crisis in retrospect. They are Romans and 2 Cor. 1–9. Riddle therefore dated them in the post-crisis

[1] *Conflict*, p. 77.   [2] *Ibid.* p. 201.
[3] *Ibid.* p. 76.   [4] *Ibid.* pp. 77, 230, n. 11.
[5] *Ibid.* p. 208.   [6] *Ibid.* p. 118.

period. None of the other letters, however, mentions this issue and for this reason he placed all of them before the crisis.[1]

In order to classify this large pre-crisis group of letters, Riddle accepted at several points the work of other scholars. He accepted Goodspeed's hypothesis that Ephesians is a covering letter written by the collector of the Pauline corpus. He accepted the hypothesis of G. S. Duncan, among others, of an Ephesian imprisonment during which all the prison letters were written. He accepted John Knox's identification of the 'fourteen year' period mentioned in Gal. 2: 1 with the reference to the same period in 2 Cor. 12: 2.[2] Finally, he accepted the opinion of many scholars about the non-integrity of 2 Corinthians and Philippians.[3] The result of all these considerations is the following rough outline of Paul's life:[4]

Paul's conversion
Short period in Arabia
First visit to Jerusalem
Work in Syria and Cilicia, then Galatia, and then Macedonia and Achaia
  1, 2 Thessalonians
Work in Asia
Ephesian imprisonment
  Philippians (except 3: 2–16), *Colossians, Laodiceans* (= *Philemon*), and possibly *1 Cor. 9* as well
Release from prison
  1 Corinthians from Ephesus
Conference visit to Jerusalem 'fourteen years later'
Judaizing crisis in Galatia and Corinth
  Galatians, 2 Corinthians 10–13, and *Philippians 3: 2–16* from Asia
Crisis resolved, at least in Corinth
  2 Corinthians 1–9 from Macedonia
  Romans 1–15, 16 from Corinth
Final visit to Jerusalem to deliver 'collection'
Rome and Paul's execution

It is important to remember that Riddle frequently maintained that the letters provide only spasmodic glimpses into Paul's life.[5] He did

---

[1] *Conflict*, p. 205.
[2] *Ibid.* pp. 209–10. This suggestion was reluctantly abandoned by Knox in *Chapters*, p. 78, n. 3.
[3] On Philippians see, for example, Edgar J. Goodspeed, *An Introduction to the New Testament* (Chicago, 1937), pp. 90–6.
[4] *Conflict*, pp. 104–24, 201–11.   [5] *Ibid.* pp. 10, 76, 107–8.

not, for example, claim that Paul had made only the three trips to Jerusalem listed above. Concerning Paul's travels before the delivery of the collection, Riddle said, 'He had made at least two visits to Jerusalem...He had more or less thoroughly covered the entire territory between Jerusalem and Illyricum'.[1]

In reflecting about Riddle's work we may note first that he consistently observed the basic distinction between primary and secondary sources. In fact, he drew very little information from Acts at all, and mainly cited it only to contrast its picture of Paul with that of the letters. Secondly, we may observe that, although the distinction between the external and internal aspects of Paul's life was not an organizing principle of his work as it was for Knox, he tended to present the two separately. He dealt with the narrative of Paul's ministry in one chapter (chapter v); the remainder of the book is, with the exception noted below, largely a topical discussion of Paul's 'religion' and personality. Thirdly, when we apply the criteria of our final distinction, we conclude that, with one major area of exception, Riddle made mainly a non-sequential use of the letters. He drew illustrative material from the letters as he proceeded from one topic to the next. He depended, that is, on what Paul said on a particular point and exhibited little concern for the historical circumstances which caused Paul to write as he did. While Riddle did discuss the order of the letters and the sequence of events in Paul's life, this discussion takes place in a brief appendix. It appears that he had understood the letters primarily without reference to their sequence and that his letters chronology was a somewhat hastily constructed second stage. His index for arranging the letters is rather crude, and it was rather crudely applied. For example, he spoke of the 'crisis' as occurring simultaneously in Galatia and Corinth.[2] He did not ask whether it is not more probable that the work of the Judaizers proceeded by stages. Riddle, in other words, did not make distinctions of sequence within his main chronological groupings.

Riddle's contribution, however, is that he did correlate the events of Paul's life with the contents of the letters at one important point: he proposed the 'crisis' as the index for the initial ordering of the letters. This index, rough perhaps though it may be, is 'sequential'

[1] *Conflict*, p. 74.   [2] *Ibid.* pp. 99–100, 118–21.

and involves the relating of Paul's thoughts about the issues of the crisis to the events which evoked them. In addition, we may note his general insistence on the need to put the letters into a new and more historical sequence. Finally, although his adoption of the 'Ephesian imprisonment' hypothesis was not argued on the basis of the sequence of Paul's thought in this period of his life, Riddle did think it necessary to suggest a few points of theological similarity between Colossians and Galatians, its neighbour in his chronological reconstruction.[1]

The limit, however, of Riddle's 'sequential' interest in Paul is indicated by his comment about the early dating of the prison letters:

Some have attempted to show from their thought and teaching that these letters reflect a late stage in the development of Paul's thought, especially in such 'doctrinal' matters as the conception of Christ and the end of the age. But no such development can be shown; none occurred. Paul insisted that he had his message from the time of his revolutionary experience; it was, he insisted, a revelation from God—certainly he would have repudiated any 'development' of it.[2]

Concerning which we may note that Paul is not always the best interpreter of his own methods and motives.

John Knox in his *Chapters in a Life of Paul* exhibits his usual clarity and orderliness.[3] After devoting a pair of chapters (I, II) to the methodological problem of the use of sources, he discussed the external aspect of Paul's career for three chapters (III–V) and concluded the book with four chapters (VI–IX) on the inner side of the career. In his discussion of Paul's public ministry, Knox quite properly began with the letters and only subsequently examined Acts. In his discussion of Paul's thought and character, Knox relied solely on the letters and only referred to Acts by way of contrast.

In reconstructing Paul's career (in chapter III) Knox, like Riddle, depended on a small selection of passages from the letters: Gal. 1:

---

[1] *Conflict*, pp. 116, 207.
[2] Riddle writing in D. W. Riddle and Harold H. Hutson, *New Testament Life and Literature* (Chicago, 1946), p. 122.
[3] He is, as someone once remarked after hearing him lecture, 'a man with a clean mind'.

13 – 2: 10; 1 Cor. 16: 1–4; and Rom. 15: 23–32. These sections all refer, he maintained, to the 'collection for the poor among the saints at Jerusalem' (Rom. 15: 26). This undertaking had its inception at the 'conference' visit of Paul to Jerusalem (Gal. 2: 10).[1] On the basis of this connexion Knox constructed a working hypothesis for the sequence of the major events in Paul's life. He next (chapter IV) examined Acts and concluded that 'a critical examination of Luke-Acts from the point of view of this hypothesis yields results which at certain points strikingly confirm the hypothesis itself'.[2] Then (chapter V) Knox proceeded to the difficult task of inserting absolute dates into the relative chronology he had constructed. It is only at the end of this chapter that he took up the problem of the sequence of the letters, and he frankly said, 'On the question of the chronological order of the letters our scheme has little bearing'.[3] One result of his argument was, of course, that Galatians had to be placed after the 'conference' visit. Further, his study of the 'collection' had led him to the following sequence for the letters relating to that project: 1 Corinthians, then 2 Cor. 1–9, and then Romans.

Beyond this point, however, it is clear that Knox did not rely on his special methodology in ordering the letters. He put the Thessalonian letters before 1 Corinthians 'on the basis of internal evidence alone', although he did not explain what the evidence is.[4] The imprisonment letters he placed very tentatively in an 'Ephesian imprisonment' just before the 'conference' visit. About the place of Galatians he was more tentative still. He dated it close to 2 Cor. 10–13 in *Chapters in a Life of Paul*.[5] Earlier, however, in his 1939 article he had suggested a date in Paul's final imprisonment.[6] This opinion he expressed again in his article on Galatians in *The Interpreter's Dictionary of the Bible* (1962).[7] On the entire problem of the letters chronology he concluded, 'No neat scheme of the order of the letters is free from objection'.[8] Inconsistencies, he said, beset every sequence known to him. For example, 2 Cor. 10–13 seemed to him later than

---

[1] *Chapters*, pp. 54–8.   [2] *Ibid.* p. 73.
[3] *Ibid.* p. 85.   [4] *Ibid.*
[5] *Ibid.* p. 98.   [6] 'Pauline Chronology', pp. 27–9.
[7] II, 342–3. See also the doctoral dissertation of his student, Howard L. Ramsey, *The Place of Galatians in the Career of Paul* (Ann Arbor, Mich.: University Microfilms, 1962).
[8] *Chapters*, p. 87.

2 Cor. 1–9, yet his chronology allows little time for it between the writing of 2 Cor. 1–9 and Paul's arrest in Jerusalem.

The sequence of Paul's life which results is as follows:[1]

Conversion in Damascus

Three years' work, mostly in Syria and Arabia

First visit to Jerusalem

Eleven or more years in Syria, Cilicia, Galatia, Asia, Macedonia, and Greece

   1 Thessalonians

   2 Thessalonians (if genuine)

Ephesian imprisonment

   Philippians, Colossians, and *Philemon*

Second ('conference') visit to Jerusalem

   1 Corinthians from Asia (probably Ephesus)

   2 Corinthians 1–9 from Macedonia (Philippi?)

   Romans probably from Corinth

   2 Corinthians 10–13 (?)

Third ('offering') visit to Jerusalem—arrest

   Galatians from prison (?)

It is important to notice that, whereas Riddle considered that his outline of Paul's life was broken by a number of unfilled gaps, Knox as the major result of his reconstruction said of Paul's visits to Jerusalem, 'Paul says there were only three visits'. And he added, 'The point is crucial'.[2] Briefly, his argument on this point is as follows:

   (*a*) The visit of Gal. 2: 1–10 was preceded by only one previous visit;

   (*b*) at the 'conference' of Galatians 2 the collection was initiated (Gal. 2: 10);

   (*c*) Romans 15 closes with Paul's forebodings about his trip to Jerusalem to deliver this same collection;

   (*d*) there is not a hint in the letters of any visit after this 'offering' visit and there is evidence in Acts that this visit resulted in Paul's arrest and eventual execution.

This three-visit pattern is exceedingly important, as we shall discuss later.

With reference to the three distinctions defined at the opening of this section, we have noted Knox's observance of the first two. Concerning the third, however, his position is similar to that of

---

[1] *Chapters*, pp. 51, 85–8.   [2] *Ibid.* p. 52.

Riddle: he had one index by which he gave sequence to the letters but beyond this his use of the letters is, in general, non-sequential. While his proposal to use the collection as the basis for reconstructing the final phase of Paul's career is sequential and of great importance, the relative order of the letters is not basically involved in his Pauline chronology. His suggestions about sequence come later and are for the most part rather tentative. His difficulties with 2 Cor. 10–13 is a case in point. So also is his uncertainty about the relative date of Galatians.

We are now in a position to compare the work of these two scholars. In presenting the outlines of Paul's life constructed by Riddle and Knox, a number of similarities both in procedure and in results became evident. In order better to assess these parallels, and in order to assess the similarities and differences between them and the traditional type of reconstruction, we may place them in parallel columns.

Traditional	Knox	Riddle
Conversion	Conversion	Conversion
Jerusalem (1)	Jerusalem (1)	Jerusalem (1)
Jerusalem (2)		
Jerusalem (3)		
1 Thess.	1 Thess.	1 Thess.
2 Thess.	(2 Thess.)	2 Thess.
Jerusalem (?)		
Ephesian prison	Ephesian prison	Ephesian prison
Phil., Col.,	Phil., Col.,	Phil., Col.,
Philem.	Philem.	Philem.
Release	Release	Release
	Jerusalem (2)	
1 Cor.	1 Cor.	1 Cor.
		Jerusalem
		Gal., Phil. 3: 2–16,
2 Cor. 10–13		2 Cor. 10–13
2 Cor. 1–9	2 Cor. 1–9	2 Cor. 1–9
Rom.	Rom.	Rom.
	2 Cor. 10–13 (?)	
Jerusalem	Jerusalem (3)	Jerusalem
	Gal. (?)	

16-2

There is no 'traditional' place for Galatians in the sequence of Paul's letters.[1] The outline presented above as the 'traditional' type of sequence is, of course, only one of several popular variations. Many scholars place some or all of the imprisonment letters late in Paul's life during his Roman or Caesarean imprisonment. The 'Ephesian imprisonment' hypothesis, however, is neither unusual today nor a special contribution of the two scholars whose work we are considering. Further, Knox expressed considerable hesitation on this point and allowed for the later dating as a distinct possibility. Scholars are also divided over the relative sequence of 2 Cor. 1–9 and 2 Cor. 10–13. The order given above is based on the conclusion that 2 Cor. 10–13 is the surviving part of the 'severe letter' mentioned by Paul in 2 Cor. 2: 3, 4; 7: 8, a theory which is probably the more popular today. On this point also Riddle and Knox do not break new ground.

Examination of the parallels given above reveals a surprising fact: although Riddle deplored the use by most scholars of a traditional sequence of the letters, his own sequence is very similar to at least one variety of the usual opinion. Both Knox and he undertook to derive their accounts of Paul's life from the letters as the primary sources, yet their sequences for these primary documents are both comparatively traditional. In this regard, at least, they cannot be considered 'radical'. They, like other scholars, have their own opinion about the point at which Galatians should be inserted. They, like other scholars, have opinions about the relative order of 2 Cor. 1–9 and 10–13 and about the place of origin of the imprisonment letters. Where they differ from other scholars is over the dates they assign to the major events in Paul's life which are known both from the letters and from Acts. More specifically, they hold a special position concerning the relationship of the visits to Jerusalem listed in Acts and those described in Galatians 1, 2.

There are three possible reasons for the large extent of the agreement between these two scholars on the one hand and the traditional view on the other.

(*a*) It could be maintained both that the traditional view is correct and that Knox and Riddle have correctly read the evidence of the letters, although in a somewhat unorthodox manner. Their work then confirms the reliability of Acts.

[1] See J. C. Hurd, Jr., *The Origin of 1 Corinthians* (London, 1965), pp. 15–18.

(*b*) Or it could be proposed that the 'traditional' sequence of the letters has not been so blindly dependent on Acts as Riddle's and Knox's protests have implied.

(*c*) Or one might suggest that the letter sequences proposed by Riddle and Knox are not as free of Acts as the methodology of these scholars would lead one to expect.

It is clear that those of Campbell's position will choose the first possibility. Knox himself has noted the similarity of his own conclusions at some points with the narrative of Acts.[1] But if we are to be faithful to our methodology, we must remind ourselves that the entertainment of this possibility must wait for the detailed analysis of the letters. Before Acts can be brought into the picture, the chronology of Paul's life and letters must be established as firmly as possible. To this end the work of Riddle and Knox may be considered an important first step.

Concerning the second alternative, we may note that Acts does not give enough information to provide a complete basis for a letters chronology. For example, the whole problem of the Corinthian correspondence must largely be settled without the help of Acts. The sequence given above as 'traditional' is based on the internal evidence of the two Corinthian letters. Moreover, the imprisonment letters are not put into sequence by the text of Acts. Paul specifically said that he had been in prison on numerous occasions (2 Cor. 11: 23). Once it is admitted that Acts has omitted an indefinite number of imprisonments, the prison letters can be inserted almost at will into the Acts account, either separately or in one or more groups. Lastly, the dating of Romans from the eve of Paul's departure to Jerusalem is also not derived from Acts but from Paul's own statement in Rom. 15: 14–29. At several points, therefore, the traditional sequence of the letters is not merely the result of the insertion of the letters into the Acts narrative at the likeliest spots. To this extent the traditional view deserves a hearing.

There is also truth in the third alternative. Riddle and Knox are not particularly free of the traditional sequence, not because they are not free of Acts, but because they, for the most part, make a nonsequential use of the letters. They are interested in giving sequence to the same major events that concerned the author of Acts. The

[1] 'Pauline Chronology', pp. 23–6; *Chapters*, pp. 51, 61–73.

sequencing of the letters they leave to last and therefore to a dependent place.

Each of them has made a vital contribution, however. Riddle has proposed a criterion which he discovered in the letters and by which he ordered the letters in a rough and preliminary way. Knox has made a similar contribution with his use of the collection as the organizing index for at least some of the letters. If, however, Knox's major conclusions are accepted, he must be considered to have made two additional contributions of a different order of importance. First, if his sequence of the major events in Paul's life stands, we do not have to contend with a series of gaping holes between the letters as in Riddle's scheme, holes several of which could have contained a visit to Jerusalem or the evangelization of Illyricum. Secondly, Knox's reconstruction means that the period of the letters covers almost the entire period of Paul's ministry. There is, therefore, reason to suppose that sequence should be discernible over the period of Paul's letter-writing activity. Knox has thus opened the door to the vigorous pursuit of the letters chronology.

It is time that we evaluated the three diagnostic distinctions offered at the opening of this section. It will have been noticed that they are of three very different kinds. The distinction between primary and secondary sources is a fundamental axiom of historical study and must, in our opinion, be observed by all who attempt to study Paul historically. Here John Knox and Donald Riddle have made an important contribution to Pauline studies.

The second distinction, however, is of a different sort. To the extent that Riddle in practice and Knox in principle have separated the outer and inner aspects of Paul's life, they have failed to correlate his thought and his circumstances, in spite of their great interest in each of these areas individually. It is clear that in writing biography the ultimate goal of the biographer is to think his subject's thoughts after him and in a sense to know him better than he knew himself. To do this the historian must connect the thoughts and events of his subject's life. The man's thought is illuminated by the original problems which were the occasions for his utterances. Some men are more systematic in their writings than others, and thus the circumstances of their lives affect the interpretation of their work to a lesser degree. Paul, however, is widely recognized to have expressed himself in direct reaction to his immediate problems. Therefore, in dealing with Paul the historian must make a special effort to present Paul's thoughts in intimate connexion with the events which evoked them. As far as possible, the inner and outer aspects of his life must be brought together; his theology and his chronology must be related. The points at which Knox and Riddle have correlated these two aspects—the collection and the Judaizing crisis—are points at which their work has added depth and importance.

When the third distinction was proposed, it was explained that the terms 'sequential' and 'non-sequential' were chosen to avoid prejudging the issue. Now it needs to be said that the 'sequential' approach is simply one aspect of sound historical method, in this writer's opinion. The sources must be understood and presented, as far as possible, within the historical sequences which gave birth to them. At some points, of course, these historical circumstances affect the thought of the letters more than at others, yet the background is always there and must be included in the calculation. Thus the interpreter of Paul should try to relate each of his letters to its immediate occasion. This occasion, in turn, should be related to the occasions of other letters. The goal is a connected sequence of events behind the letters and a sequence of the letters themselves. We maintain that it is only by a 'sequential' approach to the letters that we can make full use of these sources.

At present it is as if there were in Pauline studies a wall separating work on the 'introductory' matters and analysis of the theological problems. On the one side it is asked: What difference do Paul's theological ideas make to the task of reconstructing the chronology of his life? Thus G. S. Duncan wrote of his work on Paul's letters, 'Our study is essentially an historical one...We shall not be concerned, except in a secondary way, with...the doctrinal ideas which are expressed in them.'[1] Similarly, Riddle complained of the movements in the history of theology which had contributed to 'current misunderstandings of the real Paul...They have overemphasized the theological aspects of his messages, and thus have made a theologian of the missionary.'[2] To this side it must be said that, since the

---

[1] George S. Duncan, *St. Paul's Ephesian Ministry: A Reconstruction* (New York, 1930), p. 10. [2] *Conflict*, p. 179.

biographical data in the letters are by no means complete and unambiguous, no reconstruction of Paul's career which ignores the sequential aspects of his thought can be accepted.

On the other side it is objected, How is it possible or justifiable to interpret what we know certainly (the contents of Paul's letters) in the light of what is known to us only uncertainly (the events and motives behind them)? To this side it can be said that this dilemma is neither new nor unique. The same problem meets the historian at every turn. Why did the author of Luke-Acts write as he did? Why and how did the editors of the synoptic tradition produce the results that we have? In what manner did the early Church select, preserve, and modify the traditions about Jesus? These questions cannot be ignored merely because the answers are partially hidden from us. On the contrary, the quest for the answers to these problems has been immensely rewarding to New Testament study. In contrast, however, to these problems, the answers to which are infinitely complex and never fully obtainable, the problem of the sequence of the letters has a simple answer: Paul *did* write his letters in a sequence, and in one and only one sequence. Every clue to their order which is correctly read will point—barring the accidents of history—in the same direction. It is because of this fact that so much emphasis in this paper has been laid on the sequence of the letters. This goal is real and attainable. Knox and Riddle have prepared the way by providing the principle which requires that we concentrate our attention first on the letters alone.

The wall of separation between Pauline chronology and Pauline theology must be breached if the sources are to be studied with maximum results. Just as the 'harmonizing' of the letters with Acts is illegitimate, so too is the harmonizing of the letters with one another. Both types of harmonization are the result of a faulty historical method. On the one hand, the sequential approach to the letters is a vital element in the proper understanding of their message. On the other hand, the reconstruction of Paul's life must be based on all that Paul wrote, not just on the biographical sections. The outer and the inner aspects of Paul's life must illuminate each other.

12

THE APOSTOLIC *PAROUSIA:* FORM AND SIGNIFICANCE

ROBERT W. FUNK

In his letters Paul often indicates his reason for or disposition in writing, his intention or hope to dispatch an emissary, and his intention or hope to pay the congregation a personal visit. These items tend to converge in one more or less discrete section of the letter. This section I have identified elsewhere as the 'travelogue', and have attempted to isolate and establish it as a structural element in the Pauline letter.[1]

The designation 'travelogue' suggested itself because the passages in question appeared to be concerned primarily with Paul's movements, as indeed, in a sense, they are. Upon further reflexion, however, it became clear that Paul regarded his apostolic presence to his congregations under three different but related aspects at once: the aspect of the letter, the apostolic emissary, and his own personal presence. All of these are media by which Paul makes his apostolic authority effective in the churches. The underlying theme is therefore the apostolic *parousia*—the presence of apostolic authority and power—of which the travelogue in the narrow sense is only one element.

It is proposed here to advance the analysis of the apostolic *parousia* another step, first, by setting out the formal structure of the apostolic *parousia*, and, secondly, by considering its significance in relation to Paul's understanding of his own apostolic authority. The appropriateness of the designation will emerge in connexion with the latter. An effort will be made, finally, to draw from the analysis two specific consequences which touch two of the many provocative suggestions and proposals put forward by John Knox.[2]

[1] *Language, Hermeneutic and Word of God* (New York, 1966), chap. 10.
[2] I should like to take this occasion to acknowledge my great indebtedness to Professor Knox, especially as regards his insightful work on the Pauline corpus and Acts. His contributions have proved to be extremely fruitful in this as in other respects.

I

The following passages may be identified, on the basis of both form and content, as specifically concerned with the apostolic *parousia*: Rom. 15: 14–33 with its parallel in 1: 8 ff.; Philem. 21 f.; 1 Cor. 4: 14–21; 1 Thess. 2: 17 – 3: 13; Phil. 2: 19–24. 1 Cor. 16: 1–11, although coming under the heading of 'concerning the collection' (16: 1; cf. 16: 12), treats the movements of Paul and Timothy, and thus manifests some of the same characteristics as those passages which refer to entire letters. 2 Cor. 8: 16–23 and 9: 1–5, both of which again occur in passages (or letters?) which concern the collection, may be included for the same reason.

Phil. 2: 25–30 (Epaphroditus) and 1 Cor. 16: 12 (Apollos) treat the movements or sending of associates, and are attached in each case to sections having to do with Paul's apostolic *parousia*. They are thus secondary but related passages.

In 2 Cor. 12: 14 Paul introduces the subject of his third visit to Corinth, which leads him to remark again on the economics of his previous visits (cf. 11: 7 ff.; 12: 13); this in turn prompts him to refer to previous visits by those he had sent (12: 17 f.). In 12: 19 he reviews his reason for writing, which is directly coupled with the character of his impending visit: 'I write this in order to spare the sharp exercise of authority when I come' (13: 10). He refers to his forthcoming visit again in 13: 1 and is occupied through 13: 10 with the issue of that visit and the preparation the Corinthians should make for it. 2 Cor. 12: 14 – 13: 10 could thus be termed the section on apostolic *parousia*. It is woven, however, into the warp and woof of the letter, no doubt because 2 Cor. 10–13 as a whole is a defence of Paul's apostleship and hence of the apostolic *parousia* (cf. 10: 1 ff., 8 ff.), but it is no less discernible as a structural element for that.

In the letter to the Galatians, towards the close of his principal arguments and before beginning the *paraenesis*, Paul again (cf. 1: 6–12, with reference to his preaching in Galatia) turns to the subject of his presence in Galatia. He reviews his first welcome there and ends with the wish that he might be with them just now (4: 12–20). While this passage, as the letter elsewhere (e.g. thanksgiving, closing), skimps on formal elements, as we shall see, it nevertheless functions structurally in a way comparable to the apostolic *parousia* in the other letters.[1]

2

Rom. 15: 14–33 is the most elaborate and formally structured of these passages having to do with apostolic *parousia*. It may therefore serve as a provisional model for both individual items and order.

Paul begins (1) by stating his disposition in writing (15: 14–15 a), to which he adds (2) an elaboration of the basis of his apostolic relation to the recipients, in this case the Gentiles generally (15: 15 b–21). The implementation of the apostolic *parousia* forms the major theme of the passage (3): Paul indicates that he has been hindered from coming (15: 22), that he has longed to come (15: 23), and that he now hopes to see them (15: 24 b). The same three items appear also in Rom. 1: 11 ff. and 1 Thess. 2: 17 ff., but with the first item last. The order may be arbitrarily resolved in favour of the majority: (3 a) an expression of the desire or eagerness to come; (3 b) an expression of the hope, intention or wish to come; (3 c) the statement that he has so far been hindered or prevented from coming. He occasionally adds (3 d) the wish to be sent on by them to wherever he is going (15: 24 b). There follows in Rom. 15 the statement that when he has completed his mission to Jerusalem he will come to them on his way to Spain (15: 25–9); this item announces the definite prospect of a visit.

In parallel passages elsewhere, e.g. 1 Cor. 4: 17, 1 Thess. 3: 2 ff., before announcing a prospective visit of his own, Paul first indicates that he is dispatching an apostolic emissary. Since this item was not relevant in Romans, it may be assumed that 1 Corinthians and 1 Thessalonians represent the fuller form at this juncture. The items

---

[1] I omit consideration of 2 Cor. 1: 1 – 2: 13, 7: 5–16, the so-called 'letter of reconciliation', which is concerned as a whole with Paul's proposed and previous visits and letters, with the apostolic *parousia* in retrospect, and thus may be said to be a letter in which the apostolic *parousia* forms the body of the letter. Inclusion here would entail developing the Pauline notion of the reciprocal presence of apostle and congregation to each other—also encountered, e.g., in Philippians and 1 Thessalonians—and treating the thorny question of the integrity of 2 Corinthians. In any case, the 'letter of reconciliation' does not offer a discrete section which can be labelled apostolic *parousia*, and it is with these that we are immediately concerned.

and order would therefore be: (3 *e*) the dispatch of an apostolic emissary; (3 *f*) the announcement of an apostolic visit.

Having announced his future arrival, Paul then appeals to the recipients to join him in the prayer that he may be delivered from peril and that he may finally come to them (15: 30–2). In so doing, he suggests that his coming is dependent upon 'God's will' (15: 32). The first of these motifs may be designated 4 *a*, the second, more conventional qualification, 4 *b*.

Paul anticipates, finally, that his presence among them will bring some benefit to him (15: 32 *b*). In Rom. 1: 11, 13 he suggests that some benefit will accrue to the recipients by virtue of his presence, and in 1: 12 he modifies this note to the extent that his presence will be mutually beneficial. This theme in its various nuances may thus be designated 5 *a*, 5 *b*, and 5 *a–b*.

After making allowance for some minor modifications of the rubrics on the basis of parallel passages, and following the order proposed above, we may summarize the item analysis in tabular form:

(1) γράφω (ἔγραψα) ὑμῖν..., stating Paul's (1 *a*) disposition (participle) or (1 *b*) purpose (ἵνα-clause) in writing.

(2) The basis of Paul's apostolic relation to the recipients.[1]

(3) Implementation of the apostolic *parousia*.

(3 *a*) Desire, eagerness to see (come to) them (ἐπιποθέω, σπουδάζω and cognates).

(3 *b*) Hope (ἐλπίζω), wish (θέλω), intention (προτίθεμαι) to see (come to) them.[2]

(3 *c*) Hindrance to his coming (ἐνκόπτω, κωλύω), or delay.

(3 *d*) 'To be sent on by you' (προπέμπω).

(3 *e*) Dispatch of an emissary, which takes the form: (*a*) ἔπεμψα ὑμῖν (name); (*b*) ὅς (credentials); (*c*) ἵνα (or infinitive: purpose).

(3 *f*) Apostolic *parousia*, which takes the form of an announcement or promise of a visit, or that a visit is expected, hoped or prayed for (cf. 3 *b*, 4 *a*).

(4) Invocation of divine approval and support for the apostolic *parousia*.

---

[1] This item does not appear to be consistently accommodated in the apostolic *parousia*, being peculiar to Rom. 15 (15*b*–21) and 1 Cor. 4 (15–16).

[2] The justification for dividing into 3 *a* and 3 *b* is that both motifs appear in Rom. 15, Rom. 1, 1 Thess.

(4 *a*) The prayer for his presence may be a request for prayer, their prayer, his own prayer.[1]

(4 *b*) The convention, 'if God wills'.

(5) Benefit from the apostolic *parousia* accruing

(5 *a*) to Paul,

(5 *b*) to the recipients,

(5 *a–b*) to the two mutually.

This benefit may be derived from Paul's presence to them by letter, by emissary, or by his appearance in person. The internal relationship, but not identity, of these media is thereby confirmed.

To a certain extent this scheme is a theoretical construct, based as it is primarily on Rom. 15: 14–33. In order to indicate the range and persistence of items, together with the variety in order, it is necessary to tabulate them for each passage in the order in which they occur. It should be observed that items are sometimes worked up together, and that one occasionally finds doublets. The numerical shorthand proposed above will serve for this purpose; an item number in ( ) indicates phraseology thematically comparable, or, where two notations are given, that the first includes the function given in ( ); [ ] indicate that the theme in question does not occur in the apostolic *parousia* proper, but in proximity to it. The reference in each case is to Paul unless otherwise indicated.

Apostolic 'Parousia' : Items and Order

(1) Rom. 15: 14–33		(2) Rom. 1: 8 ff.		(3) Philem. 21 f.	
1 *a*	14–15 *a*	4 *a*	10 *b*	[5 *a*	20 *b*]
2	15 *b*–21	4 *b*	10 *b*	1 *a*	21
3 *c*	22	3 *a*	11 *a*; cf. 15	3 *f*	22 *a*
3 *a*	23 *b*	5 *a–b*	11 *b*–12	3 *b*	22 *b*
3 *b*	24 *b*	3 *b*	13 *a*	4 *a*	22 *b*
3 *d*	24 *c*	3 *c*	13 *b*		
3 *f*	28 *b*	5 *b*	13 *c*		
4 *a*	30 ff.				
4 *b*	32				
5 *a*	32 *b*; cf. 24 *d*				

[1] The prayer to be delivered from some peril (Rom. 15: 31) occurs also in 2 Cor. 1: 10, 2 Thess. 3: 2 (there also in requests for prayer). Cf. 2 Tim. 3: 11, 4: 17 f. But it does not appear to be a constitutive element in the apostolic *parousia*.

(4)		(5)		(6)	
1 Cor. 4: 14–21		1 Cor. 16: 1–11		1 Thess. 2: 17 – 3: 13	
1 *a*	14	(1)	1*	3 *a*	17 *b*; cf. 3 : 6 *b*
2	15–16	3 *f*	2 *b**	3 *b*	18 *a*
3 *e*	17	3 *e*	3 *b*†	3 *c*	18 *b*; cf. 2 : 16
3 *f*	19 *a*	3 *f*	4†	3 *e*	3 : 2–5
4 *b*	19 *a*	3 *f*	5 f.	5 *a*	3 : 6–9‡
5 *b*	18, 19 *b*–21	3 *d*	6 *b*	4 *a* (3 *f*)	3 : 10 *a*
		3 *b*+3 *b*	7	5 *b*	3 : 10 *b*
		4 *b*	7 *b*	4 *a*	3 : 11
		(3 *c*)	8–9		
		(3 *e*)	10–11		

* Ref.: collection.   † Ref.: delivery of collection.
‡ Ref.: from Timothy's return to Paul.

(7)		(8)		(9)	
2 Cor. 12:		Phil. 2: 19–24		Gal. 4: 12–20	
14 – 13: 13		3 *e*	19–23	3 *b*	20 *a*
3 *f*	14 *a*	5 *a*	19 *b*†	5 *b* (?)	20 *b*
3 *e*	17–18*	3 *f*	24		
(1)	19	In 1: 1 – 2: 18, note:			
5 *b*	19 *b*	3 *a*	1: 8		
3 *f*	13: 1 *a*	4 *a* (?)	1: 19		
(1)	13: 2	3 *f*	1: 25 f.		
1 *b*	13: 10	5 *a*–*b*	1: 25 *b*–26;		
5 *b*	13: 10 *b*		cf. 2: 16 *b*–18		

* Ref.: former sending.   † Ref.: Timothy's coming.

(10)		(11)		(12)	
2 Cor. 9: 1–5		2 Cor. 8: 16–23		Phil. 2: 25–30	
1	1	3 *a*	16–17★	3 *e*	25–28
3 *e*	3–5	3 *e*	18 ff.	3 *a*	26 *a*†
3 *f*	4	3 *e*	22 ff.	5 *a*–*b*	28 *b*‡
				5 *a*	30 *b*§

(13)	
1 Cor. 16: 12	
3 *e*	12 *a*
4 *b*	12 *b*‖
3 *f*.	12 *c*‖

★ Ref.: Titus.   † Ref. Epaphroditus.   ‡ Ref.: Epaphroditus' coming.
§ Ref.: retrospective of Epaphroditus' service.   ‖ Ref.: Apollos.

The apostolic 'parousia': form and significance

Before attempting to interpret the preceding data with respect to the shape of the whole, one item within this complex may be considered for its own internal structure.

3

The basic formula for 3*e*, the sending of an apostolic emissary, is quite similar to the formula used to express the purpose in writing (1*b*).[1] When employed in connexion with 3*e*, however, it is expanded in such a way as to give 3*e* a characteristic structure of its own.

The simple form occurs at 1 Cor. 4: 17:

a διὰ τοῦτο αὐτὸ ἔπεμψα ὑμῖν Τιμόθεον,
b ὅς ἐστίν μου τέκνον ἀγαπητὸν καὶ πιστὸν ἐν κυρίῳ,
c ὃς ὑμᾶς ἀναμνήσει τὰς ὁδούς μου τὰς ἐν Χριστῷ Ἰησοῦ,...

a stands for the introductory formula, *b* for the credentials clause, and *c* for the purpose clause.

The same structure occurs at 1 Thess. 3: 2–3*a*:

(διὸ μηκέτι στέγοντες...)
a καὶ ἐπέμψαμεν Τιμόθεον,
b τὸν ἀδελφὸν ἡμῶν καὶ συνεργὸν τοῦ θεοῦ ἐν τῷ εὐαγγελίῳ τοῦ
    Χριστοῦ,
c εἰς τὸ στηρίξαι ὑμᾶς καὶ παρακαλέσαι ὑπὲρ τῆς πίστεως
    ὑμῶν τὸ μηδένα σαίνεσθαι ἐν ταῖς θλίψεσιν ταύταις.

But Paul then expands on the theme of tribulation (verses 3*b*–4), and returns with 3: 5 to items *a* and *c*:

a διὰ τοῦτο κἀγὼ μηκέτι στέγων (renewing 3: 1) ἔπεμψα
c εἰς τὸ γνῶναι τὴν πίστιν ὑμῶν,
    μή πως ἐπείρασεν ὑμᾶς ὁ πειράζων καὶ εἰς κενὸν γένηται ὁ κόπος
    ἡμῶν.

[1] It is not possible in this context to provide an analysis of the two formulae which appear as item 1 (*a* and *b*). Suffice it to say that Paul developed his own characteristic way of expressing this theme in dependence upon the common Graeco-Roman epistolary tradition. The same could be said of items 3*a*, 3*b* and 4*b*, to cite further examples. The present analysis is thus to be understood as a preliminary step in the direction of a full comparative study. In anticipation of that study, it may be said that Paul reflects the common epistolary tradition to an extent unsuspected even by the readers of Deissmann and Moulton-Milligan, but that he deforms that tradition in characteristic ways.

The expansion in 3: 3 *b*–4 may be regarded as an expansion of *c*. Moreover, the first formulation of *c*, which expresses the immediate purpose for which Timothy is sent, is altered in the second to reflect the apostle's own perspective; it should therefore be called *c*′; *b* is omitted in the repetition.

The identical structure is found at Phil. 2: 25–30, which has to do with the dispatch of Epaphroditus:

a ἀναγκαῖον δὲ ἡγησάμην Ἐπαφρόδιτον
b τὸν ἀδελφὸν καὶ συνεργὸν καὶ συστρατιώτην μου,
     ὑμῶν δὲ ἀπόστολον καὶ λειτουργὸν τῆς χρείας μου,
a πέμψαι πρὸς ὑμᾶς,
c ἐπειδὴ ἐπιποθῶν ἦν πάντας ὑμᾶς, καὶ ἀδημονῶν,
     διότι ἠκούσατε ὅτι ἠσθένησεν.

    .   .   .

a σπουδαιοτέρως οὖν ἔπεμψα αὐτόν,
c′ ἵνα ἰδόντες αὐτὸν πάλιν χαρῆτε κἀγὼ ἀλυπότερος ὦ.

In this case, *c* states the reason Paul is sending Epaphroditus back, and that reason is expanded in verse 27. In *c*′ Paul states the reason for sending him back from the point of view of the Philippians and himself. The only variation is that *b* breaks into *a*.

With this structure may be compared Phil. 2: 19–23:

a ἐλπίζω δὲ ἐν κυρίῳ Ἰησοῦ Τιμόθεον ταχέως πέμψαι ὑμῖν,
c ἵνα κἀγὼ εὐψυχῶ γνοὺς τὰ περὶ ὑμῶν.
b οὐδένα γὰρ ἔχω ἰσόψυχον,
     ὅστις γνησίως τὰ περὶ ὑμῶν μεριμνήσει·
     οἱ πάντες γὰρ τὰ ἑαυτῶν ζητοῦσιν, οὐ τὰ Χριστοῦ Ἰησοῦ.
     τὴν δὲ δοκιμὴν αὐτοῦ γινώσκετε,
     ὅτι ὡς πατρὶ τέκνον σὺν ἐμοὶ ἐδούλευσεν εἰς τὸ εὐαγγέλιον.
a τοῦτον μὲν οὖν ἐλπίζω πέμψαι
c′ ὡς ἂν ἀφίδω τὰ περὶ ἐμὲ ἐξαυτῆς.

In this form, *b* is omitted from the initial formulation, only to be given expanded treatment in middle position. It would appear that expansion is permissible only in middle position and only in relation to the immediately preceding item. *c*′ reverses, so to speak, the perspective of *c*: just as Paul is anxious to learn about the Philippians, they are anxious to learn about him (cf. 2: 17 f.). He will send Timothy as quickly as the issue of his present crisis can be reported (cf. 1: 12–26).

The form in 2 Cor. 9: 3–5 omits *b* altogether, but is nevertheless a double form (like 1 Thess. 3: 2–5; Phil. 2: 19–24, 25–30), with an extended *c* in middle position:

a ἔπεμψα δὲ τοὺς ἀδελφούς,
c ἵνα μὴ τὸ καύχημα ἡμῶν τὸ ὑπὲρ ὑμῶν κενωθῇ ἐν τῷ μέρει
      τούτῳ, ἵνα..., μή πως... (through verse 4)
a ἀναγκαῖον οὖν ἡγησάμην παρακαλέσαι τοὺς ἀδελφοὺς
c′ ἵνα προέλθωσιν εἰς ὑμᾶς καὶ προκαταρτίσωσιν...

Once again, *c′* alters the perspective of *c*. In this instance, the immediate purpose is expressed by *c′*, while *c* views the matter from Paul's own perspective.

The forms in 2 Cor. 8: 18 ff., 22 f., on the other hand, omit *c* in the interests of the delicate situation in Corinth, but strongly emphasize *b*, which is repeated in end position:

8: 18 *a* συνεπέμψαμεν δὲ μετ' αὐτοῦ τὸν ἀδελφὸν
       b   οὗ ὁ ἔπαινος...
8: 22 *a* συνεπέμψαμεν δὲ αὐτοῖς τὸν ἀδελφὸν ἡμῶν,
       b   ὃν ἐδοκιμάσαμεν...
8: 23 *b* εἴτε ὑπὲρ Τίτου,
            κοινωνὸς ἐμὸς καὶ εἰς ὑμᾶς συνεργός ·
            εἴτε ἀδελφοὶ ἡμῶν,
            ἀπόστολοι ἐκκλησιῶν, δόξα Χριστοῦ.

2 Cor. 12: 17–18 is an allusion to a previous dispatch of emissaries, 1 Cor. 16: 10–11, 16: 12 refer to the coming of associates rather than their dispatch, with the consequence that these passages do not manifest the characteristic structure.[1] Into his discussion of the

---

[1] 1 Cor. 16: 10 f. may not be an isolated note on Timothy, with reference, perhaps, to 4: 17, but may also come under the rubric, 'concerning the collection'. Paul's discussion of his prospective sojourn in Corinth (16: 5–9) bears at least oblique reference to his instructions concerning the collection (cf. 16: 2). It is just possible that Timothy was to assist in the preparation of the collection, though this is not explicitly said. While 16: 10 f. lacks the characteristic language of 3 *e*, its structure is nevertheless suggestive:
(*a*) ἐὰν δὲ ἔλθῃ Τιμόθεος,
(*c*)   βλέπετε ἵνα ἀφόβως γένηται πρὸς ὑμᾶς·
(*b*)   τὸ γὰρ ἔργον κυρίου ἐργάζεται ὡς κἀγώ· μή τις οὖν αὐτὸν ἐξουθενήσῃ.
(*a′*) προπέμψατε δὲ αὐτόν ἐν εἰρήνῃ,
(*c′*)   ἵνα ἔλθῃ πρός με.
The terms, of course, are not those noted above, with the exception of *a* and *b*.

collection in 1 Cor. 16: 1 ff., however, Paul inserts the prospective sending of approved messengers to carry the offering to Jerusalem (1 Cor. 16: 3), with this result:

ὅταν δὲ παραγένωμαι
b οὓς ἐὰν δοκιμάσητε,
a δι' ἐπιστολῶν τούτους πέμψω
c ἀπενεγκεῖν τὴν χάριν ὑμῶν εἰς Ἰερουσαλήμ.

That Paul arrived at a consistent pattern of articulating these sections, while exercising the liberty to modify that pattern in accordance with the situation, is fairly evident. His skill in this regard goes together with the care he lavishes on the apostolic *parousia* as a whole.[1]

4

In considering the apostolic *parousia* as a whole, it should be recalled that Rom. 1: 8 ff., which anticipates 15: 14–33,[2] does not constitute an independent example of the apostolic *parousia*. 1 Cor. 16: 1–9 (10–11); 2 Cor. 8: 16–23, 9: 1–5 come, as noted, under the heading of the collection. Phil. 2: 25–30; 1 Cor. 16: 12 are notices concerning associates. Although closely related to the apostolic *parousia*, these passages cannot be pressed to the same degree for structure as can the passages which represent the apostolic *parousia* proper: Rom. 15: 14–33; Philem. 21 f.; 1 Cor. 4: 14–21; 1 Thess. 2: 17 – 3: 13; 2 Cor. 12: 14 – 13: 13; Gal. 4: 12–20; Phil. 2: 19–24.

Items 1 (letter), 3*e* (dispatch of emissary) and 3*f* (Paul's own presence) represent the implementation of the apostolic *parousia* and in ascending order of significance. The presence of Paul in person will therefore be the primary medium by which he makes his apostolic authority effective, whether for negative (1 Cor. 4: 19) or positive (Phil. 1: 24 ff.) reasons. Letter and envoy will be substitutes, less effective perhaps, but sometimes necessary. The shape of the apostolic *parousia* as a whole should be considered from this perspective.

The significance Paul attached to his personal presence in relation to letter and emissary might be deduced from the structure of the

[1] The language of 3*e*, particularly *b*, borders on the language of the letter of recommendation, e.g. Rom. 16: 1 ff.; 1 Cor. 16: 15 ff. The latter requires investigation before the relationship between the two can be determined.
[2] The significance of this point will be considered subsequently.

apostolic *parousia* itself, had Paul not made the point explicit.[1] The characteristic trajectory is from 1 through 3 *e* to 3 *f*, i.e. from the weaker to the stronger medium. As a rule, 3 *f* can be followed only by items 4 and 5 (Rom. 15; 1 Cor. 4; 1 Thessalonians; Phil. 2: 19–24), i.e. only by the invocation of divine approval and the reference to the benefits of his presence. Where this is not the case, Paul wishes to soften the coercion implied by his presence (Philem. 22—a very subtle formulation!), or his coming is advanced as an open threat and the letter conceived as a means of softening the blow (2 Cor. 12: 14 ff.).

If Paul aspired for compelling reasons to pursue his apostolic over-sight of the congregations through the medium of his own personal presence, the absence of 3 *f* in a particular case would at least require explanation. The absence of 3 *e*, on the other hand, might be occa-sioned by circumstances, and the explicit mention of his purpose in writing (1) might depend on emphasis. Among the major passages, the constellation 1 + 3 *e* + 3 *f* is found in 1 Cor. 4; 1 + 3 *f* occurs in Rom. 15; Philemon; 2 Cor. 12: 14 ff.; 3 *e* + 3 *f* in 1 Thessalonians and Phil. 2: 19–24. It is only in Galatians that not one of these items is to be found. Among the secondary passages, 2 Cor. 9 and possibly 1 Cor. 16: 1–11[2] exhibit all three elements, while 2 Cor. 8 manifests only 3 *e*: in view of the history of his relations with the congregation at Corinth, Paul may have deliberately suppressed mention of his direct role in the gathering of the collection, in order to avoid the suggestion that his coming might again be a threat (cf. 2 Cor. 1: 23 ff., 12: 20 ff., 13: 2 ff., 10). Since Phil. 2: 25–30 occurs in con-junction with 2: 19–24, the absence of 3 *f* there occasions no surprise.[3] The remaining passage, Rom. 1: 8 ff., contains only 3 *a* and *b*, i.e. the desire and intention to come, which is striking in view of Rom. 15: 14 ff. In this case, moreover, 4 *a* and 4 *b* precede even the

[1] E.g. in 2 Cor. 2: 3 f., 9 he makes it clear that he wrote instead of coming on this particular occasion in order to prepare them for his coming, or rather to spare them the pain of his coming (1: 23; if he had come under the circumstances, he would be seeking to control their faith: 1: 24 *a*). The same thought exactly is expressed in 13: 10. The letter does not therefore bear the apostolic power to the same degree as Paul's personal presence. The subordinate role of the emissary is obliquely expressed in 1 Cor. 4: 17 ff.: Timothy will remind them, but Paul will put their power to the test.

[2] See above, p. 257, n. 1.

[3] 1 Cor. 16: 12 occurs in conjunction with 3 *f*, but this point may not be relevant: is Apollos being urged to come as an envoy?

expression of his desire and intention, occasioned formally no doubt by the fact that Paul works the apostolic *parousia* into the thanksgiving. Yet there may be another reason for this arrangement, as we shall suggest.

A number of apparently heterogeneous elements are grouped together under 3. The logic of this grouping is not obvious in Rom. 14 because 3*e* is missing. When 3*e* is inserted, the logic becomes evident: Paul is eager to come (3*a*), hopes to come (3*b*), but he has suffered delay, encountered some obstacle (3*c*), which forces him to send an envoy in his place in the meantime (3*e*). However, his hopes will eventually be realized, God willing, so that he can announce his coming in advance (3*f*). The movement from 3*a* to 3*f* thus constitutes one integral unit. This structure reveals the rank of the apostolic emissary: he substitutes for the apostle himself, while the letter is at best written authority for what the emissary has to say. Since Paul gives precedence to the oral word, the written word will not function as a primary medium of his apostleship.[1] It is for this reason that item 1 does not loom so large in the Pauline letters as it does in the non-literary papyri.[2]

The complete movement 3*a*–3*f* is present only in 1 Thessalonians.[3] 1 Cor. 4 is an abbreviated example, lacking 3*a–c*, evidently because Paul wants his coming to be regarded as an imminent threat and because the expression of eagerness is not appropriate under the circumstances. It is perhaps not by accident that where 3*a–f* is curtailed, for whatever reasons, 1 tends to come to expression (Rom. 15; Philemon; 1 Cor. 4; 2 Cor. 12: 14 ff.; cf. 2 Cor. 9). Philippians is only an apparent exception, as will be seen. In this regard Galatians again constitutes the real exception, though attention should perhaps be directed to 6: 11: having failed to call atten-

[1] Such a statement as 1 Cor. 14: 37 f. must be viewed as a counterweight to the enthusiasts who placed exaggerated emphasis on the free, spirit-inspired word.
[2] Heikki Koskenniemi, *Studien zur Idee und Phraseologie des griechischen Briefes bis 400 n. Chr.* (Helsinki, 1956), pp. 77 ff., has identified the formula γέγραφα οὖν σοι ὅπως ἂν (ἵνα) εἰδῇς as a very common formula in the papyri, both in private and official letters, which extends from Ptolemaic times down into the fourth century A.D. It occurs in the Ptolemaic period characteristically as the final item before the ἔρρωσο or other closing formula, but it later occurs also elsewhere in the letter. This convention has obvious affinities with item 1*b* in the Pauline letters, as well as with the formula employed in 3*e*.
[3] Less 3*d*, which is not constitutive.

tion to the letter itself at the customary place, is he led to under-score it at the end?[1]

In sum, where the letter comes to the fore, i.e. where 3 *e* is lacking, the movement tends to be more directly from 1 to 3*f* (Philemon; 2 Cor. 12: 14 ff.; Rom. 15 nevertheless gives expression to 3 *a–c*); where emphasis is placed on the apostolic emissary, 1 tends to be suppressed (1 Thessalonians; Phil. 2: 19–24; cf. 2 Cor. 9: 1!). 1 Cor. 4 is blunt: 1–2–3 *e*–3*f*.

Items 4*a*, *b* and 5 in its various nuances, are dependent, as it were, upon 3*f*; 4*a* is a convention (well represented also in the papyri), and for that reason less subject to nuance. The authentic prayer (4*b*), on the other hand, tends to be suppressed where Paul's coming constitutes a threat (1 Cor. 4; 2 Cor. 12: 14 ff.); it is therefore the friendlier invocation (Rom. 15; 1: 8 ff.; Philem. 22; 1 Thessalonians). Item 4 is regularly omitted in passages having to do with the collec-tion and in Phil. 2: 25–30 (Epaphroditus); 4*b* is found, however, in 1 Cor. 16: 12 (Apollos).

Needless to say, benefit from the apostolic *parousia* accruing to the apostle (5 *a*) or to apostle and congregation mutually (5 *a–b*) indicates a friendlier letter than emphasis on benefit accruing to the recipients (5*b*): 1 Cor. 4; 2 Cor. 12: 14 ff.; Gal. 4.

It remains to consider the apparently chaotic order of 2 Cor. 12: 14 ff. and the apparent incompleteness of Phil. 2: 19–24 (in addition to the problem of Rom. 1: 8 ff. and Galatians). The reason for the former has already been suggested: 2 Cor. 12: 14 – 13: 10, while discernible as the apostolic *parousia*, is woven into Paul's defence of his apostleship as the final element. Because it constitutes a phase of the major argument, it is less formally structured.

Phil. 1: 1 – 2: 18, on the other hand, is a seamless robe with two parallel letters of recommendation joined on. The substance of the letter is anticipated already in the thanksgiving (1: 3–11; cf. Phile-mon); the *paraenesis* is begun in characteristic Pauline fashion in 1: 27,

---

[1] This can hardly be regarded as more than a suggestion, though the fact that the assertion of his apostolic authority in Galatia depends solely on the letter perhaps supports it. It is also worth noting that in 1 Thessalonians, where item 1 is also missing, Paul calls attention to the letter among closing matters (5: 27). The signature in his own hand at 1 Cor. 16: 21 (cf. 2 Thess. 3: 17) is another matter. Yet Philippians constitutes an important exception: Paul nowhere calls atten-tion to the letter itself.

then reintroduced in 2: 1, after a brief return to the subject of the body (1: 28 ff.); the apostolic *parousia* is anticipated by the thanksgiving (1: 8), worked into the theme of the body (the issue of Paul's current crisis; 1: 19–26),[1] alluded to twice more (1: 27, 2: 12), and expressed finally in the section having to do with the sending of Timothy (2: 19–24; note verse 24). That the apostolic *parousia* is woven into the body of the letter is indicated by the presence of language characteristic of the apostolic *parousia* in 1: 25 ff. and 1: 27 (εἴτε ἐλθὼν καὶ ἰδὼν ὑμᾶς εἴτε ἀπὼν ἀκούω τὰ περὶ ὑμῶν). The tightly conceived unity of theological body and *paraenesis*, not altogether characteristic of the Pauline letter, and the integral significance of the apostolic *parousia* to the theme of the body, explain why Paul distributes the elements of the apostolic *parousia* over the whole letter (cf. 2 Cor. 10–13) and subjoins the two recommendations which he could not easily have worked into the body so conceived. In this case, therefore, it seems legitimate to fill out the apostolic *parousia* from elsewhere in the letter (see tabular summary, above). The character of Phil. 1–2 illustrates all the more forcefully that Paul incorporates the same structural items of the apostolic *parousia*, even where he does not group them in the customary fashion.

Rom. 15: 14–33, supplemented at one point (3 e), served as the initial model for the apostolic *parousia*. It has proved to be a reliable index to Paul's pattern in the other letters. Yet it would have been possible to reconstruct the substance of it out of 1 Cor. 4, 1 Thessalonians and Philemon, in content if not in order.[2]

[1] It is very likely that εἰς σωτηρίαν (1: 19) does not refer to the immediate outcome of Paul's present crisis, but to his ultimate destiny. The prayers of the Philippians and the support of the spirit of Christ will thus also have that reference. But, as verses 20 *b* and 24 ff. make clear, Paul's ultimate destiny is intimately connected with his present dilemma: since he is confident (πεποιθώς, 1: 25) that it is necessary for him to remain in the flesh (1: 24), he knows (οἶδα, 1: 25, of his certainty in faith; cf. 1: 19) that he will remain (1: 25) in order to continue his fruitful labour (1: 22), which, through his presence again to them, will benefit their progress and joy in faith (1: 25 *b*–26). The prayers of the Philippians (1: 19) thus eventually come to bear upon Paul's presence again to them.

[2] It is of more than passing interest that the structure of the apostolic *parousia* as represented in Paul is found also in at least one of the letters emanating from a later pagan circle that worships Hermes Trismegistus; the archive in question, belonging to the fourth century A.D., includes PHermRees 2–6 and PRyland IV 616–51, and perhaps other unpublished papyri in the John Rylands Library as well (PHermRees, p. 2). The letter referred to is PHermRees 2: ll. 3 f. = item

5

It may legitimately be asked whether any significance is to be attached to the apostolic *parousia* as a structural element in the Pauline letter other than the natural inclination to issue news regarding renewed contact between apostle and/or emissary and congregation, especially, one would suppose, at the conclusion of letters.[1]

That the inclination is natural has been amply demonstrated by Koskenniemi in his ground-breaking study.[2] He has shown that *philophronesis, parousia* and *homilia* are basic motifs in both the conception and form of the Greek letter from the beginning. The letter

3 *a*; ll. 5 f. = 3 *b*; ll. 7 ff. = 3 *c*; ll. 15 ff., unfortunately defective (see n., p. 4), = 3 *e*; ll. 26 f. = 3 *f*/4 *b*. The entire archive deserves careful scrutiny in connexion with the form of the Pauline (and Christian) letter.

[1] Walter Schmithals ('Die Thessalonicherbriefe als Briefkompositionen', *Zeit und Geschichte. Dankesgabe an Rudolf Bultmann zum 80. Geburtstag*, ed. E. Dinkler (Tübingen, 1964), pp. 299, 303) is of the opinion that personal remarks having to do with Paul's relation to the congregation are found only at the beginning and end of his letters. This opinion is based in part on his view of the composite character of several of the letters, e.g. Philippians; 1, 2 Thessalonians. Even so, 1 Cor. 4: 14 ff. constitutes a notable exception (explicable, in his judgment, on the basis of 1 Cor. 16: 10 f., i.e. the sending of Timothy is reported again at the conclusion of the letter). Whether this and his other provocative suggestions concerning the structure of the letter prove to be viable depends on establishing criteria for the form and structure of the Pauline letter. With regard to the position of personal remarks, i.e. apostolic *parousia*, the question is: where do they occur in letters containing a paraenetical section? In 1 Corinthians, 1 Thessalonians and Galatians the apostolic *parousia* is found attached to the theological body of the letter, *before paraenesis*. Philemon has no *paraenesis* and 2 Cor. 10–13 has only a paraenetical summary, which *follows* the apostolic *parousia* (13: 11). The material in 1 Cor. 16: 1–10 comes under the heading of 'concerning the collection' and must therefore be considered in conjunction with other collection passages (2 Cor. 8, 9). The exceptions to the rule—body, apostolic *parousia, paraenesis*— are thus Romans and Philippians (on the view that Phil. 1–2 is an independent letter). The structure of Philippians, as we have tried to show, has its special explanation (parallel to the 'letter of reconciliation'?). It remains to account for Romans. I agree heartily with Schmithals's programme of sorting out the conflated letters in the Pauline corpus, but I am of the opinion that his specific proposals lack sufficient formal and structural control. Cf. further, 'Zur Abfassung und ältesten Sammlung der paulinischen Hauptbriefe', *ZNW* 51 (1960), 225–45; 'Die Irrlehrer des Philipperbriefes', *ZThK* 54 (1957), 297–341; 'Die Irrlehrer von Rm 16, 17–20', *ST* 13 (1959), 1–19; *Die Gnosis in Korinth* (Göttingen, 1956).

[2] Referred to above, p. 260, n. 2.

is designed to extend the possibility of friendship between parties after they have become physically separated. That friendship is dependent upon the presence of the parties to each other he traces to Aristotle's doctrine of friendship, which was taken up, extended and applied to the letter by the Peripatetics. The fundamental structure of the letter —salutation, dialogue, farewell—corresponds to the meeting between friends.

Gustav Karlsson has further shown that the motif, 'absent in body, but present through letter', can be easily traced from the beginning of the Christian era well into the Middle Ages.[1] He is of the opinion that the formulae found at 1 Cor. 5: 3 and Col. 2: 5 ('absent in body, but present in spirit') and other formulae of this type reflect well-known technical formulae of Greek epistolography.[2]

The motif of the presence of the parties to each other in one way or another is natural because it is constitutive of the conception of the letter. Koskenniemi has adduced compelling evidence from the language of the letter itself and from the theoreticians as the means of demonstrating that this motif is nearly universally presupposed in the situation to which the letter belongs. It would not be surprising, then, if this motif were to come to expression as a structural element in the composition of the letter itself, at least now and then.

Neither the naturalness of the motif nor the Aristotelian doctrine of friendship accounts, however, for the significance Paul accords his presence. Consider the startling statement in 1 Cor. 5: 3-5:

For my part, though I am absent in body, I am present in spirit, and my judgement upon the man who did this thing is already given, as if I were indeed present: you all being assembled in the name of our Lord Jesus, and I with you in spirit, with the power of our Lord Jesus over us, this man is to be consigned to Satan for the destruction of the body, so that his spirit may be saved on the Day of the Lord. (NEB.)

With this may be compared 2 Cor. 10: 3-4, in the context of his discussion of the alleged contrast between his boldness when absent and meekness when present (10: 1-2): 'Weak men we may be, but it is not as such that we fight our battles. The weapons we wield are

---

[1] 'Formelhaftes in Paulusbriefen?' *Eranos* 54 (1956), 138-41.
[2] The contrast occurs in Paul in one form or another at 1 Thess. 2: 17; Phil. 1: 27, 2: 12; 1 Cor. 5: 3; 2 Cor. 10: 1 f., 10: 10 f., 13: 2, 10; cf. Col. 2: 5. Cf. Koskenniemi, pp. 175 ff.

not merely human, but divinely potent to demolish strongholds (NEB).

Paul must have thought of his presence as the bearer of charismatic, one might even say, eschatological, power. One is reminded of the power of the apostolic presence in Acts 5: 1–11 and of the threatening character of the promise to come in the letters to the seven churches (Rev. 2: 5*b*, 16, 25; 3: 3*b*, 11). The appearance of both the motif of the apostolic *parousia* and that of the *parousia* of Christ in the letter form and in similar language (Paul and Revelation) perhaps reinforces the eschatological overtones of the former.[1]

Such an understanding of his personal *parousia* accords well with what Paul writes in 1 Cor. 4: 18 ff. Those in Corinth who are behaving arrogantly, as though he were not coming, will have the opportunity, when he does come, to match their boasting with his power (4: 19). Paul concludes, 'Shall I come with a rod?' (4: 21). Since he appeared in Corinth 'in demonstration of Spirit and power' (1 Cor. 2:4; cf. 2 Cor. 11: 12; Rom. 15: 19), the Corinthians may know whereof he speaks. It is possible, on the same basis, to understand his remark in 2 Cor. 13: 10, that he is writing them to spare himself any sharp exercise of authority when he comes (cf. 2 Cor. 1: 23). Some Corinthian braggarts apparently advanced the thesis that Paul wrote frightening letters, but that his bodily presence was beneath contempt. Now, Paul replies, 'People who talk that way should reckon with this: when I come, my actions will show the same man as my letters showed in my absence' (2 Cor. 10: 11, NEB). Paul's power is bound to the weakness of Christ, it is true, but that power, even in weakness, is capable of making itself felt: on his third visit he promises to show no leniency, when he comes (2 Cor. 13: 1–4). The word of God spoken by Paul is indeed life-giving and death-bringing (2 Cor. 2: 14–17), and this word is bound, so far as Paul is concerned, to his personal presence.

---

[1] John Knox rightly warns against views that assign to Paul an exaggerated estimate of his own role in the eschatological plan of God: 'Romans 15: 14–33 and Paul's conception of His Apostolic Mission', *JBL* 83 (1964), 3 ff. Paul does not hold the view that the eschaton depends on him. He may have thought of himself as the supreme apostle to the Gentiles, but he nowhere denies the right of others to labour among the Gentiles, and he appears to be willing to quit the scene himself (Phil. 1: 19 ff.). It follows that Paul does not regard his *parousia* as the *parousia* of Christ.

Owing to Paul's understanding of the significance of his apostolic presence to his congregations,[1] Paul gathers the items which may be scattered about in the common letter or appended as additional information, into one more or less discrete section, in which he (*a*) implies that the letter is an anticipatory surrogate for his presence, with which, however, the letter is entirely congruent (2 Cor. 10:11); (*b*) commends the emissary who is to represent him in the meantime; and (*c*) speaks of an impending visit or a visit for which he prays. Through these media his apostolic authority and power are made effective.

6

The significance of the apostolic *parousia* as a structural element in the Pauline letter may be considered for the bearing it has on the date of Galatians. Paul announces an impending visit in Rom. 15: 28*b*; 1 Cor. 4: 19 (1 Cor. 16: 5); 2 Cor. 12: 14, 13: 1; he expresses the hope to make a visit (soon), circumstances permitting, in Philem. 22; 1 Thess. 3: 10; Phil. 2: 24 (1: 25). Omitting the letter fragments, if they be such, in 2 Cor. 1–7 and Phil. 3: 2 ff., the only letter in which Paul does not anticipate a visit to the congregation in question is Galatians. In 4: 20 he does write, ἤθελον δὲ παρεῖναι πρὸς ὑμᾶς ἄρτι, a wish which, however one interprets the imperfect,[2] is clearly unattainable as expressed, i.e. he cannot be with them at the present moment since he is elsewhere. This wish nevertheless evidences the significance Paul attached to his presence. In view of the magnitude of the crisis in Galatia, it is incredible that Paul would not have backed up his letter with the hint of a future visit, had he been in a position to contemplate one, however remote, or with the dispatch of an emissary, had there been one available for the assignment. It is just this omission which prompted John Knox to conclude that Galatians was penned relatively late in Paul's career, at a time when a return to Galatia was excluded by virtue of other commitments.[3] This can only mean that it was written at the time he had already set

---

[1] And, of course, the significance of their presence to him, e.g. 2 Cor. 7: 6 f., 13 *b*–16; 1 Thess. 3: 6–8 (cf. 2: 19 f.); Phil. 4: 14–18.

[2] Cf. C. F. D. Moule, *An Idiom-Book of New Testament Greek* (Cambridge, 1953), p. 9; F. Blass–A. Debrunner, *A Greek Grammar of the New Testament* (Chicago, 1961), §359 (2).

[3] 'Galatians', *Interpreter's Dictionary of the Bible*, II (Nashville, 1962), 343.

his face to the west. Surely nothing less than that would have prompted him to turn away with the mere wish that he could be there now!

The arrangement of the apostolic *parousia* in Romans may also be revealing for the character of that letter as a whole.

It has been observed that Rom. 1: 8 ff. corresponds virtually point for point to Rom. 15: 14–33. Paul has worked the ingredients of his characteristic treatment of the apostolic *parousia* into the thanksgiving of Romans, with a consequent modification of the typical form of that unit. As O. Michel has suggested, Rom. 1: 8 ff. and Rom. 15: 14–33 serve as brackets to enclose the whole.[1]

The parallelism between these two sections is striking up to the point of particularization: Rom. 1: 8 ff., aside from the references to Rome in 1: 7, 15, is general, whereas 15: 14 ff. is highly particularized. As John Knox has pointed out, a Roman reader would not have learned from 1: 8 ff., for example, that Paul was actually coming to Rome (only that he wanted and intended to come), that he was even now setting out, that he intended to go on to Spain, nor would he have learned of the Pauline itinerary which was to bring him to Rome via Jerusalem and the further threat of delay which that route posed.[2] After reviewing the manuscript tradition which omits ἐν Ῥώμῃ in 1: 7, 15, T. W. Manson concludes: 'the context, particularly verses 8–17, imperatively demands a particular reference to a well-known community not founded by Paul or hitherto visited by him'.[3] Manson believes, of course, that the references to Rome in chapter 1 are original, but it is significant that the context, in his judgment, requires some reference to 'a well-known community not founded by Paul or hitherto visited by him'. Can we go so far as to say that this is *all* the context requires?

The double treatment of the apostolic *parousia* in Romans is exceptional for Paul,[4] and the appearance of one of these in the thanksgiving is striking, to say the least. It is curious, moreover, that what is missing from this form is precisely the particular elements,

[1] *Der Brief an die Römer* (Göttingen, [11]1957), p. 325.
[2] 'A Note on the Text of Romans', *NTS* 2 (1956), 191–3. Knox observes, p. 192, that Rom. 1: 10 is normally over-interpreted in view of Rom. 15: 14 ff.
[3] *Studies in the Gospels and Epistles*, ed. M. Black (Manchester, 1962), p. 229.
[4] Unless 1 Cor. 4 and 16 are to be regarded as doublets; see above, p. 257, n. 1 and 263, n. 1.

i.e. 1, 3*e*, 3*f.* Rom. 1: 8 ff. is parallel in this regard to Galatians. And if, as I have attempted to show,[1] the apostolic *parousia* is normally attached to the theological body of the letter, preceding *paraenesis*, this fact, too, makes the structure of Romans odd. Why did Paul anticipate the apostolic *parousia* in a general way in the thanksgiving and reserve a particular treatment of the same theme for the end of the letter?

The general character of the remarks in 1: 8 ff. (coupled with the possible absence of the references to Rome in 1: 7, 15), the near-epistolary style of the body (Romans approaches the treatise), together with the lack of certain personal references in the body of the letter, suggest that Rom. 1: 1 – 15: 13 may well have been conceived by Paul as a general letter, to be particularized and dispatched, as the occasion demanded, to other well-known churches which he had not founded or visited.[2] The double treatment of the apostolic *parousia* and the position of the particularized form (15: 14–33) at the end of the letter lend considerable weight to this suggestion, in my opinion: Paul needed only to fill in the address and, if the occasion required it, add a personalized form of the apostolic *parousia* at the end, in order to be able to dispatch this generalized summary of his gospel to yet another church. The customary form of the Pauline letter could scarcely be modified so easily, and the presence of the generalized apostolic *parousia* in the thanksgiving made it possible for him to send off another copy without doing more than adding his name.

---

[1] In the work referred to on p. 249, n. 1; cf. p. 263, n. 1.

[2] In his 1956 article Knox advances this view as something to be considered. In his 1964 essay, p. 10, n. 11, he appears to be more certain of its merits.

13

EPISTEMOLOGY AT THE TURN OF THE AGES: 2 CORINTHIANS 5: 16[1]

J. LOUIS MARTYN

I

For a number of easily understood reasons 2 Cor. 5: 16 and 17 are among the most famous verses in the whole of the New Testament. The numberless comments on verse 16 have been occasioned more often than not by the enticing hope that the verse can tell us something about Paul's relationship to Jesus.[2] And verse 17 is of such obvious theological importance that it has provided a base point not only for the work of New Testament interpreters,[3] but also for the grand construction of one of our century's most impressive theological systems.[4] Daily experience in the reading of Paul's letters teaches us, however, that the apostle's most important statements often present the greatest ambiguity. That is nowhere more obviously true than in 2 Cor. 5: 16.[5] For our present discussion I suggest that we centre our attention on this verse by reconsidering three of the dozen or so problems which it presents to us:

(1) What interpretation is to be given to the expressions μηκέτι (verse 15), ἀπὸ τοῦ νῦν (verse 16), and νῦν οὐκέτι (verse 16)?

[1] To my highly esteemed friend and colleague of seven happy years who taught me daily what it means οὐδένα εἰδέναι κατὰ σάρκα.
[2] See, e.g., the comments by R. Bultmann in an article which is probably still the most important statement of the Jesus-Paul problem, 'Die Bedeutung des geschichtlichen Jesus für die Theologie des Paulus', *Glauben und Verstehen*, I (Tübingen, 1954), 188–213. It is symptomatic, on the other hand, that the verse is not discussed by either Klaus Wegenast, *Das Verständnis der Tradition bei Paulus und in den Deuteropaulinen* (Neukirchen, 1962) or Eberhard Jüngel, *Paulus und Jesus* (Tübingen, 1964).
[3] The careful reader of Bultmann's *Theology of the New Testament*, 2 vols. trans. K. Grobel (New York, 1951, 1955) perceives that 2 Cor. 4–6 and the Fourth Gospel are two of the mountain peaks from whose heights all else is surveyed.
[4] I have in mind, of course, the creative labours of Paul Tillich who spoke so eloquently about the new being.
[5] John Knox, *Chapters in a Life of Paul* (New York, Nashville, 1950), p. 123, speaks of the verse as being 'highly ambiguous'.

J. Louis Martyn

Obviously Paul refers to some turning point of earth-shaking proportions. Is it the death/resurrection of Jesus, Paul's own conversion, these two events superimposed on one another, or something to be distinguished from both of them?[1]

(2) What role does verse 16 play in its context? It has been considered a digression between verses 15 and 17.[2] Indeed, the thesis has been boldly advanced that the verse was inserted into its context by one of Paul's opponents in Corinth who wanted to make clear that the earthly form of Jesus (Χριστὸς κατὰ σάρκα) was to be despised as the temporary dwelling place of the heavenly redeemer.[3]

(3) Are the two instances of the prepositional phrase κατὰ σάρκα to be construed adjectivally (modifying οὐδένα and Χριστόν) or adverbially (modifying οἴδαμεν and ἐγνώκαμεν)? Some interpreters believe they are asking the same question when they inquire whether the term σάρξ refers here to the flesh of the person being known or to that of the person who is the knower.[4]

Since the third of these problems is the most easily and clearly stated, we may profitably begin with it. Both alternatives have been elected and defended at length, and it is certainly true that Paul elsewhere uses the phrase κατὰ σάρκα sometimes adjectivally, sometimes adverbially.[5] Leaving aside the two occurrences in our verse, we can say with reasonable confidence that of the remaining seventeen instances of this thoroughly Pauline expression[6] four are adjectival and thirteen adverbial.[7] It may also be worth noting that when the two instances in our verse are subtracted from the six occurrences in 2 Corinthians, the remaining four are all in the

[1] Note the change of opinion in Kümmel's revision of Lietzmann's commentary, H. Lietzmann–W. G. Kümmel, *An die Korinther I.II*, HzNT 9 (Tübingen, ⁴1949), pp. 126, 205.
[2] A. Plummer, *The Second Epistle of St Paul to the Corinthians*, ICC (Edinburgh, 1915), p. 175, 'The verse is one of those parenthetical remarks which are so characteristic of St Paul'. Plummer was followed by Lietzmann, HzNT 9 (altered by Kümmel in the revised ed.) and by Wendland, NTD 7 (Göttingen, 1936).
[3] W. Schmithals, 'Zwei gnostische Glossen im zweiten Korintherbrief', EvTh 18 (1958), 552–73. Cf. 1 Cor. 12: 3.
[4] Plummer, for example.
[5] The issue is weighed carefully by H. Windisch, *Der zweite Korintherbrief*, Meyer KEK (Göttingen, 1924), pp. 184–9.
[6] Paul uses the phrase nineteen times, John once (8: 15).
[7] I count the instances in 1 Cor. 1: 26 and Gal. 4: 29 as adverbial.

adverbial column. But statistics of this sort can be very misleading. They scarcely do away with the ambiguity. One is not entirely surprised to see that a recent interpreter has come down first on one and then on the other side of this question. Indeed he has been able to do so without having to alter his interpretation of the verse because he believes the adjectival and adverbial readings are equivalent in meaning.[1] On the other hand, another scholar has recently said with emphasis that to construe the phrase adverbially is to make the second half of the verse absurd.[2] On the basis of the arguments advanced by these two scholars alone one must conclude that while the problem is obvious, the solution is not.

A way forward lies, I think, in taking seriously into account the *broad* context which stretches from 2: 14 to 6: 10.[3] When that is done, answers are readily at hand for all three of our problems. For when we allow these chapters to speak as a unit, we are struck with two facts above all others: (1) Paul defends his apostleship by various arguments, *all* of which refer to the turn of the ages;[4] (2) he mounts these arguments in a way which makes clear that only at that juncture is man granted the new means of perception which enable him to

---

[1] In 1929 Bultmann interpreted Χριστὸς κατὰ σάρκα as an expression for the 'historische Jesus' ('Die Bedeutung', p. 208). In 1947 he softened his preference for the adjectival reading by saying that while it is the better choice, in the final analysis the issue does not affect the meaning of the verse, *Exegetische Probleme des zweiten Korintherbriefes* (Nachdruck, Darmstadt, 1963), p. 16. A year later, in the first fascicle of the *Theologie des Neuen Testaments* (p. 234; Eng. 1, 238 f.), we find him opting for the adverbial reading, but still holding that the choice is interpretatively irrelevant: 'A Christ known κατὰ σάρκα is precisely what a Christ κατὰ σάρκα is.' Windisch had reached essentially the same conclusion in 1924; see p. 270, n. 5 above.

[2] Dieter Georgi, *Die Gegner des Paulus im 2. Korintherbrief* (Neukirchen, 1964), p. 291. A. Oepke, 'Irrwege in der neueren Paulusforschung', *ThLZ* 77 (1952), 449–58, used expressions equally emphatic against those who take the phrase adjectivally. Georgi seems to think that he and Bultmann stand more closely together than is actually the case. The sentence, 'Bultmann entscheidet sich für die Beziehung des κατὰ σάρκα zum Objekt' (p. 291, n. 7), is not entirely accurate. See n. 1 above.

[3] Bultmann is certainly aware of the literary piece constituted by 2: 14 – 6: 10, and he correctly identifies its major theme as that of the apostolic office (*Exegetische Probleme*, p. 3). By the time he comes to our verse, however, the context he is bearing consciously in mind has shrunk to 5: 11 – 6: 10. Georgi, *Die Gegner*, p. 291, speaks about the 'Gefälle' of 5: 11 ff.

[4] That should not surprise us in view of 1 Cor. 4: 8–13, a passage of unsurpassed lucidity with regard to Paul's understanding of his apostleship.

distinguish true from false apostles. To put it in the prosaic language of scholarly investigation, Paul's statements establish an inextricable connexion between eschatology and epistemology.

2: 14–17. The apostle stands where people are being saved and where people are perishing, i.e. he stands at the juncture of the ages. Standing at this point, he is to those on the one side a fragrance from death to death and to those on the other a fragrance from life to life.

3: 1–18. The true apostle needs no letters of recommendation. His children in the faith are his letter of recommendation, written not with material lying on the old-age side of the juncture (ink, tablets of stone), but rather with the power of the new age: the Spirit of the living God. It is God himself who qualifies the minister of the new covenant, and anyone who fails to recognize this has failed to grasp the transition from the dispensation of death and condemnation to the dispensation of the Spirit and of righteousness. Does someone fail to perceive the far greater splendour of the latter? If so, he is like those in the synagogue over whose minds a veil lies. For one beholds the glory of the Lord and is changed into his image only when the veil is taken away.

4: 1 – 5: 10. Three paragraphs, each beginning, 'Therefore we do not lose heart...' or, 'Therefore we are of good courage...'

4: 1–15. Therefore the true apostle does not lose heart. He carries out his task by the mercy of God. His gospel may be veiled as his opponents say. It is veiled, however, only to those whose allegiance to the old age (the god of this world) blinds them to the light which is streaming in from the glory of Christ, who is the *eikon* of God.

It is true that our gospel appears unglorious! We ourselves are unglorious, persecuted, afflicted, perplexed, struck down—all of which certainly shows weakness. We and our gospel appear in this way, however, in order to show that the real power belongs not to us, but to God. For that is what the turn of the ages means—that life is manifested in death. Therefore we are each day given up to death for Jesus' sake, so that the life of Jesus may be shown in our dying.

4: 16 – 5: 5. The true apostle, therefore, does not lose heart. His daily death is his daily renewal, and it points to his ultimate life. We will not always stand at the juncture of the ages. The Spirit is the down-payment of God's promise that our dying will be wholly swallowed up by life.

5: 6–10. The true apostle, therefore, is always of good courage. He who walks altogether within the old age walks by sight and will be discouraged. We walk, however, not by sight, but by faith, looking toward the *parousia* in hope.

5: 11–15. Therefore the apostle who stands at the juncture of the ages, seeking to persuade men on the one side, but being really known only to God on the other side, must give his congregation grounds for answering those who boast of their appearance, thus assuming that the congregation's way of knowing is the same as their own. He who judges ecstasy to be a reliable sign of apostleship shows that his manner of perception is bound to the old age. It is not ecstasy, but rather the love of Christ which controls us, inasmuch as we discern that one died for all. Therefore all died. He died on behalf of all for a definite purpose: that their lives might be lived *no longer* for themselves, but rather for him who for their sake died and was raised.

5: 16–21. This great turn of the ages in Christ's death/resurrection is *the fact. From now on*, therefore, we regard no one according to the flesh. Even if we formerly regarded Christ according to the flesh, *no longer* do we do so. Therefore if any man is in the realm of Christ, there is a new creation. The old age has passed away. Open your eyes, the new has come! All of this is from God who causes the new to break in by reconciling the world to himself through Christ and by entrusting his powerful word of reconciliation to the ambassador who stands at the turn of the ages.

6: 1–10. For now is the long awaited time. Now is the day of redemption. And since the old-age way of knowing is past, the old standards for identifying an apostle are shown to be invalid. The true apostle is not powerful, but rather weak. He looks like an impostor.[1] When one gazes at him, one sees a man who is unknown and therefore not worthy of regard. One sees a man who is dying, being punished, in sorrow and in poverty. Yet, paradoxically, he is true, well known, thoroughly alive, a man of joy who makes many persons rich and himself possesses everything.

---

[1] Is this a hint that Paul has been identified as a 'beguiler' (πλάνος = *messit*)? Cf. Deut. 13: 6–11; Sanh. 7: 10; John 7: 12, 47.

J. Louis Martyn

If this sketch presents the line of Paul's thought with essential accuracy, then the context alone answers all three of our questions. The expressions μηκέτι, ἀπὸ τοῦ νῦν, and νῦν οὐκέτι are quite harmonious with the clear indications which Paul gives throughout chapters 3–6 that he is centrally concerned with the turn of the ages in the death/resurrection of Jesus. The decisive point is not a private event, treasured by Paul as a radical change in his self-understanding.[1] As the apodosis of verse 17 shows, it is an event of cosmic proportions, and Paul describes it in a manner worthy of an enthusiast: καινὴ κτίσις, τὰ ἀρχαῖα παρῆλθεν, ἰδοὺ γέγονεν καινά. Secondly, verse 16, far from being a digression, is precisely the explicit statement of the epistemological concern which has been the twin to Paul's discussion of eschatology right from 2:14 onward. That, in turn, tips the balance decisively in favour of reading the κατὰ σάρκα phrases adverbially.[2] Paul is not speaking about a Christ κατὰ σάρκα. He is certainly not saying that he was acquainted with Jesus prior to the crucifixion. Nor is he considering *in the first instance* 'how a man should be understood and regarded'.[3] He is saying that there are two ways of knowing and that what separates the two is the turn of the ages, the eschatological event of Christ's death/resurrection. There is a way of knowing which is characteristic of the old age (γινώσκειν or εἰδέναι κατὰ σάρκα),[4] and by clear implication there is a way of knowing which is proper either to the new age or to that point at which the ages meet.[5]

But now that we have reached these conclusions, we recall that the

---

[1] Bultmann sees this quite clearly, *Exegetische Probleme*, p. 17; cf. N. A. Dahl, *Das Volk Gottes* (Oslo, 1941), p. 250.

[2] There are, of course, other arguments which support the adverbial reading. See the commentaries and Oepke, 'Irrwege'; also P. Schubert, 'New Testament Study and Theology', *Rel in Life* 14 (1945), 556–74 (especially pp. 565 f.).

[3] Bultmann, *Exegetische Probleme*, p. 16, 'Im Zusammenhang handelt es sich um die Frage, wie ein Mensch verstanden und beurteilt werden soll'. I should be satisfied had Bultmann said, 'wie ein Mensch *versteht*'.

[4] The εἰ καί clause of verse 16 apparently tells us that at one time Paul himself regarded Christ in accordance with the old-age way of knowing. Lietzmann was quite right in his initial comment: 'Er [der Satz] hat nicht die Form des Irrealis (εἰ ἔγνωμεν), sondern die des Realis, und reinsprachlich ist es erlaubt und naheliegend, ihn zu verstehen: "Wenn ich auch, wie es ja der Fall ist..."' (p. 125).

[5] We will see in a few moments that it is *quite important* to ask whether we are dealing with a theory of knowledge proper to the new age or with one which is proper to the point of juncture.

answer to a problem is more often than not a problem itself. Why does Paul speak somewhat cryptically on the negative side, and why is he satisfied merely to *imply* a positive epistemological statement? What precisely are the two ways of knowing? What Greek words would Paul have used in order to speak directly about the new way of knowing? Unless we are willing to speak in a vaguely 'edifying' manner, we must ask the Apostle to tell us specifically how the epistemological question is related to the eschatological one.

Our ability to hear his answer will depend to a large extent on our being able to listen first of all with the ears of his original readers. Against what conceptual background did the Corinthians hear Paul's words about knowing κατὰ σάρκα?[1]

2

It is apparent that between the writing of 1 Cor. and that of 2 Cor. 2: 14 – 7: 4 (and 10–13) there was a shift in the front which stood opposed to Paul.[2] At a later point we will take that seriously into account. For the moment we ought to ask how our verse was understood by the Gnostic Christians against whom Paul had to fight when writing 1 Corinthians.[3] The invasion of Corinth by the new 'super-apostles' of 2 Corinthians scarcely caused the Gnostics to evaporate. And from an abundance of data in 1 Corinthians we know not only that they were keenly interested in the epistemological question, but also that by the time Paul wrote our verse he had already had

[1] For reasons which will become obvious as we proceed, I think it likely that the Corinthians grasped Paul's intention to link the prepositional phrase to the verbs. Contrast Schmithals, 'Glossen'.

[2] The research which has been most successful in identifying the opponents in 2 Corinthians is indebted to the very important study by E. Käsemann, 'Die Legitimität des Apostels', *ZNW* 41 (1942), 33–71, even though some of the aspects of Käsemann's thesis are scarcely convincing. See Bultmann, *Exegetische Probleme*, pp. 20–31; G. Klein, *Die Zwölf Apostel* (Göttingen, 1961), p. 58 n.; D. Georgi, *Die Gegner*; G. Bornkamm, 'Die Vorgeschichte des sogenannten zweiten Korintherbriefes', *SHAW*, 1961 (2), particularly pp. 10–16; H. Köster, 'Häretiker im Urchristentum', *RGG*³, 3 (1959), 17–21; D. Lührmann, *Das Offenbarungsverständnis bei Paulus und in paulinischen Gemeinden* (Neukirchen, 1965), pp. 45 ff. Unfortunately Lührmann's study came into my hands after the present article had been completed.

[3] See especially the highly illuminating work of U. Wilckens, *Weisheit und Torheit* (Tübingen, 1959) and the review by H. Köster, *Gnomon* 33 (1961), 590–5.

exchanges with them on precisely this issue. Indeed it is worth noting that, while Paul shows little inclination in his other letters to discuss the subject of epistemology, he returns to it time and again in the Corinthian correspondence. It would not be incorrect to say that what justification by faith is to Galatians and Romans, the epistemological issue is to 1 and 2 Corinthians.[1]

A philosophically inclined citizen of Corinth would have had no difficulty with Paul's expression γινώσκειν κατὰ σάρκα. To him it would have meant to know on the basis of sense perception, for there is a time-honoured connexion between the term σάρξ and speculation of an epistemological sort. Alexander Aphrodisiensis, for example, queried whether it is the flesh itself or something in it which has the power of perception.[2]

Many persons of the Hellenistic age would have answered Alexander's question not so much in a philosophical as in a religious way. Agreeing that the flesh is somehow the seat of a certain kind of perception, they would have gone on to say that the power of true perception stems neither from the flesh nor from something in it. On the contrary, sense perception is so misleading that the bodily senses must be curbed before one can truly know. Consider the opening paragraph of *Poimandres*:

One day, when I had begun to reflect on the things that truly exist and my thoughts had soared aloft, while my bodily senses were bridled like those borne down by sleep through surfeit of food or fatigue of the body, it seemed to me that a being of vast, immeasurable size drew near and called me by name and said, 'What do you wish to hear and see and by thinking come to learn and know?'[3]

---

[1] The situational character of Paul's writings is reflected in both cases. The Galatians assumed a stance which compelled the apostle to discuss justification. It was, initially, the Corinthians' openness to wisdom speculation of a Gnostic type which compelled him to take up the epistemological question. Verbs of perception are particularly numerous in 1 and 2 Corinthians.

[2] Cited by E. Schweizer in the article on σάρξ, *ThWNT* 7, 2/3 (1960), 103.25. That Alexander was active about A.D. 200 is not important here. Earlier references are readily available, as one would surmise from Parmenides' reproach of those who trust daily experience as the basis for knowledge, from Protagoras' theory that knowledge is perception, and from Plato's concerted argument against Protagoras' theory. A Platonist reading Paul's expression would surely have thought of his master's careful distinction between ἐπιστήμη and δόξα.

[3] I have given the translation of Nock's text by F. C. Grant in R. M. Grant (ed.), *Gnosticism* (New York, 1961), p. 211.

Philo too considered the flesh to be the seat of sense perception (*Agric* 97), and he viewed that fact as a liability to true knowledge.[1] The understanding which is endowed with vision is unfortunately weighed down by the pleasures of the flesh (*Migr Abr* 14). Indeed, 'there are no two things so utterly opposed as knowledge (ἐπιστήμη) and pleasure of the flesh' (*Deus Imm* 143).[2] Thus, the royal way which is Philo's passionate concern (ὁδός equals σοφία) is 'a straight high road, and it is when the mind's course is guided along that road that it reaches the goal which is the recognition and knowledge of God. Every comrade of the flesh hates and rejects this path and seeks to corrupt it' (*ibid.*). From such texts it is obvious that there are two kinds of men for Philo: he who is a representative of the many and he who is the true mystic. One of the things which distinguish them is of considerable importance. The many do not have God's spirit abiding in them, whereas the mystic does. Here we encounter a suggestion that, while the flesh is a deterrent to true perception, the divine spirit which abides in the mystic makes knowledge possible. 'One sort of man only does it (τὸ θεῖον πνεῦμα) aid with its presence, even those who have disrobed themselves of all created things and of the innermost veil and wrapping of mere opinion (δόξα). With their minds unhampered and naked they will come to God' (*Gig* 53).[3]

It is the mass of men who know κατὰ σάρκα, whereas the initiate knows in a higher way by the aid of the divine spirit. A good many other texts could be cited to show that for various kinds of religious circles in the first century Paul's words about knowing κατὰ σάρκα would be readily understandable. But we may profitably return to

---

[1] Just how Philo's thought is related to Gnostic speculation of the sort represented by Poimandres is a very large problem in itself. Cf. H. Köster who refers to Gnosticism as a presupposition of Philo's philosophy on p. 191 of 'Paul and Hellenism', in J. Philip Hyatt (ed.), *The Bible in Modern Scholarship* (Nashville, 1965), pp. 187–95.

[2] Here and subsequently I cite Philo according to F. H. Colson, G. H. Whitaker, and Ralph Marcus, *Philo*, 12 vols. (London, 1929–53).

[3] Here I have altered somewhat the translation of Colson and Whitaker. My attention was called to this passage by U. Wilckens, *Weisheit*, p. 140. One should also consider passages from the literature of Qumran, e.g. 1QS4: 20 ff., 'He will... clean His flesh by a holy spirit from all ungodly acts. He will sprinkle upon it a spirit of truth...so that upright ones may achieve insight in the knowledge of the Most High', P. Wernberg-Møller (Grand Rapids, 1957), p. 27. Cf. further 1QH7: 26; 12: 11 f.; 13: 18 f.

the Corinthian correspondence itself, for the best text we could possibly desire is a remarkable paragraph from I Corinthians in which Paul himself literally speaks like one of the Corinthian Gnostics. Of course his intention is to convict them of being σάρκινοι. But in the course of his argument he reveals quite plainly the Gnostics' understanding of the epistemological question, and that is what interests us just now. The passage is I Cor. 2: 6–16.[1] Notice particularly verse 14 in its context. The major points are:

(a) In order to know the things of a person, one must have the spirit of that person.

(b) We who are the *pneumatikoi* have received the Spirit of God which searches the deep things of God.

(c) Therefore, unlike the *psychikoi* who have only the spirit of the world, we are able to receive the things of God's Spirit. For having God's Spirit, we discern in a spiritual manner.

With regard to our present concern the key expression is ἀνακρίνειν πνευματικῶς. The Gnostic who used it clearly meant to say that there are two ways of knowing: there is an ἀνακρίνειν ψυχικῶς, and there is an ἀνακρίνειν πνευματικῶς.[2] What separates the two from one another is quite simply the *natural* distinction between the ψυχικοί and the πνευματικοί. Of course the Christian Gnostics in Corinth were sure that it was Christ, the Lord of Glory, who awakened the πνευματικοί. The point of major importance is that in their view he did so by granting them γνῶσις regarding their con-substantiality with him. They had his νοῦς, his πνεῦμα. They therefore knew πνευματικῶς.

Now we may return to our text, 2 Cor. 5:16. When a leader in the Corinthian congregation read aloud the words of Paul about knowing κατὰ σάρκα, the Gnostic members must have understood that expression in itself as a reference to the way of knowing characteristic of the natural man. He lives in the realm of the flesh and knows in a way which takes the flesh as its norm. But Paul's negative words about knowing κατὰ σάρκα must also have brought immediately to their minds the

---

[1] Wilckens, *Weisheit*, has convincingly shown the history-of-religions background of this astounding paragraph.

[2] We know remarkably little about the nuances of Greek words in the first century. It may be somewhat accidental that the adverb σαρκικῶς occurs only once in literature which has come down to us (Ign *Eph* 10: 3). Perhaps Paul *could* have placed opposite one another ἀνακρίνειν σαρκικῶς and ἀνακρίνειν πνευματικῶς.

positive counterpart. He who is naturally spiritual and who has been initiated by baptism knows in a spiritual way (γινώσκειν κατὰ πνεῦμα ≅ πνευματικῶς ἀνακρίνειν). In short, the Gnostics may have failed to hear Paul's words as a criticism of their epistemological position. Of all people on earth, they were convinced that they did not know κατὰ σάρκα. They may, therefore, have welcomed Paul's words, appropriating them as an accurate (though partial) expression of Gnostic epistemology.

Of course if one considers our verse in the context, it is obvious that a number of factors are left out of account in this appropriation. We will return to the matter at a later point. Here I want only to underscore the absence of eschatology. While Paul's Gnostic opponents were keenly interested in the epistemological issue, they did not consider that issue to be related in any essential way—one might also say in any sophisticated way—to the question of eschatology. The basic distinction between those who know ψυχικῶς and those who know πνευματικῶς is not a matter of eschatology but rather of nature.[1]

3

When we turn our attention from the Gnostics to the 'super-apostles' whose coming to Corinth spelled so much new trouble for Paul, we are conscious of moving into a conceptual orb which, externally at least, is somewhat more Jewish. These persons claimed, in fact, to be superbly Jewish, Hebrews, Israelites, descendants of Abraham (11: 22). They lay great store by their tradition in which Moses was probably celebrated as a divine man (θεῖος ἀνήρ). But they were, of course, Christian apostles. Their tradition extended into the present via Jesus who was the divine man *par excellence*. Indeed they themselves were divine men, as anyone should have seen who beheld their mighty works of spiritual prowess.[2]

Before we ask specifically how these men must have understood Paul's words about knowing κατὰ σάρκα, we ought to consider one of the implications of their quickly won influence over the Corin-

---

[1] If one asks how the Corinthian Gnostics must have understood the expressions νῦν οὐκέτι, etc., the answer is clear. They understood the decisive turning point as their own baptism/initiation, at which time they were awakened to their true nature as πνευματικοί.

[2] I take for granted the essential accuracy of Georgi's major thesis in *Die Gegner*.

thian Gnostics. The latter, we will recall, believed that their initiation into Christ granted them *all* of the blessings of the new age. Not only their knowledge, but also their way of knowing (πνευματικῶς) was complete and perfect. The super-apostles are sure to have claimed at least as much.[1]

But in doing so, they must have encountered a serious problem. Indeed, we ought to take fully into account the problem faced by any Jew, including Paul, who affirmed, in however guarded a manner, the presence of eschatological blessings in the midst of an unchanged world.[2] In such a world where will one look and how will one look in order to see the new age? This form of the epistemological question must have been faced by the super-apostles before they ever laid eyes on the Corinthian church.

There are strong indications that they answered the question—at least in part—by a sophisticated use of the term 'face'. I have referred above to the passage in 1 Corinthians in which Paul speaks of the two ways of knowing almost as if he were a Gnostic (2: 6–16). There is another passage in 1 Corinthians in which he again speaks of the two ways, but this time as a good Jew: 'Is there knowledge? it will vanish away; for our knowledge... [is] partial, and the partial vanishes when wholeness comes...Now we see only puzzling reflections in a mirror, but then we shall see face to face' (1 Cor. 13: 8–12 NEB).[3] We may be sure that the super-apostles did not impress their Corinthian hearers by claiming to see puzzling reflexions in a

---

[1] Contrast Paul's own use of the terms ἱκανότης and ἱκανός (2 Cor. 2: 16; 3: 5), and see Georgi's comments, *Die Gegner*, pp. 220 ff.

[2] For a modern parallel consider the marvellously illuminating letter written by Martin Buber in 1926 and recently published in F. Hammerstein, *Das Messiasproblem bei Martin Buber* (Stuttgart, 1958). I quote two sentences as they are given in the review by H. J. Schoeps, *TL* 84 (1959), 348 f.: 'Meinem Glauben nach ist der Messias nicht in einem bestimmten Augenblick der Geschichte erschienen, sondern sein Erscheinen kann nur das Ende der Geschichte sein. Meinem Glauben nach ist die Erlösung der Welt nicht vor 19 Jahrhunderten geschehen, sondern wir leben noch immer in der unerlösten Welt...'

[3] In rabbinic Judaism seeing and/or knowing perfectly appears to be consistently reserved for the messianic age or the age to come. 'The things that are concealed from you in this world, you will see in the World to Come, like a blind man who regains his sight', Num. R. 19. 6 (quoted in W. D. Davies, *Torah in the Messianic Age and/or the Age to Come* (Philadelphia, 1952), p. 69). See also Str-B 1. 207 ff. Dr Ed P. Sanders has kindly provided further examples which include Koh.R. 2. 1, Pes 50*a*, Ber 34*b*, Nidd 70*b*, Gen R 98. 9.

mirror. That is surely the old-age way of seeing. On the contrary
there are good reasons for thinking that in some sense they claimed to
have seen God, perhaps even face to face.[1] Here again Philo may be
our best guide. 'If...thou art worthily initiated and canst be
consecrated to God..., (then) instead of having closed eyes, thou
wilt see the First (Cause)...For the beginning and end of happiness
is to be able to see God (*Quaest in Ex* ii. 51).'[2] Of course the super-
apostles would scarcely have found it sufficient merely to claim that
they had seen God. They must have provided proof (2 Cor. 13: 3).
How? By reminding their hearers that he who sees God (especially
face to face) experiences a remarkable change in his (own) face. The
classic example in their store of tradition was probably Moses, whom
God knew face to face (Deut. 34: 10).[3]

For we read that by God's command he [Moses] ascended an inaccessible
and pathless mountain...Then after...forty days...he descended with a
countenance far more beautiful than when he ascended, so that those who
saw him were filled with awe and amazement; nor even could their eyes
continue to stand the dazzling brightness that flashed from him like the rays
of the sun (*Vit Mos* ii, 70).[4]

[1] Cf. 2 Cor. 12: 1, 11. The ancient Israelite traditions which speak of seeing God
face to face clearly imply that the experience should bring death. But a bold
interpreter could have taken advantage of certain ambiguities (e.g. Exod. 24:
9 ff.), especially if he claimed his vision as an eschatological blessing. The author of
the Fourth Gospel evidently had in mind persons who made a similar claim (for
Moses? Compare Exod. 33: 20 with Deut. 34: 10) when he said pointedly,
'No one has ever seen God' (1: 18). Cf. also the opponents mentioned in
Col. 2: 18.

[2] I should not want to present Philo as a clear witness for the super-apostles' views.
His comments about seeing God reflect an ambivalence. He was careful to say that
mortals cannot see God *in his being* (*Poster C* 168). He took seriously the famous
passage in which God tells Moses that 'man shall not see me and live' (Exod. 33:
20; e.g. *Fug* 165). To boast of seeing the invisible God is to yield to arrogance
(*Quaest in Ex* ii. 37). On the other hand, to speak of seeing God is to refer to
the goal of the entire Jewish mystery, and Philo was so attracted by the goal
that on this subject, as on others, he had a somewhat divided mind. See E. R.
Goodenough, *By Light, Light* (New Haven, 1935), pp. 212 ff., and Wilckens,
Weisheit, pp. 140 f., where Pascher is quoted. What I am suggesting above is
that the super-apostles who came to Corinth were not so scrupulous as was
Philo.

[3] LXX renders the well-known Hebrew expression πρόσωπον κατὰ πρόσωπον.
Philo uses the preposition πρός (*Rer Div Her* 262); cf. 1 Cor. 13: 12.

[4] My attention was called to this passage by Georgi, *Die Gegner*, p. 259.

J. Louis Martyn

It seems quite likely that the super-apostles did in fact speak explicitly about Moses' face, affirming its remarkable radiance.[1] In doing so they were scarcely interested in Moses himself. He was for them a *type* of the divine man. They may have compared themselves not only with Moses, but also with Jacob/Israel, who is said to have seen God (Gen. 32: 30), and with Abraham, about whom Philo writes in a revealing way:

> Thus whenever he was possessed, everything in him changed to something better, eyes, complexion, stature, carriage, movements, voice. For the divine spirit which was breathed upon him from on high made its lodging in his soul, and invested his body with singular beauty, his voice with persuasiveness, and his hearers with understanding (*Virt* 217).[2]

The super-apostles evidently referred to such ancient divine men in order to say with emphasis that their own status as divine men was attested by their ecstatically radiant faces.[3]

From all of this we can see how important the term 'face' is for the epistemological question. Where will one look in an unchanged world in order to see the signs of the new age? 'Look at our faces!' reply the super-apostles. And should a loyal Corinthian convert of Paul call attention to the one who first brought the gospel to Corinth, the answer is simple: 'Look at his face. It is weak and inferior, not glorious like our faces and that of Moses. He lacks the signs of a true apostle. He does not provide proof that Christ speaks in him. Indeed, when one considers his general demeanour, one sees that he lives on a purely human level' (κατὰ σάρκα περιπατεῖν; 10: 1; 12: 11; 13: 3; 10: 2).

These are thoroughly epistemological affirmations. Notice also that the opponents themselves use the prepositional phrase ad-

---

[1] S. Schulz, 'Die Decke des Moses', *ZNW* 49 (1958), pp. 1 ff., has shown it to be probable that in 2 Cor. 3 Paul corrects his opponents' *midrash*. Cf. also Georgi, *Die Gegner*, pp. 258 ff.

[2] Cf. Georgi's comments on this passage, *Die Gegner*, pp. 80 f.

[3] Notice Paul's own statements in 2 Cor. 3: 18 and 4: 6. He claims to behold the Lord's glory (Shekinah) with an *unveiled* face, being thereby changed into the Lord's likeness from one degree of glory to another. But he is careful not to say that his own face is what is changed. The face-heart polarity which is an overt part of Paul's polemic in 5: 12 lies behind 4: 6. God has shone in *our hearts* to give the light of the knowledge of the glory of God in the face of Christ.

verbially. They must, therefore, have grasped Paul's words about knowing κατὰ σάρκα quite as readily as did the Gnostics. Like the Gnostics the super-apostles doubtless agreed with Paul that knowing in a way which takes the flesh as its norm is a thing of the past.[1] In the old age one knew in a partial manner (1 Cor. 13: 12).[2] They too must have thought of the positive statement implied: Now we know in a spiritual manner. And the meaning which that positive expression had for them is clear from what we have said about their use of the term 'face'. When they stood before the congregation, they boasted on the basis of their faces (2 Cor. 5: 12), and in doing so they obviously presupposed that the Corinthians would be properly impressed.[3] Of course that does not mean that they consciously embraced a theory of knowledge which placed confidence in sense perception. The face on the basis of which they boasted was that of an ecstatic (2 Cor. 5: 13), one who was possessed by (or who possessed) the spirit. In the state of ecstasy the true divine man knew face to face, and his knowing in that way was reflected on his own face. The Corinthians—so the super-apostles assumed—had at least a portion of the spirit. Spirit is perceived by spirit (1 Cor. 2: 14). Therefore the Corinthians perceived the superiority of the divine man as they gazed into his face.

Thus, the super-apostles must have agreed with the Gnostics that

---

[1] By now it should be clear that the adjectival/adverbial choice is quite important (*contra* Windisch; Bultmann). Did the opponents in 2 Corinthians *proudly claim* to know the κατὰ σάρκα Christ (F. C. Baur; E. Käsemann, 'Die Legitimität des Apostels', p. 49, says he will leave open the famous question of the Christ κατὰ σάρκα, but he also says that the opponents 'ihre Beziehung zum historischen Jesus gegen Paulus ausspielten.'); did they *despise* the κατὰ σάρκα Christ (Schmithals 'Glossen'); or did they agree with Paul in rejecting all *knowing* κατὰ σάρκα? It is important to see that in the first instance Paul does not speak in our verse about Christology (Georgi; Lührmann), but about epistemology.

[2] So far as I can see the expression *lᵉ pi habaśar* is foreign to first-century Hebrew. This is not surprising. *Miḳṣat*, on the other hand, is used with a verb of perception in Koh R. 1. 8 (from A. Schlatter, *Paulus, der Bote Jesu* (Stuttgart, 1934), p. 361 n.). Therefore while γινώσκειν κατὰ σάρκα is apparently non-Semitic, the same is not true of γινώσκειν ἐκ μέρους (1 Cor. 13: 12).

[3] If this line of interpretation is correct, 2 Cor. 5: 12 is somewhat undertranslated when ἐν προσώπῳ is rendered by such expressions as 'on a man's position' (RSV), 'in outward show' (NEB), or 'nach Vorfindlichkeit' (Bultmann, *Exegetische Probleme*, p. 16, taking verse 16 as parallel to verse 12). With regard to the Corinthians' ability to perceive the meaning of their preacher's radiant faces, compare the final words of Philo *Virt* 217 quoted above.

J. Louis Martyn

the true way of knowing is κατὰ πνεῦμα. But by that expression they surely meant γινώσκειν κατὰ πρόσωπον or, perhaps, γινώσκειν κατὰ δυνάμεις.

4

More than one interpreter has suggested that when Paul denied a knowing κατὰ σάρκα, he himself intended to imply a knowing κατὰ πνεῦμα. In light of 1 Cor. 2: 14 we can be confident that this suggestion is not altogether incorrect. The norm of the old-age way of knowing, the power referred to as σάρξ, has been replaced by the norm of the new-age way of knowing, the πνεῦμα which God has given us. Paul was quite uninhibited in his own type of enthusiasm: 'Behold now is the day of salvation' (2 Cor. 6: 2).

But if the argument advanced in the preceding sections is essentially valid, then it is obvious that when Paul came to speak about the epistemological issue in a direct way, he had every reason to choose his words carefully. We can see that he consciously avoided certain expressions, allowing the positive side of the epistemological issue to be inferred from the context.

For the Gnostics, the epistemological dualism was essentially a matter of the natural distinction between the ψυχικοί and the πνευματικοί. Therefore, however 'enthusiastic' Paul may have been, he probably realized that he could not use again the expression ἀνακρίνειν πνευματικῶς (1 Cor. 2: 14).

The super-apostles claimed to have seen God and to have radiant faces by which they should be known. Paul himself had spoken of knowing face to face as an eschatological gift. One might expect that kind of knowing to be realized in 'the day of salvation' (2 Cor. 6: 2). But Paul is sure that those who boast on the basis of their faces show, paradoxically, that they still hold fast to the old-age way of knowing.[1] For in the final analysis what Paul places opposite the old-age way of knowing is not that of the new age—this point must be emphasized —but rather the way of knowing which is granted at the juncture

---

[1] The parallelism so often noted between verses 12 and 16 of 2 Cor. 5 is surely one of Paul's clever means of argument. He wants to say that his opponents who claim to be freed from the bonds of sense perception in their states of ecstasy only demonstrate by those very claims that they know κατὰ σάρκα.

of the ages. He does not speak of seeing God's face (contrast Rev. 22: 4). And when he is exercising great care, he does not speak of knowing by means of the Spirit, the gift of the new age. Why? Because he does not live entirely in the new age, but rather at the painful and glorious juncture where some are being saved and some are perishing (2 Cor. 2: 15). Then what is the way of knowing which is granted at this juncture of the ages?

The context provides the answer. Were Paul describing life as it is experienced by one who exists completely and exclusively in the new age, he would no doubt speak of the fundamental epistemological antithesis between knowing κατὰ σάρκα and knowing κατὰ πνεῦμα. But in the context which we have summarized above (pp. 272f.) it is clear that the implied opposite of knowing κατὰ σάρκα is not knowing κατὰ πνεῦμα but rather knowing κατὰ σταυρόν.[1] He who recognizes his life to be God's gift at the *juncture* of the ages recognizes also that until he is completely and exclusively in the new age, his knowing κατὰ πνεῦμα can occur only in the form of knowing κατὰ σταυρόν. For until the *parousia*, the cross is and remains *the* epistemological crisis. The essential failure of the Corinthians consists in their inflexible determination to live either *before* the cross (the super-apostles of 2 Corinthians) or *after* the cross (the Gnostics of 1 Corinthians) rather than *in* the cross.[2] So also the essen-

---

[1] The word σταυρός, so important in 1 Corinthians, is absent from 2 Corinthians, but it is certainly absent only in a literal sense. A more important problem is raised by my expression 'knowing κατὰ σταυρόν'. Can one speak of a *way* of knowing by allowing the preposition κατὰ to govern a noun which refers to something *outside* the knower (as opposed to σάρξ and πνεῦμα which are, so to speak, inside the knower)? A full answer to this question would be constructed, I think, on the following points: first of all, when Paul speaks of knowing κατὰ σάρκα, he does not intend the term σάρξ to refer *exclusively* to the flesh of the knower. He intends it to point also to the realm of the old age. So also πνεῦμα points not only to an entity which is now in the believer, but also to the new age. Conversely, the σταυρός is not entirely outside the knower whose way of knowing is granted neither in the old age, nor in the new age, but rather at the painful and gracious juncture (Gal. 2:20; Rom. 6:3). Of course Paul's opponents know the σταυρός as an object of knowledge (although even this affirmation would be qualified by the apostle). They do not know κατὰ σταυρόν, inasmuch as to do so is to have one's own σταυρός.

[2] The Gnostics affirmed the cross, of course, but evidently only as the door through which the *essential* redeemer momentarily passed. See Wilckens, *Weisheit*. The super-apostles must also have affirmed the cross in some sense, but they seem to have desired union with the *pre*-Easter Christ whom they considered to be a

tial flaw in their epistemology lies in their failure to view the cross as the absolute epistemological watershed. On a real cross in this world hangs the long-awaited Jewish Messiah. How can that be anything other than an epistemological crisis? The divinely authorized herald of the glorious new age comes to Corinth bringing this foolish word of a crucified Messiah, and he himself has a weak and inferior face. That too is an epistemological crisis. For the riddle, How can the best of news be proclaimed in the midst of an unchanged world?, a riddle to which the super-apostles had a ready but false answer, is precisely the riddle, How can the resurrection be proclaimed in the midst of the cross? This is just the point. The cross is *the* epistemological crisis for the simple reason that while it is in one sense followed by the resurrection, it is not replaced by the resurrection.[1]

The new way of knowing is not in some ethereal sense a spiritual way of knowing. It is not effected in a mystic trance, as the super-apostles claimed, but rather right in the midst of rough-and-tumble life. To be sure, the veil is taken away, the creation is new, the old has passed away, look !, the new has come. Yet all of this can be seen only by the new eyes granted at the *juncture* of the ages. Thus, the man who knows κατὰ πνεῦμα cannot show that he knows κατὰ πνεῦμα by performing mighty works. Seeing in a partial way has not yet been replaced by seeing face to face. On the contrary, it has been replaced by faith (2 Cor. 5 : 7). The marks of the new age are at present hidden *in* the old age. At the juncture of the ages the marks of the resurrection are hidden and revealed in the cross of the disciple's daily death, and *only* there.[2]

divine man in his earthy manifestation, much as Moses was a divine man. See Georgi, *Gegner*. On the basis of 1 Cor. 2 : 2 Paul must be numbered among the prophets !

[1] In the course of twenty centuries the spiritual disciples of the super-apostles have been legion. The thirteenth-century artist who designed the famous church and synagogue statues which stand on opposite sides of the Strasbourg cathedral's south portal showed himself to be their follower. To be sure, he took his theme from Paul's *midrash* in 2 Cor. 3, placing a veil over the eyes of the young lady who represents the synagogue. But one can imagine Paul's looking at the statues and ordering a radical change. 'Replace the veil so that it is the proud figure with the crown, the noble bearing, and the mace-like cross who is blindfolded and the weak figure with the broken lance and the humiliated countenance (κατὰ πρόσωπον ταπεινός) who is able to see.'

[2] Several important *limitations* are set to the epistemological question by Paul himself; our concentration on the single verse, 2 Cor. 5 : 16, must not be allowed

to obscure that fact. (1) 2 Cor. 5: 17 ff. makes it quite clear that God's deed of reconciliation in Christ is a cosmic event (cf. the hymns in Phil. 2 and Col. 1). It involves far more than the granting of a new way of knowing. (2) In 1 Corinthians Paul was very careful to limit the epistemological question by means of an insistence on God's election. The datives of 1 Cor. 1: 18 certainly point to different perceptions on the part of different groups, but by means of the surprising *imbalance* between μωρία and δύναμις θεοῦ, Paul says forcefully that the preached word is not served up as a first step so that as a second step the Corinthians may apply to it their superior powers of discernment. Rather, in the preached word God is himself powerfully present and active. (3) 1 Cor. 4: 3 tells us that the Corinthian Gnostics had a propensity for judging others. That is not at all surprising. But notice that in this passage Paul, far from claiming for himself the capacity to judge (contrast 2: 15!), insists that only the returning Lord is capable of judgment. These three passages should suffice. By citing them we may return to our theme: until we all stand before the βῆμα τοῦ Χριστοῦ, there is only one point at which the epistemological question can be legitimately posed: the death/resurrection of Christ and the daily death/life of the disciple.

14

'THE WORD IS NEAR YOU': ROMANS 10: 6–10 WITHIN THE PURPOSE OF THE LETTER

M. JACK SUGGS

The honoree of this volume discovered in an essay by Anton Fridrichsen[1] reason for considering 'with a new seriousness the proposal that the letter to the Romans represents one form of a document which Paul composed for more general distribution'.[2] Fridrichsen had employed the view that Paul understood his vocation as that of the apostle to the Gentiles to suggest that the 'main motive of Romans is to assert, in a discreet way, the apostolic authority and teaching of Paul in the church of Rome'.[3] Professor Knox finds that to be in agreement with the hypothesis that the letter was a circular. In his opinion this would ease the way to a solution of two problems connected with the text of Romans: (1) the eccentricity of G and its associates in 1: 7, 15, which attest a form of the letter from which the word 'Rome' is missing,[4] and (2) the evidence of the absence of chapter 15 from some ancient witnesses. It would also explain why there is in chapter 1 neither mention of the intended journey to Spain nor even clear promise of an impending visit to Rome; '...the phenomenon is more easily accounted for if Paul is simply leaving as

---

[1] 'The Apostle and His Message', *Uppsala Universitets Årsskrift*, 3 (1947), 1–23.
[2] 'A Note on the Text of Romans', *NTS* 2 (1955–6), 191.
[3] *Op. cit.* p. 7.
[4] The well-known textual problems involved in these two verses will not be discussed in this study. It is obvious that G and company testify to a form of chapter 1 from which all mention of Rome had been deleted. Any explanation of the deletion is speculative. It does not appear likely to me that it was made out of antagonism to the Roman church, nor does it seem probable that a late effort was made to *transform* a universally-known letter to a local church into a general epistle. At the same time, we cannot explain the textual phenomena as due to accidental omission. If Romans was a circular, the deletion might be explained as the effort of a scribe to *restore* the letter to its original form. In the light of the problems of text in chapters 15–16, this solution has considerable appeal. However, it is clear that Rom. 1: 7, 15 cannot be made the cornerstone of a circular theory; it may, however, lend support to such a theory.

it stood a letter which was originally composed for a type of gentile church with which Paul is seeking to establish contact—a letter intended not to announce a visit but to take the place of a visit which was having to be postponed',[1]

I

If this proposal is taken seriously, it has far-reaching consequences for our treatment of Romans. Two recent studies related to the question of the occasion of the letter may be seen to lend support to the proposal.

The first is an important essay by Günther Bornkamm which strongly challenges the propriety of efforts to understand the content of Romans on the assumption that it reflects a special situation of conflict within the Roman congregation. It does not have in view 'two factions in Rome, on the one side the Judaizers, who retained the Law and circumcision, and on the other side spiritualizing antinomians'.[2] Nor is it possible to accept the traditional understanding of the letter as 'a timeless theological treatise, a textbook of Paul's dogmatics, which accidentally happens to be clothed in the form of a letter'.[3] It is thoroughly grounded in a specific historical situation, for which the circumstances surrounding the collection are especially important. As Rom. 15: 31 shows, Paul approaches the visit to Jerusalem with two fears—that he will face persecution at the hands of the Jews who regard him as an apostate and that the offering which his gentile congregations have gathered will not be accepted by the Jerusalem church. It is not possible to imagine why the Jerusalem community, in its need, would not receive the offering with joy unless the significance of the collection itself had become an occasion for controversy between Paul and the Jewish Christians. '...this collection was closely associated with the old question contested already at the Apostolic Council in Jerusalem, that is, whether the Gospel free from the law can be legitimate and whether

[1] Knox, *NTS* 2 (1955–6), 192. A footnote to his presidential address for the Society of Biblical Literature indicates that by 1963 he was persuaded of the correctness of the proposal; see 'Romans 15: 14–33 and Paul's Apostolic Mission', *JBL* 83 (1964), 10.
[2] G. Bornkamm, 'The Letter to the Romans as Paul's Last Will and Testament', *AusBR* 11 (1963), 5.
[3] *Ibid.* p. 7.

the Gentile Christians can be recognized as members of equal rank in the church as a whole'.[1] The content of the letter is thus to be understood in the light of the forthcoming trip to Jerusalem and the preceding history of Paul and the Pauline congregation, for Romans in large measure echoes the major themes of the Galatian, Corinthian, and Philippian correspondence.[2] But these themes received their original explication in Paul's conflict with identifiable opposing fronts. While Romans itself is still polemic, these fronts can no longer be seen. The opponent now is an ideal figure (the Jew, who 'represents man in general', and is indeed 'hidden within each Christian')—so that the ideas have outgrown their original polemic dress and have become universal. Not in a literal sense, but nonetheless truly, 'this letter, even if unintended, has in fact become the historical testament of the Apostle'.[3]

But Bornkamm's solution, though eminently attractive, is not finally persuasive. If, as Bornkamm correctly believes, the old problems clustering around the issues Jew-and-Gentile, law-and-gospel were still so acute that there was a question of the acceptability of the offering, how did Paul escape to the heights of serenity from which such a universalization of the old but still persistent themes could be issued? Granted that Paul's 'opponent' in Romans is an ideal figure in some sense, how does it happen that it is precisely in Romans that the diatribe dominates so completely the style of the letter? In view of the way the letter reflects so much of the correspondence from the period of the collection, a fact to which Bornkamm properly gives the stress it deserves, are we really to suppose that the identifiable fronts are so out of sight as to be out of mind? And, even if all this is conceded, why should such a letter be addressed to the church in Rome? What makes it a proper piece of correspondence to send to an unknown church? Bornkamm has pin-pointed a moment in Paul's career when the writing of a testament (or, at least, a 'summing-up') would have been appropriate, but he has not explained why the Roman church would be an appropriate recipient of the testament. He has demonstrated that the content of the letter cannot be explained by hypothetical tensions

---

[1] G. Bornkamm, 'The Letter to the Romans as Paul's Last Will and Testament', *AusBR* 11 (1963), 4.
[2] *Ibid.* pp. 8–12.   [3] *Ibid.* p. 14.

and conflicts in Rome, but he has left unexplained why a letter which does not deal directly with Roman problems should have been sent to Rome at all. Or, rather, his treatment of the latter question does not appear to me to match his masterful exposition of the issues that must be faced in dealing with the occasion of the letter. For at this point Bornkamm goes back to the treatment of Romans as a letter of 'self-introduction'. To be sure, by 'self-introduction' he means 'the presentation of Paul's message itself including also the exposition of his deepest convictions in view of the impending discussions at Jerusalem'.[1] But it is not at all clear that this is the 'natural' form for a letter of introduction to take—especially if these convictions have been shaped by Eastern controversies and an imminent trip to Jerusalem in which Rome was not involved.

In some respects, the letter which Bornkamm describes is one which might have been composed under circumstances such as those proposed by T. W. Manson in 'St. Paul's Letter to the Romans—and Others'.[2] Manson, like Bornkamm, thought that the controversies of the collection period had much to do with the content of Romans,[3] and he finally concluded that the phenomena of the letter are best explained by regarding it as a 'circular'. Most of Manson's essay consists of a careful sifting of textual evidence. He discusses the problem of the variant readings in Rom. 1: 7, 15. But in his opinion the readings extant in G and a few other witnesses are hardly part of the evidence concerning the intended recipients of the letter; they are, rather, probably the result of Marcionite excisions from the version of the epistle which belonged to Rome.[4] The more complicated evidence bearing on the text of the final two chapters requires a more complicated solution. He discusses three ancient

[1] G. Bornkamm, 'The Letter to the Romans as Paul's Last Will and Testament', *AusBR* 11 (1963), 9.
[2] *BJRylL* 31 (1948), 224–40; reprinted in *Studies in the Gospels and Epistles*, ed. M. Black (Manchester University Press, 1962), pp. 225 ff.
[3] Bornkamm recognizes the kinship between his own position and that of the British scholar, but he objects to Manson's abandonment of 'the close and original connection' of the letter with Rome and of the 'old common notion that Romans was a letter of self-introduction'. Moreover, he thinks that Manson's view of the letter as a summary of the position reached by Paul is too narrow (Bornkamm, *AusBR* 11 (1963), 7–9).
[4] See above, p. 289, n. 4.

forms of the text: (1) chapters 1–14, (2) chapters 1–15, (3) chapters 1–16. The first he dismisses as Marcion's truncation of (2). He considers that the evidence of $\mathfrak{p}^{46}$ decisively demonstrates that a form of the letter circulated without chapter 16 and that this (2) was the letter to Rome. Chapter 16 is a 'covering letter' attached to a copy of the same letter, which (3) was sent to Ephesus and was preserved 'in the archives of the Ephesian community. From Ephesus copies reached Egypt at an early date, and the sixteen chapters were well known to Clement of Alexandria as well as to the translators of the Sahidic versions.'[1] At this point, Manson's argument almost treats the 'Ephesian copy' as an afterthought—a 'carbon' sent along to Ephesus in connexion with Phoebe's letter of introduction. But, when Manson's discussion actually turns to the question of motive for the composition of the letter, he immediately rejects the idea that it is 'a simple letter to Rome' and that its purpose was to introduce Paul to a congregation which did not know his theological position. He calls attention to 'the careful and judicious way' in which Rom. 1–11 takes up again the issues of Galatians, Philippians, and 2 Corinthians. 'These chapters may fairly be regarded as Paul's considered judgment on the whole issue'.[2] The 'opponent' who faces Paul in these chapters may be only an imaginary antagonist, but Manson is 'inclined to think that we have here a record made by Paul and his clerical helpers of a real discussion.... The material used in putting it together may well have come in large part from the actual debate'.[3] Looked at in this way, the document in our possession is hardly a letter at all. It is really Paul's 'summing up' of the matter at the end(!) of the controversy.

Having got this statement worked out to his own satisfaction, Paul *then* decided to send a copy of it to his friends in Ephesus, which he did not intend to visit on his way to Jerusalem (Acts xx.16)...*At the same time*, he *conceived the idea* of sending a copy to Rome with a statement of his future plans.[4]

Manson's final word about the nature of the letter is that it is a 'manifesto'.

I do not suppose that Manson intended 'manifesto' to be taken any more literally than Bornkamm meant 'last will and testament',

---

[1] Manson, *op. cit.* p. 238.   [2] *Ibid.* p. 239.
[3] *Ibid.*   [4] *Ibid.* p. 240. (Italics mine. M.J.S.)

though the former seems to me the more appropriate metaphor. Manson's solution appears to answer Bornkamm's analysis of the nature of the letter. In my opinion, Manson has pointed in the right direction. But, in doing so, he has left untouched problems that are of crucial importance. Perhaps the concluding section of Manson's presentation is too compact to be fully clear, but it gives the appearance of asking us to believe that Paul worked up such a summary largely for his own benefit—without advancing an adequate motive for the undertaking. If one assumes that such a summary was prepared, it perhaps requires little stretch of the imagination to understand why it was sent to Ephesus, from which he had written most of the letters related to the controversy and where a lively interest in Paul's conclusions might be expected. Conceived in this way, the letter can no longer be a 'mere letter of self-introduction' to Rome. But can it be a letter of any kind to Rome? I think it can, but Manson has not told us how.

The essays of Bornkamm and Manson call attention to four factors that must be explained by any attempt to establish the occasion of the letter:

(1) The double fear of the apostle in view of his impending visit to Jerusalem: on the one hand, of persecution by the Jews; on the other hand, of the refusal of the Jerusalem Christian community to accept the offering.

(2) The heavy use of themes with which we are familiar from the correspondence of the collection period.

(3) The altered character of the polemic in relation to these themes—which for Bornkamm and Manson alike is explained by its being divorced from a specific situation in a particular congregation.

(4) The sending of a letter with this content to Rome, for there can be no doubt that—even if the letter is a circular—a copy did go to Rome.

If only because the letter shows no sign of previous communication *from* Rome to Paul, Bornkamm and Manson rightly reject efforts to explain the content of the letter as a response to circumstances which have arisen there. But, since Paul was not intimately acquainted with the Roman church,[1] it is precisely as a letter to Rome that it creates difficulties whether the letter is regarded as a

---

[1] I will assume as established that chapter 16 is in the main addressed to Ephesus.

testament or as *a summary at the end of a period of controversy*. As the latter, it would be intelligible as a communication addressed (let us say) to the churches of Galatia, where Christians would presumably have a natural interest in Paul's calmer judgment of the period. As the former, it would be treasured in (for example) Philippi, where there was a congregation to which Paul had been bound by particularly close ties from 'the beginning of the Gospel' (Phil. 4: 15; 1: 5). But in neither case would Rome come to mind as a recipient of the letter—except, of course, for the all-important fact of 1: 7, 15.

It is significant that Manson's article, although it bears the title 'St Paul's Letter to the Romans—and Others', finally describes the document in effect as 'St Paul's letter to others—and the Romans'! And that discrepancy between title and description suggests what in my opinion is the most likely explanation of the letter. To employ a metaphor, the letter is a brief drawn up by Paul in anticipation of the renewed necessity of defending his gospel in Jerusalem. The period of the collection has indeed been a period of continuing controversy. With the possible exception of 1 Corinthians, the literary remains of the short time between the Jerusalem conference and the final visit exhibit evidence of repeated conflicts characterized by such antitheses as Gospel–Law, Christian–Jew, Church–Judaism. This is not to say in advance that the opponents of Paul always occupy the same ground in Galatians, 2 Corinthians, and Philippians 3,[1] but it is to recognize

---

[1] It seems to me equally clear that the controversies in these letters are both distinct and related. Is it possible that the explanation can be found along these lines: (*a*) that the division of field responsibility at the Jerusalem conference (Gal. 2: 6–10) was ethnic and not geographical (so, quite recently, W. Schmithals, *Paul and James* (*Studies in Biblical Theology*, 46, Naperville, Ill., 1965), 45 ff.), (*b*) that this agreement led to a large 'invasion' of the Pauline field by Jewish Christian missionaries to the Jews, and (*c*) that this resulted in a series of difficulties of an essentially local nature, varying according to situations peculiar to each locality, but all occasioned by the unprecedented experience of parallel Jewish and gentile missions? That might account for the series of brush fires which demanded Paul's attention during the relatively short period of the collection, but *it is also only a question raised by facts which are assured*. The facts still point in one direction: the continuing necessity for Paul to concern himself with problems having to do with the relation of gentile Christianity to Jewish norms. What D. Georgi writes at the end of his study of 2 Corinthians, in which he brilliantly argues an entirely different position, provides an instructive example of how the problem of understanding Jewish tradition remains with Paul and demands consideration in connexion with the occasion of Romans: 'Es darf nicht übersehen werden, dass diese erneute Besinnung auf das Wesen nicht nur

that issues revolving round these poles remain at the forefront of concern. This is no accident but is the product of the historical situation. But the course of recent events has demonstrated that the agreement of the conference left unsettled issues that must yet be resolved.

However, it is not only the unsolved and recently aggravated tensions within the Christian fold which cause Paul concern. It is from the unbelieving Jews that he prays to be delivered (Rom. 15: 31). If he should excite fierce opposition from that quarter, an open show of unity between Jewish Christians in Jerusalem and his gentile constituency would lead to disaster. The Jerusalem Christians might be charged as 'fellow-travellers' with opponents of the Torah. Such an eventuality would greatly complicate the already ticklish situation relative to the offering as a symbol of unity. Thus, the questions whether the Jews will permit Paul's visit to be a peaceful one and whether the Jerusalem church can receive the offering which is an expression of the solidarity of Jewish and gentile Christianity turn out to be, in Paul's mind, one question. The question boils down to this: whether the apostle to the Gentiles—who will in no wise place himself under his own anathema by preaching 'another gospel'—can nonetheless cope with attacks on his attitude toward Israel and the Law. With that in view, he advances both the objections to his position and his reasoned, strangely passionless (in comparison with Galatians) answers. He develops a brief. It necessarily goes back over the ground which the controversies of the collection period have occupied; it is here that the shape of the discussion has been hammered out.

The brief is not prepared as a mere summary of controversies now ended, but in anticipation of a situation in which they may break forth afresh. On the outcome of that hangs the future of the relation

der christlichen Existenz im allgemeinen, sondern auch der missionarischen Existenz im besonderen Paulus aufgezwungen wurde durch christianisierte Vertreter der universalistischen Traditionen und Tendenzen des Judentums. Insofern musste es für ihn eine erneute Aufforderung sein, noch einmal sein Verhältnis zu seiner jüdischen Tradition zu überprüfen und verschärft nach dem Recht christlicher Verkündigung angesichts des aus dem alttestamentlichen Wort und seiner Überlieferung erschallenden Anspruchs zu fragen. In dem wenige Monate später als unsere Fragmente geschriebenen Römerbrief legt Paulus endgültig Rechenschaft darüber ab' (*Die Gegner des Paulus im 2. Korintherbrief*, (*Wissenschaftliche Monographien zum alten und neuen Testament*, 11, Neukirchen-Vluyn, 1964), 302–3).

between gentile and Jewish Christianity in the territories of the East where the offering has been taken—and also in the West where the strategic and perhaps powerful church in Rome is tactfully reminded that Paul has an apostleship to all the Gentiles, 'including yourselves who are called to belong to Jesus Christ' (1: 6). Among such churches the brief is circulated as a letter which states the Pauline 'party line' in A.D. 53. The importance of communicating his partially moderated position to gentile churches *in advance* of the delivery of the offering to Jerusalem would have been shown by the recent uproar in Galatia. It must be plain that his stance is independent of Jerusalem and consistent with his previous proclamation.

How many churches received copies of the letter cannot now be determined. Perhaps, as Manson thought, no copy would have gone to congregations which Paul intended to visit on his way to Jerusalem. Perhaps, as Knox tentatively suggests, it was sent to a number of churches with which Paul's desire for contact was frustrated by circumstance. Almost certainly, a copy went to Ephesus, including at least the larger part of chapter 16. So crucial are the issues for all gentile Christianity that it is, thus understood, an appropriate 'mailing' for all. Naturally, the copy which went to Rome speaks at its close of an anticipated visit (15: 22–4, 28–9).[1] But this addendum, which furnishes the news that Paul intends a visit, leaves the document what it is for all who receive it: a pre-Jerusalem brief prepared 'for others—and Rome'.

This hypothesis answers to the four factors outlined above which require explanation in any attempt to define the occasion of the letter.[2]

With Jerusalem in view Paul is at pains to develop a defence of his gospel which provides minimal offence to the Jews. If the collection is to serve as a bond of unity for the whole Church, Paul's position *vis-à-vis* the issues clustered around the poles Law–Gospel, Jew–Christian, Judaism–Church must be clarified in such a way that the Jerusalem community's identification with him and his churches will not increase the threat to its existence in Judaea.

[1] Knox, *NTS* 2 (1955–6), 192, rightfully contrasts the indefiniteness of all references to a visit in chapter 1, which may have been directed in substantially its present form to a number of churches.

[2] It may be added that the hypothesis would also explain some features of the ambiguous textual phenomena of chapters 1, 15, 16.

Without intending to renounce the principle that 'there is neither Jew nor Greek' (Gal. 3: 28, cf. Rom. 10: 12–13), Paul exalts his 'kinsmen' in Romans as in no other letter. It is probably no new development in his understanding of his mission when he speaks of magnifying his ministry to the Gentiles 'in order to make my fellow Jews jealous, and thus save some of them' (11: 13–14). But the letter betrays repeatedly, and especially in chapters 9–11, a preoccupation with the priority and election of Israel which points toward a pressing need to justify his gentile mission in a manner which salvages Israel's *heilsgeschichtlich* role.

Without turning aside from the fundamental position that 'the righteousness of God has been manifested apart from the law' (3: 21) so that both Jew and Gentile 'are justified by grace' (3: 24) on the ground of faith, he nonetheless insists that this does not do away with the law. 'On the contrary, we uphold the law' (3: 31). The letter is repeatedly punctuated by exclamations which defend the law (6: 15; 7: 7, 12, 16). 'For God has done what the law, weakened by the flesh, could not do: sending his own Son in the likeness of sinful flesh and for sin, he condemned sin in the flesh, in order that the just requirement of the law might be fulfilled in us, who walk not according to the flesh but according to the Spirit' (8: 3–4).[1]

It is not that Paul sacrifices his theological position 'in order to please men' (Gal. 1: 10)—or for any other reason. He is as determined as ever not to yield 'submission even for a moment, that the truth of the gospel might be preserved for you' (Gal. 2: 5). But it is his aim to make his position as palatable as possible, both because of the Jews whose knowledge of his reputation would make them dangerously suspicious of him, and because of his determination to make it possible for the collection to serve as an efficacious symbol of the oneness of the Church.

---

[1] John Knox, 'The Epistle to the Romans, Introduction and Exegesis', in *The Interpreter's Bible* 9 (New York, 1957), 508–9, writes: 'Paul makes in this verse and in the sentence immediately following (verses 5–17) a somewhat different, and (would one not say?) a somewhat more adequate, answer to...the question of the ground of ethical behavior in the believer and especially of the relation in which the believer stands to the law...One may reasonably believe that in the words *that the just requirement of the law might be fulfilled in us* a needed balance is being restored.' That this verse represents a new plateau in Paul's effort to find a viable place for the law in his proclamation should be stressed.

2

Now, if the purpose thus sketchily outlined answers at all to the situation in which Romans was produced, then in our interpretation of particular passages in the letter we should rely on Paul's desire to mollify (if not to pacify) the Jewish opposition and thus to satisfy the needs and feelings of the Jewish–Christian community in Jerusalem. Since the brief which he circulates among gentile Christian churches has in view the sensitivities of a Jewish third party, he must himself be sensitive in his appropriation and utilization of Jewish tradition.

A case in point is Rom. 10: 6–10, where Paul's treatment of Deut. 30: 11–14 is too often dismissed as an instance of the apostle's eccentric handling of scripture. Immediately following Rom. 10: 5 ('Moses writes that the man who practises the righteousness which is based on the law shall live by it'), Paul introduces his interpretation of the Deuteronomic passage:

But the righteousness based on faith says, Do not say in your heart, 'Who will ascend into heaven?' (that is, to bring Christ down) or 'Who will descend into the abyss?' (that is, to bring Christ up from the dead). But what does it say? The word is near you, on your lips and in your heart (that is, the word of faith which we preach); because if you confess with your lips that Jesus is Lord and believe in your heart that God raised him from the dead, you will be saved. For man believes with his heart and so is justified, and he confesses with his lips and so is saved.

While our view of the occasion and purpose of Romans makes it difficult to believe that Paul would lay himself open to the charge of careless and inept treatment of the Old Testament, this is in fact what modern commentators commonly allege that he has done. Their most charitable judgment is that Paul's use of the ancient material was merely allusive or illustrative. The few recent expositors who support the idea that Paul intended to be explicating the Deuteronomic verses also customarily conclude, 'This drastic and unwarranted allegorizing must have exposed him to attack'.[1] In either case, the apostle's adversaries would have found him guilty of an irresponsible use of scripture, which would have undone every effort to persuade either friend or foe of his positive attitude toward the law.

[1] K. E. Kirk, *The Epistle to the Romans* (*The Clarendon Bible*, Oxford, 1950), p. 225.

On the surface there are two strong arguments on the side of modern interpreters who doubt that Paul meant this reference to Deut. 30: 11–14 to be taken as a quotation.

(1) There is first of all the striking divergence of Rom. 10: 7 (τίς καταβήσεται εἰς τὴν ἄβυσσον;) from Deut. 30: 13 (τίς διαπεράσει ἡμῖν εἰς τὸ πέραν τῆς θαλάσσης;). C. K. Barrett declares that the freedom of Paul's citation here 'suggests that he is not using his quotation as a rigid proof of what he asserts, but as a rhetorical form'.[1] This explanation of the wording adopted by Paul is frequently associated with the observation that the expression 'ascend to heaven and descend to the abyss' had become proverbial. Lagrange goes so far as to cite a rabbinic ruling on the sincerity of a suitor who offers to marry a girl 'if she will mount to heaven or descend into the abyss'![2]

It is, of course, possible that Rom. 10: 7 is simply a careless citation from memory (cf. Ps. 106 [107]: 26), and I think it is even probable that Paul's form has been influenced by 'proverbial' usage. Further, the close connexion between 'abyss' and 'sea' in the Old Testament suggests another possibility, one which recognizes such influence and still allows that the apostle is basing his argument solidly on the passage in Deuteronomy. Perhaps with the words 'Who will descend into the abyss?' he has already introduced a step in his interpretation of Deut. 30: 13. That is, what we find in Paul is neither a careless allusion nor an attempt at quotation. Rather, on the assumption that his (real or imagined) adversary will be familiar with Moses' words, he furnishes a paraphrase which is itself a move toward interpretation. As we shall see, the paraphrase utilizes a wisdom tradition which had prepared the way for his own understanding.

(2) The second objection to accepting Paul's words as based solidly on Deut. 30: 11–14 is stated directly by Lagrange: 'It is neither Moses who speaks, nor is it the scripture. Paul attributes the word to the righteousness based on faith.'[3] This is to argue that in ascribing the saying to ἡ ἐκ πίστεως δικαιοσύνη Paul indicates that the following material is not intended as a quotation from the Old

[1] *A Commentary on the Epistle to the Romans* (*Black's New Testament Commentaries*, London, 1957), p. 199.

[2] M.-J. Lagrange, *Épître aux Romains* (*Études Bibliques*, Paris, 1914), p. 255.

[3] *Ibid.* p. 254.

Testament. This consideration weighs heavily in Sanday and Headlam's assertion that 'the context of the passage shows that there is no stress laid on the fact that the O.T. is being quoted'.[1] Such an argument would be more significant if there were good reasons for regarding 'the righteousness based on faith' as anything other than a rhetorical personification. But it is hazardous exegesis to assume that this phrase is more than a stylistic flourish adopted to assist the apostle's interpretation.

Moreover, contrary to the views so often expressed, the context offers strong support for the opinion that sober, responsible citation is intended.

(1) The ten verses which precede and the ten which follow Rom. 10: 6–10 contain eleven Old Testament quotations. In no instance can any of these citations be regarded as allusive; each is made to score a point—creating a presumption in favour of the notion that the three references in our five verses were similarly intended.

(2) Phrases within our passage found at any other location in Paul would be regarded as signs of careful citation or serious interpretation of scripture. The form of Deut. 30: 14 found in verse 8 is altogether too close to the LXX to be regarded as allusive. Further, it is introduced by the phrase ἀλλὰ τί λέγει, which surely is best explained as an abbreviated version of the citation formula ἀλλὰ τί λέγει ἡ γραφή which with insignificant variations appears in Gal. 4: 30, Rom. 4: 3, 11: 2, 11: 4 (in the latter instance with ὁ χρηματισμός as the subject of λέγει). The effort of scribes to 'improve' the text at Rom. 10: 8 by supplying ἡ γραφή as the subject of λέγει (D G 33 sa vg^cl) shows that ἀλλὰ τί λέγει would naturally be understood as introducing a quotation from scripture.

Moreover, in verse 8, the words, 'But what does it say? The word is near you, on your lips and in your heart', are followed by an epexegetic 'parenthesis': 'τοῦτ' ἔστιν, the word of faith which we preach'. Apart from our passage, τοῦτ' ἔστιν is used following scripture citations only three times in the New Testament (Rom. 9: 7–8; Heb. 7: 5; 1 Pet. 3: 20). But in all of these cases (as would be expected) it introduces a comment that is intended to be a serious

[1] W. Sanday and A. C. Headlam, *A Critical and Exegetical Commentary on the Epistle to the Romans* (*The International Critical Commentary*, New York, 1899), p. 289.

explication of the cited material. Within our passage it occurs again in Rom. 10: 6, where this understanding of it occasions no real difficulty since the words quoted from Deut. 30: 12 approximate the LXX text closely. It is only in Rom. 10: 7 that the parenthesis introduced by τοῦτ' ἔστιν offers problems—and that because the preceding reference to Deut. 30: 13 diverges so radically from the Old Testament passage. But, with so many signs in the context that Paul is dealing with scripture seriously, surely this circumstance ought to drive us to ask if there is a more plausible explanation of Paul's reference than careless allusion. We have already suggested that verse 7 is to be understood neither as an allusion nor as a faulty quotation, but as a first step in the interpretation of Deut. 30: 13. The second step is now provided by the 'parenthesis'; 'τοῦτ' ἔστιν, to bring Christ up from the dead'.

In view of these considerations, it is not correct to conclude that '...the Apostle does not intend to base any argument on the quotation from the O.T., but only selects the language as being familiar, suitable, and proverbial, in order to express what he wishes to say'.[1] On the contrary, Paul is basing his argument directly and solidly on Deut. 30: 11–14.

But once this decision is reached, what are we to make of the allegation that the apostle's interpretation deserts the plain meaning of Deuteronomy and substitutes a diametrically opposed idea? Even if Paul is not guilty of flippant citation—that is, even if Paul does intend to explicate the Deuteronomic verses—has he nonetheless used the material in so fanciful a fashion as to make it meaningless to his readers? Professor Knox has commented that 'it is hard to see why Paul should have chosen for use a passage for whose clear original meaning he must substitute a meaning almost the exact opposite'.[2] It was this difficulty which led Bishop Kirk, in a sentence

---

[1] W. Sanday and A. C. Headlam, *A Critical and Exegetical Commentary on the Epistle to the Romans* (*The International Critical Commentary*, New York, 1899), p. 289. Cf. O. Michel, *Der Brief an die Römer* (Meyer KEK Göttingen, 1957), p. 226, n. 1: 'τοῦτ' ἔστιν (bzw. τοῦτο δέ ἔστιν) stammt nicht aus der hellenistischen Rhetorik...sondern aus der exegetischen Terminologie des Judentums...Entscheidend ist, dass man seine *exegetische* Bedeutung erkennt... Hier bei Pls leitet es eine exegetische Deutung ein. Pls verwendet also Dt 30, 11–14 in ganz strengem Sinn als exegetischen Schriftbeweis (gegen Str. B. III 281).'

[2] *Romans, Interpreter's Bible,* 9, 557.

already quoted, to describe Paul's interpretation as a 'drastic and unwarranted allegorizing' which 'must have exposed him to attack'.

It is precisely in connexion with this point that the whole issue of Paul's treatment of the Deuteronomic passage must be examined. If in this 'brief' Paul is working his way toward a statement of his proclamation which will allay suspicion sufficiently for the collection to be received, then *there is no place in the letter where a reckless disregard for Jewish interpretative tradition would land him in more hot water*. Deut. 30: 11–14 *does* read like a sermon text for his Jewish adversaries. This is so obviously true that I would concur in Bishop Kirk's judgment that Paul probably did not introduce it into the picture himself but that it was at some time 'quoted against him in defence of the *righteousness which is by the law*'.[1] To Paul's 'Moses writes that the man who practises the righteousness which is based on the law shall live by it', the proper Jewish rebuttal might run: 'But Moses also writes, "This commandment which I command you this day is not too hard for you, neither is it far off, etc.... The word is near you".' But it is just because it is a text of that kind that we should be hesitant to assume that Paul's interpretation is completely out of contact with contemporary Jewish tradition. For Paul to throw caution to the wind at this point, to essay a treatment so novel as to prove incongruous, would be wholly inconsistent with the type of polemic which both Bornkamm and Manson have shown to be typical of Romans.

Nor need we assume with Kirk that Paul, when the passage was adduced against him, was pushed into a corner where 'he had to make shift to dispose of it somehow'.[2] In fact, we must assume that Paul took up the response of his adversary with confidence, because he believed that he had an adequate rejoinder. For, while the Deuteronomic quotation may at some time have been introduced by a real antagonist in the course of debate, there can be no question as to how it found its place in Romans: it was placed there by Paul because he believed he had a viable interpretation of it. Straw men are set up only by writers who have a match that will set fire to them! *We* may not approve of his exegesis; yet Paul had not only confidence, but reason for confidence, that his readers would. This may be seen in the way his understanding of 'the word is near you'

[1] *Romans*, p. 225.   [2] *Ibid.*

(verse 8) is made the basis of the following discussion (see, especially, verses 17–19).

That Paul was able to take up an opposition proof-text with such boldness is to be explained by the foundation provided his interpretation by the Jewish wisdom tradition. The apostle had already drawn upon this tradition, with its speculation concerning the personified Sophia, to identify Christ and wisdom in 1 Corinthians.[1] This identification offered obvious values in a situation involving a Gnosticizing spiritualism. But, once it had been made, it also furnished Paul with a new means of relating law and gospel. The intimate connexion between Torah and Wisdom—indeed, the view that Torah is the embodiment of Wisdom (cf. Rom. 3 : 20)—paves the way for the view that Christ = Wisdom = Torah.[2]

3

The sources of late Jewish speculation about Wisdom and her roles as creatrix, revealer, and redeemer are so complex that they will never be fully recovered. It is, in my opinion, highly unlikely that all the traits associated with this figure in wisdom and apocalyptic literature are traceable to an ancient myth of the heavenly being Sophia—a myth which, largely repressed in the literature of the canonical Old Testament, burst forth anew about the turn of the Christian era to provide inspiration for Gnostic religiosity.[3] Nevertheless, there is,

[1] It is important to recognize that 'vorher Paulus der einzige war, der eine solche Identität behauptete'—so H. Köster, *Gnomon* 33 (1961), 594, in a review of U. Wilckens, *Weisheit und Torheit* (Tübingen, 1959).

[2] On this whole question, see W. D. Davies, *Paul and Rabbinic Judaism* (London, 1955), chapters 6–7. No attempt will be made to document in detail this paper's heavy indebtedness to Davies.

Much of what will be said in the following has been anticipated in one compact paragraph in T. Arvedson, *Das Mysterium Christi* (Uppsala, 1937), pp. 216–17. However, the Jewish background for Paul's interpretation of this particular passage is considerably richer than Arvedson could indicate on scarcely more than a page. Moreover, Arvedson's ingenious but rather indiscriminate accumulation of *religionsgeschichtlich* materials in the interest of his understanding of primitive Christianity as a mystery cult places his discussion in a misleading context. Cf. B. W. Bacon, *The Story of St. Paul* (New York, 1904), pp. 316–18; F. F. Bruce, *The Epistle of Paul to the Romans* (London, 1963), p. 204.

[3] But see U. Wilckens, *op. cit.* pp. 97–213, and article on Σοφία, *ThWNT*, 7, 497–514 (esp. pp. 508–10).

In a paper published after the present article was completed, H. Conzelmann speaks of three major types of Jewish wisdom speculation reflected in the Pauline

towards the beginning of the Christian era, a cluster of traits connected with Wisdom that begin to hang together. But is this evidence of an old myth resurrected? Or do we have, instead, an emerging synthesis of several older strains—traditions with a degree of independence but with a long history of mutual interaction?

However those questions are to be answered, certain elements which are present in the tradition available to Paul and important to the understanding of Rom. 10: 6–10 can be identified. Without any attempt at establishing temporal priority among them, these motifs may be mentioned:

(1) The Old Testament probably preserves traces of an old myth of a primal man who sat in the council of God and possessed divine wisdom (e.g. Job 15: 7–8). It is possible that the difficult passage Prov. 30: 1–4 may have been influenced by such a tradition; in any case, this text furnishes an example of the question, 'Who has ascended to heaven and come down?' following the confession, 'I have not learned wisdom' (contrast LXX).

(2) Sceptical sages denied the accessibility of wisdom to men, frequently using terms like 'heaven', 'deep', 'sea', etc., to express the idea that wisdom cannot be obtained. Thus the preacher testifies: 'I said, "I will be wise"; but it was far from me. That which is, is far off, and deep, very deep; who can find it out?' (Eccles. 7: 23–4). The classical statement of this theme is in Job 28, which asks where wisdom may be found. For the most part, the answer given to that query is couched in the familiar type of saying which expresses the value of wisdom: it 'cannot be gotten for gold, and silver cannot be weighed as its price' (verse 15), 'Gold and glass cannot equal it, nor can it be exchanged for jewels or fine gold' (verse 17). But while

---

correspondence: (1) die *entschwundene* Weisheit (1 Cor. 1: 18 ff.), (2) die *verborgene* Weisheit (1 Cor. 2: 6 ff.), (3) die *nahe* Weisheit (Rom. 10: 6 ff.) ('Paulus und die Weisheit', NTS 12 (1966), 236 ff.). The categories will certainly cover most of the tradition and demonstrate the danger of thinking of a cohesive myth, but I wonder if Conzelmann's description is not a bit too precise for a fluid tradition.

Conzelmann's thesis concerning Paul's relation to a wisdom tradition is that 'im Hintergrund ein von Paulus bewusst organisierter Schulbetrieb, eine "Schule des Paulus", zu erkennen ist, wo man "Weisheit" methodisch betriebt...' (p. 233). 'Als Sitz der Schule bietet sich Ephesus an' (*loc. cit.*). If the thesis could be established, it would serve our understanding of Rom. 10: 6–10 well; cf. Conzelmann's paragraph on p. 242 and especially n. 5.

such statements might be employed to extol the value of school wisdom, the context in Job requires that they be understood in a different way. Here, wisdom is a magnitude beyond the reach of men.

> Man does not know the way of it,
>> and it is not found in the land of the living.
> The deep says, 'It is not in me,'
>> and the sea says, 'It is not with me.'

> (verses 13–14; cf. Job 11: 5–12)

(3) An important element in the complex tradition is the personified figure of Wisdom who appears repeatedly in Prov. 1–9[1] and frequently in later literature. In this form, Wisdom is assigned a special status in relation to creation (the first of God's works [Prov. 8: 22 ff.], co-worker with God in creation [Prov. 8: 30?, Wisd. of Sol. 9: 1 ff.]). She dwells 'in high places' (Ecclus 24: 4) and 'sits by God's throne' (Wisd. of Sol. 9: 4).

Most important, for our purposes, is her gracious coming to men to reveal the ways of truth. It is not the intention of Wisdom to remain remote from men. She is a prophetess who 'calls' (Prov. 8: 1–3); she is the sage-mother who implores her sons to listen (Prov. 8: 32–5), she spreads her feast and invites her devotees to sup with her (Prov. 9: 1–6).

As Revealer, Wisdom delivers her message through representatives who are bound to her in the most intimate fashion and are conscious of their inspiration. Sirach lays claim to prophecy (Ecclus 24: 32–3). Even in the Elihu section of Job, it is affirmed that inspired youth may claim, 'We have found wisdom'. The language which describes the relation of Wisdom as Revealer to her disciples progressively approximates that of mysticism. She is the bride or paramour of her follower (e.g. Ecclus 14: 23–4; Wisd. of Sol. 8: 2, 16); the discovery of 11 QPs[a]—which includes a hymn previously known from a bowdlerized version in Ecclus 51: 13–30—confirms that this picture of Wisdom was widespread in late Judaism.[2] This aspect of

---

[1] It is not necessary for our purposes to determine the origin of this figure. H. Ringgren, *Word and Wisdom* (Lund, 1947), has made it very unlikely that the explanation of the figure is to be found in any single mythological parallel. A good discussion of possible sources and influences is to be found in O. S. Rankin, *Israel's Wisdom Literature* (Edinburgh, 1954), chapter 9.

[2] See J. A. Sanders, *The Psalms Scroll of Qumran Cave 11*, in *Discoveries in the Judean Desert of Jordan*, 4 (Oxford, 1965), 79–85.

the tradition about wisdom reaches its climax in Wisdom of Solomon, 'In every generation she passes into holy souls and makes them friends of God, and prophets' (7: 27).[1]

Because the language descriptive of Sophia's relation to her representatives includes the vocabulary of erotic mysticism, a word of caution should perhaps be urged. So intimate is the relation that Bultmann declares, 'It is therefore really Wisdom herself who again and again comes down to earth out of her hiddenness and becomes incarnate (*sich verkörpert*) in her envoys, the prophets'.[2] One hesitates to express reservations about such a statement, since *it certainly represents the direction in which this speculation moves*. But to speak of a *Verkörperung* in connexion with Sophia's *human envoys* at this stage appears to me to be overinterpretation—even in the Wisdom of Solomon (for which it would represent only mild exaggeration).

(4) The crucial step in the development of the tradition—in so far as our present interest is concerned—is the definition of Wisdom in terms of Law.

Precisely when this way of understanding Wisdom emerged is difficult to say, but Fichtner observes that there is no *nomismusfrei* wisdom writing later than Ecclesiasticus.[3] The range of literature in which the connexion between Wisdom and Law is important is quite broad. Even in the Wisdom of Solomon, the connexion is significant beyond the idea that 'wisdom...knows...what is right according to thy commandments' (9:9);[4] in 6:4, 9 'keeping the law' means 'learning wisdom and not transgressing.' Syr. Apoc. Baruch sets 'wisdom' and 'law' in synonymous parallelism on several occasions (see 38: 1 – 39: 1; 48: 24; 51: 3–4, 7). This identification can be taken for

[1] Wisdom's approach to men is often marred by their rejection of her and her messengers. This is the tragedy reported in John 1: 9–11. What the Fourth Evangelist says of the Logos, the wisdom literature says repeatedly of Sophia (cf. Prov. 1: 20–33; Ecclus 24: 6–7; Baruch 3: 13; 1 Enoch 42, 93: 8).
[2] R. Bultmann, 'Die religionsgeschichtliche Hintergrund des Prologs zum Johannes-Evangelium', in *Eucharisterion* [Gunkel Festschrift] (*Forschungen zur Religion und Literatur des Alten und Neuen Testaments*, nF 19, 1923), 18.
[3] J. Fichtner, *Die altorientalische Weisheit in ihrer israelitisch-jüdischen Ausprägung* (Giessen, 1933), p. 95.
[4] *Ibid.* p. 81: 'Wer von Jahves Willen redet, redet von seinem *Gesetz*...Sap. 9, 9: Die Wsht "weiss, was in deinen Augen wohlgefällig (!) und nach deinen Geboten (!) recht ist".'

20-2

M. Jack Suggs

granted in the Pirke Aboth, about which Fichtner could write that everything 'which Proverbs says about wisdom holds good for the law'.[1] It goes without saying that this development stands behind the rabbinic identification of Wisdom and Torah.

It is only here that it is proper to speak of an 'incarnation' of Wisdom. In support of his statement cited earlier to the effect that Sophia 'becomes incarnate in her envoys', Bultmann argued further in this fashion:

'Thus even the remarkable verse Baruch 3 : 38 is not to be removed as a Christian interpolation, but rather is an element of the old Wisdom-speculation, which the author has worked over: μετὰ τοῦτο ἐπὶ τῆς γῆς ὤφθη (Wisdom) καὶ ἐν τοῖς ἀνθρώποις συνανεστράφη.[2]'

It is very possible that this verse is not a Christian interpolation. But, if it is not, then it should not be isolated from its succeeding context: 'She is the book of the commandments of God, and the law that endures forever' (Baruch 4: 1). This kind of *specific identification* of wisdom with another subject occurs only in relation to the Torah (prior to 1 Cor. 1: 24; Matt. 11: 19; John 1: 14). Its first indisputable occurrence is in Ecclus 24: 23 where, at the conclusion of the famous 'Praise of Wisdom', the sage writes: 'All this is the book of the covenant of the Most High God, the law which Moses commanded us as an inheritance for the congregation of Jacob.'

4

It is against this background that Paul's interpretation of Deut. 30: 11–14 in Rom. 10: 6–10 is to be understood. Jewish wisdom speculation, upon which Paul has drawn for the identification of Christ and Sophia in 1 Corinthians, also provides the ground for a more positive statement of the relation of law and gospel.

Windisch appealed to our passage in Romans in discussing Paul's wisdom Christology and cited in this connexion the passage in Baruch which parallels Paul's use of Deut. 30.[3] Baruch asks concerning Wisdom:

[1] J. Fichtner, *Die altorientalische Weisheit*, p. 96.   [2] 'Hintergrund' *loc. cit.*
[3] H. Windisch, 'Die göttliche Weisheit der Juden und die paulinische Christologie', in *Neutestamentlich Studien für Georg Heinrici* (*Untersuchungen zum Neuen Testament*, 6, Leipzig, 1914), 224.

308

'Who has gone up into heaven and taken her,
   and brought her down from the clouds?
Who has gone over the sea and found her,
   and will buy her for pure gold?   (3: 29–30)

The significance of this sermon of Baruch is not merely that Deut. 30: 11–14 has been interpreted as referring to divine Wisdom. It is, rather, that the use of Deuteronomy in this way demonstrates that the words 'She is the book of the commandments of God, and the law that endures for ever' (Baruch 4: 1) are not an appendage to a passage dealing with Sophia. From beginning to end the sermon in Baruch 3: 9 – 4: 4 is the 'gospel' of the Torah. The identification of Wisdom and Law is made at the very outset: 'Hear the command-ments of life, O Israel; give ear, and learn wisdom!' While the opening section of the sermon reads like a conventional rebuke and demand for repentance directed to those who are 'in the land of your enemies' (verses 1–14), and the bulk of the sermon frequently echoes the mood of Job 28 and 38 (verses 15–37a), the heart of the message is neither the call to repentance nor the inaccessibility of Wisdom. The theme, rather, is God's gracious election of Israel and his gift of the Torah (Wisdom) 'to Israel whom he loved' (verse 37). Thus, although only Deut. 30: 12–13 is 'quoted' by Baruch, this does not mean that the declaration, 'The word is very near you, etc.' (Deut. 30: 14) is ignored. On the contrary, the Wisdom who is unheard of in Canaan and unseen in Teman (verse 22), unknown even to the giants of ancient fame (verse 26), has been given to Jacob (verse 37). 'She is. . . the law that endures for ever' (4: 1). Baruch affirms of the Torah what Paul affirms of Christ: that by this instrument 'the word is near you'.

The influence of thought of this type on the interpretation of Deut. 30: 11–14 may be seen frequently in the Rabbis. To cite only one clear example, Baruch's position is echoed plainly in R. Samuel ben Nahman's (third century) treatment of the phrase, 'The word is near you':

It is as if there was a king's daughter who was not acquainted with any man, and the king had a favourite who could visit him at any time, and the princess waited on him. Said the king to him: 'See how I love you; no one is acquainted with my daughter, yet on you she waits.' So the Holy

One, blessed be He, said to Israel: 'See how beloved you are upon Me, for no being in My palace is acquainted with the Torah, yet to you have I entrusted it', as it is said, Seeing it is hid from the eyes of all living (Job 28: 21). But as for you, IT IS NOT TOO HARD FOR THEE...BUT THE WORD IS VERY NIGH UNTO THEE. God said to them: 'My children, if the words of the Torah will be near unto you, I too will call you "near ones".' For so Scripture says, *Even for the children of Israel, a people near unto him. Hallelujah* (Ps. 148: 15).[1]

The statement that 'no being in My palace is acquainted with the Torah' is probably to be referred to the futility of seeking some one to 'ascend to heaven' to bring the word near. The quotation from the Wisdom hymn in Job 28 makes it clear that Samuel ben Nahman, like Baruch, teaches that though Wisdom is hidden from all eyes, God has graciously brought Wisdom near Israel in the Torah.

A similar theme is developed in the hymn found in Ecclus 24, where 'heaven' and 'abyss' again express the other-worldly character of Wisdom:

Alone (μόνη) I have made the circuit of the vault of heaven,
And have walked in the depths of the abyss (ἐν βάθει ἀβύσσων).
(verse 5)

Wisdom pictures herself as roaming the earth in search of a people with whom she might dwell until 'the one who created me' said, 'Make your dwelling in Jacob' (verse 8). Here, too, Wisdom is fully identified with Torah (verse 23).[2]

In summary, it is plain that proverbial expressions using the terms 'heaven' and 'abyss' (or, 'sea') were adapted to serve a significant Wisdom motif. 'Heaven' and 'the abyss' are symbols of the inaccessibility of Wisdom. In the late literature, Deut. 30: 11–14 is employed to show how God in his goodness has brought this hidden Wisdom 'near' in the Torah.

The familiar 'heaven-abyss' manner of describing Wisdom in her hiddenness has apparently influenced Paul's citation of the Deutero-

[1] *Midrash Rabbah, Deuteronomy* (translated by J. Rabbinowitz) in H. Freedman and M. Simon (eds.), *Midrash Rabbah* (London, 1951), p. 155.
[2] H. Windisch, *The Meaning of the Sermon on the Mount* (Philadelphia, 1951), pp. 99–100, found a reference to the 'near-by word' of Deut. 30: 14 in Ecclus 51: 26.

nomic passage, but the apostle is not thereby convicted of levity of citation or interpretation. And, if Bultmann is correct in thinking that the hidden Wisdom hovers behind Deut. 30: 11–14 as the counterpart of the revealed law,[1] then the apostle stands far closer to the original meaning of his source than is generally recognized. But that is hardly necessary to our argument here. It is enough that the late wisdom tradition provides a framework within which his interpretation can be understood.

The importance of establishing a link between Paul and the wisdom tradition is not merely that the apostle is thereby acquitted of gross mishandling of Deut. 30: 11–14. The greater significance lies in his appropriation of that tradition in relation to the continuing problem of Gospel and Law. In Rom. 10: 6–10 Paul has taken up the familiar identification of Wisdom and Torah and added a third term: Jesus Christ. The tension between Gospel and Law is resolved by the identification of Christ with Wisdom–Torah. The apostle hopes in this way to rescue his gospel from the stigma of absolute opposition to the law, while fully preserving the freedom of his own churches. To obey Christ in faith is to obey the law in truth. The (probably) inherited formula, 'Love is the fulfilling of the law' (Rom. 13: 8–10; Gal. 5: 14), is provided with a new rationale. The righteousness based on faith does not annul the law but brings it to its true goal, for 'the word of faith which we preach' is Jesus Christ, incarnate wisdom,[2] τέλος νόμου (10: 4).

Rom. 10: 6–10 thus provides a crucial point in the argument prepared by Paul in advance of the final visit to Jerusalem. The time leading up to the visit has not been characterized by peace. Rather, as the correspondence of the collection period shows, old wounds have been aggravated and new tensions have arisen. The impending journey to Jerusalem poses threats which the apostle takes with the utmost seriousness. The whole collection enterprise is endangered by persistent problems associated with Jew–Gentile, Gospel–Law tensions. The success of the visit hinges, in Paul's mind, on whether he can define his position in relation to Israel and the Law in such a way that the unity symbolized by the offering is protected from Jewish animosities and Jewish-Christian suspicions. In the interest of this cause he composes the document which we know as Romans, a

---

[1] 'Hintergrund', p. 8.   [2] Cf. Arvedson, *Das Mysterium Christi*, p. 216.

review of areas of prior dissension and a projection of solutions to possible future conflicts. This is the ground he presently occupies as he looks toward Jerusalem. And, since in this matter the whole of gentile Christianity has a stake, the 'brief' is issued as a letter—one copy of which went to 'all God's beloved in Rome', who are numbered among 'all the ἔθνη' to whom Paul has been sent as apostle (1: 5–7).

15

PAUL AND THE CHURCH AT CORINTH
ACCORDING TO 1 CORINTHIANS 1:10 – 4:21

NILS A. DAHL

When Ferdinand Christian Baur in 1831 published his famous article on 'The Christ-party in the Corinthian Church',[1] he was not raising a new question but making a fresh contribution to a discussion which had already begun. Yet his article is generally considered to have inaugurated a new epoch in the history of New Testament scholarship. Dealing with one specific question, Baur in his article gave a first sketch of his understanding of the historical dialectic in primitive Christianity. The main ideas were later developed in voluminous works by Baur and his pupils in the 'Tübingen School', and have exercised a considerable influence upon students of the New Testament up to the present day.

In his essay Baur argued that in spite of the four slogans reported in 1 Cor. 1: 12 there were, in fact, only two parties involved in the strife at Corinth: over against the adherents of Paul and Apollos stood those of Cephas, who claimed to be those who belonged to Christ. As the weaknesses of this theory have often been pointed out, there may be some reason for calling attention to its strength. On the basis of his theory, Baur was able to account for the fact that in 1 Cor. 1–4 Paul does not deal with a variety of parties, but in 'this first apologetic section' gives a justification for his apostolic authority and ministry. Further, he was able to trace a continuity between 1 Cor. 1–4 and the later controversy of which 2 Corinthians, especially chapters 10–13, is evidence. More especially, he could relate the enigmatic slogan 'I belong to Christ' to Paul's remark in 2 Cor. 10: 7: 'If any one is confident that he is Christ's, let him remind himself that as he is Christ's, so are we.' Finally, Baur was able to integrate the Corinthian controversy into a comprehensive view of the earliest

---

[1] 'Die Christuspartei in der korinthischen Gemeinde, der Gegensatz des paulinischen und petrinischen Christentums in der ältesten Kirche, der Apostel Petrus in Rom', *Tübinger Zeitschrift für Theologie* (1831), Heft 4, pp. 61–206. Cf. Baur, *Paulus* (Stuttgart, 1845), pp. 259–332.

history of Christianity which he found to be determined by the tension between Paulinists and Petrine Judaizers. Yet, the arbitrary reduction of the four slogans to two parties caused numerous modifications of Baur's theory even within his own school.

More than one hundred years of research since Baur has made it clear that there is no real trace of 'Judaizers' at Corinth, at least not at the time of I Corinthians. According to Wilhelm Lütgert, Paul's chief opponents at Corinth, identified with the 'Christ party', were spiritualistic enthusiasts, an early type of libertinistic Gnostics.[1] This theory has been very influential in Germany. Adolf Schlatter modified it by tracing a Palestinian background for the 'Corinthian theology'.[2] The philologist Richard Reitzenstein explained both Paul's terminology and the Corinthian piety on the background of contemporary hellenistic religiosity, mystery religions and syncretistic 'Gnosis'.[3] More recently W. Schmithals[4] and, in a different way, U. Wilckens[5] have tried to reconstruct the doctrines of the Gnostics in Corinth.

Outside Germany scholars have been more reluctant to assume that Paul's polemic had to be directed either against Judaizers or against Gnostics. Johannes Munck published an essay on I Cor. 1–4, later incorporated in his book *Paul and the Salvation of Mankind*, with the provocative title 'The Church without Factions'.[6] He held that there were neither 'parties' nor 'Judaizers', and, we may add, no 'Gnostics' at Corinth. What caused the trouble was that the Corinthians, owing to their Greek background, misunderstood Christianity as wisdom: they took the Christian leaders to be teachers of wisdom, like rhetors and sophists, took themselves to be wise, and made all this a cause for boasting. More recently, John C. Hurd,

[1] *Freiheitspredigt und Schwarmgeister in Korinth.* (*BFTh* 12, 3, Gütersloh, 1908.)
[2] *Die korinthische Theologie.* (*Ibid.* 18, 2, Gütersloh, 1914.) Cf. also Schlatter's commentary, *Paulus, der Bote Jesu* (Stuttgart, 1934).
[3] *Die hellenistischen Mysterienreligionen* (1910; 3rd ed., Leipzig, 1927), esp. pp. 333–93, 'Paulus als Pneumatiker'.
[4] *Die Gnosis in Korinth.* (*FRLANT*, 66, nF 48, Göttingen, 1956; 2nd ed. 1965.)
[5] *Weisheit und Torheit.* (*BhTh* 26, Tübingen, 1959.)
[6] 'Menigheden uden Partier', *Dansk teologisk Tidsskrift*, 15 (1952), 251–53. Incorporated as chapter 5 in *Paulus und die Heilsgeschichte* (*Acta Jutlandica*, 26, Aarhus/Copenhagen, 1954; Eng. Trans., *Paul and the Salvation of Mankind*, London, 1959).

Jr, has written a very stimulating book on *The Origin of 1 Corin-thians*.[1] Following good traditions of American scholarship, he avoids the generalizations of theology and comparative religion and tries to reconstruct the stages of the relations between Paul and the Church at Corinth prior to 1 Corinthians. The result is that the controversies behind 1 Corinthians were not due to any extraneous influence upon the congregation, but to Paul's own change of mind in the time between Paul's Corinthian ministry and the 'previous letter' referred to in 1 Cor. 5: 9–11. This change is explained as due to the apostolic decree to which Paul in his 'previous letter' felt obliged to be loyal; in accordance with John Knox and others, Hurd argues that the Corinthian ministry preceded the 'Apostolic Council', according to a chronology based upon Paul's letters and not upon the secondary evidence of Acts.[2]

This brief and eclectic, but fairly representative summary shows that while there is a wide negative agreement that in 1 Corinthians Paul is not opposing Judaizers, there is no consensus with regard to the background and nature of the controversies. As to questions of exegesis, it is fairly generally agreed that in 1 Corinthians 1–4 Paul is addressing the church at Corinth as a whole, and that it is not possible to take any one section to refer to any one of the 'parties', if there were any parties at all. Likewise, while 1 Cor. 5–16 may attest the presence of various trends within the congregation, it has not proved possible with any degree of certainty to relate these trends to the slogans reported at the beginning (1: 12). But this exegetical consensus is only a negative one.

No clear interpretation has been given to the slogans of 1: 12. If there were no factions, but merely quarrelling, jealousy and strife, the difficulties are increased. Why does Paul, then, set the slogans forth in such a prominent place? The major difficulty lies in the words ἐγὼ δὲ Χριστοῦ which quite a few scholars regard as a gloss.[3] The combination with 2 Cor. 10: 7 favoured by Baur and, on

---

[1] *The Origin of 1 Corinthians* (London, 1965).
[2] Cf. John Knox, *Chapters in a Life of Paul* (New York, 1950), pp. 13–88 (in *Apex Books* edition).
[3] J. Weiss and others, including Wilckens. For reference cf. Hurd, *Origin*, pp. 96–107, and (Feine–Behm) W. G. Kümmel, *Einleitung in das Neue Testament* (14th ed., Heidelberg, 1965), pp. 201–2; Eng. trans., *Introduction to the New Testament*, (Nashville, 1966), p. 201.

different presuppositions, by Lütgert and Schmithals, seems to provide the relatively best possibilities of interpretation, but the theories of these scholars are open to other objections.

No clarity has been reached with regard to the relation between chapters 1–4 and the rest of the epistle. An increasing number of scholars doubt the integrity of 1 Corinthians; the present epistle is assumed to be a composition of fragments from two or more letters.[1] Hurd offers a valuable survey and critique of these theories, but fails himself to provide a reasonable explanation of the function of the first major section (1: 10 – 4: 21) within the letter as a whole. On the fairly dubious principle that 'clearly the greater objectivity attaches to the written portion of the information',[2] he bases his understanding of the background of 1 Corinthians entirely upon the hypothetical reconstruction of the letter from the Corinthians to Paul and Paul's previous letter. This may represent a sound reaction against other scholars who have based their theories mainly upon 1 Cor. 1–4. Munck deals only with these chapters, and Wilckens concentrates on 1 Cor. 1–2 alone! But personally I cannot share the optimism with regard to the objectivity of written documents like statements issued by ecclesiastical bodies, and often find oral information more revealing with regard to what has been going on. In fact, Hurd is hardly able to make anything out of 1 Cor. 1–4, and the 'tentative suggestion' which he finally makes is a bad relapse into a method which he has in principle overcome.[3]

Finally, no clarity has been reached with regard to the relation between the situations reflected in 1 Corinthians and in 2 Corinthians. Is Paul in 2 Corinthians, or in the fragments of which the epistle is often assumed to be composed, dealing with later developments of the same controversy as in 1 Cor. 1–4, or is he facing entirely new problems? Both views are held, and there are arguments which

---

[1] Cf. Hurd, *Origin*, pp. 43–7, 69–71, 86–9, 131–42. Kümmel, *Introduction*, pp. 202–5.

[2] *Origin*, p. 62. But cf. also p. 113: 'Paul knew from his oral information that the Corinthians had not been altogether candid with him in the letter they addressed to him.'

[3] *Origin*, pp. 269–70. Cf. the summary on p. 295: '1 Cor. 1–4 and 11. 17–34 concern the "parties" which we suggested were the result of disagreement over the effect of the Previous Letter on the table fellowship between Jewish and Gentile Christians.'

seem to favour both of them.[1] In the following pages it will be argued that while Ferd. Chr. Baur was wrong in taking Paul's opponents in 1 Cor. 1–4 to be Judaizers, he was fully right in speaking of these chapters as an 'apologetic section' in which Paul justifies his apostolic ministry. It is a main failure of theories like those of Munck and Hurd that they do not really take account of this.[2]

An attempt to reach beyond the present impasse in the interpretation of 1 Cor. 1–4 must be performed according to a strict method if the result is not going to add to a chaos which is already bad enough. I would suggest the following principles:

(1) The controversy must be studied as such. Due account must be taken of the perspective under which Paul envisages the situation at Corinth. But as far as possible, we must also try to understand the Corinthian reaction to Paul.

(2) While 1 Cor. 1–4 must be understood against the historical background, any reconstruction of that background must mainly be based upon information contained within the section itself. Relatively clear and objective statements concerning the situation at Corinth must serve as a basis. Evaluations, polemical and ironic allusions, warnings and exhortations may next be used to fill out the picture. Only when these possibilities have been exhausted, and with great caution, Paul's own teaching should be used as a source of information concerning views held by the Corinthians; Paul may have adapted his language to theirs, but this assumption remains highly conjectural.

(3) The integrity of 1 Corinthians may be assumed as a working hypothesis which is confirmed if it proves possible to understand 1 Cor. 1: 10 – 4: 21 as an introductory section with a definite purpose within the letter as a whole. Materials from 1 Cor. 5–16 should therefore be used for the sake of comparison. Special atten-

---

[1] Examples are given by Kümmel, *Introduction*, pp. 209f. Cf. also W. Schmithals, *Paulus und die Gnostiker* (*Theologische Forschung*, 35, Hamburg-Bergstedt, 1965), pp. 175–9.

[2] Without making any impression upon Munck, I tried to draw attention to the apologetic aspect in an article, 'Paulus apostel og menigheten i Korinth (1. Kor. 1–4)', *Norsk teologisk tidsskrift*, 54 (1953), 1–23. The present essay is an attempt to restate and elaborate my case, with less attention paid to exegetical details, and with the addition of some new, more conjectural hypotheses. My interest in the topic has been renewed by the work of Hurd, but it is not a main purpose to discuss his theories.

tion should be paid to chapters 5 and 6 which in the present context stand at the transition from 1–4 to those sections of the epistle in which Paul handles questions raised by the letter from Corinth.

(4) In so far as they do not directly serve the purpose of philological exegesis, but provide materials for a more general, historical and theological understanding, information from other Pauline epistles, Acts, and other early Christian, Jewish, Greek, or Gnostic documents should not be brought in until the epistolary situation has been clarified as far as possible on the basis of internal evidence. Points of similarity, especially with 2 Corinthians, should be noted, but not used in such a way that the results of contextual exegesis are pre-judged.

(5) Any reconstruction of the historical background will at the best be a reasonable hypothesis. A hypothesis will recommend itself to the degree to which it is able to account for the total argument and all details within 1 Cor. 1–4 with a minimal dependence upon hypothetical inferences derived from extraneous sources. The results achieved will, on the other hand, gain in probability if they can without difficulty be integrated into a comprehensive picture of the history of primitive Christianity in its contemporary setting.[1]

The basic information contained in 1 Cor. 1: 10 – 4: 21 is what was reported by Chloe's people: There was quarrelling (ἔριδες) among the Christians at Corinth, each one of them saying, 'I belong to Paul', or 'I to Apollos', or 'I to Cephas', or 'I to Christ'. In 3: 3–4, where only the names of Paul and Apollos are mentioned, Paul speaks about 'jealousy and strife' (ζῆλος καὶ ἔρις). As the implication of the slogans is controversial, only the fact of the quarrels is unambiguous. Another piece of evidence is, however, added at the end of the section: ὡς μὴ ἐρχομένου δέ μου πρὸς ὑμᾶς ἐφυσιώθησάν τινες (4: 18). That the persons in question were 'arrogant' (RSV), or 'filled with self-importance' (NEB), is Paul's evaluation. But we do get the information that some persons assumed that Paul would not come back to Corinth. It seems more likely than not that they brought this assumption to an open expression.[2] In view of this

[1] The statement of methodological principles will make it clear why I discuss the theories of Munck and Hurd rather than those of Schmithals and Wilckens. This does not reduce the value of the immense material gathered especially by Wilckens.
[2] This is made fairly unambiguous by the emphatic ἐλεύσομαι δέ at the beginning of verse 19, cf. verse 21 and 16: 5–7.

statement, the idea that Paul all the time deals with the congregation as a whole needs some modification; there are some special persons whom he regards as being 'arrogant'. As fairly often, he uses the indefinite pronoun τινές to refer to some definite persons whose names he does not want to mention.[1] Thus we get an indication that Paul is aware of the existence of some centre of opposition against him within the church at Corinth.

The results of this search for objective information may seem to be very meagre. But if combined they may disclose some important insights; the quarrels and the slogans at Corinth were linked with the assumption that the apostle would not return. That the combination really ought to be made is strongly supported by the contexts in which the information appears.

The whole section begins by Paul's appeal to his brethren in Corinth that they should agree and avoid divisions (1: 10). It ends with an equally urgent appeal that they should be imitators of Paul: to that purpose he sends Timothy who will remind them of his instructions (4: 16–17). Both in 1: 10 and 4: 16 we find periods headed by the verb παρακαλῶ, a formal pattern which Paul uses when he sets forth what is a main purpose of his letters, expressing what he wants the addressees to do.[2] The παρακαλῶ-periods are distinguished from strict imperatives in that they call for a voluntary response. But Paul makes it quite clear that as the Corinthians' only father in Christ he does have authority to command, even if he does not do so, and hopes that he will not have to use his rod when he comes to Corinth, as he certainly will, if that is the will of the Lord (4: 14–15, 19–21). At the beginning Paul asks for the mutual concord of the brethren; at the end of the section if not before, the reader understands that Paul at the same time asks his children to concur in harmony with their father in Christ. This is well brought out by John Knox, who has written, with reference to 1 Cor. 1–4: 'He

---

[1] Cf. Rom. 3: 8; 1 Cor. 15: 12, 34; 2 Cor. 3: 1; 10: 2, 12; Gal. 1: 7; Phil. 1: 15; 2 Thess. 3: 11 (1 Tim. 1: 6, 19; 4: 1; 6: 10, 21). Sometimes even τις or εἴ τις is used in a similar way.

[2] The clearest example of this epistolary use of παρακαλῶ is found in Philemon, verses 8 ff. Cf. John Knox, *Philemon among the Letters of Paul* (1935; 2nd ed. New York, 1959), pp. 22 f. A full treatment of the form and function of the periods by Carl J. Bjerkelund is to be issued by Oslo University Press under the title ΠΑΡΑΚΑΛΩ. *Studien zu Form, Funktion und Sinn der παρακαλῶ-Sätze in den paulinischen Briefen.*

wants his converts to stand firm, not only in the Lord, but also in their loyalty to him.'[1]

The general content of the section adds further confirmation to this. It deals with four main themes:

(1) The unity in Christ and the quarrels at Corinth, 1: 10–13. This initial theme is taken up again in 3: 3-4 and 21–3.

(2) Wisdom and foolishness, the power and wisdom of God over against the wisdom of men. Various aspects of this main theme are handled in 1: 17 – 3: 2, and taken up again in 3: 18–21 and 4: 7–10.

(3) The function of the apostles and Christian leaders, and the esteem in which they should be held, 3: 5 – 4: 6, cf. 4: 9–13.

(4) Paul's relations to the Church at Corinth. This theme is implicit throughout the whole section from 1: 13 onwards and comes into the foreground at the end, 4: 14–21.

It is fairly clear how the first and the third theme are related to one another. The Corinthians are quarrelling because they 'boast of men', i.e. of one of the teachers, and are 'puffed up in favour of one (of them) against the other' (3: 21; 4: 6). It is somewhat less evident why the wisdom theme is given such a prominent place. However, Paul takes the boasting of the teachers to imply boasting of their own wisdom (cf. 3: 18–21; 4: 7–10). On the other hand, he sees the quarrelling as clear evidence that the Corinthians are not so wise and spiritual as they imagine themselves to be (3: 3–4). But in order to understand the structure of the total argument we have to realize that the fourth theme, the apostle and his relations to the church at Corinth, comes in at all important points of transition.

The initial appeal to unity immediately leads over to Paul's activity at Corinth and his commission as messenger of the gospel (1: 13–17). In 2: 1–5 and 3: 1–2 Paul returns to his own first preaching at Corinth, so that this provides the framework within which he deals with the word of the cross and the way in which the Corinthian brethren were called (1: 18–25; 1: 26–31), as well as with the wisdom which is reserved for the mature ones (2: 6–16).

From his first preaching at Corinth Paul comes back to the present situation (3: 2c–4, cf. 1: 11–12). Even when he deals with the questions, 'What then is Apollos? What is Paul?' he does not merely make statements of principle, but points to the special ministry

---

[1] *Chapters in a Life of Paul*, p. 95.

assigned to him (3: 10–11), and asserts that no human court, but only the Lord is to pass judgment upon him (4: 3–4). Even when he contrasts the predicaments of the apostles with the riches of the wise Corinthians, Paul has first of all his own ministry and sufferings in mind (4: 8–13). Thus the whole argument quite naturally leads up to the conclusion, 'For though you have countless guides in Christ, you do not have many fathers. For I became your father (ὑμᾶς ἐγέννησα) in Christ Jesus through the Gospel.' It would be unfair to take preparation for this statement to be the main function of everything that has been said; yet, one aim of what Paul has to say about the strife at Corinth, about wisdom and foolishness, and about the function of Christian leaders, is to re-establish his authority as apostle and spiritual father of the church at Corinth.[1]

From the statement, 'With me it is a very small thing that I should be judged by you or by any human court' (4: 3), we may safely infer that some kind of criticism of Paul has been voiced at Corinth. And it is not difficult to find out what must have been the main content of this criticism. That becomes evident in phrases like, 'Not with eloquent wisdom' (οὐκ ἐν σοφίᾳ λόγου, 1: 17), 'Not in lofty words of wisdom' (οὐ καθ' ὑπεροχὴν λόγου ἢ σοφίας, 2: 1), 'Not in persuasiveness of wisdom' (οὐκ ἐν πειθοῖ σοφίας, 2: 4),[2] 'Milk, not solid food' (γάλα...οὐ βρῶμα, 3: 2). To what extent the phrases, and not merely their content, allude to what was reported to have been said, is immaterial. Since the Corinthians evidently understood themselves as wise because they thought themselves inspired, pneumatic persons (cf. 3: 1), we must conclude that Paul was not merely held to lack the oratorical ability of a Greek rhetor, but also the gift of pneumatic wisdom. In 4: 8 the apostles are not only said to be 'fools for Christ's sake', but also 'weak,' and 'in disrepute'.[3]

---

[1] On several occasions the point that is most directly relevant to the actual situation comes towards the end of a section or an epistle, cf. 1 Cor. 10: 23 – 11: 1; 11: 33–4; Rom. 15: 30–3; Gal. 6: 11–17; Phil. 4: 10–18; 2 Thess. 3: 6–15. Thus there are good analogies for the assumption that the issue involved in 1 Cor. 1–4 is most clearly to be seen in 4: 14–21.

[2] I am inclined to take this as the original text which by an early error was misspelt as οὐκ ἐν πειθοῖς σοφίας. The other variant readings can all be understood as attempts to improve this. The problem has no material importance.

[3] Adducing very interesting evidence, Munck demonstrates that Greek rhetors and sophists could be regarded as wise, powerful, and honoured: *Paul and the Salvation of Mankind*, pp. 158f. and 162f., with notes. But he does himself see that

In addition to Paul's alleged lack of wisdom, some other factors may also have been voiced by his critics. He had not baptized many (cf. 1: 14). The catalogue of sufferings in 4: 11–13 deserves close attention. Hunger, thirst, and nakedness are common features in descriptions of persons in need (cf. e.g. Matt. 25: 35–6). That he is 'roughly handled' (NEB, κολαφιζόμεθα) refers in a more specific way to afflictions suffered during the apostolic ministry (cf. 2 Cor. 11: 23–5). The lack of stability (ἀστατοῦμεν) is characteristic of the apostle who is 'homeless' (RSV) and has to 'wander from place to place' (NEB); but the choice of the term may very well allude to what was said at Corinth about the unstable apostle who was not likely ever to come back (4: 18, cf. 2 Cor. 1: 15 ff.). An unambiguous reference to a practice of Paul, which is known to have caused objections at Corinth, is contained in the clause 'We labour, working with our own hands' (cf. 1 Cor. 9: 3–18; 2 Cor. 11: 7–11; 12: 13). Paul goes on: 'When reviled, we bless; when persecuted, we endure.' This is what a follower of Christ should do (cf. Luke 6: 27–9; Rom. 12: 14). But adding, 'When slandered, we make our appeal', he once more alludes to the actual situation; at Corinth he is slandered and responds, not with harsh words, but by making his friendly—though not exactly 'humble' (NEB)—appeal.

Since the entire section contains an apology for Paul, and the strife at Corinth was linked up with opposition against him, it becomes fairly easy to interpret the slogans reported in 1: 12. Those who said 'I belong to Paul' were proud of him and held that his excellence surpassed that of Apollos or Cephas. The other slogans are all to be understood as declarations of independence from Paul. Apollos is mentioned as the most outstanding Christian teacher who had visited Corinth after Paul. Cephas is the famous pillar, the first witness to the resurrection, an apostle before Paul. The slogan 'I belong to Christ' is not the motto of a specific 'Christ-party' but simply means 'I belong myself to Christ—and am independent of Paul'. Understood in this way, all the slogans give a clear meaning in the context and in the situation. Paul had no reason to deal in

the Corinthians thought of their power as participation in the kingdom of God (p. 165). The Greek analogies therefore do not suffice. At this date there hardly were any sharp distinctions between philosophers, sophists, rhetors, hierophants and mystagogues. For Jewish analogies cf. D. Georgi, *Die Gegner des Paulus im 2. Korintherbrief* (*WMANT* 11, Neukirchen, 1964).

detail with the various groups, and it becomes quite natural that he should concentrate his presentation on the relationship between himself and Apollos.

It may be added that on the interpretation proposed, the analogy between 1 Cor. 1: 12 f. and 2 Cor. 10: 7 becomes lucid. In 2 Cor. 10: 7 there is no trace of a specific 'Christ-party': the wandering apostles simply attacked Paul and claimed to belong to Christ as his servants (cf. 11: 23). Paul's answer is that he too belongs to Christ, and more than they he is distinguished as a servant of Christ, by virtue of his sufferings. Here and there Paul finds it an anomaly that someone at the same time can claim to belong to Christ and oppose his apostle and faithful servant.

There is no reason to think that either Apollos or Cephas was in any way responsible for the use that was made of their names by people at Corinth who claimed to be independent of Paul.[1] Paul himself stresses their solidarity and dependence upon God's work (3: 5–9; 3: 22; 4: 6; 15: 11; 16: 12). But what was then the occasion for the strife and the opposition to Paul? One fact, especially, is in need of explanation. The church at Corinth had sent Stephanas, Fortunatus and Achaicus as a kind of official delegation to Paul. According to all probability they had commissioned these delegates to bring a letter from the congregation to Paul, asking for his opinion on a number of questions. And in this letter it was stated that they remembered Paul in everything and maintained the traditions he had delivered to them.[2] Thus, the official attitude of the congregation seems to have been one of loyalty to the apostle. But on the other hand, Chloe's people could orally report that there was a strife in Corinth and that there was some opposition against Paul. This tension between the written document and the oral report requires some explanation.

We do not know anything either about Chloe or about her

[1] The Corinthians may well have derived their knowledge of Cephas from what Paul had told them; at least Peter may have been a great authority far away, in spite of the renewal of the theory that he had visited Corinth by C. K. Barrett, 'Cephas and Corinth', *Abraham unser Vater: Festschrift O. Michel* (*Arbeiten zur Geschichte des Spätjudentums und des Urchristentums*, 5, Leiden, 1963) pp. 1–12.

[2] 1 Cor. 11: 2. It is fairly generally agreed that Paul here alludes to what was said in the letter from Corinth. Cf. Hurd, *Origin*, pp. 52 and 90 f.

people. From what Paul writes we do, however, learn one thing, namely that it was not Stephanas and the other members of the delegation who reported the quarrels at Corinth. Possibly, this was the most important point even to Paul and the recipients of his letter. It may mean that the quarrels had started after the departure of the delegation, or it may mean that the delegates had not gossiped. In any case, Paul had his information about the quarrels and the opposition from some other source. The name of Stephanas is mentioned at the beginning of our section, in a very curious fashion. Paul first states that he baptized none of the Corinthians except Crispus and Gaius. But he has to correct himself and add that he also baptized the household of Stephanas. This lapse of memory may be due to the simple fact that at the moment Stephanas was together with Paul and not at Corinth. But even without much depth psychology one might suspect that Paul first forgot to mention the household of Stephanas because he did not wish that his name should be mixed into the discussion of the strife.

Considerably more importance should be attached to the way in which Stephanas is mentioned at the end of the letter. First Paul recommends Stephanas and his household; they were the 'first-fruits', i.e. the first converts of Achaia, and have devoted themselves to the service of the saints, which may mean that they have taken an active part in the collection for Jerusalem.[1] With remarkable emphasis Paul urges the congregation to be subject to such men and to every fellow worker (16: 15–16). After 1: 10 and 4: 16 this is the third παρακαλῶ-period of the letter! Next Paul speaks about his joy at the presence of the delegation, adding a new injunction: 'Give your recognition to such men' (16: 17–18). It is risky to draw conclusions from such injunctions as to the state of affairs which is presupposed. But the double emphasis gives some reason to suspect that not everybody in Corinth was inclined to pay due recognition to Stephanas, his household, and his fellow delegates. The evidence is so far inconclusive, but an hypothesis may be ventured: the quarrelling Corinthians were opposing Stephanas as much as they were opposing Paul. As Stephanas was the head of the delegation, he was

---

[1] R. Asting mentions this possibility, but is more inclined to think that Paul refers to service rendered to Christian preachers, including himself. *Die Heiligkeit im Urchristentum* (*FRLANT* 46, nF 29, Göttingen, 1930), pp. 151 and 182–3.

quite likely also its initiator, and a chief advocate of writing a letter to Paul to ask for his opinion on controversial questions.[1]

The advantage of my conjecture is that it makes it possible to account in a simple, perhaps somewhat trivial way for the data contained in 1 Cor. 1: 10 – 4: 21. The cause of the quarrels was the very fact that a delegation and a letter were sent to Paul. I can imagine myself hearing the objections, and I put them in my own language:

Why write to Paul? He has left us and is not likely to come back. He lacks eloquence and wisdom. He supported himself by his own work; either he does not have the full rights of an apostle, or he did not esteem us to be worthy of supporting him. Why not rather write to Apollos, who is a wise teacher? I am his man! Or, if we do turn to anybody, why not write to Cephas, who is the foremost of the twelve. I am for Cephas! But, why ask any one for counsel? Should we not rather say: I belong myself to Christ? As spiritual men we ought to be wise enough to decide for ourselves.

The details of this picture are of course pure imagination. But they may help us to visualize the delicate situation Paul was facing when he set out to write his answer to the Corinthians. He had to answer a polite and official letter, asking for his advice. But he had also received an oral report, stating that some brethren at Corinth had objected to the idea of asking Paul for instructions. Quite likely, latent objections had become more open and caused a good deal of quarrelling after the departure of the delegation. As a consequence, Paul had to envisage the possibility that his letter containing his reply might easily make a bad situation worse. Quarrel and strife might develop into real divisions of the church, if his recommendations were enthusiastically received by one group and rejected by others.[2]

---

[1] Hurd argues that the Corinthians' questions were veiled objections, *Origin*, p. 113 and chapter 5, pp. 114–209. In that case, the role of Stephanas may have been that of a mediator who succeeded in persuading the brethren that the objections should be presented to Paul in the form of a polite letter. But cf. below, p. 330, nn. 2 and 3.

[2] While Munck rightly argues that the term σχίσματα used in 1 Cor. 1: 10 (cf. 11: 18 and 12: 25) does not prove that there were 'parties' or 'factions', he has a tendency to play down the serious danger of divisions within the Church. *Paul and the Salvation of Mankind*, pp. 136–9. I am still inclined to think that σχίσματα corresponds to the term *maḥᵃlākōt* used in rabbinic literature. Jonathan ben Uzziel, for instance, is said to have translated the prophets 'in order that divisions should not multiply in Israel', Bab. Megilla 3*a*. Cf. N.A. Dahl, *Das Volk Gottes* (1941, repr. Darmstadt, 1963), p. 224.

If the situation was anything like what I imagine, Paul could not possibly go right ahead and answer the questions raised in the letter from the Corinthians. He had first of all to make it clear that he did not speak as the champion of one group but as the apostle of Christ, as the founder and spiritual father of the whole congregation. The first section, chapters 1–4, is therefore a necessary part of the total structure of the letter and has a preparatory function. This also explains the somewhat unusual pattern that a short thanksgiving (1: 4 ff.) is immediately followed by the first παρακαλῶ-period.[1] Paul had first of all to urge the Corinthians to agree and be of one mind. Only on the presupposition that they did so, and no divisions were caused, would whatever else the apostle had to write be of any help.

Answering his critics Paul is very careful to avoid giving the impression that he favours any one group in Corinth. There is no competition between himself and Apollos or Cephas, and still less between Christ and himself. Therefore even the slogan 'I belong to Christ' is in an appropriate way encountered by the questions, 'Is Christ divided? Was Paul crucified for you? Or were you baptized in the name of Christ?' There is only one Christ, and therefore no distinction between the Christ to whom the Corinthians belong and the Christ preached by Paul. Paul is Christ's delegate and in no sense his rival. At Corinth he laid the foundation, and it is impossible to belong to Christ without building upon this foundation, which is Jesus Christ himself (cf. 3: 10 – 11, 21–3).[2]

---

[1] The closest analogy is the period introduced by the equivalent ἐρωτῶμεν in 2 Thess. 2: 1. At this point I am indebted to the forthcoming work of Bjerkelund, cf. above, p. 319, n. 2.

[2] Even in 2 Cor. 11: 4 the point is the identity of Jesus and not a variety of Christologies. The true Jesus is identical with himself, as Paul preached him and made him the foundation of the church at Corinth. A 'Jesus' who does not recognize this foundation must be another, a false Jesus. The same holds true for a Spirit and a 'gospel' which is received as if Paul had not already preached the gospel and as if those who then believed had not already received the Holy Spirit. In *Origin*, pp. 104–5, Hurd has well summarized the arguments against the existence of a separate 'Christ party'. Paul's replies would 'simply further the claims' of the party. But Hurd has failed to take account of the possibility that 'I belong to Christ' could be an anti-Pauline slogan even if it is not the device of a special party. On that presupposition the replies become highly relevant just because 'It is axiomatic that Christ is a unity', as Hurd says himself; Paul is not a rival, but the apostle, servant, and steward of Christ. The argument in 1 Cor. 1: 13–15 is analogous with 3: 5–11 and 3: 21–3; 2 Cor. 10: 7; 11: 1–4, and 11: 23.

The fact that Paul did not baptize many is for him a reason for thanksgiving. Thus there is no risk that any one will say that he was baptized in Paul's name and has been made his man. The task of the apostle was not to baptize but to proclaim the gospel (1: 14–17). That he did not preach with eloquent wisdom was to the benefit of the Corinthians, and in accordance both with his own commission and with the nature of the gospel, which is the word of the cross. What may appear as sheer folly is God's saving power and wisdom (1: 18–25). The Corinthians ought to know this from their own experience (1: 26–31). When Paul in Corinth concentrated on preaching Jesus Christ as the crucified one, this was due to a conscious decision. He renounced all the effects of rhetoric and human wisdom, in order that the faith of the converts might rest in the power of God alone (2: 1–5). But when he did not in Corinth elaborate the secret wisdom of God's way of acting, it was not because Paul lacked the pneumatic gift of wise speech, but because the Corinthians were immature (2: 6 – 3: 2).

My one-sided and incomplete summary of 1: 14 – 3: 2 may be sufficient for the purpose, to show that everything Paul here says was relevant to the situation he faced. From 3: 3 onwards he turns more directly to the present state of affairs. Using himself and Apollos as examples, he stresses their solidarity as servants and fellow workers for God. Those who make comparisons and are proud of the excellencies of their favourite fail to realize their own dignity as God's field, building, and temple (3: 5–17). All things, including Paul, and Apollos, and Cephas, belong to those who themselves belong to Christ (3: 21–3). Yet it is also stressed that Paul had a special task of his own. He was the one who planted and laid the foundation, and this he did as a skilled master builder (ὡς σοφὸς ἀρχιτέκτων). Certainly he did not lack wisdom, after all (3: 6 and 10). While Paul has no authority of his own, all others have to build upon the foundation laid by him. They have to take care, lest they build with materials that will perish, or even destroy the temple of God (3: 10–17). By the context it is suggested that those who vaunt that they are wise might easily be found to be doing this. (I see no reason for making 3: 18 the beginning of a new section.) When speaking about faithfulness as the one duty required of stewards, Paul once more immediately turns to the relations between the Corinthians and himself (4: 2–5).

Even the riddle of the enigmatic statement in 1 Cor. 4: 6 may possibly find a solution. The phrase μὴ ὑπὲρ ἃ γέγραπται is widely assumed to be the quotation of a slogan used in Corinth.[1] I would suggest that even this slogan was part of the discussions and quarrels connected with the delegation and the letter to Paul. The point would then be: 'We need no instructions beyond what is written. As spiritual men we can interpret the Scriptures for ourselves. Why ask Paul?' Paul picks the slogan up and returns it. There is no contrast between the apostle and 'What is written', but there might be one between the scriptures, Paul and Apollos on the one side and the assertive and quarrelling Corinthians on the other. By the example of Paul and Apollos they should learn not to go beyond what is written, viz., not to be puffed up, but faithfully to perform the allotted service, knowing that everything is a gift of God. In the context the slogan gets its content from the preceding citations from and allusions to what is written concerning the wisdom of God in its contrast to the wisdom of men (cf. 1: 19 f.; 1: 31; 2: 9; 3: 19 f.).

Paul does not, as his adherents are likely to have done, deny the facts which his opponents alleged against him. But what they meant as objections Paul interprets as indications of the faithfulness with which he has carried out his commission. Lack of wisdom, power, and honour is part of the lot that God has assigned to the suffering apostles of the crucified Christ (4: 9–13). In order to prevent the possibility that the quarrellings could lead to divisions, Paul the whole time deals with the church at Corinth as a unity. Only at the end he singles out some persons and flatly denies what they have pretended, 4: 18 f. That he will not return to Corinth, and therefore no

---

[1] In addition to the commentaries, cf. O. Linton, '"Nicht über das hinaus was geschrieben steht" (1 Kor. 4. 6)', *Theologische Studien und Kritiken*, 102 (1930), 425–37; L. Brun, 'Noch einmal die Schriftnorm 1. Kor. 4, 6', *ibid.* 103 (1931), 453–6; M. D. Hooker, '"Beyond the things which are written"', *NTS* 10 (1964), 127–32. Miss Hooker deals very well with the terminology and context, but I have not been convinced by her renewal of Lütgert's and Schlatter's suggestion that the Corinthians ventured to go beyond what was written. It seems much more likely to me that they exercised their wisdom as interpreters of scripture as suggested by the terms σοφός, γραμματεύς, and συζητητής in 1 Cor. 1: 20. Only in 1 Corinthians Paul uses quotation formulas like, 'It is written in the law', and 'The law says' (9: 8 and 9; 14: 21 and 34); the reason might be that he agrees to play the game according to the rule set by the Corinthians themselves.

more cares for the brethren there, is simply not true. They are his dear children, and certainly he will come very soon, if the Lord will. This assertion is repeated at the end of the epistle (16: 5–7, cf. also 16: 24).

We can now draw some conclusions: (1) the section 1 Cor. 1: 10 – 4: 21 is correctly, even if not exhaustively, to be characterized as an apology for Paul's apostolic ministry. (2) The quarrels at Corinth were mainly due to the opposition against Paul. (3) Probably, the quarrels were occasioned or at least actualized by the letter and the delegation which were sent to Paul. (4) The section has a clear and important function within the total structure of 1 Corinthians; before Paul could answer the questions raised, he had to overcome both false appraisals and false objections, and to re-establish his apostolic authority as the founder and spiritual father of the whole church at Corinth.[1]

A number of problems remain. I have to deal briefly with some of them. The first is the function of 1 Cor. 5–6. Why does not Paul after the introductory section immediately proceed to give his answer to the questions raised by the Corinthians? It is hardly more than a partial answer that in chapters 5–6, as in 1–4, he deals with matters on which he has got oral information only.[2] In spite of some theories that fragments from several letters are combined, chapters 5–6 seem to be closely related to their context. There are several points of contact between the preceding section and the beginning of chapter 5.[3] In 6: 12–20 a number of items in the latter part of the epistle are preluded.[4] 6: 1–11 is related to chapter 5 by the idea of judgment, the question of the relation to those outside the Church, and especially by the catalogues of sinners in 5: 10 and 11 and 6: 9–10. Finally, 6: 9–11 serves not only as a conclusion to 6: 1–8 but also as an introduction to 6: 12–20. There is no reason to doubt the literary integrity. The problem is that of the epistolary function of these short sections.

---

[1] As to Paul's authority, cf. 1 Cor. 5: 3–4; 7: 40*b*; 9; 11: 16 and 34*b*; 14: 37–8; 15: 1–2, 10, and 2 Corinthians, *passim.*

[2] The section 11: 17–34 is an example of material based upon oral information and dealt with at a later place in the letter. Cf. Hurd, *Origin*, pp. 79–82.

[3] πεφυσιωμένοι, 5: 1, cf. 4: 19. Paul's absence and presence, 5: 3, cf. 4: 19 f. καύχημα, 4: 6, cf. 3: 21; 4: 7. Cf. Hurd, *Origin*, p. 89, n. 1.

[4] Cf. Hurd, *Origin*, pp. 87–9.

The most important point in this connexion may be the allusion to the previous letter, 5: 9–11. I have elsewhere argued that the content of what Paul wrote may best be reconstructed by a combination of 5: 9–10 with 6: 9–10.[1] He must have written something like: 'Neither immoral men, nor the greedy, nor robbers, nor idolaters, etc., will inherit the kingdom of God. Do not associate with them, nor even eat with them.' If this reconstruction is approximately correct, the fragment 2 Cor. 6: 14 – 7: 1 is hardly likely to have been part of the previous letter. Closer parallels are found in the catechetical instructions in Eph. 5: 3–7 and Gal. 5: 19–21, cf. also Col. 3: 5–6; 1 Thess. 4: 3–6, and the free, epistolary variation in Rom. 1: 18 – 2: 11. Thus, the previous letter is likely to have contained a restatement of Paul's oral instructions, just like 1 Thess. 4: 2 ff.[2]

It is fairly generally assumed that in Corinth what Paul had written was taken to imply that all social relations with unbelievers had to be broken off, and that, in 1 Cor. 5: 9–13, Paul is correcting this idea, whether (as is sometimes assumed) it was his own original intention, which he subsequently altered, or whether it was the Corinthians' misunderstanding of what he wrote. Certainly the scope of his instruction may have been open to several interpretations, as can be seen by the analogous passage in Eph. 5: 3 ff. But neither theory—self-correction or misunderstanding—is necessary.[3] The point in 1 Cor. 5: 9 ff. may simply be a matter of clarification, with the purpose of stressing that what Paul wrote was highly relevant to the church at

[1] Nils Alstrup Dahl, 'Der Epheserbrief und der verlorene, erste Brief des Paulus an die Korinther', *Festschrift O. Michel* (see p. 323, n. 1), pp. 65–77.

[2] Hurd has seen that there are some signs of similarities between 1 Thessalonians and the previous letter, *Origin*, pp. 231–3. In addition to the analogies between 1 Thess. 4: 2–6 and 1 Cor. 5–6, statements like 4: 4–5, 4: 13–18, and 4: 19–20 might in fact have occasioned questions like those which are treated in 1 Cor. 7, 15, and 12–14. But, instead of following this track, Hurd has elaborated the much less attractive hypothesis that the previous letter was occasioned by the apostolic decree.

[3] I owe this observation to one of my graduate students at Yale, C. Douglas Gunn. To state 'that we have in 1 Cor. 5: 9–11 Paul's own word for the fact that his earlier statement on the subject had been misunderstood by the Corinthians', as Hurd does on p. 215, is not correct. But even if one accepts the probability of the inference, as I have earlier done myself, there is not sufficient evidence to justify the shift from Hurd's first conclusion that it is not possible to know whether or not the section 5: 9–13a was occasioned by the Corinthians' letter, to his later assumption that this was indeed the case (*Origin*, p. 83, and on the other hand pp. 149–54, 215 and 219 f.).

Corinth. I am therefore inclined to think that chapters 5–6 are still closely related to the controversies which the first main section of the epistle sought to clear up.

At Corinth someone may have felt that even in his previous letter Paul had only given them milk and not solid food; why ask for a new letter from him? Dealing with two concrete cases, and adding some general warnings against sexual licence, Paul is able to illustrate his point, viz., that the brethren at Corinth are still in bad need of the milk of elementary instruction concerning a Christian way of life. Understood in this fashion, chapters 5 and 6 can be seen to have an important function as the transition from the introductory section to the answers given to the questions raised by the letter from Corinth. To put it more bluntly: Paul did not want to shame his children at Corinth by what he wrote concerning their quarrels and the opposition to him (4: 14); but before he proceeded to answer their questions he did point out that there were cases of which they ought to feel ashamed (5: 1–6; 6: 5). If the incestuous man is to be identified as one of those who were puffed up, assuming that Paul would not return (4: 18), the reasons for this would be quite obvious; but I see no possibility for deciding whether he was or not.[1]

In my essay I have explained the controversies reflected in 1 Cor. 1–4 in terms of the church policy and personal matters involved. This does not mean that I take the theological aspects to be of minor importance. But in actual practice theological debates are usually mixed up with questions of church policy and personal relations. I see no reason to assume that this was different at the time of Paul. But, whereas we have a tendency to regard theology, church policy, and personal relations as belonging to separate departments and yet, in practice, to allow them, illegitimately, to influence each other, Paul makes no such distinctions. He does not separate between person and office, but identifies himself and wants to be identified by his apostolic ministry.[2] Even his theology and his policy cannot be kept separate from one another. His theology is flexible according to the

[1] In case he was, the further identification with Paul's opponent in 2 Cor. 2: 5 ff. and 7: 12 would be somewhat less improbable than it is found by most contemporary commentators.
[2] On Paul as an 'eschatological person' cf. A. Fridrichsen, *The Apostle and his Message* (Uppsala Universitets Årsskrift, 1947, 3, Uppsala/Leipzig, 1947).

situations. Yet it has a firm core. In shorthand fashion it may be called a theology of the cross, a term that is especially appropriate with regard to 1 Cor. 1–4. From this basis, he evaluates the trends within the church at Corinth. He finds that the Corinthians do not recognize the wisdom of God, manifested at the cross of Christ. Claiming to have a wisdom of their own, they fail to appreciate that wisdom which, to paraphrase a Lutheran term, is an alien wisdom, *sapientia aliena*. They think already that they possess the coming power and glory, not realizing that in this world the glory of the Church and its leaders is, like the glory of Christ himself, veiled under weakness and sufferings (cf. 4: 8 ff.). Likewise, by passing judgments themselves, they fail to take account of the judgment that is to come, which both the apostle and his critics have to face (3: 11–15; 4: 5). Boasting that they are pneumatic, they prove by their behaviour that they are psychic, sarkic, just ordinary men (2: 14 – 3: 4). Still using Lutheran theology, we may say that in the eyes of Paul the Corinthians uphold a false theology of glory.

To an adherent of *theologia crucis* any doctrine which he dislikes may appear to be *theologia gloriae*. So far, the term is not very useful for characterizing any specific type of theology. We have to raise the question whether or not this does in an analogous way hold true of Paul's picture of the 'Corinthian theology'. And certainly, Christians at Corinth may have quarrelled and passed critical judgments, both against Paul and against one another, they may have appreciated wisdom and rhetoric, and they may have been proud and even arrogant, without having any profound theological reasons for all this. Much of what Paul writes does not give us any information whatsoever of what was involved in the theological aspects of the con- troversies. And yet, there are some clear indications that Paul really did hit the nail on the head when he found that the main tendency in Corinth was to anticipate the eschatological glory to such a high degree that almost nothing was left for the future. To use modern slogans: The Corinthians upheld an 'over-realized eschatology', overstressing the 'already' and neglecting the 'not yet'.

The clearest evidence is to be found in 1 Cor. 15. Whatever may have been the exact views of those who said, 'There is no resurrec- tion of the dead', they evidently saw no reason why there should be a future resurrection, as those who were baptized did already participate in the heavenly glory.[1] That this was the attitude is affirmed both by the sacramentalism and by the pneumatic enthusiasm at Corinth (1 Cor. 10: 1–13; 12–14).[2] The encratitic tendencies with regard to marriage and sexual intercourse, as well as the custom of allowing women to prophesy and speak in the assembled congregation, without restrictions, are likely to reflect the idea that there was no longer to be a distinction of 'male and female', as those who belonged to the new mankind were like the angels (1 Cor. 7; 11: 2–15; 14: 34–5). Even the knowledge and liberty claimed in relation to meat sacrificed to idols point in the same direction of eschatological enthusiasm (chapters 12–14).

To Paul this type of enthusiasm is a perversion of the message he preached at Corinth. Yet it is conceivable that it may have emerged spontaneously as a result of Paul's own activity.[3] To some degree the tendencies may also have been stimulated by the preaching of Apollos. I see no necessity for assuming any other extraneous influence at work. If the term 'Gnosis' is to be applied, one would probably have to assume that in the spiritual climate of those days various types of 'Gnosticism' could emerge and be mutually independent of one another.[4] But these are complicated questions. The short survey of theological trends at Corinth has only one purpose in this context: to show that the section 1 Cor. 1: 10 – 4: 21 not only has the function of re-establishing the authority of Paul

---

[1] Cf., long ago, Schlatter, *Die korinthische Theologie* (as in p. 314, n. 2, above), pp. 28, 62–6, etc. Many details are still under discussion, as, for instance, how far 2 Tim. 2: 18 would be an adequate summary of the Corinthians' position; but a fairly wide consensus seems to be emerging, cf. Hurd, *Origin*, pp. 195–200 with references, and further Munck, *Paul and the Salvation of Mankind*, pp. 165–7, and E. Käsemann, 'Zum Thema der urchristlichen Apokalyptik', *ZThK* 59 (1963), 257–84.

[2] In their letter the Corinthians must have written about their zeal for spiritual gifts, 1 Cor. 14: 12 and 39. This explains the somewhat forced transitions in 12: 31 and 14: 1. This allusion is more obvious than others which have been widely recognized, but is not taken account of in the literature surveyed by Hurd, *Origin*, pp. 67–8.

[3] Hurd's reconstruction of Paul's first preaching in Corinth is fairly independent of the dubious theory concerning the impact made upon the previous letter by the Apostolic Decree. Several points deserve serious attention. Cf. *Origin*, pp. 273–88.

[4] If Wilckens is right that there was a fully developed Gnostic Christology at Corinth, the balance of probability would weigh in the other direction. The data discussed in my paper are not favourable to this hypothesis, but it is not excluded by my own reconstruction.

as the founder and father of the entire church at Corinth, but also prepares for the content of the answers given to the questions raised and indicates the theological basis from which these answers are given.

The way in which Paul identifies his cause and his person, his policy and his theology may be astonishing and strange to us. We know that even at Corinth the reactions were mixed. The letter apparently made its impact. In 2 Corinthians we hear no more about the concrete questions discussed in 1 Corinthians; probably Paul's instructions were accepted. The proposals to appeal rather to Apollos or Cephas may not have been very serious, and proved to be failures. What did not come to an end was the criticism directed towards the apostle. Many of the objections which Paul countered in 1 Cor. 1–4 were voiced again, partly in modified, partly in sharpened forms.[1] The relations between the apostle and the Church at Corinth in the time between 1 and 2 Corinthians were both complex and troublesome. It is easy to understand that many were quite willing to listen when some new, wandering apostles arrived. And thus, the apostle had once more to write an apology for his apostolic ministry, this time in a sharper and more direct form (2 Corinthians, especially chapters 10–13). The picture here drawn of the situation in Corinth at the time of 1 Corinthians does therefore very well harmonize with our general knowledge of the Corinthian church and of primitive Christianity as a whole.

In later days, and even in scholarly literature, the Corinthians' mixed feelings with regard to Paul have found many echoes. Paul has been hated and loved more than most persons of the past. The book on Paul by Vilhelm Grønbech, the Danish historian of religion, might be mentioned as a highly sophisticated version of such reactions with many features in common with the Corinthians' portrait of Paul.[2] John Knox is one of the few who have tried to do justice both to the opponents and to the admirers of the apostle in past and present.[3] While the debate will go on, we should not forget that

[1] When Paul is said constantly to recommend and defend himself, this might well be a direct reaction to 1 Corinthians. Cf. 2 Cor. 3: 1; 5: 12; 12: 19. It was admitted, however, that 'His letters are weighty and strong', 10: 10.

[2] V. Grønbech, *Paulus. Jesu Kristi Apostel* (Copenhagen, 1940). Cf. E. Hirsch, *ZNW* 40 (1941), 229–36.

[3] 'The Man and His Work', *Chapters in a Life of Paul*, pp. 89–107.

Paul did not care about judgments passed by the Corinthians or any human court. He would hardly have cared more about the tribunal of history if he had been familiar with that concept. His only ambition and passion was to be found a faithful servant in the judgment of his Lord. For the historian, the chief task must be, not to express sympathy or antipathy or to evaluate virtues and short-comings, but to try to understand Paul as he wanted to be understood, as an apostle of Jesus Christ. He is an amazing person. In 1 Cor. 1–4 he proves able to handle delicate and fairly trivial matters of church policy in such a way that his words are still worth reading. He has something to say which is potentially most important, and which remains reasonably clear in spite of the hypothetical nature of our historical reconstructions.[1]

[1] The book by R. Funk, *Language, Hermeneutic, and the Word of God* (New York/Evanston/London, 1966), includes a chapter on 'Word and Word in 1 Corinthians 2: 6–16'. It appeared too late to be taken into consideration, but makes me aware of the fact that I have overlooked H. Köster's important review of Wilckens, *Weisheit und Torheit*, in *Gnomon*, 33 (1961), 593ff. These authors approach the problems of 1 Cor. 1–4 from another angle than mine. The question, to what extent the approaches are mutually exclusive or, rather, supplementary to each other, calls for more hermeneutical reflection than I am ready for at the moment of proof-reading.

16

CHURCH DISCIPLINE AND THE INTERPRETATION OF THE EPISTLES TO THE CORINTHIANS

G. W. H. LAMPE

The word 'excommunication', with its sinister and somewhat melo-dramatic associations, probably seems to most people to have more to do with the world of the historical novelist than with that of twentieth-century Church life. Yet by a strange paradox excommunication, if we understand the term to mean the exclusion of fellow-Christians by their brethren from participation with them in the Eucharist, is the state in which all Christians live at the present time: many of them either unconscious of the fact or accepting it as normal and inevitable. The denominational discipline of some churches has accustomed their members to a situation in which other Christians are regularly debarred, except perhaps under special ecclesiastical regulations, from sharing with them in the Lord's Supper, and in which they themselves are in turn excluded elsewhere. Even those branches of the Church which profess the practice of 'open Communion' are excluded from the Lord's Table in the greater part of Christendom. Separation at the focal point of Christian worship may be, as in the past, accompanied by mutual hostility, accusations of heresy and schism, and outright persecution. In better times such as the present, anathemas may be lifted and denominations may regard one another as 'separated brethren' moving towards greater unity. Yet the condition of perpetual excommunication, whether one-sided or reciprocal, still persists.

It requires an effort of the historical imagination to appreciate the gulf which, in this respect, divides the world-wide denominational churches of today from the local churches of the first century, in which every baptized Christian who had not repudiated his baptism or been specifically debarred from the assembly of his own congregation was accepted, on the commendation of that congregation, at the Eucharistic meeting of Christians wherever he might find himself. For in the early Church baptism is the primary point of acceptance and of division. The unity of the scattered local churches is a baptismal unity, and eucharistic fellowship automatically follows from it. The most paradoxical aspect of the modern situation, from the standpoint of primitive Christianity, is that for the most part baptism is mutually acknowledged by the churches, and yet that the one baptism is deemed insufficient as a basis for fellowship in Communion between Christians of whom none could allege that they had in any way repudiated or forfeited their baptismal status. This shift of emphasis from baptism to the Eucharist as the focal point of unity or of disunity has had profound consequences for the life and thought of the Christian Church. The way in which it took place, and the reasons for it, still call for fuller investigation. Certainly, it has had a far-reaching effect in the sphere of ecclesiastical discipline and of excommunication, and it makes it hard for us, accustomed as we are to eucharistic disunity, to understand the very different attitude of New Testament writers to the privileges and obligations of Church membership.

In part, this change is traceable to a depreciation of the central significance and supreme importance which baptism possessed in the early Church. Here was the real dividing line, the point of transition from darkness to light, from death to life, from the unredeemed 'world' to the fellowship of God's people, the 'saints', from the realm which lies under the domination of Satan and the demons to the kingdom of the Son of God's love. J. C. Hurd describes, as one of the characteristics of the Corinthian community, a 'conviction that the Church was an island of life in Christ, surrounded by a sea of death ruled by Satan'.[1] This is no doubt true; but it was shared by Paul himself as 1 Cor. 5: 5 and Gal. 1: 4 plainly indicate, and it is a characteristic conviction of the early Church as a whole. The clearest expression of it is in 1 John 5: 19, 'We know that we are of God, and the whole world is in the power of the evil one'. The sharpness of this dichotomy would probably come to be ever more vividly experienced as the Church moved beyond the sphere of Judaism and found itself in immediate confrontation with the polytheism, which it held to be demonic, of the gentile world. Hence, perhaps, there came into being the elaborate system of exorcisms in

[1] *The Origin of 1 Corinthians* (London, 1965), p. 285.

the catechumenate and the formal pre-baptismal renunciation of Satan.

Baptism is therefore a true antitype of the salvation of Noah's family by water (1 Pet. 3: 20–1); for it is the sacramental moment of washing, sanctification (that is, transition into the community of God's 'saints'), and justification 'in the name of the Lord Jesus Christ and in the Spirit of our God' (1 Cor. 6: 11). In such passages as the latter, where the allusion to baptism is clear, 'baptism' is a term of wide significance; for upon the rite itself there is focused the entire complex meaning of the converts' 'illumination': their turning from darkness to light, their reception of the gift of sonship to God through Christ, their response to the hearing of the word of the gospel, and their entry into the new life in the Spirit, which is marked by obedience answering to grace.

Yet in the primitive Church baptism, with all its wealth of significance, appears to have stood, chronologically as well as theologically, at the very beginning of the Christian's life. Echoes of catechetical teaching abound in the New Testament, but it is not clear to what extent this may represent pre- or post-baptismal instruction; and even if the extraordinarily sudden baptisms recorded in Acts should not be regarded as typical, there seems to have been nothing corresponding to the long and rigorous period of probation demanded of prospective Church members by the catechetical discipline that became normal by the beginning of the third century and is described in Hippolytus' *Apostolic Tradition*. Once the candidate for initiation had come to be required to prove his fitness for membership in this way, it was easy to regard baptism, if not as the sacrament of Christian perfection, at least as the moment when, after full preparation and warning, the candidate receives a once-for-all forgiveness of his sins, after which he can be expected to 'keep his baptism pure and undefiled' and preserve 'the "seal" unstained' (2 Clem. 6: 9; 8: 6). Moral perfection thus tended to be transferred from the sphere of eschatology to the moment of initiation. Baptism then becomes a seal set upon repentance instead of the beginning of repentance; a sacrament of fully-developed faith rather than the ground and starting-point of faith; the sign that the believer has received forgiveness rather than the gateway to a life of continual forgiveness.

22-2

In these later circumstances the problem of post-baptismal sin, if difficult to solve in practice, at any rate presents in theory a clear-cut issue. Grave sin either annuls the sinner's baptism completely (so that to receive baptism is to incur a risk to which, as Tertullian maintained, children ought not in fairness to be exposed and which the adult convert might well wish to postpone until the near approach of death), or, on the more lenient view which prevailed in the Great Church, it may be remedied by penitential discipline which, though not equivalent to the total re-creation and renewal conferred through the initial repentance in baptism, is a 'second repentance'.[1]

Certain passages in the New Testament, notably Heb. 6: 4 ff., 10: 26 ff. and 12: 17, seem at first sight to be open to an ultra-rigorist interpretation which would, as K. E. Kirk observed, make them 'strike a discordant note in the midst of so much mercy' and anticipate the Novatianists' attitude to post-baptismal sin. Other texts, again, might appear to foreshadow another doctrine which was to cause trouble in the second century: that the believer has already entered into the completeness of the age to come and so is secured by his baptismal illumination against all possibility of sinning. It would perhaps be possible to interpret Paul himself in this way, particularly when he speaks of believers as being 'dead to sin' (Rom. 6: 11), 'emancipated from sin' (6: 18), being 'not in flesh but in spirit' (8: 9), and a 'new creation in Christ' (2 Cor. 5: 17). 1 John could still more easily be misunderstood when its author asserts that no one who is born of God commits sin, for God's seed abides in him (3: 9); and the statements of Ignatius could be even more dangerous, that the fleshly *cannot* do spiritual things nor the spiritual do fleshly things (*Eph.* 8: 2) and that no one who professes faith sins (14: 2). The opponents against whom the polemic of 1 John is directed do in fact seem to have professed sinlessness (1: 8–10), and this may have been the attitude of the Corinthians whose slogans were 'all things are lawful' (1 Cor. 6: 12; 10: 23) and 'food for the belly and the belly for food' (6: 13), and who claimed, as those who

---

[1] Cf. Tert. *paenit.* 7, 9, Clem. *str.* 2. 13, Epiph. *haer.* 59. 5, etc.,; also the frequent orthodox insistence against the Novatianists that Hebrews (6: 4 ff.; 12: 17) does not exclude post-baptismal forgiveness but merely asserts that baptism is unrepeatable (e.g. Ath. *ep. Serap.* 4. 13 and the commentaries of Chrysostom and Theodore on Hebrews).

were already living fully in the new age, to be strong enough in their spiritual self-confidence to ignore the risk of contamination through retaining a grave offender in their ranks (1 Cor. 5: 2, 6 ff.).

Generally speaking, however, the primitive Church clearly understands that moral perfection is an object of eschatological hope; that the Spirit enables the believer to possess the assurance and first-fruits of the age to come, but that he still lives in the flesh and stands within the present order; that in this life the implications of his baptismal enlightenment have to be worked out in the daily following of Christ and in daily dying and rising with him. Baptism is the beginning of life as a justified sinner rather than the end of sin. The emancipation from, or death to, sin of which Paul speaks is clearly to be understood as an object of faith and hope rather than of perfect realization in this world. The author of 1 John knows that cleansing is not begun and ended at baptism but that the cleansing by the blood of Jesus is a continuous process (1: 7); and, assuming any reasonable measure of unity in that epistle, his antithetical statements about sinlessness and confession of sins point to a doctrine of 'simul justus, simul peccator'. In the case of Ignatius' apparently rash statements quoted above full allowance has to be made for their context and their hortatory character. The writers of the primitive Church are aware that the Church must contain sinners in its midst so long as the present age endures. The tares cannot be separated from the wheat until the final harvest.

It follows from this that the discipline of the first-century Church is pastoral rather than penal, directed towards mutual support and encouragement, and towards the reclamation of sinners rather than their exclusion. This principle finds expression in the pastoral exhortations of Paul, most notably in Gal. 6: 1: 'Brethren, if a man is overtaken in any trespass, you who are spiritual should restore him in a spirit of gentleness. Look to yourself, lest you, too, be tempted.' His injunctions here stand in strong contrast both to the rigorism so often displayed in later times by those who claimed to be 'spiritual' and also to the arrogant complacency towards offenders shown by the Corinthians in the episode of the incestuous man. A similar spirit pervades 2 Cor. 2: 5–11, 2 Cor. 7: 9 (perhaps to be connected with the last-named passage), and 1 Thess. 5: 14; and it is in harmony with the admonitions given by other early writers, such as 2 Tim. 2:

25–6 and Jas 5: 16, 20, and with Polycarp's attitude to the erring presbyter Valens (*ep.* 11: 4). It accords, too, with the teaching on private reconciliation in Luke 17: 3–4 and Matt. 18: 21–35. This pastoral care may involve the temporary exclusion of an impenitent offender from the fellowship, and in particular from the Eucharistic meal, in order to secure his repentance and prevent the community from being implicated in his sin. The local church may have to express its disapproval of a disobedient member by boycotting him: yet not in a hostile spirit but by way of brotherly admonition (2 Thess. 3: 14–15; cf. also 6–10 where 'let him not eat' may refer to exclusion from the common meal).

To this pastoral and remedial discipline, however, the treatment of the incestuous man at Corinth (1 Cor. 5: 1–6) appears, at least at first sight, to present a striking contrast. The passage offers many notorious difficulties. These include the problem of determining the circumstances in which Paul is writing; the reason for Paul's singular vehemence and severity in this case, and for his rebuke to the Corinthians for their 'boasting' (5: 6); the vexed question whether the offender whose restoration to fellowship is enjoined in 2 Cor. 2: 5–11 is to be identified with the incestuous man or with the offender to whom Paul vaguely alludes in 2 Cor. 7: 10–12, or with both; the connexion between this case and Paul's allusion to instructions previously sent by him to Corinth to the effect that the company of fornicators is to be avoided (5: 9); the manner in which judgment is passed on the offender and the nature of his punishment: whether he is both cursed and excommunicated, or simply expelled; and how his being consigned to Satan for the destruction of the flesh could result in the salvation of the spirit in the day of the Lord.

The first of these problems involves the relation of verses 9–13 to the preceding passage. Paul had included in a previous letter (if ἔγραψα (verses 9, 11) is to be taken as a true aorist) a warning against association with fornicators, idolaters, drunkards and other wrongdoers in the Christian community (verses 9 ff.). Such people are to be boycotted. Verse 11, τῷ τοιούτῳ μηδὲ συνεσθίειν, may possibly refer to exclusion from the Eucharistic meal, but if so the emphatic μηδέ is perhaps surprising; one would suppose that to exclude such notorious offenders, while still impenitent, from the agape-Eucharist would be the natural first step for the community to take, and not an extreme measure. More probably, therefore, the injunction is to avoid all social intercourse with them.

2 Cor. 6: 14 – 7: 1 is possibly part of the same letter, but if so that fragment of it is not being referred to here. It concerns mixed marriages with pagans, whereas Paul says most emphatically that the previous instructions to which he is alluding had nothing to do with relations between Christians and pagans, but were concerned solely with the internal discipline of the Church. So strongly and sarcastically, indeed, does Paul emphasize that he would not be so foolish as to recommend the Corinthians to refrain from all dealings with immoral heathens (since to do this would be to make ordinary life impossible) that it is difficult to believe that 2 Cor. 6: 14 – 7: 1, with its rigid insistence on the total separation of God's spiritual 'temple' from the realm of lawlessness and 'Beliar' (strongly reminiscent of the Qumran literature),[1] could have been included anywhere in the letter to which he is now referring. It is by no means impossible that Paul should have sent more than one letter to Corinth before he wrote our 'first epistle'. J. C. Hurd's theory[2] is attractive, that the Corinthians had affected to misunderstand Paul's warning against associating with Christian backsliders, and had objected that, the world being full of fornicators and idolaters, so puritanical an attitude would be impossible to maintain. The motive of their objection was their confidence that truly enlightened believers are beyond the reach of any defilement from sinners. To this arrogance of theirs verses 9–13 are Paul's reply.

Whether or not this reconstruction be correct, and even if there had been no previous correspondence between Paul and the Corinthians on this point (ἔγραψα being then an epistolary aorist: yet the allusion to 'the letter' (verse 9) tends to tell against this), it is likely that the Corinthians' 'boasting' (verse 6) was of this kind: that a 'spiritual' church cannot be defiled by the presence of gross sinners. This was in all probability the reason for their 'arrogant' failure to mourn the calamitous case of incest and to take steps to expel the offender (verse 2); and this is why, assuming that ἔγραψα does indicate that Paul had sent an earlier warning, Paul alludes to his previous

[1] As has been pointed out by K. G. Kuhn (*RB* 61, 1954) and others. Cf. especially 1QS 5.
[2] *Origin*, pp. 149 ff.

letter here in connexion with this new scandal which had been 'reported' to him (verse 1), probably by Chloe's people.

If the Corinthians, as J. C. Hurd supposes, had retorted with a sarcastic objection to Paul's warning not to consort with evildoers in the community, the singular vehemence of his condemnation of this sinner is easy to understand. Not only was the offence peculiarly shocking, even when judged by the standards of pagan morality (verse 1), but it had afforded a focal point for the disobedience of the Corinthian Church towards its apostle. Hence the extraordinary severity with which Paul himself anticipates the judgment which the Church must proceed to pass on the offender. He acts vicariously on the Church's behalf, in the name of the Lord; he is present in spirit, though physically absent, in the formal assembly which is now to be convened (verses 3–4). At this meeting judgment is to be delivered by the power of the Lord Jesus; for whether it be the apostle alone (but acting as 'spiritually present' with the congregation) who pronounces sentence, or whether it be the corporate body of the Church, the judgment is really Christ's.

The conviction that Christ is the real agent in either case is similar to the belief expressed in Matt. 18: 18–20: the verdict of the Church is ratified in heaven (and possibly, even, the final judgment is thereby anticipated), because, when the congregation is assembled in prayer with the intention of exercising discipline, Jesus is in their midst and God will act in response to their petitions. In this context 'binding and loosing' must surely signify the discipline exercised by the community over its members. But this meaning is to be distinguished from the sense of the same phrase in Matt. 16: 19, where it probably alludes to the opening of the kingdom of heaven to men through the preaching of the gospel, Peter, by the fact of being the leader of the apostolic mission, being entrusted with the keys which admit or exclude men from repentance and faith. The authority to forgive and to retain sins (John 20: 23) is also probably to be understood in the latter sense, that is, as a commission to the disciples to proclaim the gospel which, according to the manner in which it is received, brings forgiveness or condemnation.

The whole of the passage Matt. 18: 15–20 is important in relation to this case at Corinth. The procedure to be adopted by the Church is in some respects similar to that which Paul enjoins. It also has parallels in the discipline of the Qumran community (e.g. 1QS 5: 26 – 6: 1). If a brother sins (the variant ἁμαρτήσῃ εἰς σε, which would restrict the procedure to private wrongs, is probably to be rejected: personal injuries are dealt with in 18: 21 ff. by the very different method of unlimited forgiveness), he is to be privately rebuked. If he does not repent, the brother who has taken the matter up with him is to do so again in the presence of the witnesses required by regular judicial procedure. If he rejects this appeal, he is to be treated as an outcast from the fellowship, just as the Gentile and the publican were excluded from Israel. There are echoes here of Lev. 19: 7 f. and Deut. 19: 15.

The rigorism of this passage, and the formality of the ecclesiastical discipline here described, stand in striking contrast to Luke 17: 3–4 where, in a parallel context of 'scandals' in the community, a command to rebuke a brother who sins adds no directions about what is to be done if he proves obdurate but only the further injunction to set no limit to the forgiveness of private wrongs. It also forms a contrast to the Matthaean parable of the tares, and to other less rigorist teaching such as we find in the *Didache* (14: 2; 15: 3), Ignatius (*Philad.* 8: 1), and Polycarp's attitude to Valens. Possibly this passage reflects a Jewish tradition, perhaps of a sectarian type; at any rate, it bears a close relationship to Paul's conception of the community, and the apostle, acting in the Lord's name and in his power, assembled to deliver the offender to Satan.

It is true that Matthew tones down the severity of the passage by placing it in the context of the parable of the lost sheep, here applied to the Church's pastoral care of its erring members, and of the subsequent teaching about the forgiveness of private injuries, leading on to the parable of the unmerciful servant. It is also true that it is not explicitly stated in the pericope that the exclusion of the disobedient members is irrevocable; but the natural inference is that it is meant to be permanent, like that of the most recalcitrant offenders at Qumran. The procedure here laid down thus represents an even greater degree of rigorism than we find in the Pauline case, where at least concern is shown for the ultimate salvation of the offender's spirit. It is worth notice, however, that it is not the initial sin of the erring member which is punished by relegation to the ranks of the outcast; it is the sin of obdurate refusal to repent in response to brotherly admonitions. It is a direct offence against the fellowship: contempt for the brethren.

We are introduced to the Corinthian story at a late stage. We do not know whether a similar process of private reproval and appeals for penitence had taken place there. It may reasonably be assumed that the sinner had refused to amend. If so, his case might perhaps be classed with that of the sinner in Matt. 18. He would have directly injured the fellowship itself; and the injury would be more than ever damaging, from Paul's standpoint, if the effect of his obduracy had been to encourage the Corinthians to use his case as an occasion for arrogant 'boasting' and contempt for Paul's instructions.

Sins which are direct injuries to the community receive severe treatment in the primitive Church. There should probably be included in this category the eating of the bread and drinking of the cup 'unworthily' (1 Cor. 11: 27). 'Unworthily' seems to be equated with failure to 'discern the body' (verse 29). It is notoriously difficult to elucidate Paul's meaning here, partly because the situation which he has in mind is not clearly indicated and partly because his language is obscure and elliptical. He is alluding to matters which his readers are familiar with, but we are not. It is particularly hard to tell whether 'the body' which the unworthy do not 'discern' is the community as the body of, or in, Christ, or the body of Christ whose death is proclaimed in the Supper, or, as is probable, the two are so closely interrelated as to be indistinguishable from each other in this context. A man who eats and drinks unworthily is guilty of the body and blood of Christ. This suggests that to violate the solemn fellowship of Christ's people, as had been done by the scandalous selfishness of some participants in the Corinthian Eucharist, is to become implicated in responsibility for the death of Christ, just as for the baptized person to commit apostasy is, according to the writer to the Hebrews, to crucify the Son of God.

Profanation of Christ's body, represented in the Eucharist and in the assembly of the congregation, has resulted in many being weak and ill, and in some having died (verse 30). Paul does not directly connect this punishment with expulsion from the Church; indeed, the conduct of the Corinthians over the case of incest makes it highly improbable that they would have taken any action against those whose scandalous behaviour consisted in profaning the sacred character of the corporate meal. The physical penalties which had afflicted them are not, therefore, any automatic consequence of exclusion from the community, and we need not suppose that Paul thought that a baptized person who loses his place in the Christian body and returns to the world of darkness and demons would automatically suffer in body as well as in soul. They may rather represent the way in which direct divine judgment had been vindicated upon them, even though the Church had neglected to subject them to proper discipline. This is, incidentally, some indication that the consignment of the offender to Satan (1 Cor. 5: 5) is not simply to be identified with excommunication as such.

These physical penalties are in line with the general severity shown towards offenders who injure the 'body' of the Christian fellowship. The case of Ananias and Sapphira is relevant here, for they profaned the Spirit in the community by their attempt to deceive the apostles, and through them to lie to God, for selfish ends. It seems improbable that Paul believed the physical penalties that had been visited upon the profaners of the Supper to be due to some inherent potency in the sacrament itself, so that their fate would be somewhat comparable with that of Uzzah (2 Sam. 6: 7), despite the number of scholars, including Allo, Héring, Lietzmann and Bultmann, who have taken this view.[1] We are not, of course, entitled to assume as an axiom that Paul was free from superstition. Moreover, it would not be impossible to interpret such a belief at a rather higher level than that of crude magic. Supposing Paul to have anticipated the belief of Ignatius that the Eucharist is the 'medicine of immortality', it is arguable that he might have drawn the negative inference that if it were partaken of unworthily it would become a means of dis-grace and bring about death. But it is extremely unlikely, though again it has been maintained by some, that Paul, whatever he may have thought about his own prospect of surviving until the *parousia*, believed that no Christian who continued within the fellowship and partook of the Eucharist would encounter physical death. In view of his treatment of the problem created for the Thessalonian church by the deaths of some of its members (1 Thess. 4: 13–18 and especially verse 16: 'the dead in Christ shall rise first'), and in view, also, of his words in 1 Cor. 15: 52, 'the dead shall be raised incor-

[1] It is shared by J. C. Hurd, who discusses the question, *Origin*, pp. 135 ff.

ruptible', it is surely impossible to interpret his πάντες οὐ κοιμηθησό-μεθα in the last-named verse so as to mean, 'none of us shall die', even though the grammatical construction might indicate this, and to suppose that this expectation was linked in his mind with a belief that its fulfilment could be guaranteed by the fact of participating in the Eucharist. It is therefore most unlikely that Paul believed that those who had profaned the sacrament had been relegated to a condition of illness and death from which they would otherwise have been exempt. Nor does anything else in Paul's teaching on death and resurrection lead us to think that his beliefs about the Eucharist anticipated Ignatius' φάρμακον ἀθανασίας, but in a more crudely materialistic form than Ignatius himself would have acknowledged. It seems much more probable that Paul is pointing to the sickness and death of some Corinthians as a divinely inflicted punishment for a grave offence against the Christian society, which implied a direct repudiation of its essential character in its relationship to the Lord whose death was proclaimed at every Eucharistic assembly.

Even this harsh punishment, however, seems to have had a re-formative aspect. To be judged by the Lord is to be chastened, and the purpose of chastisement is deliverance from the general condemnation to which the 'world' is doomed (verse 32). How this can be effected is not made clear; but it would seem, at any rate, that these offenders will not be condemned, along with the unredeemed world, at the final judgment; that is to say, they have not simply forfeited their baptismal status. The Lord's judgment in this world is thus reckoned to be merciful and remedial. Presumably this means that the possibility of repentance remains open to them, and this in turn implies that the infliction of physical penalties is intended to evoke repentance. Such an idea would be in harmony with much Old Testament and Christian thinking: the threat of destruction pronounced by Peter against Simon Magus, and the latter's response to it (Acts 8: 20–4), afford an obvious example. At the same time, it is certainly difficult to see how death could serve as a means of promoting repentance, and one can only speculate on the possibility that Paul envisages a divine sentence of death, which continues to take effect even after illness has induced the offender to come to a better mind, but which does not, in such a case, form a prelude to final condemnation at the *parousia*. Difficult as it is to make sense of Paul's words along these lines, it is easier than to suppose that he regarded the mere fact of having been baptized as a guarantee of salvation: that is to say, that he believed that although a Christian may be visited with punishments his baptism in itself secures him against ultimate condemnation. The language of verse 32, κρινόμενοι δὲ ὑπὸ τοῦ κυρίου παιδευόμεθα, ἵνα μὴ σὺν τῷ κόσμῳ κατακριθῶμεν, is enough to rule out that possibility; and it is clear from his teaching as a whole that he did not in fact hold that every baptized person was automatically assured of salvation.

This brings us back to the parallel problem of the judgment passed in the case of incest. Action is taken against the man by Christ himself, for since it is done in his name and by his power the human agents are his instruments. It is thus a kind of negative counterpart to a miracle of healing, for it is with positive 'mighty works' of that kind that the name of Jesus and the divine δύναμις are regularly associated. Its effect is to 'deliver him to Satan for the destruction of the flesh, in order that the spirit may be saved in the day of the Lord'. What this may mean it is extraordinarily difficult to discover. 'The destruction of the flesh' is most naturally to be taken to mean the kind of affliction which also overtook those who profaned the Supper: weakness, illness and death. Then it may be supposed, once again, that the object of this physical suffering is to induce repentance. The idea of sinners being forced to repent under the torture of wasting sickness is repugnant to us. Even more odious is the picture of God as a kind of Grand Inquisitor with Satan playing the role of the secular arm. But it is by no means improbable that Paul would see it in a wholly different light and approve of the notion that illness may be a form of remedial chastisement. There was much scriptural precedent for such a conception of God's dealings with sinners, and the idea continued to commend itself to Christians until modern times. The Office for the Visitation of the Sick in the Book of Common Prayer is full of it. There remains the difficulty that if the destruction of the flesh is carried out thoroughly, to the point of death, as ὄλεθρος naturally suggests, it could hardly be said to serve a remedial purpose. Again, therefore, we shall have to assume that the intention was that the sinner should be brought to repentance, though it might be on his death-bed.

However mysterious the operation of this may seem, it is at least

349

clear that the object of the condemnation to 'destruction of the flesh' is ultimately remedial: 'that the spirit may be saved in the day of the Lord'. The language is difficult. 'Flesh' and 'spirit' in Pauline usage most often denote the totality of man's being under different aspects: in Adam, or in his unredeemed nature, he, including his mind and will as well as his body, is 'flesh'. In so far as he is open to the Spirit of God, or in a positive relationship to God, he is 'spirit'. These terms refer to man's condition and relationships rather than to distinct elements or 'parts' in his make-up. Paul's usage, however, is not entirely firm or consistent, and there are passages in which he contrasts 'flesh', in the sense of 'body', with 'spirit' in the sense of 'soul'; and he does this in such a way as to make it possible that this contrast, in a particularly precise and vivid form, is intended here. 2 Cor. 7: 1 (possibly part of an earlier letter to Corinth and, according to some, exhibiting striking similarities in language and thought to the Qumran literature) is a case in point. So, too, is Col. 2: 5 if this is authentically Pauline; and a parallel contrast in which 'spirit' and 'body' (not 'flesh') are set in opposition to each other occurs in the present passage (1 Cor. 5: 3), as well as in 1 Thess. 5: 23.

It is interesting, however, to notice that another interpretation, corresponding more closely to the usual Pauline sense of 'flesh', was current in the early centuries. Tertullian's well-known discussion of 1 Cor. 5: 1–13 (*pudicit.* 13–15) is important in this connexion; for Tertullian, in presenting an extreme 'rigorist' interpretation of the passage, is well aware that his own exegesis of it is novel and that the accepted understanding of the incident, which links it with 2 Cor. 1: 5–11, makes it an example not of apostolic severity, but of mercy in the exercise of church discipline. According to the usual exegesis, which Tertullian is opposing, the 'destruction of the flesh' meant the conquest of the flesh, in the ethical, not the physical, sense of the term: the annihilation of the principle of sin in the offender by the subjugation of his rebellious nature through penance (in the sense of satisfaction made by means of fasting and self-humiliation). If this pericope was an embarrassment to Tertullian's rigorism, it is also true that Paul's vehement order to 'drive out the wicked person from among you' put a powerful weapon in the hands of Novatianists and other rigorists. Orthodox commentators therefore do their utmost to persuade themselves that Paul did not really sentence the offender to permanent exclusion and to bodily death. Thus the passage is often interpreted with a strong bias on the one side or the other. It is still, however, conceivable that we ought not to dismiss out of hand the idea that 'the flesh' means the φρόνημα σαρκός. Origen thought that it did. He believed that Paul expelled the offender from the Church so that the φρόνημα σαρκός might be destroyed through confession, sorrow and fasting, and that the spirit (by which Origen thought that Paul meant the whole man, body, soul and spirit) might be saved in the end. Chrysostom and Theodore of Mopsuestia, among other ancient commentators, held that the 'flesh' meant 'the lusts of the flesh', and that their destruction was to be effected through penitential discipline. The former, too, knows of a view, though he does not endorse it, that the 'spirit' does not mean the offender's soul but the baptismal charisma of the Holy Spirit which persistent sin would quench but which could be preserved intact through penitence.

Such an interpretation would save us from having to ascribe to Paul a somewhat extreme dualism of soul and body, and possibly also the idea that the destruction of the physical body might in itself assist the salvation of the soul. It would save us, in fact, from the embarrassment of perhaps discovering in Paul the germ of the principle that it may be the Church's duty to put people to death in order to save them from hell. But it is not really a tenable interpretation. The clear parallel between the case of this offender and that of the profaners of the Eucharist compels us to interpret the destruction of the flesh in terms of physical punishment; Paul's use of ὄλεθρος would be unnatural if he meant the overcoming of the φρόνημα σαρκός through penitence; above all, it is unthinkable that victory over the 'flesh', in the ethical sense of the term, could be brought about by the agency of Satan.

Even if, however, we must accept the fact that Paul intended that the sinner should be physically punished, his object was the ultimate salvation of his spirit, or soul, at the *parousia*. We must therefore assume that the sentence of physical destruction was meant to produce repentance at some stage; for the death of the body cannot in itself be conducive to salvation. Repentance alone can avail for this, for only by faith and repentance can there be a death to sin. When

Paul says that 'he who is dead is freed from sin' (Rom. 6: 7), he is referring to the death of the 'sinful body' through union with Christ in his crucifixion and resurrection, not to the mere physical death of an impenitent sinner.

Many commentators, including Theodore of Mopsuestia among the ancients, have held that the consignment to Satan means simply the cutting off of the offender from the fellowship. On this view, delivery to Satan was not part of the actual sentence pronounced by the Church; it was rather the inevitable consequence of expulsion. On the other hand, there is no evidence in Paul, or in other New Testament writers, that the exclusion of impenitent sinners from the community was generally regarded as tantamount to handing them over to Satan and destruction. It may have been otherwise in the case of apostates and of those false teachers whose attitude also seems to have been treated as amounting to a total repudiation of their baptism. A solemn curse (anathema) is invoked by Paul, in general terms, upon 'anyone who does not love the Lord' (1 Cor. 16: 22). 'To love (φιλεῖν) the Lord' is an unusual expression: a comparison with Matt. 10: 37, John 16: 27, 21: 15, suggests that it denotes discipleship, so that the anathema is directed against any who forsake the way of discipleship. But this is not a specific curse against named individuals. In Gal. 1: 8 Paul pronounces it against enemies of his gospel. This curse implies a cutting off from Christ (Rom. 9: 3), and it clearly means something more, and harsher, than disciplinary excommunication. In the case of Hymenaeus and Alexander (1 Tim. 1: 20), if this is a genuine historical incident and not a fiction based on 1 Cor. 5: 5, those who are 'delivered to Satan' are followers and propagators of false doctrine and opponents of the apostolic gospel (1 Tim. 1: 19–20; 2 Tim. 2: 17–18, 4: 14–15). They are delivered to Satan 'that they may be taught not to blaspheme'; and since this is probably not meant ironically, in the sense of the English, 'I'll teach you to do so and so', but literally (as Tertullian's opponents maintained, to his great scandal, as he tells us in his discussion of 1 Cor. 5: 5), their delivery to Satan is intended in the long run to be reformative. The parallel with 1 Cor. 5: 5, whether real or fictitious, is therefore exact. It seems likely, then, that the consignment to Satan is not simply to be identified with excommunication itself, but that some kind of solemn curse is indicated. Curses invoked for disciplinary reasons figure prominently in the apocryphal Acts (e.g. *Acts of Thomas* 51–2), and the case of Simon Magus affords some parallel. It is less probable that the phrase 'by the power of our (or, the) Lord Jesus' is an echo of the formal pronouncement of the sentence. It is not part of a formula but, as we have seen, it expresses Paul's conviction that in this judgment it is the Lord who acts.

Satan, then, is in the last resort an agent of God's saving purposes, enabling the offender, through the chastening of his flesh, to come to repentance so that his spirit may be saved. This idea is by no means unthinkable. Paul's own 'thorn in the flesh' was a 'messenger of Satan' (2 Cor. 12: 7); but it was given him for a beneficent purpose, to make him wholly dependent upon the grace of God. The work of Satan is evil, but it serves God's ultimate object, almost as in the Book of Job.

The question remains: was this drastic action successful, and did the sinner repent? The general belief in Tertullian's time, which he himself contradicts most vehemently, was that the incestuous man is the same as the person whom later on Paul urged the Corinthians to forgive and comfort (2 Cor. 2: 5–11). Most ancient commentators shared this opinion, but the possibility that they were influenced by anti-Novatianist motives must be borne in mind. In modern times it has tended on balance to be unfashionable: the offender in this passage is often thought to have been a personal opponent of Paul (2 Cor. 2: 5) rather than a scandalous sinner; his restoration appears to be rather easy in comparison with the extreme severity of the condemnation pronounced in 1 Cor. 5: 5; if it was the incestuous man who was restored, then the 'destruction of the flesh' must have stopped short of the death which this phrase itself seems to indicate; 2 Cor. 2: 5 ff. seems to be echoed in 7: 11–12, and there the allusion to 'the one who did the wrong' and 'the one who suffered the wrong' suits a situation in which Paul or one of his associates (possibly Timothy) has been insulted by someone at Corinth rather than the circumstances of the incestuous man, for the one who suffered the wrong would then presumably be the man's father and γυναῖκα τοῦ πατρὸς ἔχειν (1 Cor. 5: 1) might suggest that the father was dead when the scandal took place.

On the other side, the case for the ancient interpretation is strong. Paul was more concerned with the attitude of the Corinthian church than with the individual offender, and we need not expect him to dwell more fully on the latter's repentance than he does in 2 Cor. 2: 5 ff.; his words in 2: 9, however, 'this is why I wrote, that I might test you, and know whether you are obedient in everything', and in 2 Cor. 7: 12, 'I wrote to you...in order that your zeal for us might be revealed', are exactly appropriate to what he wrote in 1 Cor. 5 about the attitude of the Corinthians and to his insistence that the Corinthians must take decisive action against the sinner. The phraseology of 2 Cor. 2: 9–11 strongly recalls that of the earlier passage, particularly in the reference to Satan and in the use of the phrase ἐν προσώπῳ Χριστοῦ. The danger of Satan 'gaining the advantage over us' is most easily understood if it means that whereas the offender had been handed over to Satan for chastisement until he should repent, to leave him in Satan's power after he had once shown penitence would be to allow Satan to exceed the limits of his permitted task. To give him more scope would be to allow him a victory. The restoration of the sinner in verses 7 ff. is to be a corporate act of the Church; the apostle again joins his personal action to theirs: 'anyone whom you forgive, I also forgive'; and all this is done 'in the person of Christ', that is to say, as by an agent of Christ and with his authority. This procedure is therefore closely parallel to that of the condemnation, and it may well seem too formal and ecclesiastical to be appropriate to the forgiveness by Paul of a personal insult, even if the wronged person were not himself but one of his companions and envoys. The language of 2 Cor. 7: 11, 'See what earnestness this godly grief has produced in you...what zeal, what punishment! At every point you have proved yourselves to be pure in the matter', would admirably suit a situation in which, obeying Paul's rebukes and injunctions in 1 Cor. 5, the Corinthians had punished the sinner and he had now repented. Reference back to 1 Cor. 5 would also be a very natural explanation for the allusions in 2 Cor. 2: 9 and 7: 12 to previous correspondence (ἔγραψα). On balance, then, the probability is quite strong that in 2 Cor. 2: 5–11 we have evidence that the severe sentence passed in 1 Cor. 5: 5 was not only intended to be, but actually was, remedial: an extreme and painful form of pastoral discipline rather than capital punishment.

This being so, it would seem that while sins which directly injure the Christian brotherhood as such were treated most severely, Paul and his communities did not regard any moral offender, however grave his sin might be, as standing outside the scope of pastoral discipline and beyond hope of repentance and restoration. At the same time, it was vitally important that pastoral discipline should in fact be exercised. To tolerate the presence of an impenitent offender would indicate a false and presumptuous sense of security and would lead to the moral contamination of the brotherhood; hence Paul is concerned above all, throughout this correspondence, with the reactions of the Corinthian congregation and with the paramount need for them to realize their duty to purge out the leaven of malice and evil from their midst.

If such was the situation with regard to moral offences, it is worth while to inquire what reasons there might be for regarding any Christian as having forfeited his membership of the Church altogether. One answer seems clear: apostasy, in the sense of deliberate denial of Christ, especially in the circumstances of persecution, was tantamount to the repudiation of baptism and was generally regarded as unforgivable. To refuse to acknowledge Christ in this present age entails being disowned by him at the *parousia* (Mark 8: 38; Luke 9: 26). Confessors of Christ before men will be themselves 'confessed' by him before his Father in heaven; to deny him will lead to being denied by him before his Father in heaven (Matt. 10: 32–3, Luke 12: 8–9). The same thought is vividly expressed in the hymnal fragment preserved in 2 Tim. 2: 12. The words ὁμολογεῖν and ἀρνεῖσθαι recur again and again in the New Testament as virtually technical terms for the profession of Christian faith in the face of persecutors and for formal apostasy; and Luke's setting of these terms in 12: 8–9 is particularly illuminating, for he puts into the same context the logion concerning blasphemy against the Holy Spirit. His handling of that saying shows that he has persecution in mind. On the one hand, the faithful confessor need not be anxious how to make his defence, for he is promised the direct inspiration of the Holy Spirit. The confessor shares the gift which the prophet possesses. By contrast, there can be no forgiveness for the man who blasphemes against the Holy Spirit; and by this, as the context shows, Luke means the apostate who repudiates the promised inspiration and denies Christ. This text is of the highest importance for our understanding both of the status of confessors and martyrs in the eyes of their fellow-

Christians and also of the reluctance of so many in the later Church to allow any reconciliation to those who abjured Christ in times of persecution.

To deny Christ was, in fact, to annul and repudiate the baptismal profession of faith that Jesus is Lord (cf. Rom. 10: 9–10 and especially 1 Tim. 6: 12–13), whether in the face of Jewish opposition, to which most, if not all, allusions to persecution in the New Testament probably refer, and which is directly reflected in John 9: 22, 12: 42, or, later, in response to the demand of the Roman authorities to confess Caesar as Lord (*mart. Polyc.* 8: 2). Such a denial set the apostate on the side of the old Israel which had denied Jesus in the presence of Pilate (Acts 3: 13–14), and against Jesus himself who had set the pattern for confessors in his testimony before Pilate (1 Tim. 6: 13). The author to the Hebrews is therefore not adopting a peculiarly rigorist attitude, out of harmony with that of the primitive Church as a whole (as some have supposed), when he says bluntly that 'it is impossible to restore again to repentance those who have once been enlightened, who have tasted the heavenly gift, and have become partakers of the Holy Spirit...if they then commit apostasy (παραπεσόντας), since they crucify the Son of God on their own account and hold him up to contempt' (6: 4–6). The writer is not speaking of sins in general, nor even of specially grave moral offences, but of apostasy; and this, as he makes plain in the words just quoted, he considers to be a repudiation of baptism, and therefore a crucifixion of Christ, into whose death and resurrection the believer is baptized. Heb. 10: 26–31 is also concerned with apostasy. 'If we sin deliberately' cannot be intended to allude to wilful, as opposed to unwitting, sins; for the old distinction between ritual offences, committed without intent, and deliberate disobedience to God has no place in the Christian dispensation. For the same reason, the 'sin unto death' of 1 John cannot refer to deliberate, as contrasted with unintentional, sin. Heb. 10: 26 ff. is speaking of sin which is tantamount to spurning the Son of God, profaning the blood of the covenant, and outraging the Spirit of grace. This clearly means the repudiation of the name of Christ, the tearing up of the covenant in Christ's blood, to which the Christian comes to adhere through his baptism, and blaspheming against the baptismal gift of the Spirit by denying Christ. The thought here has much in common with Luke 12: 10.

If, too, as is likely, πόρνος and βέβηλος (Heb. 12: 16) denote an apostate, then Esau, who sold his birthright and found no place for repentance (12: 17), is presented by this writer as a type of those who repudiate their Christian heritage. In all this Hebrews is fully in line with the general position of the New Testament writings.

One passage alone stands out as a striking exception to the view that apostasy admits of no restoration: the story of Peter's denial. This goes so far as to make the apostle an archetypal pattern of those who 'lapse' in times of danger. All the versions of the tradition lay stress on the fact that Peter was thrice questioned and expressly repudiated Christ three times. It may not be a coincidence that the threefold question and answer correspond fairly closely to the Roman magistrate's procedure in the interrogation of Christians. 'I ask them if they are Christians', says Pliny (*epp.* 10. 96. 3). 'If they admit it I repeat the question a second and a third time, threatening capital punishment; if they persist I sentence them to death.' If Christians recanted, Pliny applied certain tests to prove that they had completely denied their faith, the final one being that they should curse Christ (*maledicerent Christo*), a thing which, he says, 'those who are really Christians cannot be made to do'. So, too, Polycarp was required to 'swear (i.e. by the τύχη of Caesar) and revile Christ' (ὄμοσον, λοιδόρησον τὸν Χριστόν). According to Mark, Peter, in response to the third interrogation, ἤρξατο ἀναθεματίζειν καὶ ὀμνύναι ὅτι Οὐκ οἶδα τὸν ἄνθρωπον τοῦτον. 'Αναθεματίζειν is usually here rendered absolutely: 'to curse', but there seems to be no parallel to this usage of the word. In Acts 23: 12, 14, 21, it is used reflexively, 'to bind oneself by a curse'; in the Septuagint it is used transitively with the meaning 'put to the ban'; and in Christian authors it occurs frequently as a transitive verb meaning 'pronounce a curse upon' or 'anathematize'. Very possibly Mark uses the verb in this normal sense, understanding τὸν 'Ιησοῦν as the object. If this is the correct interpretation Peter carried his apostasy to the extreme limit; he cursed Christ (cf. ἀνάθεμα 'Ιησοῦς) and swore that he did not know him. It is not easy to see what motives were responsible for the transmission of the story of Peter's denial. In later times it served as a warning against apostasy; but in times when it was believed that it was impossible 'to restore again to repentance those who have been once enlightened' it could scarcely serve that purpose. For the sequel was known: the apostate had not merely been restored, as Mark 16: 7, Luke 22: 32, and John 21: 15 ff., state or imply, but had become, as all the churches knew, the leader of the apostolic mission. Here, then, was a primary instance of forgiveness being granted for the most explicit and formal act of apostasy.

It might be possible to argue, on lines suggested by the logion concerning 'saying a word against the Son of Man' (Matt. 12: 32; Luke 12: 10), that Peter's case might be on a different footing from that of apostates who, after the resurrection, denied the glorified Lord who was present through the Spirit in the Church: he had not, that is to say, received the Holy Spirit and did not blaspheme against the Holy Spirit. But it seems much more probable that the transmission of the story indicates that it was not universally believed in the primitive Church that the Lord would never forgive those who denied him. It is tempting to wonder whether it may be connected with the situation of the Church at Rome in the Neronian persecution. We do not know whether this produced a problem of the *lapsi*, nor whether those of whom Tacitus says *qui fatebantur* were confessors of the faith or informers against their brethren (but the fact that their capture led to wholesale arrests might suggest the latter). If, as is likely in the nature of the case, apostasy presented a problem to the Roman church in the sixties, the tradition of Peter's denial may have been directly relevant to this, and may indicate that Hermas was not wholly an innovator when he announced the possibility of one reconciliation, to include even those who had previously failed to confess the faith under persecution.

False teachers rank with apostates as people who are to be summarily expelled from the community. Sometimes it is difficult to distinguish Christian heretics from teachers whose aim is to persuade Christians to lapse into either Judaism or idolatry. This is especially true in 1 John. Certain false teachers who have created schism are equated by the writer with antichrist; they are a sign of the approach of the end (2: 18). They are false prophets (4: 1): another characteristic of the last times; and the spirit of false prophecy is in conflict with the anointing of the Holy Spirit which the Christian community possesses (2: 26–7), and by which all its members can know the truth. This false teaching or prophecy seems to have involved the repudiation of Jesus as Messiah; so that the 'spirit which does not confess Jesus' (4: 3) is parallel to the false prophetic inspiration which, according to Paul, may cause men to say 'anathema Jesus' (1 Cor. 12: 3). This denial of Christ seems to be contrasted, as in Matt. 10: 32–3, with the boldness and confidence which the faithful will have at the *parousia* (2: 28): those, that is to say, who maintain the credal (baptismal) confession that Jesus is the Son of God (4: 15; cf. 5: 1, 10); and the allusion to 'fear' in 4: 18 may indicate that the writer envisages a situation of persecution.

The question here is whether the false teachers are trying to induce Christians to renounce their faith completely, or to propagate an heretical Christology. From 2: 22–3 it would seem that they are denying that Jesus is the Messiah; and hence, from the Christian point of view they are denying both the Father and the Son. This is consistent with the statement that the spirits speaking through the false prophets do not confess Jesus, and the parallel assertion (4: 2) that the spirits which are of God confess 'that Jesus Christ has come in the flesh' does not necessarily conflict with it. That Jesus Christ has come 'in the flesh', which the deceiver and the antichrist denies (2 John 7), may mean that Jesus is the Messiah who has really come, and need no longer be awaited. The denial of this assertion, then, may represent, not a form of Docetism but rather an out-and-out rejection of the gospel, and the baptismal creed, that Jesus is the Christ. This interpretation could find support in the language in which the writer (5: 20–1) contrasts the believers' faith and knowledge of Jesus Christ as Son of God with the total apostasy ('idols') involved in the false teaching. It is true that Polycarp (*ep.* 7: 1) understands the denial that Jesus Christ has come in the flesh in a Docetic sense, and this in turn might find support in the enigmatic assertion that Jesus Christ came not with water only, but with the water and the blood (5: 6), but the hands of redactors have been discerned in 1 John[1] and anti-Docetism may not have been the original motive of the letter's polemic. If the false teachers were directly attacking belief in Jesus as the Christ it is easy to understand the writer's sharp distinction between sins 'not unto death', for the doers of which the brethren ought to intercede, and which are continually cleansed by the blood

---

[1] See, e.g., H. Braun, *ZThK* 48 (1951); E. Haenchen, *TRev*, nF 26 (1960). J. C. O'Neill, *The Puzzle of 1 John* (London, 1966), appeared too late for consideration in this essay, and should be consulted on this question.

of Jesus, and a 'sin unto death' for which prayer (for the sinner's repentance) may not be made (5: 16–17). The latter is the false teaching and prophesying which denies the basic creed that Jesus is the Christ: and 1 John is echoing the ideas of Hebrews about the unforgivable character of deliberate apostasy.

Possibly these false prophets resembled the Jewish false prophet, bar-Jesus, who tried to obstruct Paul's preaching to the proconsul in Cyprus (Acts 13: 6 ff.). Certainly, false prophesying directed against the gospel was a serious threat to the Christian mission, as is attested by Matt. 7: 15, 22, Mark 13: 22, Matt. 24: 11, 24, 2 Pet. 2: 1–3, and by the warnings of Paul and 'John' to test the prophetic spirits by the criterion of their consistency with the gospel (cf. 1 Thess. 5: 20–1; 1 Cor. 12: 3; 1 John 4: 1). The connexion of false prophecy with deception, and the likening of false prophets to wolves in sheep's clothing, together with the statement in 1 John 2: 19 that 'they went out from us, but they were not of us', suggest that these false prophets, who seem to have been almost as great a menace to the Christian preachers as the Hebrew false prophets were to Jeremiah, acted as a kind of 'fifth column' within the community; and 2 Pet. 2: 1–3 and Jude 3–4 expressly affirm this. 1 John, then, has in mind, as the sinners 'unto death', enemies who pretended to belong to the Church while they undermined the faith of its members.

But perhaps the question whether their teaching denied Christ outright or admitted his coming only in a Docetic sense is after all unimportant for us. For in either case the basic truth of the gospel was being denied, and the offence was therefore deadly and unforgivable. The same is true of all the heresies in the New Testament whose propagators are excluded from the community or refused recognition by local churches when they travel from place to place. They represent a fundamental opposition of one kind or another to the essential gospel, and their effect is to disrupt the fellowship. Of those who 'hold the form of religion but deny the power of it' the writer of 2 Timothy says, 'Avoid (i.e. refuse communion with) such people' (3: 5). Subversive Judaizers, not unlike Paul's opponents in Galatia, are to be silenced (Titus 1: 10–11), and it is probably such people who, being 'factious', are to be boycotted by the community after one or two admonitions (3: 10).

A very curious case occurs in 3 John 9–10. Diotrephes, the chief person in a local church, quite possibly, as has often been supposed, an early monarchical bishop, has refused to receive brethren commended by the presbyter who writes the letter. He even 'stops those who want to welcome them, and puts them out (ἐκβάλλει) of the church'. Ἐκβάλλειν in this context must denote excommunication. In John 9: 34–5 the word is evidently meant to indicate expulsion from the synagogue. This passage therefore speaks of a formal act by the leader of the Church, and, since this could hardly be done without the consent of the 'majority' (cf. 2 Cor. 2: 6), or simply as a mere piece of personal spite, it is likely that Diotrephes, however mistakenly,[1] believed the presbyter's emissaries to be purveyors of false teaching. It is scarcely possible that even the worst of bishops could have used this ultimate sanction of church discipline quite irresponsibly.

The answer, then, to our inquiry into the reasons for which Christians in New Testament times might be deprived of the Communion-fellowship which was otherwise universally enjoyed by all the baptized, notwithstanding much diversity in doctrine and practice, must be that complete excommunication was generally imposed on those who repudiated their baptismal faith, either by denying Christ in the face of opposition and persecution or by propagating or accepting those kinds of false teaching which led to apostasy, or to a form of belief which contradicted the gospel that Jesus Christ is the Son of God incarnate through whom alone salvation is to be gained. The impenitent sinner also had to be excluded in order to prevent the community from being implicated in his transgressions and to induce him to repent; but in no case, not even, it would seem, in the shocking instance of the Corinthian offender, did repentance fail to meet with forgiveness and restoration.

[1] See, however, E. Käsemann, *ZThK* 48 (1951).

17

PAUL AND THE NEW TESTAMENT ETHIC
IN THE THOUGHT OF JOHN KNOX

PAUL SCHUBERT

Ever since the publication of Knox's *Chapters in a Life of Paul* (Nashville, 1950, subsequently cited as CLP) one particular passage together with the context of the preceding and following analysis of Paul's thought has haunted me:

When Paul speaks of 'justification' and 'reconciliation', therefore, he is distinguishing elements which actually belong to the meaning of God's forgiveness of us; and we might argue that his neglect of the term 'forgiveness' itself involves no loss—indeed, means gain, since his analysis prevents our ignoring either element in its meaning, either the justice in it or the mercy. The fact and importance of this gain should be gratefully recognized; nevertheless, it must be said that the division which Paul made in the meaning of forgiveness was one of the most tragically fateful developments in the whole history of Christian theology and therefore in the intellectual history of mankind. For although both justice and mercy are in forgiveness, they are there together—not simply combined and therefore separable, but united indissolubly. The justice is not mere justice, and the mercy is not mere mercy; each is modified by the other so as to make a mercy that is also just and a justice that is also merciful. When we say that God forgives, we are saying that this is the character of his justice and of his mercy. But Paul by dividing forgiveness into two parts opened the way to division in the nature of God himself—his justice is seen as mere justice and his mercy as only mercy. He is the just Judge and the merciful Father; He is not, as he is for Jesus, a Father who is both just and merciful—truly (that is, appropriately) just only because he is also merciful, truly (that is, authentically) merciful only because he is also just. We must not fail to note that this dichotomy in Paul's view of God is far from complete or consistent: it is God's grace alone which makes possible our justification as well as our reconciliation; it is God who by offering his own Son in love provides the basis for our acquittal. But division within the character of God and within his reconciling act, while by no means complete (as it later became in Marcionism), is nevertheless undeniably present. And this division is not supported either by the teaching of Jesus or by the church's experience of the forgiveness of God in Christ—experience which immeasurably deepens for us the meaning of forgiveness but does not modify its essential structure as Jesus' teaching sets it forth (pp. 147 f.).

Add to this a related, equally thematic passage from *The Ethic of Jesus in the Teaching of the Church* (1961; subsequently cited as EJ):

I venture to say that the question of antinomianism would never have arisen in the church if Paul had not interpreted God's act in another way. Paul identified God's saving act as an act of justification, and in doing so, as I see it, set grace and law against each other in a way that seriously distorts both Jesus' teaching and the realities of the Christian's experience. It is not an accident that the only places in the New Testament where the antinomian question is explicitly raised are in Paul's letters. Paul quotes his opponents as raising it and, of course, vigorously and with indubitable sincerity, repudiates the ascription of antinomian implications to his doctrine; but I do not believe that we can deny the fact of these implications, however remote they may be from Paul's intention. Paul's doctrine of justification has in itself the seeds of antinomianism, and Paul's critics, or perhaps heretical followers, were not being merely perverse in saying so (pp. 75 f.).

These two passages illustrate the outstanding characteristics of all Knox's works—meticulous attention to the material details and their expression put into a broad perspective of historical and theological thought; fearlessness and fairness born of modesty and the sense of uncompromising obligation; deceptive simplicity, almost super-human clarity and coherence in thought and expression.[1]

In other words, the incisiveness of Knox's affirmations and denials sometimes invites or provokes contradiction, as the simplicity of his style may mislead the simple-minded, unwary reader to conclude that Knox has little to say. That is to say that Knox's work, seen as a whole in its wording and in ultimate intention, cannot be easily contradicted and need not be. And this, in turn, is not to say that other scholars or 'teachers in the church'[2] may not see many tech-

[1] To put it differently, John Knox is not only one of the leading technical scholars in the field of the New Testament, as many items in his bibliography testify, but one of America's outstanding and influential interpreters of the New Testament to the twentieth century, alongside Amos N. Wilder and Paul S. Minear. What they have in common most significantly is their strong hold on empirical reality as the base, medium and goal of their interpretation.
[2] A characteristic term of Knox's in EJ.

nical details in a specifically but not ultimately different total perspective. The purpose of this essay is a critical appreciation and
appreciative criticism of Knox's work at one particular but all-
pervasive point on the part of a fellow-scholar who has, in the words
of H. Richard Niebuhr, 'no absolute notions, but only notions of
the absolute'.[1]

The two quotations also suggest the outline for this essay. What is
the early Christian understanding of God's saving act in Christ (1. A)
which according to Knox results in God's gracious forgiveness dependent on repentance (1. B). Here especially it is necessary, because
of the remarkable and impressive coherence of all of Knox's writings,
to give an account of his whole constructive thought. Although
Knox is second to none in the appreciation of Paul as a 'man in
Christ' and as a Christian theologian, he is quite frankly and un-
waveringly dissatisfied with Paul's understanding of justification and
of law in the gospel. I shall therefore attempt to sketch an alternative
interpretation of Paul's understanding of justification (2. A) and of
the place of law in Paul's theology (2. B), thus hoping to lay the ghost
that has haunted me, or, perhaps preferably, to bring it to real,
full-bodied life.

I

A. Every theology or philosophy worth its salt deals with a multiplicity of items and unifies them into an organic whole. In Knox's case
one might list four factors which provide this unity; first, the insistence, empirically philosophical and theological, that reality has
event character, that an historical event has a characteristically social
aspect. Thus the event of Jesus Christ is no event, unless the society in
which the man Jesus lived, opponents, friends, and 'neutrals' alike,
are acknowledged as a constitutive part of the event. Second, the
earliest Christian communities by their common faith in Jesus
Christ, variously expressed by the various authors as leaders and

[1] H. Richard Niebuhr, *The Meaning of Revelation* (New York, 1940). The term
scholarship—an abstraction, an idol to be worshipped—is a term which Knox
never (or nearly never) uses. For him (and for me) there is only a community of
persons who are scholars, who realize in fact that they are interdependent, so that
often they talk only to each other. This is true of physicists, archaeologists,
numismatists, philosophers and theologians; they realize that they are a community with special functions in a community which ultimately includes all
mankind.

mouthpieces of various groups, constitute by virtue of that faith a genuine community which is fully recognizable to all critical historians, but that faith is not necessarily shared by them. Third, there is an all-pervasive consistent insistence on an empirical approach, the results of which are invariably confirmed by 'human experience'. Fourth, this earliest Christian community was born and lived by the man Jesus, who 'was remembered and still known' in the Church as the risen and living Lord Jesus Christ.

This is little more than a bare listing of basic aspects of Knox's work as a whole, as seen by this observer. It is based on the well-known 'Trilogy' of John Knox's, *Jesus: Lord and Christ* (New York, 1958), which contains *The Man Christ Jesus* (1941), *Christ the Lord* (1945) and *On the Meaning of Christ* (1947). The first book sets the perspective and even in part the terminology of the second and third books; the second sets forth fully and in detail the Christology of the New Testament under the tripartite heading 'he [i.e. Jesus] was remembered', 'he was known still', and 'he was interpreted'. The third book analyses and demonstrates fully the constitutive factors or elements in the one organic, indivisible, indissoluble, revelatory event of Jesus Christ. We can do no better than to listen to Knox's own words:

One might think, for example, of the life and death of the man Jesus as a single factor, rather than two; or of the deepening response of his disciples to the total event—earthly life and resurrection—as one factor instead of two. Likewise the resurrection and the coming of the Spirit and perhaps also the creation of the community might be conceived of as a single element.[1] But the possibility of such modifications in the form which analysis may take does not alter the fact of the complexity of the event we are considering or allow for the exclusion in substance of any of the factors I have mentioned.[2]

It was necessary to summarize, however briefly, Knox's total critical-exegetical and theological position, first, because of its simplicity, profundity, clarity and fruitfulness, and second, because it bears at every point directly on the specific issues of this essay.

[1] I have no doubt that Knox commends this simplification of the number of elements in the event as a whole, because he himself uses similar simplifications for practical purposes, but the whole context of the quotation above indicates that a 'multiplication' of them is also desirable and necessary.

[2] *On the Meaning of Christ* (Nashville, 1947) (subsequently cited as MC), p. 36.

Three more specific amplifications of Knox's total position or, perhaps better, of his total attitude toward New Testament interpretation
are necessary before we are ready for our much more limited
topic.

First, with all of Knox's deep insight and constant insistence that
the memory and knowledge of Jesus Christ are an indissoluble part
of the empirically ascertainable aspect of the event as a whole, it
is important to note that Knox is free from the anxiety to base
the Christian faith on the '*ipsissima verba* and *acta*' of 'the so-called
historical Jesus' established 'by methods of literary and historical
criticism'.[1] This effort is indeed a temptation to which many conservative scholars—fundamentalist as well as liberal—fall victims. I
am not sure whether Knox uses the designations 'Jesus' and 'Christ'
with absolute consistency, but I have the impression that Knox talks
about both 'Jesus' and 'Christ' as 'remembered and known still' in
the early community of believers, using 'Jesus' when he emphasizes that 'Jesus was a man like ourselves'; this 'is to make a vital
affirmation of Christian faith', and generally using 'Christ' and/or
'Lord' when he emphasizes the divinity of Jesus: 'The divinity of
Jesus was the deed of God. The uniqueness of Jesus was the absolute
uniqueness of what God did in him.'[2] At any rate, it will be important to keep in mind the rough generalization that 'there are not many
particular points where we can feel absolute assurance [about the
ipsissima verba and *acta*]. We can be sure that Jesus said a certain kind
of thing: but not that he said just this thing or that.'[3]

---

[1] The small quotations in this paragraph are taken from MC, pp. 62–4; see the whole
section, pp. 60–8; also, *The Death of Christ* (DC) (Nashville, 1958), pp. 121–3,
and many other passages throughout Knox's works.

[2] See DC, pp. 122–3.

[3] See MC, p. 62. It is indicative of the objectivity of scholarly work that in this
whole discussion there are partial but nevertheless significant family likenesses at
various points with the well-known views of R. Bultmann, and even more so
with Ernst Käsemann; see the latter's 'Das Problem des historischen Jesus',
1, 187–214, and his follow-up essay 'Sackgassen im Streit um den historischen
Jesus', 2, 31–68, of *Exegetische Versuche und Besinnungen* (Göttingen, 1960 and
1964). See also H. J. Cadbury, *Jesus: What Manner of Man?* (New York, 1947). See
also Knox's 'A Note on Rudolf Bultmann and "Demythologization"' (DC,
pp. 175–82). This is a very significant contribution to the predominantly German,
lively debate on the issues discussed and related ones. It is also a clarification of
Knox's own views, in which he makes some telling points against Bultmann's
existentialist individualism.

This last sentence makes a sharp and subtle distinction which today is widespread among historians and theologians.[1] In Knox's case it may be remarked that in this passage and elsewhere the continuity between the historical Jesus and the Christ of faith is in principle over-emphasized at the expense of the discontinuity between the two, which deserves equal consideration in the interests of both the New Testament faith and of secular historical methods. Of course, contingency is not revelation, but a specific contingency, which any historian, if he is more than a museum-custodian, may and must circumscribe, is the locus which the theologian may and must describe as revelation.

However this may be, free from the enslaving anxiety of attempting to base the Christian faith on the *ipsissima verba* and *acta* of the Jesus of Nazareth, Knox regards the 'quest for the historical Jesus' as an indispensable theological task,[2] for in Knox's view revelation is not a 'language-event' or an event of *bruta facta*, isolable from time and space, but it is always tied to the man Jesus of Nazareth as he was remembered by his contemporary first disciples and is known still in the Church throughout the centuries.

The second special item is a corollary to the first. In EJ the whole third chapter is characteristically written as a description of the exalted task of the teacher of the New Testament ethic in the Church. There is one particularly eloquent and impressive paragraph, from which the following sentences are quoted, because they are applicable not only to the Christian teacher of the New Testament ethic, but surely—*mutatis mutandis* and in Knox's spirit—to every responsive and responsible New Testament scholar of whatever faith:

Such a responsibility, if adequately borne, implies enormously high qualifications. Not only must he be keenly sensitive to...the New Testament ethic...but he must also know how...Christians in various generations have found it possible to express in actual deeds their submission to the law of love. He must be able to draw upon the ethical [read: literary, historical and theological] *insights of prophets, poets, and teachers of all cultures and traditions* [the present writer's italics]. He must know the world he and his hearers live in—the political, economic, social and intellectual environment...[And he must] know all one can know of the human

[1] See the references in the preceding note to Bultmann, Käsemann, and Cadbury.
[2] MC, pp. 64 f.

heart[1]...His task must be freshly done in every generation, indeed, in every new historical or personal situation. Ultimately the decision of what, if anything, is to be said in any particular moment must be his. Like Paul he must rely finally on his own informed and...inspired 'judgment'.[2]

If this somewhat truncated version of this quotation finds Knox's approval in its wider application to all serious work on the New Testament, it is indeed a very significant statement. The final sentence puts full and final responsibility on the individual scholar's judgment. But his judgment and argument must be communicable, verifiable and objective, because they are based on social realities,[3] realities outside himself which yet make him fully what at any moment he himself is or has. Paul says (1 Cor. 4: 7), 'What have you that you did not receive? If then you received it all as a gift, why take the credit to yourself?'[4] This is a profound theological, sociological and even physiological truth.

A third aspect of Knox's exegetical and theological work to be singled out here goes to the very heart of his thought and of the experience which the thought conveys. It is the most central, suggestive and also the most baffling part of Knox's thought—the event of the resurrection of Christ. It is treated from every angle throughout all his major works. One of the compact statements is the following:[5]

This new Spirit,[6] which emerged with the event of Christ and was embodied in the community of Christ, could thus be called the Spirit of Christ. The living reality of this Spirit was the real ground of the resurrection faith. To know the Spirit was to know Christ, and in the most vital parts of the New Testament the terms can be used almost interchangeably. The resurrection of Jesus as an incident in time and space was an inference from, and became a symbol of, this identity. Christ, without ceasing to be the master whose death was remembered, is now known as the Spirit; the event, without losing its character as historical event, is perpetuated in the community. This is the real and ineluctable miracle in Christianity. All other 'miracles' are signs and symbols of this one inexplicable but empirically given fact.

---

[1] EJ, p. 64.   [2] *Ibid.* p. 65.

[3] MC, p. 85. '—the historical is essentially social.'

[4] The second part of this translation is from the NEB.

[5] *The Early Church and the Coming Great Church* (Nashville, 1955), pp. 61 f.

[6] See *ibid.* p. 60: 'God's love is God's Spirit, and God's Spirit is his love.'

The most noteworthy feature here—and elsewhere in Knox—
is the identity of Christ, the Spirit and the community as one
historical event. In the community the event itself finds its culmination and is perpetuated in it. This, of course, is the conception
maintained in several variations by Roman Catholic and Anglican
theologians. Knox has breathed new life into it by bringing to bear
on it in his own way the up-to-date views and terminology o,
most modern thinking of theologians like W. Norman Pittenger.
H. Richard Niebuhr and—most importantly perhaps—Charles Cf
Morrison and many other Chicago thinkers, not forgetting the
tremendous amount of exegetical groundwork laid by Knox in a
grand reinterpretation of the New Testament, especially but not
exclusively of the letters of Paul. Thanks to the work of Knox and of
a few others those issues will and should be vigorously debated; in
fact, they are beginning to be discussed with new vigour and in a
new spirit without dogmatic literalism and without the all-too-
human boasting of being in the right.

Exegetically as well as theologically I have some trouble with
some of Knox's identification-statements which are contained in
the quotation just given and especially with the one quoted in my
footnote, p. 369, n. 6 above: 'In a word, God's love is God's Spirit,
and God's Spirit is his love.' They occur frequently and typically in
Knox's works. Are they to be taken as fully ontological statements
(especially in this case: $x = y$ and $y = x$)—this seems to me exegetically questionable (see, e.g., Rom. 5: 5 and 2 Cor. 3: 17)—or
do they mean that whenever x is given then y is also present? In this
case both x and y maintain their own identity, while the temporal
and/or logical correlation between x and y has to be decided on the
grounds of the context of each particular passage.

Be that as it may, the over-all conception of the event of revelation as a whole, which includes the resurrection and is socially,
historically and empirically knowable in one important aspect, is a
grand one. It brings assured findings and new perspectives to the
work of New Testament scholars and to theologians today.

B. We can now turn to an analysis of Knox's affirmations and
denials in regard to New Testament and Pauline ethic. We begin
with a quotation from the early MC (1947). Thus we shall be able

to see that all of Knox's works form an astoundingly organic whole, and that Knox's deepest impulse as a New Testament scholar and as a theologian is to get at—and to come from—the experience of the essentially ethical and moral character of revelation. His own deeply pietistic heritage, in which all Christians of the last two hundred years have in some degree a share and which has its roots in the decision-evoking character of the Old and the New Testaments, is not diminished by his characteristic and deep sense of the communal character of the 'new life', but finds its true fulfilment in community and nowhere else:

It is sin and death which confront faith in God with its severest (indeed with its only severe) test. No 'revelation' of God which does not show him dealing effectively with these enemies of man, these destroyers of the meaning of his life, can be a saving revelation. It was seen very early by the first witnesses of the event that its unique character consisted largely in the fact that this was precisely what God had been doing. It was not a matter of theory or even of faith, but of fact, that, as a result of what had occurred, forgiveness had been made available to them.[1]

Add to this from the same context:

Thus we know that the event...culminated in the formation of the community in which God makes Himself known in a particular concrete way as both righteous and forgiving and through which the new life of the Spirit, the distinctive Christian life, is imparted.[2]

Note in this double-quotation the decisive emphasis that God's saving act is itself moral, that it was particular and concrete, that God is righteous and forgiving, and that the distinctive Christian communal life is the new life of the Spirit. The key term 'forgiveness' comes primarily from the synoptic gospels, or, as Knox puts it, from 'the ethic of Jesus' (as he was remembered and is known still) in the teaching of the church', and the other key term 'life in the Spirit' comes from Paul. All these themes are fully developed and argued in Knox's CLP and in EJ.

In the final chapter (ix) of CLP, 'The Life in Christ', from which the quotation at the beginning of this essay comes, Knox develops the ethical aspect of the revelatory event further, by comparing and contrasting Jesus' teaching about repentance and forgiveness with Paul's teaching of justification and reconciliation.

[1] MC, pp. 104 f.   [2] *Ibid.* p. 103.

Knox finds it is 'nothing short of astounding' (p. 142), 'surprising' (p. 143), 'most amazing' (p. 144) and all the 'more remarkable' (p. 145) that 'Paul, knowing so well the reality of repentance and forgiveness, makes so little use of those terms' (p. 145), which were profusely and centrally used in the Old Testament, in rabbinic Judaism and, most emphatically, in the teaching of Jesus (*ibid.*). In his context Knox needed no answer to this 'astounding, surprising, most amazing and remarkable' problem. However, his way of putting the problem shows the importance of answering it. It is indeed fairly obvious. In rabbinic thought, on its highest as well as its lower levels, repentance and forgiveness are part and parcel of that conception of the law of God which Paul combated with all his heart and mind, not because this conception was particularly Jewish, but because it is universally human. We shall have more to say on this later.

Here it is important to take note of Knox's positive evaluation of Paul's experience as a 'man in Christ' and of his thought. On p. 145 Knox says 'the idea of salvation by God's mercy rather than by our merit was for [Jesus] central, decisive and constant, and...Paul in his characteristic emphasis upon redemption rather than attainment, upon "grace" rather than "works", is only following where Jesus has led the way.' 'The *substance* of repentance and forgiveness is surely here.' In so far as this is an historical judgment on the historical dependence of Paul on Jesus' own teaching it is shared by a large number of fundamentalist and liberal scholars, with some notable exceptions. But it is hardly necessary, or at least the dependence of Paul on Jesus' own teaching can be reduced to a minimum, if Knox's concluding appraisal of Paul a few pages later is taken seriously, as I think it should. Thus greater allowance can be made for—to use Knox's terminology—the creativity of the Spirit of Christ at work in Paul:

Although no interpretation of that event [i.e. God's revelatory act in Jesus Christ] which is not consonant with Jesus' teaching could be true, nevertheless it was impossible that the event should have been fully interpreted—impossible both because the teaching was itself a part of the event and because the event had not fully transpired when the teaching was given. Paul became the first great interpreter of the complete event,[1] as

---

[1] Does this statement mean that Paul belongs to the event itself, or that he takes his exalted place simply as one of the first and greatest among other members of the Church (including numerous avowed atheists and even non-Christians?) in

he became the first great apostle of Christ among the nations. In him was first fulfilled in a conspicuous way the word of Christ: 'Greater works than these will he do, because I go to the Father.'...as interpreter [Paul] set the lines which Christian theology was to follow through Mark, to John, and beyond;[1] and at many points he spoke what has proved to be the final word. The marks of human frailty can be discerned on his work, but to the really discerning they serve only to make clear the supreme greatness of his achievement—or rather the supreme greatness of what God wrought through him.[2]

This passage calls for several comments: (i) the greater allowance for the creativity of the Spirit of Christ is made by applying to Paul the eschatological words of the Johannine Christ (John 14: 12 and 16). To what extent and how Paul was influenced by the Jesus tradition, and whether any of the Gospel writers—Mark, Matthew, Luke and John—were in turn influenced by Paul, these questions are still great puzzles. These more or less technical questions have occupied scholars a great deal for a long time, but none of them has commended itself very strongly even to its own proponents. The strong interest of contemporary scholars in all phases of *Traditionsgeschichte* (history of tradition) may yet achieve considerable results and even contribute substantially to our understanding of earliest Christian experience and thought all along the line. The impatient scepticism voiced now and then regarding the limited value of these 'technical' questions is hardly becoming. It simply points out their complexity.

(ii) I cannot rid myself of the deep impression that Knox himself could not have chosen 'repentance and forgiveness'—this double-term is given thematic significance in Luke-Acts (see Luke 24: 47 and Acts 5: 31, and many other passages in which one of the terms is used, but the other is implied)—as the master concept of his conception of the New Testament ethic without saturating this double-term thoroughly with the experience of Paul as a 'man in Christ' and with the characteristic terms of his thought. It is particularly Paul's emphasis on grace and on faith which Knox reads into the synoptic gospels and their witness to the teaching of Jesus. Thus, and

---

which the event 'culminates' and is 'perpetuated'? Or is it answered by the statement that 'the event culminates and is perpetuated in the Church'?
[1] Does Knox mean that Mark and John are influenced by Paul, as does E. J. Goodspeed, or that all three are divergent witnesses who have a special common ground in pre-Pauline Hellenistic churches?   [2] CLP, p. 159.

thus only, can Knox understand repentance and forgiveness as gifts of God, ever renewed, the God of righteousness and of his coming kingdom as the God of love.

This is typically exemplified by Knox: 'Repentance is necessary, but repentance is all God asks.'[1] This statement is a fair summary of how repentance is regarded in the synoptic gospels (Mark 1: 15 and Matt. 4: 17, the two formal topic sentences of the gospels of Mark and Matthew respectively; cf. also Matt. 11: 20–4). There is a noticeable legalistic element both in these texts and in Knox's statement. But Knox immediately continues by giving to this call to repentance concreteness, depth and universal theological significance: 'Repentance, however, is no small or easy thing; it is an act of realization so radical and costly that only God's grace can move us to it or make us capable of it'.[2] Thus one can agree that 'the *substance* of repentance and forgiveness is surely here' [i.e. in Paul]; one might even go further and say it is only here, without use of the terms. It is with two of Paul's terms and ideas that Knox voices dissatisfaction, and this essay is still engaged with laying the appropriate foundations before discussing them.

Of course, Knox has a much broader and more solid exegetical basis for the three components of his ethic than we have indicated. Very little of the positive evidence escapes his attention. As to repentance and forgiveness he makes much, and rightly so, of the Lucan parables, especially the Lost Son,[3] the Pharisee and the Publican at Prayer; the Good Samaritan illustrates the law of love; the Sermon on the Mount[4] is in fact the basis for our obligation to the perfect will of God.[5] 1 Cor. 13 is equally often referred to. It helps Knox to call the law of God[6] also the 'law of love'.[7] 'But even in

[1] CLP, p. 149. [2] *Ibid.*
[3] The references to it are profuse; MC, pp. 81–6 offers a moving detailed interpretation of it. [4] See the 'Index of Scripture References' in MC, p. 119.
[5] MC, p. 67, 'We have no right to identify as the will of God anything short of perfect obedience to the law of love.'
[6] EJ, p. 97: 'By "law of God" is meant God's categorical demand upon my moral life with all that the fulfilment of that demand involves. The "law of God" is what God requires of me. Because this requirement is not fortuitous or whimsical or arbitrary, but is consistent with his nature and with the nature of his relations with me and with his creation—it is basically the same requirement of me and of all men—it can properly be called his "law".'
[7] See EJ, p. 49: 'I see no objection to speaking of the *law* of God or the *law* of love.'

this passage love is God's love, not ours, that is why it is "the greatest of [them]". "Faith" and "hope" represent human responses; "love" is the reality to which the response is made.'[1] The last sentence of this statement is right if one reads 1 Cor. 13 in the light of Rom. 5: 5–11, and 8: 35 and 38 f. and similar passages elsewhere, because the interpreter *must* do so. But reading 1 Cor. 13 by itself, as he must also do, from the first verse to the last and in its immediate context (chapters 8–14), shows that it speaks of love only as the 'more excellent way' of responding *in kind* to God's love for man.[2] This indeed is unusual for Paul, for his characteristic and normal term is faith, as Knox points out. Love, as response, is 'a still more excellent way' (1 Cor. 12: 31*b*). That is the reason why it is the greatest of the three great responses (1 Cor. 13: 13); and faith and hope remain indispensable.

With Knox's own conclusion of this whole section of EJ (pp. 89–97) I can fully agree; this shows that exegetical differences may not materially affect theological unity: 'It is worth saying again that an ethic having its root, as the Christian ethic does, in the experience of God's love in Christ…does not need to be thus limited' [i.e. to the Johannine brotherly love.][3]

(iii) We have seen so far that Knox's understanding of the Christian ethic is quite consciously—but also quite unconsciously—deeply indebted to Paul, even if one doubts that he said 'the final word' (CLP, p. 159) on anything. In his many better moments, Paul would have repudiated such a claim or such an accolade in the interest of the whole meaning and purpose of his theology. (See, e.g., Rom. 11: 36; 1 Cor. 13: 8–13 (not an unimportant part of this famous chapter!); Phil. 3: 12–16; 1 Cor. 7: 40*b* (NEB is the preferable translation), etc.). Even the Lord Jesus Christ, the *pantocrator*, is ultimately (eschatologically) provisional, as 1 Cor. 15: 28 clearly shows. The purpose of Paul's theological work is not primarily

---

[1] MC, p. 97.
[2] Both Knox and I have a powerful ally in Hans von Soden's *Urchristentum und Geschichte*, 1, ed. Hans von Campenhausen (Tübingen, 1951), 'Sakrament und Ethik bei Paulus', pp. 239–75: 'Die Agape ist hier [1 Cor. 8: 1] wie in I Kor. 13 durchaus die Liebe die Gott liebt, aber eben als solche die Bruderliebe einschliesst' (p. 244), Knox in the first half of the sentence, I in the second. Von Soden holds very suggestively that chapters 8, 9, 10, 11 and 12 work up gradually to chapter 13.
[3] EJ, p. 94.

in setting forth theological doctrines, but in showing the directions in which faith in Christ is to move, and therefore subjecting even that faith itself to searching theological reflexion (Rom. 4 and 10; Gal. 2: 20 and 3: 23–6; I Cor. 1: 18 – 2: 5, etc.).

Yet, it is equally clear that Knox is decidedly dissatisfied with Paul at two decisive and important points, namely, first, at Paul's theory of justification and atonement, and second at Paul's incipient anti-nomianism. Certainly Knox has long earned the right and has a profound obligation to engage in what our German colleagues call 'material criticism' (*Sachkritik*), i.e. to distinguish between the various grades of good and bad in a given author from the point of view of the author as well as of the scholar's own theology. Not only does a Christian scholar share the right and obligation to engage in such material criticism with non-Christian scholars, but he has the additional obligation 'to test the spirits, whether they are from God' (I John 1: 4). I shall try to argue that in both cases another exegesis of Paul is possible and preferable and to show that the alternative exegesis, though it is in some respects a minority report, does not weaken but strengthen Knox's total theological perspective.

2

A. (i) 'The division which Paul made in the meaning of for-giveness' is the division between justification and reconciliation, the two terms which Paul uses in the place of forgiveness, so that Knox's chief horror is the Pauline theory of justification. I have always fully shared this horror of the predominantly forensic, juridical interpreta-tion of justification which became so entrenched in Germany and elsewhere through the powerful Lutheran scholasticism of the seventeenth century, not through Luther himself, so that few German scholars have managed to free themselves from it.

'Reconciliation' is also derived from the language of the courts, but the term has become so thoroughly 'personal'[1] for obvious reasons, that no one has any difficulty with it, but the 'legal' root-meaning still shines through in Paul's usage of 'reconciliation', though Paul himself has essentially personalized it.

[1] See CLP, p. 146.

This can and must, however, also be said *mutatis mutandis* of the meaning which justification has for Paul.

(ii) Justification becomes a highly social and personal figure of speech in Paul, by being always qualified, explicitly most of the time and implicitly all the time, as justification *by faith*. If there is anything in Pauline thought approaching 'the final word', it is his understanding of the all-dominating significance of faith. Habakkuk says (2: 4), 'he who is righteous (keeps the law of Jahwe) shall live by his faithfulness (to Jahwe's covenant-law with Israel)'. Paul quotes this verse twice quite literally, but the over-towering significance he attaches to faith—in Jesus Christ who also evoked it and evokes it still and ultimately in the God 'who raised Jesus our Lord from the dead' (Rom. 4: 24)—now reads the sentence in a new relationship of its syntactical components, 'he who is justified by faith shall live'. From here to Gal. 2: 20 is only a tiny step, 'the life I now live in the flesh I live by faith in [and from] the Son of God who loved me and gave himself for me'. Here we need not elaborate the point, except to say that 'faith' has for Paul the full meaning which it has in the Old Testament, namely faith as faithfulness, trust and obedience to God as having revealed himself in the law, but Paul has so radicalized faith from and in Christ that the law is absorbed, not abolished by faith.

(iii) As far as I can see Knox never or hardly ever deals with this crucially important, revolutionary relationship of faith to justification; he relates justification rather to atonement; they are related as the two sides of a suspected coin; they are viewed, in a large part at least, as if they were for Paul descriptions of objectively real, unilateral transactions on the part of a God of wrathful, retributive and juridical justice.

Atonement and justification are indeed closely related, but the relationship is that both are *in the same decisive way* related to faith from and in Christ; they are no longer descriptions or even symbols of transactions of God but personal and social symbols applied to the one 'God and Father of Jesus Christ', who is both all justice and all grace. Thus the meaning of the death of Christ to Paul, in the passage which comes closest to an atonement theory, is emphatically and thoroughly personal, social and symbolic: 'But they are justified as a free gift, by God's grace, through the act of redemption which he performed in Christ Jesus. This Christ Jesus God publicly set forth in his bloody sacrificial death as his means of dealing with sin, received through faith' (Rom. 3 : 24 f.).[1]

Thus one may legitimately ask with Knox,[2] whether one can do better justice to the total intention of Paul by omitting the term atonement from the agenda altogether, asking simply for the meaning of the death of Christ in the reflexions of Paul. Here it must suffice to quote one of Knox's illustrious predecessors, to summarize and reinforce Knox's thought:

The language is necessarily symbolic, the language of myth. Nobody knows what it can mean literally for God, the Creator and Lord of a universe measured in light-years, to have an 'only Son' on the earth, in whom God has himself come in human form to save men from themselves. But though the language has to be that of myth it gives expression to a faith that has thrived on suffering and has rallied men time after time through dark centuries of struggle.[3]

(iv)[4] The fact that justification, like faith, is in Paul strongly eschatological points in the same direction, namely, that for Paul justification is not a purely forensic, but a social, personal and ethical symbol. This eschatological character of justification also has its deep and vigorous roots in the Old Testament and in Judaism. It is indeed the event of Christ, which is for Paul—as for John and the synoptic gospels (in significantly different ways)—the eschatological event κατ'ἐξοχήν, that gives to the eschatological hope as a present gift conveyed by the Holy Spirit (Rom. 5 : 5 and 8 : 24 f.) the great significance he assigns to it in 1 Cor. 13 : 13 and in Rom. 5 : 5; 8 : 24 f., etc., and is the power which, according to Rom. 5 : 1–3, enables him

[1] Translation by C. K. Barrett, *A Commentary on the Epistle to the Romans* (New York, 1957).
[2] See DC, especially pp. 142–57.
[3] R. L. Calhoun, *What is Man?* (New York, 1939), p. 92; pp. 92–3 are well worth reading, and they further illuminate other aspects of Knox's thought. The book antedates Bultmann's publication (1940) of his demythologizing programme.
[4] The reader will be aware, particularly in this paragraph, of some major affinities with and differences from E. Käsemann's very important article 'God's Righteousness in Paul' in the *Journal for Theology and the Church*, 1 (Tübingen and New York, 1965), 100–10. It is a notable example of the fact that German scholars also are struggling to overcome the time-honoured domination of a purely or even predominantly forensic notion of justification by faith.

who is justified by faith to live his daily life physically, morally and victoriously. It is, perhaps, an oversimplification (in the direction of the truth) that the eschatology of the synoptic gospels stresses the expected, future consummation, and the Fourth Gospel stresses, on any reading, the consummation as essentially present. For Paul eschatology is consciously dialectic, based on his experience and on profound theological reflexion: the consummation is present *and* future. It would be an un-Pauline reductionism (which Knox does not share !), namely, to reduce this dialectic to a mere chronological sequence: partial or even relatively decisive fulfilment now—consummation later. No, history and man in history are not eliminated by Paul's dialectic, they are transcended by it. 'The life I now live in the flesh (in history) I live by faith in the Son of God' (Gal. 2: 20), and, 'though we live in the world (in history and in "nature") we are not carrying on a worldly war...we destroy arguments and every proud obstacle to the knowledge of God, and take every thought captive to obey Christ' (2 Cor. 10: 3 and 5). Paul does not know our modern common-sense division of common-sense time into past, present and future, but only the division between τὰ ἐνεστῶτα (the present time of which all the past since Adam is and so far remains constitutive) and τὰ μέλλοντα or τὸ μέλλον (the future which comprises and transcends him who is justified by faith). (See 1 Cor. 3: 12; Rom. 8: 38 and Gal. 1: 3; also Rom. 8: 18 and Gal. 3: 23; also 1 Cor. 7: 26.) Pauline eschatology is not the temporal sequence between what happened two thousand years ago in and around Jesus of Nazareth and the expected event of the return of Christ making an end of history, with a lot of history thrown in between the two events, events connected only by faith, hope and love. Such faith, hope and love even at their best would be no more than wishful thinking, hoping for things that are seen, faith that looks for works and love considered as good business. Paul's eschatology expresses a dynamic tension in which faith apprehends in the Greek folly of the cross the wisdom of God, and over against the Jewish demand of creditable 'miracle' the power of God. Hope is not determined by what it seems to see but is faith directed toward the future. Love is given, because it was received, and thus it is kept alive and growing in strength.

This dialectic theory of eschatology enabled Paul to give expression to his experience as a man in Christ that faith lives socially, personally and individually, at every moment of history in which the event of two thousand years ago impinges upon, yea determines every moment of history and therefore all history. In a dynamic, creative tension the old present, of which the past is constitutive, and the new present, which is assured by the ever-new future, meet and become one. 'To this hope we are saved. Now hope that is seen is not hope. For who hopes for what he sees? But if we hope for what we do not see, we wait for it with steadfastness' (Rom. 8: 24 f.).

When and how this consummation takes place in empirical history faith in Christ does not know and does not wish to know; nor does it wish to point to any personal, social or political achievement as its fruit or as its prop, because that would be a form of the righteousness by works, but it does know it is happening now in empirical history.

What does this interpretation of Paul's 'doctrine' of justification as eminently eschatological have to do with the ethic of Paul? A great deal, from the ground up. The *function* of the eschatological sanction for a Christian ethic is in fact the same as the sanction of God himself. So the absolute will of God of the Sermon on the Mount is God acting in his coming with his kingdom *and* (epexegetical καί) the coming of his absolute righteousness. As far as Paul is concerned at this specific point Käsemann's words[1] are unexcelled.

[Christ's] dominion over us is precisely then totally effected when it masters our heart and takes us into its service. Conversely, every gift which is no longer interpreted as the presence of its giver and therefore loses the character of a claim is an abused and detrimental grace. *Justification and sanctification must coincide, if indeed justification means that Christ assumes power over our life.*[2] At the same time this understanding excludes the possibility of righteousness by works and of boasting on the basis of one's own accomplishment. The same Lord who calls us to his service makes possible this service which he demands in such a way that his gift is passed on.

This understanding of Paul's symbolic, metaphorical concept of justification fits beautifully in the perspective of the Christian ethic which Knox bases chiefly on the Christ of the synoptic gospels.

---

[1] For the reference see 'God's Righteousness in Paul' (as in p. 378, n. 4 above), pp. 104–5.

[2] The italics are mine. On the coinciding of justification and sanctification see Rom. 6: 19; 1 Cor. 1: 30; 1 Thess. 4: 3, 7.

B. The third (in an important sense the first) cornerstone of Knox's New Testament ethic is the 'law of God', which is identical with 'the law of love'. It is understood despite his profound appreciation of 'the grace of God' as—quite explicitly—more Matthaean than Pauline. Correspondingly, Knox's understanding has throughout, like Matthew's, recognizably legalistic flavour.[1]

A constructive and suggestive solution of the relationship between the 'legalistic' Matthaean Christ of the Sermon on the Mount and the 'antinomian' Christ of Paul is offered in an essay by R. Bultmann.[2] I would put the matter as follows: Matthew (and Knox too), by using legalistic language for the absolute demand of absolute obedience to the absolute 'law of God', explodes legalism from within, while Paul absorbs and truly establishes the absolute will of God in his theology of grace.

Knox says that Paul wrestled strenuously with the problem of finding an adequate and convincing place for the law of God in his theology of the grace of God; the nearest Paul comes to an answer is in Romans 6: 14, 'since you are not under law but under grace'. This, according to Knox, makes Paul, as a *theoretic* ethicist, that is, as a theologian of ethics, suspect of fatal antinomian tendencies.[3]

In view of the fact that Knox speaks of Paul's inability to offer a sufficiently convincing theoretical basis for his own high standards as a 'man in Christ', and that, in wrestling with the problem why the man of faith should not 'remain in sin', Paul only repeats subsequently the question of Rom. 6: 1, still failing to answer it convincingly, it becomes necessary to sketch the movement of Paul's thought from Rom. 6: 1 – 8: 30, for it is in this whole section, step by step, that it is Paul's intention and purpose to answer the question. As far as it is necessary, we must, because of the importance

---

[1] E.g. in the quotations above, in nn. 6 and 7, p. 374, and various other places, such as CLP, p. 142. Here he says of repentance disapprovingly that Paul 'never uses it so as to make it a condition of salvation', and EJ, pp. 97 f. (in his comments on the 'law of God'). Knox calls the Epistle of James the 'most simply ethical of all the New Testament books' (EJ, p. 94). This is descriptively true, but I can only regard James' attempt (2: 8–26) to combine legalism with a theology of grace and faith such as Paul's as unsuccessful.

[2] See in the collection of Bultmann essays, *Existence and Faith*, tr. and ed. Schubert M. Ogden (New York, 1960), the essay 'Jesus and Paul', pp. 183–201.

[3] CLP, p. 154, and the whole of chapter IX; see also EJ, pp. 75–7; 97–104.

Paul attaches to the issue, connect it backward and forward to the train of thought of the whole letter.

In Rom. 3: 31 Paul first states his thesis: 'Do we then abolish the law by this faith? By no means. We establish it.' A very clear putting of the question and of the answer. It is also a thesis very emphatically put, because in 3: 21-30 he makes, in Romans, the first explicit statement of his faith- and grace-theology. This means that the first and most important question that comes to his own mind on stating the leading, principal thesis of his whole theology, is the question: What happens to the law? The importance of the thesis of verse 31 is further underlined by the fact that Paul, in order to argue it effectively, first discusses five prior issues which were raised in 3 : 21-31: (i) Although the righteousness of God has been revealed apart from any assistance by the law, it was nevertheless witnessed to by the scriptures (4: 1-15). (ii) The most striking and notable feature of Rom. 3: 21-31 is the close and far-reaching correlation of the righteousness of God and of faith. Therefore these complementary terms receive substantial, if incomplete, clarification throughout ch. 4, but especially in its second part (4: 16-23; see earlier 3: 3-6 and also 9: 30-10: 17). (iii) In 5: 1-5 faith and grace (thematically stated in 3: 24*a*), are shown in their essential relationship, and are related to hope and love and to the Holy Spirit. These *new* thematic terms are not yet elaborated—in a well-planned sequence and not by the hindsight of the exegete—until chapter 8: 1-30 (Spirit) and 8: 18-25 (hope). (iv) In 5: 6-11 justification by faith, the love of God, and the reconciliation which God brought about are shown in their correlation; justification and reconciliation are two alternate symbols with important different connotations of the saving act of God through Christ rather than a sequence of acts. (v) 5: 12-21, besides serving other basic, Christological interests of Paul's, emphasizes and argues dialectically the over-towering significance of the grace of God; the term occurs in emphatic positions no less than six times in verses 15-21, eight times really if 'free gift' (verse 16) is regarded, as it should, as expressing the essential meaning of grace, namely, as the all-embracing gift and power of God.

Here my main thesis is, contrary to Knox, that the whole section 6: 1 – 8: 30 addresses itself to the same question (of 3: 31) and not to the question of 6: 1; this latter question is just the first specific step of seven further specific steps which follow in a dialectic, progressive order, i.e. organically and dynamically, from the preceding ones. Here it may be helpful to say that dialectic does not mean an esoteric, independent kind of the art of reasoning (logic) or of the results of reasoning (whether scientific, or historical, metaphysical, ontological or theological), but it simply means one of the special techniques of reasoning, employed characteristically, as can be shown historically and phenomenologically, by at least some thinkers and poets whose total concern is with reality as in some way dynamic, by thinkers who apprehend reality as a complex event or process. Each of these 'dialecticians' may profitably use and detrimentally abuse this particular technique of practically universal reasoning, but to make such judgments one has to do it with the aid of this particular method in order to be effective. Each of the dialectic thinkers, including Paul, will have to be judged not only in the light of his own thought, but especially in the light of his own basic, ultimate intuition or axiom, which is non-dialectic.

For Paul, this unstated intuition *and* the explicit axiom is in the living faith inherited *and* 'digested'[1] from a living tradition many centuries old in the faith which Israel had held to. Paul's 'ultimate, explicit axiom' is also a significant element in the first and basic statement of Rom. 3: 21–30 already characterized above. 'Or is God the God of Jews only? Is he not the God of Gentiles also? Yes, of Gentiles also, since God is one' (see also Gal. 3: 25–9; 1 Cor. 8: 5–6, etc.).

Now, to trace the progressive, dialectical arguments of Rom. 6: 1 – 8: 30. The organic unity and orderliness of the whole section is indicated by the repetition in truly dialectical style of the same formal question of the successive arguments, namely, the basic question formally expressed by τί οὖν ἐροῦμεν; the answer by μὴ γένοιτο. This formulation of 6: 1 is the base of τί οὖν; and μὴ γένοιτο (verse 16); in 7: 7 we read τί οὖν ἐροῦμεν; and μὴ γένοιτο; verse 13 omits the formal interrogatory formula altogether, but states the new question only in substantive terms; the sub-sections of chapter 8 are not introduced by questions at all, because Paul is now ready for the

---

[1] 'Digested' is my attempt to translate the meaning of Goethe's 'winged word', 'was Du ererbt von Deinen Vätern, erwirb es um es zu besitzen', especially of the key-verb 'erwirb es'.

ultimate answers (8: 1–11, 12–17, 18–25, 26–30). This is followed by (31–9) the evocative, climactic question τί οὖν ἐροῦμεν πρὸς ταῦτα (add: πάντα); This question does not belong to the section (6: 1 – 8: 30) alone, but sums up the whole of the letter so far written. It is the literary as well as the confessional-liturgical climax of 1: 16 – 8: 30. Indeed it is a direct response, greatly enriched by all the matters considered so far, to the thanksgiving (1: 8–15) which precedes it and lends to the whole letter not little of its coherence and tone.

A second thematically literary as well as theological clue is the constructive and positive denotation and connotation ascribed to the law (verse 12), especially in the conclusion of the section extending from 7: 7–12, 'the law is good, and the commandment (which promised life, verse 10) is holy, just and good'. In the immediately following section (7: 13–25) this conception of the law is indeed profusely thematic; the law is called twice more good (verse 13); in 14 it is holy; in 16 good; in 19 and 21 good; 22 says, 'I delight in the law of God', and in 25 again it is called once more the law of God; as now Paul's final conclusions begin (8: 1–11), the law is characterized in a significant and not simply casual, rhetorical or homiletic way 'the law of the Spirit of life' (verse 2). Here, in the first step of the concluding answer, the relation between law and Spirit is first, and decisively defined; the power of the law is described in an unheard of, yet dialectically logical way no longer as its own (7: 10 f., 13, 23) but as the Spirit's; in fact, it is God's own power (8: 3*a*); verse 4 concludes in a ἵνα-clause, that due to the power of God made manifest through faith in Christ 'the just requirement of the law is to be fulfilled in us', because we walk according to the Spirit, for 'the mind of the flesh is hostile to God; it does not submit to God's law, indeed it cannot' (8:7). This is the last time that the law of God as permanently valid is used in Romans, nor is it called again the law of the Spirit (after verse 2). But the whole of 8: 1–30 does much to show why from now on in Romans—and the Corinthian letters as well as Galatians show the same thing in significantly different situations and in noteworthy, theological variations—the Holy Spirit, the Spirit of God or of Christ takes its place, i.e. the Spirit can and must eliminate the *term* law—thus eliminating the last trace of legalistic wording from the Pauline vocabulary without in any way eliminating—theoretically for ethical theory or practically for moral conduct—anything of the rigorous and absolute demand or claim conveyed by the positive but basically dispensable term 'law of God'—by absorbing its full, new and permanently revolutionary substance, whose transcendent power is—with Knox—the power of love. The Spirit does not have the power to set up extraneous conditions; it is itself the truly irresistible power of the love of God at work in all men, set to work among, in and through them.

This finds its truly final, but still incomplete expression—incomplete because the power of the Spirit is transcendent, and therefore also is experientially confirmed by those who live and walk by the Spirit (see also, besides Romans, Gal. 5: 25)—in Rom. 12: 1–2, which is in the whole letter, alike from the literary, theological and experiential perspective, the Paul of Romans in a nutshell. 'Be ye transformed by the renewal of your minds'—this typically Pauline wording probably comes closer to the meaning of Jesus Christ as remembered and known still in and by the Church than does any other Pauline text. This wording means what is said in 6: 4, 7: 6 and in chapter 8 about the new and ever new life in the power of the Spirit as over against any law or code, written or oral. This text also says that by the power of the Spirit the man in Christ is enabled to know the *will* of God in every concrete situation, as the illustrations of 12: 3 – 15: 13 show. This will of God, which we can experience and know by life in the Spirit, is good, acceptable and perfect, just as the 'law of God' is holy, just, good, spiritual and promised life (Rom. 7: 12–22).

It remains to indicate the basically dialectic, substantive issues in the four progressive steps of Romans chapters 6 and 7, of which chapter 8 gives the solution.

At the end of chapter 5 (verses 18–21) Paul states the realities of man's situation in the most appropriate dialectical terms. To conceive of the Adam-Christ typology (verses 12–21) merely as 'text' on which to base the history-of-salvation theology of Paul, thus dissolving the Adam-Christ relationship into mere chronological sequence, is to fail to understand the dialectic character of verses 18–21, which are the basis and the topic sentence for chapters 6 and 7. The nature and purpose of this Pauline dialectic comes out clearly in the following scheme:

(18) Then as one man's [Adam's] trespass
  leads to condemnation
  for all men

     so one man's [Christ's] act of
     righteousness leads to acquittal
     and life for all men.

(19) For as by one man's disobedience
  many were made sinners,

     so by one man's obedience
     many will be made righteous.

(20) Law came in
  to increase the trespass;
  but where sin increased,

     grace abounded all the more,

(21) so that,
  as sin reigned in death,

     grace also might reign
     through righteousness
     to eternal life
     through Jesus Christ our Lord.

The left-hand column shows man's solidarity with Adam, i.e. man's solidarity with all other men by nature and by fate resulting in death, the ambivalence of his existence, his disobedience to God; in short, it shows man as he is. The right-hand column shows what man may be in solidarity with the one man Christ and his obedience to God, what he may be, ought to be and can be, if he accepts the abounding power of the grace of God by faith in (solidarity with) Christ. It has become abundantly clear that the main function of Pauline dialectic is to lead man to a full understanding of his situation by comprehensive and incisive analysis in the light and power of his life as a 'man in Christ'.[1] A few bold strokes to characterize the substantive arguments of the four steps 6: 1–14, 6: 15 – 7: 6, 7: 7–12 and 7: 13–25 serve to confirm our whole argument.

In 6: 1–14 the issue starts from a focusing on 5: 20*b*, itself dialectic-ally arrived at from the argument of 1: 16 – 5: 20. 'Are we to

---

[1] It is not necessary, and perhaps not possible, to trace the dialectic of Paul to his environment, although it would be a rewarding task otherwise. At all events, the deepest roots and the finest fruits of his dialectic lie in and come from his experience of Christ.

continue in *sin* that grace may abound? By no means' (6: 1 f.). Our baptism (immersion!) was a sign that we died with Christ to sin that we too might walk in newness of life (verse 4). Death no longer has dominion over Christ (verses 7–8), and therefore sin has no longer dominion over those who belong to him; they are no longer under law but under grace (verses 11–14). It is clear the dialectic of 5: 18–21 is maintained and carried forward.

On the basis of 6: 1–14 the issue is now, 'are we to sin, because we are not under *law* but under grace? By no means!' (verse 15). Correspondingly attention is focused on obedience and freedom (verses 16–22). Slavish obedience to the law is turned into obedience to righteousness for sanctification (verses 19 and 22 b); conversely, freedom from righteousness (verse 20 b) is turned into the slavery of righteousness (verse 18). Where else could the absolute demand of the absolute law of God find a more profound expression than in this radical theology of grace? This 'demand', this imperative is to be carried out in daily life: 'yield your members', i.e. yield your life in the flesh by faith, 'to righteousness' (verse 19 c). In its final part (7: 1–6) the conclusion is reached, 'so that we serve no longer under the old written code, but in the new life of the Spirit' (7: 6), laying the ground for the dialectic steps of the final answer in chapter 8.

The third step before the final answer is taken in 7: 7–25. Again its dialectic is based on that of the topic sentence (Rom. 5: 18–21), and similar to it, but the details are adjusted to the new subject-matter of this later step. The issue is, 'did that which is good', i.e. the law of God (verses 22 and 25), 'bring death to me? By no means!' (verse 13). In 7: 7–25 the dialectic has reached its highest point in its statement of man's situation as it is before the final answer of 8: 1–30. The dialectic is between sin which leads to death (verse 13 b) on the one side and the law of God (verses 22 and 25) which is good (verses 13 a and 16) and spiritual (verse 14) on the other side. It is between the law of sin in my members and the law of God in my inmost self in which I delight (verses 22–5). It is the miserable tension (verse 24 a) between 'I do not do the good I want, but the evil I do not want is what I do' (verses 15–19). This is the climactic tension in man's situation and its dialectic expression before the coming of faith, which frees man from *this* tension.

C. The end is reached. Is the ghost laid, or is it brought to life, or does it simply remain an unlaid ghost? At any rate, my comments are to a large extent the product of my reactions to John Knox's impressive challenge, which is a significant part of my experience. Our differences are not important, if it is true that we have not yet reached the time when we can understand the New Testament ethic and Paul's without steering between the Scylla of legalism and the Charybdis of antinomianism, for both are still the product of deep instincts in 'human nature', and it is therefore hard for the interpreter of the New Testament, as it was for its own writers, to avoid the dangers of being shipwrecked on either rock, because theology as a whole still has to steer between the extremes of deism and mysticism, of which legalism and antinomianism may only be the ethical equivalents. Our differences may even be regarded as constructive, if it is true that we share the perspective of biblical and of contemporary modern theology which speaks of Jesus Christ as a revelatory *event*. Such an ecumenical theology would still be today and perhaps tomorrow a theology expressing the experience of the 'pilgrim's progress of the reasoning Christian heart'.[1]

[1] See H. Richard Niebuhr, *The Meaning of Revelation* (New York, 1940), p. 137.

18

OBLIGATION IN THE ETHIC OF PAUL

C. F. D. MOULE

In *The Ethic of Jesus in the Teaching of the Church* (New York, 1961; London, 1962), Professor John Knox analyses the dilemma facing the Christian when he recognizes at once the inescapability and the impossibility of the demands of Christ. The demands of Christ are self-authenticating; they are such that the honest conscience is bound to accept them. And yet they are unattainable. Therefore the Christian is forced into a tension, a tension which would be unendurable—'how can we be really obligated to do the impossible?' (p. 15)—were it not for the accompanying forgiveness which is offered—a forgiveness, however, which, because it is real forgiveness and not a mere forgetting or ignoring, involves not the slightest relaxation of the demand.

This characteristic of the ethic of Jesus—namely, the undiminished costliness of repentance—is described with the writer's usual clarity and feeling, and in an entirely convincing manner. Professor Knox has brought back into view an element in the teaching of Jesus which had tended to be forgotten; and I have no intention of making clumsy attempts to improve on it. It is in connexion with the treatment, in the same book, of Paul's standpoint that I venture to offer some further reflexions. In this part of his argument, Professor Knox reiterates a conclusion which he had expressed some ten years earlier in *Chapters in a Life of Paul* (New York, 1950; London, 1954), chapter 9. He accuses Paul (*The Ethic of Jesus*, p. 76)[1] of, unconsciously and unintentionally, relaxing the demand and sowing the seeds of antinomianism by his doctrine of justification. Paul's opponents and his heretical followers did interpret his gospel in an antinomian sense; and Professor Knox suggests that such was, indeed, the logic of his position, though not, of course, his intention—still less, his experience.

The Pauline doctrine of justification, Professor Knox maintains,

[1] All page references without further designation will henceforth relate to this book.

divides forgiveness into two parts—justice and mercy; and this is a disaster, because it tends to make us see God's justice as mere justice and his mercy as mere mercy, whereas, in reality, God's justice and mercy are never thus divided. For 'when we say that God *forgives*, we are saying that *this* is the character of *his* justice and of *his* mercy' (*Chapters in a Life of Paul*, p. 148). It is not that there is a shadow of doubt about the depth of Paul's own experience. The 'single act' of God's forgiveness 'has unquestionably taken place within Paul's experience' (*ibid.* p. 150). It is only his interpretation and explanation of it that Professor Knox questions. Paul's interpretation, he holds, 'obscures the fact that love has its own way of dealing with sin—a way which is compatible with the highest demands of truth, but which does not need to make use of the terms or devices of either the law court or the market place. We do not have to be 'acquitted' before the Judge in order to be reconciled to the Father' (*ibid.*). In short, Professor Knox expresses surprise and regret that Paul, using the potentially misleading category of justification, did not make more use of the category of *penitence*, which is used with such effect in the teaching of Jesus. Had he done so, he might have safeguarded mercy against being thought of as 'mere mercy'. As it is, he speaks of God justifying the ungodly 'not on the ground of his repentance (what can repentance have to do with justification?), but on the ground of Christ's expiatory act, which one appropriates by faith' (*ibid.* p. 153).

In this complaint, Professor Knox is by no means alone, for Paul's failure to reckon with penitence is a charge frequently levelled against him (see further p. 398, n. 1, below). But it is precisely this charge that the present essay attempts to re-examine; and, to that extent, it is a modest contribution to the larger problem of the relation of Jesus to Paul,[1] as well as a grateful acknowledgment of the stimulating and challenging character of what Professor Knox has written.

Accepting Professor Knox's challenge, and believing that he will

[1] On this, particularly valuable light has been shed by W. G. Kümmel (see the three papers on Jesus and Paul in his collection, *Heilsgeschehen und Geschichte* (Marburg, 1965)) and by E. Jüngel, *Paulus und Jesus* (Tübingen, 1964). See also the important survey by V. P. Furnish, 'The Jesus-Paul Debate: from Baur to Bultmann', *BJRylL* 47 (1965), 342 ff.

treat this attempt to hold dialogue with him as the sincerest token of my regard, I shall put forward the view that Paul's alleged neglect of penitence is only apparent, not real, because the Pauline conception of faith-union with Christ itself presents a profound analysis of penitence, albeit translated into other terms. Thus, the logic of obligation is not surrendered by Paul, for he has as demanding a doctrine of repentance as Jesus had. Indeed, I would go further, and suggest that Paul offers an analysis of penitence where the teaching of Jesus does not, Paul making explicit what, in the teaching of Jesus, is only implicit. Conversely, I would suggest that the teaching of Jesus was as anti-legalistic and—if one may put it so—as 'situational' as Paul's. For Jesus himself, as for Paul, it was the new eschatological situation which was the decisive factor.

But, before I reach my main point, it will be useful to discuss two related matters: first, the legitimacy and value of the term 'legalism' to characterize what Paul is attacking; and, secondly, the relation of 'legalism' to sin.

I

The term 'legalism', although deplored by some scholars, can be a useful tool; and I suggest that, if it can be legitimized, its use may help to clarify something of considerable importance for the present investigation. What Paul means by νόμος is a thorny and endlessly debated problem.[1] But the term 'legalism' conveniently summarizes an important aspect of the subject; for I suggest that, in the tangled thickets of discussion, it is more important to draw a distinction between different uses of law and attitudes to law, than between different conceptions of its nature or contents: and this is usefully done in terms of 'legalism'. In other words, more important than whether law is viewed as a code or as a necessary ground of obligation, is the question whether a man is trying to justify himself by keeping the law, or whether he allows law to be a medium through which God reveals himself. On the basis of this approach, a provisional answer may at once be offered to one vital question. (The answer is a drastically simplified one, and ignores, no doubt, many

---

[1] Besides the well-known discussions in E. de W. Burton, *Galatians* (I.C.C., Edinburgh, 1921), pp. 443 ff., and G. Kittel, *ThWNT* I (Stuttgart, 1940), 1061 ff., see, more recently, the analysis on p. 44 of C.E.B. Cranfield, 'St Paul and the Law', *SJT* 17 (1964), 43 ff.

nuances and subtleties, but perhaps it is adequate as a start.) The short answer to the question 'In what sense, if any, did Paul speak of law as abrogated?' is that Paul saw Christ as the *fulfilment* of law, when law means God's revelation of himself and of his character and purpose, but as the *condemnation* and *termination* of any attempt to use law to justify oneself. And it is this latter use of law which may conveniently be called (for short) 'legalism'. It has been objected that '...the Greek language used by Paul had no word-group to denote "legalism", "legalist", and "legalistic"'.[1] But, for that matter, neither has he a distinctive word for any other aspect of law. The many shades of meaning attaching to νόμος have to be deduced from the ways in which the word is used; and it is clear that νόμος is used by Paul in (among others) the two quite distinct connexions which may be called respectively 'revelatory' and 'legalistic'.

Thus—to take only some very obvious examples—νόμος is used in allusion to the revelation of God's requirements and character in the two following passages:

So the law is holy, and the commandment is holy and just and good. (Rom. 7: 12.)
The commandments, 'You shall not commit adultery, You shall not kill, You shall not steal, You shall not covet', and any other commandment, are summed up in this sentence, 'You shall love your neighbour as yourself'. Love does no wrong to a neighbour; therefore love is the fulfilling of the law. (Rom. 13: 9, 10.)

In the former of these two passages, even the more specifically imperative word, ἐντολή (commandment), is equally recognized as representing something good and permanent.

In sharp contrast to these, there are well-known passages in which law is disparaged. In such a passage as Rom. 3: 20, for example, νόμος is recognized as impotent to save, though able to pass sentence: 'For no human being will be justified in his sight by works of the law, since through the law comes knowledge of sin.' Even more explicit is Gal. 3: 21 b, 22a: '...for if a law had been given which could make alive, then righteousness would indeed be by the law. But...' The same applies to Rom. 3: 28: 'For we hold that a man is justified by faith apart from works of the law.' And, to make it

---

[1] C.E.B. Cranfield, 'St Paul and the Law', p. 55.

doubly clear that this is not a denial of the validity of νόμος as a statement of God's requirements and character, Paul adds (verse 31), in so many words: 'Do we then overthrow the law by this faith? By no means! On the contrary, we uphold the law.'

This contrast between the two contexts in which νόμος is used is perfectly familiar to all students of Paul. The only point I want to make is that it is here that the word 'legalism' comes in useful as 'shorthand' for an idea which is of primary importance in the discussion of obligation in the ethic of Paul. If by legalism we understand the intention to claim God's favour by establishing one's own rightness, then legalism is a convenient summary of what Paul is alluding to when he speaks of justification by works of the law.

What I am saying, then, is that, for the purposes of this debate, it is not so important to define the law as to define a man's motives in relation to it and his methods of using it; and the vital distinction is not between law *in itself*, whether as a code or as a ground of obligation (p. 97), but between two different attitudes to and uses of law—on the one hand, the recognition of law as a revelation of God's will and purpose, and, on the other hand, the attempt to use it 'legalistically', to establish one's rightness.

Gal. 5: 3 is a verse which, perhaps, throws light on this distinction. Here Paul says that anyone who gets himself circumcised is under an obligation to keep the whole law. He is apparently referring to Christians who became converts to Judaism and who were circumcised as adults. That is, they had come to the conclusion that trust in Christ was not enough: they must add the safeguard of Judaism. If so, Paul says, then you must accept Judaism as the mechanical system which your decision to make use of the law implies: having adopted the law as a 'safeguard', you must abide by it in a spirit of meticulous literalism. What Paul indicates as, by contrast, desirable is not the abolition of law. What needs to be abolished is the arrogantly human use of the law for the purposes of human 'safety'.

2

Thus, it is legalism that Paul consistently attacks. Indeed, for him it is a symptom of *the* essential sin, namely, Adam's self-centredness. And this brings me to the second of my two preliminary points—a point concerning the relation of legalism to sin. Paul's contention is not only that, since man is never going to be able to keep the law merely by trying, therefore the intention to claim God's favour by establishing one's justice is *futile*. Worse than that—such an intention is positively *sinful*, because it implies an uncreaturely refusal to accept man's need of God and dependence on him.

Thus, when Paul contrasts grace with law, he is not for a moment setting up some supposed gracious indulgence over against the absolute demands of God, in such a way as to relax these demands. On the contrary, he is declaring that the only realistic step towards meeting God's inexorable demands is to recognize them as frankly unattainable without the power of God; and to recognize, further, that to presume to try to attain them without God's aid is man's essential sin. It is not that grace abolishes law, but that dependence on grace, instead of the attitude of legalism, is the only way to fulfil God's law. There is obligation, but it is to grace, not law.

That this is Paul's meaning is, I think, evident in the contrasting uses of νόμος that have already been referred to. But, given this conclusion, there are other passages which, in their turn, seem to be illuminated and to be given their proper point. For instance, Rom. 6: 14: 'For sin will have no dominion over you, since you are not under law but under grace.' This sounds paradoxical, because one might expect that subjection to law would provide precisely the firm discipline and obligation that would make for the avoidance of sin. In any normal ethical context, it would have made good sense to say: 'sin will have no dominion over you, since you are securely under law.' But, instead, Paul inserts his 'not': it is precisely because you are *not* under law that you can escape from the dominion of sin.[1] Are not those commentators right who interpret this in the light of legalism? Professor C. K. Barrett's comment puts this interpretation as clearly as possible:

Law means the upward striving of human religion and morality, and therefore colours all human activity with sin, for it represents man's attempt to scale God's throne. Those who live under the reign of grace, however, have given full scope to God's freedom, since instead of pressing upward towards God they humbly wait for his descent in love.

[1] Perhaps the extremely obscure passage, Gal. 5: 17 f., is akin to this passage in its logic.

Ultimately, therefore, justification by faith, which means living under grace, though it is rooted in a region of divine-human relation which lies beyond morals, becomes the one hope of a truly moral life. (*A Commentary on the Epistle to the Romans* (London, 1957), p. 129.)[1]

On this showing, the very essence of sin is precisely the human attempt to establish autonomy; and it is only by ceasing to be 'under law' in that sense—the sense, namely, of attempting to establish for oneself one's own law-abidingness—that one may begin to gain release from the tyranny of sin. The very paradox of the 'not' seems to point to an interpretation in terms of legalism. And this is borne out by the rest of the chapter; for Rom. 6: 15 ff. urges that release from νόμος (in the sense implied by the context) means *not* antinomianism (verse 15), but a firmer obligation than ever: to be released from the self-concern of legalism is to be free to devote oneself as a slave (verses 16 ff.) to 'obedience' (verse 16) or to the shaping force of Christian teaching (verse 17), or to 'righteousness' (verses 19 f.). It is possible, I think, that Rom. 8: 3 may stand within the same circle of ideas. It says that the law was impotent διὰ τῆς σαρκός. This is generally interpreted in some such sense as (RSV) 'weakened by the flesh'. But may it not rather mean that law, in the nature of the case, can only operate externally, on the physical level? The law is impotent and weak because its scope is limited to a man's material, physical aspects, and does not touch his motives (τὸ... ἀδύνατον τοῦ νόμου, ἐν ᾧ ἠσθένει διὰ τῆς σαρκός). It can, at best, only coerce a man's body, not affect his will. In other words, a mere statement of God's will—however excellent in itself—cannot be *applied* to man except in terms of external restraint or compulsion. When law has

---

[1] Somewhat differently, O. Kuss (*Der Römerbrief*, II (Regensburg, 1959), 384), who takes it to mean that one is removed from the domain of a law which could only demand but not succour, and transplanted to a realm of grace which brings God's help and strength. Professor Knox himself, in his commentary in *The Interpreter's Bible*, edd. G. A. Buttrick and others, 9 (New York, Nashville, 1954), 480 f., stresses the future tense ('will have no dominion') as indicating that Paul recognizes that the release is not yet accomplished in the present age; and, for the meaning of 'you are not under law...', asks whether it is that (*a*) all of the commands of the law are now invalid, no longer binding, for the believer; or (*b*) the believer, because of the power of the Spirit, now finds himself able to fulfil the law and is therefore not aware of its restrictions and demands; or (*c*) the believer does not now have to rely upon his obedience to the law for his acceptance with God. Of these, (*b*) is nearest to the meaning indicated by Barrett, but not quite the same.

made its announcement—its good and holy announcement—it still remains for something less external to put it into effect. But to proceed from law to legalism is precisely to remain on the level of externals.

Thus, it is not that one is released from obligation by ceasing to be under law (p. 103). Rather, it is that only by abandoning the self-centred and self-chosen obligation may one hope to fulfil the genuine obligation. But even if one agrees to all this, Professor Knox's complaint is still not met. He does not question Paul's recognition that Christians are under the obligation to live a life of love nor Paul's own experience of the joyfully accepted 'bondage' to God's love. What he questions is whether Paul's 'understanding of what God had done in Christ and of the corresponding status of the believer provided any *adequate theoretical and theological basis* for the obligation' (p. 97, my italics). For—so Professor Knox maintains—Paul's *theory* really does represent a radical rejection of law. Thus he writes:

But, it may be asked, is Paul's rejection of the law as binding on the believer so radical as this? Is not the 'law' he rejects simply an external code, a list of thou shalt's and thou shalt not's, in particular the code of Judaism? Whatever may seem to be implied in some of his practical teaching, I feel sure that in his 'theory' of the Christian life Paul went much further than this. Although undoubtedly he is frequently referring to the Jewish law, one cannot deny the presence—often, if not always—of a more radical, more inclusive, reference. The Gentiles also are subject to law (Rom. 2: 15); will they not share, with redeemed Jews, in release from the burden of its demands? And when Paul speaks of this release, can he have only an external code in mind? Would he have said, 'God has freed us from a code of particular rules by making us subject to a higher, more exacting law—a law which lays its demands upon the very thoughts of our hearts and calls for an absolutely unremitting obedience?' Jesus speaks to this effect, but I do not believe Paul would have done so. Certainly he does not in fact speak so. It is striking that when, in the seventh chapter of Romans, he is telling of the difficulties he himself had under the Jewish law, he mentions particularly only the one commandment of the Decalogue which involves a demand upon the inner life, 'You shall not covet'. Now many of us would make a significant distinction between 'rules' and 'principles', and would say that whereas the law in the external sense of rules is abrogated in Christ, the principles remain valid and binding. In line with this distinction we might insist that the Christian is no longer under any specific command touching outward behaviour, even a command as important as 'Thou shalt not kill'. But would we not concede that he is still subject to the law against covetousness? But can we think of Paul as making any such concession? Would he have allowed continuing validity to the law at the very point where it had caused him the greatest pain and anxiety? There is no evidence that Paul differentiated between various elements within the law—or various kinds of law—as, for example, between the ceremonial and moral, or the general and the particular. Law, as such, is no longer valid for the Christian. We are not under law, but under grace (pp. 98 f.).

Agreed—Paul did not distinguish explicitly between ceremonial and moral law. But I question whether he disallowed the continuing validity of 'thou shalt not covet'. What he is affirming is that the law against coveting could not be achieved by 'law' in the sense of 'legalism'. I do not think that he is denying that the law, pronouncing the words 'Thou shalt not covet', continued to be a revelation of God's will. But it was, Paul saw, disastrous to adopt, as one's way of life, a self-centred, ambitious determination to establish oneself as a keeper of the law. The moment law is accepted in that light, one is as good as dead.

Thus, Paul did not claim release from the law of coveting, but only from an inability to keep it arising from a fatal and futile determination to establish one's own success. It is necessary, then, I would hold, to interpret Paul as seeing the antithesis to grace, not in law so far as it is the revelation of God's character and demand, nor even in law as obligation, but in law as an arrogantly and arbitrarily chosen target of human ambition and as a system of human achievement, that is, legalism. This brings us back to the matter of essential sin. On p. 28, Professor Knox writes: 'We are as natural finite men self-centered—this is neither wrong nor avoidable; it is our nature— but as sinful men we are also, equally inescapably, corrupted by pride. Our self-centeredness passes inevitably into selfishness.' Now, Professor Knox may be using 'self-centred' here in a special way (reflecting, possibly, a Tillichian vocabulary); but I wonder whether this distinction between a self-centredness that is natural and right and a sinful self-centredness, is Pauline. Paul would, I think, identify self-centredness *tout court*, as Adam's primal sin: it is mistrust of God; it is a refusal of creaturely dependence; it is legalism. And is not this essentially in line with the teaching of Jesus—for instance, in the

Sermon on the Mount, where the ideal attitude depicted is that of a son in full dependence on his Father? There is no other state that is not sinful.

3

So far, I have asked for a recognition that it is 'legalism' (as defined), rather than 'law' that Paul opposes to grace; and that this legalism is seen by Paul as a symptom of man's essential sin. It is this, and not law, from which he claims release. But the main point of this inquiry is concerned with the remedy for the ill; for it is here, if anywhere, that the logic of obligation will be found. If the law, as an exhibition of God's Name and Nature, is holy and just and good, but man, in his self-centredness, continually imagines that to have seen it is to be able to achieve it, and, by his very efforts to achieve it, expresses this essential self-centredness and so plunges deeper into sin, who can deliver him? If God's good law is constantly turned, by man's self-centredness, into legalism, who will break the vicious circle?

Now, Christ's answer to man's inability to meet God's demand, the answer so movingly described by Professor Knox in his exposition of the teaching of Jesus, lies, in essence, in penitence, for penitence is a realistic way of meeting failure without lowering the sights. Without for a moment relaxing his absolute requirements, God constantly offers his forgiveness. And forgiveness (as I have already said) means no relaxation of demand, because, infinitely costly to give, it is notoriously costly also to receive: true penitence is itself costly and demanding. It accepts, unabated, the stringency of God's demand. Though it does not earn forgiveness, it is the only way in to forgiveness. True penitence, so far from bringing a relieved sense that 'Allah is merciful' and will not be exacting, means a renewed committal to the ideal. Forgiveness means no relaxation of the stringency of demand, as the extreme painfulness of true penitence shows. Logically, the obligation is perfectly clear.

But, it is precisely in this connexion that a charge is frequently levelled against Paul; and this charge now requires careful examination. Paul has often been accused of paying scant attention to repentance;[1] and Professor Knox repeats the charge (pp. 86, 87):

[1] See, for instance, H. J. Schoeps, *Paul* (English version, London, 1961, of *Paulus* (Tübingen, 1959)), p. 188, and many before him, both Christian and non-Christian.

Those who find an antinomian tendency in the Christian doctrine of grace, who say, 'Let us then sin that grace may abound', who ask, 'Why should we try to fulfil God's law when we know not only that we cannot succeed, but also that God stands ready graciously to receive us even in our sinfulness?' or who take the even more radical position of saying, 'Christ has destroyed the law', all of these (and, I think, Paul is included here) forget or neglect the great significance of repentance in the Christian doctrine of grace.

A little further on (p. 90), he points out also that Paul, while speaking often of God's love for man, has comparatively little to say about the response of love from man to God.

Now, it is indeed true that μετανοεῖν occurs in the Pauline corpus only at 2 Cor. 12: 21, and μετάνοια only at Rom. 2: 4, 2 Cor. 7: 9 (and 2 Tim. 2: 25); and the statistics for man's loving God are comparable. The same, it may be said in parenthesis, is true of the word 'will': it is usually God's will, not man's. It is true also (pp. 76 ff.) that Paul's 'justification', though sometimes claimed as his equivalent for penitence, is not strictly equivalent. All this is undoubtedly true; and it can be argued that the nearest parallel to justification is, in fact, not penitence but forgiveness. But if 'justification' is not an equivalent for penitence, that is not to say that no equivalent is known to Paul. One only needs to ask what penitence and love really mean, to find that Paul is full of them. For what is penitence, and what is love? Penitence, in contrast to mere remorse, is genuine concern for the injured party. Remorse is the sinner's concern for himself, it is his mortification over failure or exposure. Penitence, by contrast, is distress over the wrong done to the other; and its positive side is obedient self-surrender to God—the offering to God of one's will and one's person, for him to use in the repair of the damage done. It is a voluntary entering with God into the pain and distress which one's own sin has caused, and which, in God's hands, can be turned into the creative means of healing and repair. For the teaching of Jesus, Professor Knox makes very compelling use (pp. 80 ff.) of the story of the prodigal son. But that story is not explicit about the meaning of penitence. If we are to be explicit, we must follow the direction of the parable, and ask: What form is the prodigal son's penitence, if it is real, going to take when it is translated into practical terms? The answer, clearly, is that it will mean alining himself with the father's self-sacrificing, eirenic, forgiving appeal to the elder brother. Instead of resenting and reciprocating his brother's caustic words, he will join his father in patient entreaty. This, I believe, is exactly what is implied by Professor Knox when (p. 75) he says that 'forgiveness in its very nature presupposes the acknowledgment of, and submission to, a moral requirement'. True repentance is going to be shown in the same kind of costly suffering for others as was shown in the initial act of forgiveness: it means responding in kind to the creative effort of reconciliation: 'Forgive us our debts, as we also are forgiving our debtors.'[1] This is what repentance and love mean.

But, if so, all this, I would contend, is precisely what Paul is all the time expressing, although without using μετάνοια or ἀγάπη. It may be true that a doctrine of 'justification', by itself, would divide justice from mercy and remove all logical grounds from obligation. But is this true of Paul's justification *by faith*? And has not Paul, in addition to 'faith', an impressive array of other expressions for the meaning of penitence? For he not only speaks of faith,[2] but also uses terms borrowed from cultus and sacrifice, and the figures of death and burial, and of union with Christ. It is a familiar fact that, for Paul, faith has far-reaching connotations of trust and self-sur-render and loyalty. And, even if this were not clear in itself, he re-inforces it by such phrases as 'present your bodies as a living sacrifice ...that you may prove what is the will of God...' (Rom. 12: 1, 2); 'we were buried...with him by baptism into death' (Rom. 6: 4); 'I have been crucified with Christ' (Gal. 2: 20). So, too, by his use of the preposition ἐν, he denotes incorporation in Christ and the identification of the will with his. In a word, all that is meant by ὑπακοή, 'obedience' (which, incidentally, is an important word in Romans and 2 Corinthians), implements in a very realistic way the content of penitence and love. Justification, in Paul's use, is no doubt based on the finished work of Christ, quite independently of man's worth or effort. But justification *by faith* denotes such a response to that finished work as identifies the believer most intimately with the

---

Cf. J. Jeremias, 'The Lord's Prayer in Modern Research', *ExpT* 71 (1960), 141 ff. (p. 146, 'as we herewith forgive our debtors').

[2] On faith in Paul, as contrasted with Jesus' idea of faith, see M. Buber, *apud* Kümmel, *Heilsgeschehen und Geschichte*, p. 442.

costly work of Christ, involving him inescapably in the cost and pain of repentance. It may be added that, conversely, there are areas of Christian literature where, although actual words for repentance are more prominent, the inner meaning of it is seriously misconstrued, and where the idea of merit is evident. This is well brought out by S. Laeuchli in *The Language of Faith* (New York, 1962; London, 1965), p. 94.

It would appear, then, that, so far from ignoring repentance, Paul offers a profound and realistic analysis of it, even when he does not use the word. And if he is constantly saying that we must become what, in Christ, we already are (as, for instance, in Gal. 5: 25, 'If we live by the Spirit'—that is, if we owe our very 'existence', as Christians, to the Spirit—, 'let us also walk by the Spirit'—that is, let our conduct conform to this), is this any more a mark of inconsistency (p. 100) than the constant appeals of Christ himself? The *datum*, both for Jesus and Paul, is always God's initiative in Christ and the individual's initial decision and response in faith and baptism. But the ἐφάπαξ of the *datum* has as constantly to be re-appropriated by repeated 'becomings'.

On p. 63 Professor Knox acknowledges that the teaching of Jesus himself did not show *how* his demands were to be met. But Paul, if I have at all justly represented him, does attempt to analyse how the dominical commands may be met, without abating one jot of them. It is not that he preaches the abrogation of the demands in favour of a reign of gracious relaxation. Rather, he penetrates to the heart of the ethical dilemma by recognizing that the attempt to meet the demands in one's own strength had always been self-frustrating and of the essence of sin; and that the first step towards meeting the demands is to acknowledge one's need and one's inability to do so in one's own strength, and to capitulate, in penitence and love or, in Paul's vocabulary, in the self-surrender of faith and obedience, to God's forgiveness. Paradoxically, it is the most costly process imaginable, although it cannot start until we have confessed that we can give nothing out of our own resources.

This brings us to a reconsideration of one of the most hotly debated passages in the Pauline epistles—Rom. 10: 4: τέλος γὰρ νόμου Χριστὸς εἰς δικαιοσύνην παντὶ τῷ πιστεύοντι. Up to the time of writing, the controversy is still swinging to and fro. E. Bammel argues for τέλος meaning 'termination',[1] C. E. B. Cranfield, for its meaning 'fulfilment'[2]—to quote only two of multitudes of debaters. The decision depends upon whether one takes νόμος in the first or the second of the meanings I have tried to isolate; or, to put it syntactically, on whether one construes εἰς δικαιοσύνην with νόμος or Χριστός. The Revised Standard Version renders it: 'For Christ is the end of the law, that every one who has faith may be justified.' The Jerusalem Bible (*Le Nouveau Testament, traduction nouvelle*, Paris, 1955) renders it: 'car le terme de la Loi, c'est le Christ, pour que soit justifié tout croyant.' The New English Bible (text) has: 'For Christ ends the law and brings righteousness for everyone who has faith', or (margin): 'Christ is the end of the law as a way to righteousness for everyone who has faith.' Cranfield (*loc. cit.* p. 49) suggests: 'For Christ is the goal of the law, so that righteousness is available to everyone that believeth.' Of these versions, Cranfield's clearly construes εἰς δικαιοσύνην with Χριστός, and the New English Bible margin almost as clearly with νόμος. The New English Bible text's 'brings righteousness' would be compatible with τέλος meaning goal, though 'ends' would be difficult to treat as though it meant 'brings to fulfilment'.

If one takes τέλος as 'termination', and construes νόμος with εἰς δικαιοσύνην to mean 'law used as a means to righteousness', Paul is saying that Christ put an end to legalism. This would, I know, be strictly illogical, because, on Paul's own showing, legalism (as we have called it) had never at any time been valid or other than sinful, so that Christ could not, strictly and correctly, be spoken of as terminating it. But it is intelligible, nevertheless, that Paul should so speak of Christ, in the sense that the Christian era constituted at any rate the final exposure and discrediting of legalism. If, on the other hand, one adopts the alternative and takes τέλος to mean 'purpose' or 'goal', then Paul is saying that Christ, as the way to righteousness, constitutes the goal and fulfilment of that revelation of God's way and character which the law contains.

Either interpretation is compatible with Paul's thought, but I suspect that he mainly intended the former—Christ put an end to

---

[1] 'Νόμος Χριστοῦ', *Studia Evangelica*, 3 (ed. F. L. Cross, *Texte und Untersuchungen* 88, Berlin, 1964), pp. 120 ff. Cf. H. J. Schoeps, *Paul*, pp. 171 ff.
[2] 'St Paul and the Law', *SJT* 17 (1964), pp. 43 ff.

legalism (this is borne out by verse 3, and, perhaps, by the fact that, in his 'targum' on Deut. 30: 12 ff., in Rom. 10: 6 ff., he seems to substitute Christ for Torah), although (he might have added) legalism, it is true, never was really valid. But Paul is by no means incapable of intending double meanings, and, especially in view of Rom. 13: 10, '...love is the fulfilling of the law', he could simultaneously have meant it in the second sense—Christ fulfils all that the law stands for.[1] As W. D. Davies has pointed out (*The Setting of the Sermon on the Mount*, Cambridge, 1964, p. 356), Jesus is, for Paul, parallel, not so much with Moses as with the law. If there is a new Moses, it is Paul; the new law is Christ himself.

I have discussed this famous phrase in Rom. 10: 4 at some length because the very fact of its ambiguity and of both senses being compatible with Paul's thought illustrates well the double meaning attaching to νόμος in respect of its use rather than of its contents. It is legalism that Paul is forever attacking and renouncing, and that he sees finally and decisively exposed and rejected by Christ; but the Mosaic Law as a revelation of God's will and purpose, so far from being abrogated, is seen as finding its fulfilment and culmination in Christ. Once this is recognized, Jesus and Paul can be seen to be speaking, at least on this matter, with one voice. As E. Jüngel points out (*Paulus und Jesus*, pp. 266, 267), Paul retains the idea of judgment according to works, regarding it as a criterion of responsibility no less than Jesus' teaching on rewards and penalties expresses responsibility. Similarly, Jesus and Paul both show the grace of God meeting responsible but sinful man. It is not the validity of a code that Paul is denying. He is only denying that a code can or should be used for uncreaturely attempts at boasting and autonomy. And the rejection of this use means no relaxation of the code.

But Paul does much more than merely reaffirm what had, all the time, been the right use of the law. He interprets it in a new and distinctively Christian way. He finds in Christ the embodiment and implementation of that relation between God and man which was represented by the law as a revelation of God, and he does, therefore,

---

[1] Professor Knox himself, in his commentary (*Interpreter's Bible*, 9, 554), says: '...meaning probably that in Christ the law is superseded (cf. 3: 21; Gal. 3: 25), rather than that the goal of the law is reached, although that too is a perfectly congenial Pauline idea.'

26-2

see Christ as superseding the law—but only in the sense that Christ, by totally and completely obeying the will of God revealed in it, includes and transcends it. To be united with Christ is, therefore, not to by-pass law, but to fulfil it in a supremely costly way. For instance, the death of Christ is seen by Paul as the surrender of Christ's entire body, his whole self, and, thus, as the greater, the all-inclusive 'circumcision'. To be baptized into Christ's death is, therefore, to have surrendered one's whole self with him in death, and thus to obviate the need for circumcision: the greater includes the less. But does this eliminate the logic of obligation? In a striking phrase of R. T. Brooks,[1] we who are forgiven are 'ruled more firmly by the pardon than we ever were by the law'. And, if the acceptance of the pardon is analysed into a total giving of oneself in union with the self-giving of God in Jesus Christ, is not this a sufficiently clear logic of obligation? If the Pauline faith and death with Christ are given their full value, then it would seem to me that the judgment and mercy of God are as inseparable in Paul's logic as in that of the teaching of Jesus.

4

In conclusion, then, it would appear that, conversely, the element of obligation in the teaching of Jesus is similar to that in the teaching of Paul and as free from 'law', in any legalistic sense, as Paul's. When Paul attacks legalism, he is attacking precisely what Jesus attacked in the Pharisees of his day. Jesus attacked the Pharisees; Paul attacked the Pharisee he had himself once been. The use of the law in an attempt to establish one's righteousness was condemned by Jesus every bit as much as by Paul, and, indeed, perhaps, by most other Jews except the most rigorous Pharisees.

In neither case is there antinomianism. Neither the ethic of Jesus nor that of Paul was exercised in a vacuum. The great presuppositions and principles of Jewish morality—rectitude, integrity, honesty—

---

[1] *Person to Person* (London, 1964), p. 66: 'Those who reject the code and those who bewail its rejection are alike in the belief that the only possible pattern of relationship between God and man is that of ruler and ruled, and that the only possible way of operating such a relationship is by the inexorable application of a code of prohibitions and punishments. That we are both condemned and pardoned—and ruled more firmly by the pardon than we ever were by the law—that is the missing insight.'

were obviously axiomatic for both. But actual moral decisions have to be taken in a situational way, and were evidently so taken by Jesus as much as by Paul. Man was not made for the sabbath, but the sabbath for man; and general rules about the details of ethical practice are as lacking in the traditions of Jesus as in Paul's writings. Both Jesus and Paul attacked legalism, and both affirmed law. But both Jesus and Paul did still more than that, for both speak with the voice of the new age. What Jesus brought to the Law of Moses was not only a repudiation of its legalizing and a reaffirmation of its broad and religious sense, but, still more, the new light of the new age in his own Person. E. Jüngel, in *Paulus und Jesus*, p. 269, remarks that the validity of the law was treated by Jesus as self-evident; but that, when one asks how Jesus implemented its validity, the answer is, by treating men as responsible in the light of the nearness of the kingdom and in the light of the new strength of love. In other words, Jesus' approach to the law is eschatological.

What Paul added to the teaching of Jesus, maintaining to the full the eschatological dimension, was not a relaxation of ethical principles but a definition and analysis of the relation between, on the one hand, law (in the good sense) and grace, and, on the other hand, legalism and merit.

W. G. Kümmel, in *Heilsgeschehen und Geschichte*, p. 19⁷, analyses Klausner's misunderstanding of Paul as bound up with a failure to recognize Jesus as the eschatological Bringer of Salvation and as thus bringing about the end of the Old Testament epoch of salvation (cf. Luke 16: 16). This is why Klausner has to drive a wedge between Jesus and Paul and represent Paul as the enemy of true Judaism. But in reality, Paul stands on the same side as Jesus. In both Jesus and Paul, love, in an urgently demanding, eschatological embodiment, is the essence of the law.

The conclusion, then, that I would venture to draw in this last section is that Paul shows as much and as little of the logic of moral obligation as Jesus himself; and that the essentially eschatological character of the tension between demand and succour which Paul so firmly grasped is precisely what was presented by the Person of Jesus himself. And the logic of it, it seems to me, is as taut in Paul as in Jesus. Indeed, it is Paul who analysed the meaning of the repentance by which the tension is made endurable.[1] Justification and faith, burial with Christ and incorporation in him, self-surrender, and obedience—all these in Paul's teaching represent an analysis of forgiveness and repentance. He thus makes explicit—although perhaps without conscious reference to the teaching of Jesus—something which, in the teaching of Jesus is only implicit.

That is the kind of apologia I would offer for Paul against the charge that the logic of his position is a relaxation of obligation, and that he neglects the elements of forgiveness and penitence. Very likely I have misinterpreted Professor Knox; perhaps I have misconstrued Paul. But I offer these reflexions on Professor Knox's delineation of Paul as a token of my serious concern to wrestle with the implications of what he writes and of the way in which he stimulates a reader; and I know that he will welcome friendly debate on paper in exactly the same spirit in which he has always welcomed and engaged in it, with lively and genial interest, in verbal dialogue.

[1] P. G. Verweijs, *Evangelium und neues Gesetz in der ältesten Christenheit bis auf Marcion* (Utrecht, 1960), p. 77, commenting on the essential agreement between Jesus and Paul about the fulfilling of the law, remarks that the distinctiveness of Paul's teaching is in keeping with 'die neue pneumatische Heilszeit'.

GENERAL INDEX

Abbahu, Rabbi, 135
Abdimi of Haifa, Rabbi, 131
Aboth, the (Pirqê Aboth), 307; nature of, 127, 142; Greek words in, 143 n. 3; not explicitly anti-Christian 154; summary of relevance, 156–9
Aboth de Rabbi Nathan, 131, 155
Abraham, 85–6, 282; 'lost sons' of, 114
Achaia, Paul in, 238
Acts, the, 153, 166, 226, 244–5; kerygmatic passages in, 186; as evidence for Paul's life, 226–8, 229–34, 241, 244–5
Apocryphal Acts, 353
Adam, 385–6; self-centredness of, 393, 397
Adars, 134–5
ages, old and new, 272–3, 286; juncture of the, 272–4, 284–5, 286
Aher (Elisha b. Abuyha), 138 n. (c)
Akabya b. Mahalaleel, Rabbi, 149–50
Alcimus, 130 n. 4, 136
Alexander Aphrodisiensis, 276
Allo, E. B., 347
Ambrose, St, 88 n.
America (North), tendencies in, 11–12, 45
Amos, 137
analogy, use of, 31, 69
Ananias, 347
ἀναθεματίζειν, 357
Anselm, St, 58, 72
    Cur Deus homo, 72
Antigonos Monophthalmos, 159
Antigonus of Soko, 130, 142–5
antinomianism, in Paul, 364, 381, 388, 389, 395, 399
Antiochus Epiphanes, 145
'Apocalypse, Synoptic', 172–3
apocalyptic, 129, 137 n. 5
Apocrypha, 42
Apocryphal Acts, 353
Apollos, 250, 254, 259 n. 3, 261, 326, 327–8; adherents of, 313; in relation to Paul, 322–3, 326; preaching of, 333
Apophthegms, 124 n.
apostasy, 355–8, 360; of Aher, 138 n. (c)
apostles, 320; mission of, 162, 165–6, 168; designation of, 209; 'super', 275, 279–84, 285 n. 2
apostleship, true nature of, 272–3
Arabia, Paul in, 238, 242
archegos, 87

arguments (theistic), ontological, 58–66; cosmological, 66–71; teleological, 71–3; moral, 73–5
Aristotle, 264; school of, 140
Arvedson, T., 304 n. 2
Asia, Paul in, 238, 242
atonement, 6, 53, 376; and justification, 377–8
Atonement, Day of, 43, 137 n. 5
atonement, the, 35; theory of, 36; Taylor on, 39–41; Knox on, 47–9, 56
Augustine, St, 83 n. 2, 92; conversion of, 88 n.

Bacher, W., 133
Bammel, E., 401
baptism, 164–5, 338–41, 349, 387, 401; repudiation of, 356, 361
bar-Jesus, 360
Barrett, C. K., 300, 394
    Commentary on Epistle to Romans, quoted, 394–5
Barth, Karl, 33, 58, 62, 69, 107; on human relation of Christ, 81 n. 3
Baruch, 159, 308, 308–9; Syriac Apocalypse of, 307
Baur, Ferdinand C., 104; concept of Jesus, 101–2; on parties at Corinth, 313–14, 317
    'Christ-Party in Corinth Church', 313
Beare, Frank W., **161–81**
beatitudes, the, 105
Berdyaev, Nicholas, 12
Bethsaida, blind man of, 205
Bible, the, 13, 68
Bickerman, E., 140, 143–4
    'La Chaîne de la Tradition Pharisienne', 140
blasphemy, 355
Bornkamm, Günther, essay on Romans, 290–2, 294
Branscomb, B. H., 201, 205
Britain, theology in, 11
Brooks, R. T., 404
    Person to Person, quoted, 404 n.
Brunner, E., 107
Buddhism, 65
Bultmann, Rudolf, 69, 72, 107, 124 n., 269 n. 2, 271 nn. 1 and 3, 347, 367 n. 3, 381; Knox and, 32, 83 n. 2, 218; on

General Index

Daniel, Book of, 137 n. 5
Daube, D., 151
David, 85, 136
Davies, W. D., 51, 53, **127–59**, 231–2, 403; on formation of early doctrine, 42–5
Invitation to New Testament, 231; quoted, 231
Paul and Rabbinic Judaism, 42
Setting of Sermon on the Mount, 403
demoniac, Gerasene, 81
demons, exorcism of, 170–1, 338
Denney, James, 51, 53; on doctrine of reconciliation, 36–8
Christian Doctrine of Reconciliation, 36–8; quoted, 37, 38
Death of Christ, 36
despair, preparatory nature of, 93–4
Deuteronomy (30: 11–14), 299–304, 308–12
dialectic, Paul's, 386 n.
Diatessaron, 162
Dibelius, M., 180, 201, 218
Dictionary of the Bible, The Interpreter's, 241
Didache, 345
Dillistone, F. W., **35–56**
Dilthey, William, 80
Diogenes Laertius, 148
Diotrephes, 360–1
disciples, mission of, 168, 176–7, 190; incomprehension of, 170; relation of Jesus to, 183–4, 196–8
Docetists, the, 118, 359
Dodd, C. H., 106, 138, 171, 173 n. 1, 175, 179, **183–98**, 201
Historical Tradition in Fourth Gospel, 195 n.
Parables of the Kingdom, 175
Duncan, G. S., 238, 247

Ebeling, G., 60
Ecclesiastes, 145
elders, the, 129, 132–3
Eleazer b. Arach, Rabbi, 146–7
Eleazer b. Jacob, Rabbi, 131
Eleazer of Modiim, Rabbi, 152, 153 n. 3
Eliade, M., 23
Eliezer b. Hyrcanus, Rabbi, 147, 156 n. 1
Elijah, 85, 87
emissaries, apostolic, 252, 255–8, 260
Emmaus, 167
Epaphroditus, 250, 254, 256, 261
Ephesians, Epistle to, 225, 238
Ephesus, 293; Paul at, 238, 242; 'imprisonment' at, 238, 240, 241, 242, 243, 244
Epictetus, 145
Epicurean school, 140, 145–7
'epicurean', as 'unbeliever', 146
Episcopacy, 25

Episcopal Church, Knox's affiliation with, 3
Esau, as a type, 357
eschatology, Pauline, 379
Essenes, 159
Eucharist, the, 337; profanation of, 346–7, 351; as 'medicine of immortality', 347–8
Eupolemos, 141
Eusebius, 141, 165
'events', 19; Knox's conception of, 4, 14–15, 20, 50, 365; Denney on, 37–8
excommunication, 337–8, 346, 361
existentialism, 12, 367 n. 3
exorcism, 170–1, 338
Ezekiel, 179
Ezra, 132, 159

'face', use of term, 280, 282
fact, two types of, 28; as basis of faith, 69
faith, 4, 9–10, 17, 29, 57, 75, 100, 373, 379–80, 382; invulnerability of, 23–4; Bultmann on, 46; and reason, 62–4, 75–6; and natural science, 69, 76–7; Jesus as author of, 88–90, 98–9; pre-existent, 90 n. 1, 93, 96; and passion, 90–1; sacrament of, 339; baptismal, 339, 356, 361; of early Christian communities, 365–6; meaning for Paul, 377, 400–1
Farmer, William R., **101-26**, 124 n.
feeling, Knox on, 27
'fence', image of a, 151
Festugière, A-J., 149–50
Fichtner, J., 307
Finkelstein, L., 141, 155
flesh, 295; 'destruction' of, 349–51
forgiveness, 37, 371–2, 389, 399; Pauline thought on (Knox), 363–5, 376, 389–90, 406; Knox on, 373–4, 400
form-criticism, 102, 105, 200 n. 2, 201, 218
Foster, A. Durwood, Jr, **57-77**
Frankel, Z., 151
freedom, 73, 75, 154
Freer logion, 162, 163–4
Fridrichsen, Anton, 289
friendship, Aristotle's doctrine of, 264
Funk, Robert W., **249-68**
Language, Hermeneutic, and the Word of God, 335 n.

G, codex, 289, 292
Galatia, 261 n.; crisis in, 237, 238, 266, 297; Paul in, 238, 242, 250; opponents of Paul in, 360
Galatians, Epistle to, 236, 237, 238, 240–4 *passim*, 250, 259, 260, 263 n. 1, 293, 295; date of, 266–7

General Index

Galilee, return to, 164, 166
Gaunilo, 58, 59
Gautama, 65
Gavin, Frank, 9
Geiger, A., 153
genealogies, 141 n. 2
gentiles, mission to, 165, 166 n., 176–7; faith of, 190; Christian, 237, 291; relation of Paul to, 251, 265 n., 297; God of, 383
Georgi, Dieter, 227, 279 n. 2, 295 n.
  Geschichte der Kollekte des Paulus für Jerusalem, 228
Gerhardsson, B., 158 n.
Gnostics, the, 118, 149–51, 153, 277 n. 1, 284, 285 n. 2; in relation to Judaism, 149 n.; at Corinth, 275, 278–9, 280, 286 n. 2, 314
God, as love, 5–6, 30, 370; as living, 6–7; saving action of, 20–1, 365, 371; relation to history, 29–32; knowledge of, 32–4, 69; ontological argument for, 58; cosmological argument, 66; teleological argument, 71; moral argument, 73–5; kingdom of, 83, 97–100, 167, 189–91; catholicity of, 85 n.; authority of, 95; in Lucan parables, 110–11; relation of Jesus to, 185–6, 192–4; as ultimate source, 272–3; seen face to face, 281 nn. 1 and 2, 284–5; law of, 374 nn. 6 and 7, 381, 384–5, 387; man's need of, 394
Gogarten, F., 72
Goldin, J., on the Aboth, 145–9
good, concretions of, 5; with evil, 66
Goodspeed, Edgar J., 225, 238, 373 n.
gospel, dissemination of, 165, 344; purpose of, 210; appearance of, 272; law and, 308, 311; denial of, 360
Gospels, the, 37, 101, 110 n., 158; date of, 105, 109; historicity of, 199, 201–8, 222; commentator's function, 210, 211; *see also* Synoptic Gospels
grace, 374, 381, 386–7, 394; significance of, 382; legalism and, 397
Great Synagogue, the, 129, 131, 151 n. 3, 155
Greece, Paul in, 242
Greek philosophy, in relation to Judaism, 138–51; schools of, 140
Grønbech, Vilhelm, 334

Habakkuk, 377
haggadah, 128 n. 2
Haggai, 131–2, 134, 137
Halafta b. Dosa, Rabbi, 152
halakah, 128, 133, 152

Hallel Psalms, 135
Hanah, Rabban ben, 131
Hananiah b. Akashya, Rabbi, 154
Hanson, A. T., opinions examined, 199–222 *passim*
  Vindications (ed. A. T. Hanson), 199; cited, 200–20 *passim*
Harnack, A., 157
Hartshorne, Charles, 4, 6, 11–12, 58, 62
Harvey, Van A., 232
  Historian and Believer, 232
Headlam, A. C., 301
healers, Christian, 205
healing, of deaf mute, 205; of blind man, 205; of Peter's mother-in-law, 206
Hebrews, the, lost gospel of, 105; writer to, 346, 356
Hegel, G. W. F., 58, 64
Heidegger, M., 12, 72, 201 n. 2
Herford, R. T., 127–8, 149
Héring, J., 347
Hermes Trismegistus, 262 n. 2
Herrmann, W., 60
Heschel, A. J., 128 n. 2, 137 n. 5
Hillel, 132, 134, 138 n. (c); House of, 133
Hippolytus, 339
  Apostolic Tradition, 339
Hirsch, E., 105
historicity, of gospel stories, 201–8, 222; of Mark, 202, 208, 210–11, 213
historiography, 57, 69, 77
history, dynamic view of, 4–7, 8; as social anamnesis, 11; in relation to Christian faith, 17, 18–20, 26; meaning of, 22–3; purpose of, 24–5; reality in, 26–9; relation of God to, 29–30
Ḥiyya b. Abba, Rabbi, 132
Hobbes, Thomas, 91, 92
  Leviathan, quoted, 91
Hodgson, Peter C., 101 n., *The Formation of Historical Theology*, 101 n.
Hooker, M. D., 328 n.
hope, 375, 379-80
humanity, the new, 60
Hume, David, 66
Hurd, John C., Jr, **225–48**, 314–17, 325 n. 1, 326 n. 2, 330 n. 2, 333 n. 3, 338, 343–4, 347 n.
  Origin of I Corinthians, 315; quoted, 316 nn. 2 and 3, 338
Hymenaeus, 352

Ignatius 340–1, 345, 347–8
illness, as remedial chastisement, 349
Illyricum, 239, 246

General Index

Martyn, J. Louis, **269–87**

Matthew (evangelist), 85, 101, 152, 164, 166, 174, 187, 345, 373; Baur's reliance on, 105; parables of, 112, 118–21; tradition in, 122–4; anti-Paulinism of, 176 n. 1; major discourses in, 180; use of Mark, 212

Mead, George H., 9, 12

Meir, Rabbi, 144, 152

Meland, Bernard, 12

memory, 19, 27, 29, 50

Messiah, 41, 42, 85, 286, 358–9

metaphysics, 16, 31

Michel, O., 267

Minear, Paul S., 364 n. 1

miracle stories, 22

Mishnah, the, 127, 211 n. 1; translations from, 129 n. 2

Montefiore, H. W., 138, 201

moral argument, 73–5

moral birth, 92

Morrison, Charles C., 370

Moses, 85–6, 119, 129, 133, 279, 281–2, 403

Moule, C. F. D., 14, **389–406**

Munck, Johannes, 231, 314, 316–17, 321 n. 3, 325 n. 1

Paul and Salvation of Mankind, 314

'Church without Factions', 314

myth, 22–4, 30, 53

Nahman, Rabbi, 132

Nahman b. Hisda, Rabbi, 134

Nathan, Aboth de Rabbi, 131, 155

Neusner, Jacob, 117 n.

New Testament, 17, 27, 50, 52, 53, 70; Knox's work on, 3, 367–70, 370–6; central message of, 36–7; unity of, 37, 39; reading of, 79–84; definition of, 84–5; relevance of Aboth to, 128; tradition in, 156–9; students of, 212 n. 1, 225, 313; on privileges and obligations, 338; teaching of ethic, 368–9

Niebuhr, H. Richard, 26 n. 2, 365, 370

Meaning of Revelation, 26 n. 2, 365 n.

Niebuhr, Richard R., **79–100**

Nineham, D. E., **199–222**; relation to Bultmann, 200–1; on historicity of gospel stories, 201–8, 215; on commentator's function, 210, 211

Historicity and Chronology of N.T., 217

Saint Mark, cited, 202–15 *passim*

'History and the Gospel', 199 n. 3

Ninevites, the, 191–2

νόμος, 391

Novatianists, the, 340, 350

obedience, 100, 387, 395; in relation to Christ's death, 43–5; to God's commands, 111, 144

obligation, 396, 398, 404

Ogden, Schubert, 12, 14

Christ without Myth, 14

Old Testament, 129, 348, 377, 378; background of symbolic terms, 39–41; interpretation of, 167–8, 169–70; relation to Mark, 208–9; cited by evangelists, 216–17

Onkelos, 132

ontological argument, 58–66; apologetic use of, 62–4

Origen, 351

'ought, the', man and, 74–5

Outler, A. C., 118 n.

Oxford Conference (1937), 42

𝔓⁴⁶, 293

Palestine, conditions of, 202

papyri, 43, 260 n. 2

parables, 106; in Luke, 110–12, 118–21, 124, 374; in Matthew, 112, 118–21, 122–3; of vineyard labourers, 115, 122; of prodigal son, 115–16, 374, 399; ben Zakkai's, 119–20; of sower, 171–2, 174; of tares, 174–5, 345; modification of, 179; of Son as apprentice, 186; of two builders, 191

Parmenides, 276 n. 2

parousia, divine, 173, 179, 265, 273, 347, 355; apostolic, 249, 250, 251 n., 253–4, 258–9, 262 n. 2, 265, 268

passion, faith and, 90–1

passion, the, 40–1, 42; necessity of, 169

Passover, 43

Paul, St, 20, 22, 37, 42–5, 85, 101, 138, 262 n. 1, 338; as founder of Christianity, 104; theology of, 43, 111, 246–7, 331–2, 375–6; attacks on, 152–4, 321–3; commission of, 165, 176 n. 2; time sequence of, 226; life of, 238–40, 240–3, 243–6; apostolic authority of, 249, 251–2, 258–9, 265–6, 271–3, 289, 313, 329; emissaries of, 252, 255–8, 260; conversion of, 270; on ways of knowing, 274–5, 275–9, 280, 284–7; fears of, 290; defends his gospel, 295–7; treatment of O.T., 299–304, 308–12; Corinthian ministry of, 315, 331; relation to Church at Corinth, 319–23, 327, 334; delegation of Stephanus to, 323–5, 329; reply of, 326–9, 334; as apostle of Christ, 335; on association

INDEX OF REFERENCES

A. THE OLD TESTAMENT

Index of References

B. EXTRA-CANONICAL JEWISH LITERATURE

C. THE NEW TESTAMENT

Index of References

Romans (*cont.*)

10: 12–13	298
10: 17–19	304
11: 2	301
11: 4	301
11: 13–14	298
11: 36	375
12: 1–2	385, 400
12: 3 – 15: 13	385
12: 14	322
13: 8–10	311
13: 9	392
13: 10	392, 403
14	260
14: 10	186
15	242, 259, 260, 261, 289, 297 n. 2
15: 9–33	237
15: 14–29	245
15: 14–33	250, 251–3, 258, 259, 262, 265 n., 267, 268, 290 n. 1
15: 15–21	252 n. 1
15: 19	265
15: 22–4	297
15: 23–32	241
15: 28	266
15: 28–9	297
15: 30–3	321 n. 1
15: 31	290, 296
16	289, 293, 294 n., 297 n. 2
16: 1 ff.	258 n. 1

1 Corinthians

1–2	316
1–4	313–19, 326, 331, 332, 334, 335
1: 4 ff.	326
1: 10	319, 324, 325 n. 2
1: 10–13	320
1: 10 – 4: 21	316, 317, 318, 325, 329, 333
1: 11–12	320
1: 12	313, 315, 322
1: 12 f.	323
1: 13–15	326 n. 2
1: 13–17	320
1: 13 ff.	165
1: 14	322
1: 14–17	327
1: 17	321
1: 17 – 3: 2	320, 327
1: 18	286 n. 2
1: 18 – 2: 5	376
1: 18–25	320, 327
1: 18 ff.	304 n. 3
1: 19 f.	328
1: 20	328 n.

1: 24	308
1: 26	270 n. 7
1: 26–31	320, 327
1: 30	380 n. 3
1: 31	328
2–4	265
2: 1	321
2: 1–5	320, 327
2: 2	285 n. 2
2: 4	321
2: 6–16	278, 280, 320, 335 n.
2: 6 ff.	304 n. 3
2: 6–3: 2	327
2: 9	328
2: 14	283, 284
2: 14–3: 4	332
2: 15	286 n. 2
3: 1	321
3: 1–2	320
3: 2	321
3: 2–4	320
3: 3–4	318, 320
3: 5–9	323
3: 5–11	326 n. 2
3: 5–17	327
3: 5 – 4: 6	320
3: 6	327
3: 10	327
3: 10–11	321, 326
3: 10–17	327
3: 11–15	332
3: 12	379
3: 18	327
3: 18–21	320
3: 19 f.	328
3: 21	320, 329 n. 3
3: 21–3	320, 326, 327
3: 22	323
4: 2–5	327
4: 3–4	321
4: 4–5	330 n. 2
4: 6	320, 323, 328
4: 7–10	320
4: 8	321
4: 8–13	271 n. 4, 321
4: 8 ff.	332
4: 9–13	320, 328
4: 11–13	322
4: 13–18	330 n. 2
4: 14	331
4: 14–15	319
4: 16	324
4: 16–17	319
4: 17 ff.	259 n. 1
4: 18	318, 322, 331

Index of References

424

D. CLASSICAL AND HELLENISTIC AND EXTRA-CANONICAL CHRISTIAN LITERATURE

Index of References

Index of References